Sustainable Consumer Behavior

Special Issue Editor
Gerrit Antonides

MDPI • Basel • Beijing • Wuhan • Barcelona • Belgrade

MDPI

Special Issue Editor
Gerrit Antonides
Wageningen University
The Netherlands

Editorial Office
MDPI AG
St. Alban-Anlage 66
Basel, Switzerland

This edition is a reprint of the Special Issue published online in the open access journal *Sustainability* (ISSN 2071-1050) from 2016–2017 (available at: http://www.mdpi.com/journal/sustainability/special_issues/consumer_behaviour).

For citation purposes, cite each article independently as indicated on the article page online and as indicated below:

Author 1; Author 2. Article title. *Journal Name* **Year**, *Article number*, page range.

First Edition 2017

ISBN 978-3-03842-583-0 (Pbk)
ISBN 978-3-03842-584-7 (PDF)

Table of Contents

About the Special Issue Editor v

Preface to "Sustainable Consumer Behavior" vii

Gerrit Antonides
Sustainable Consumer Behaviour: A Collection of Empirical Studies
Reprinted from: *Sustainability* **2017**, *9*(10), 1686; doi: 10.3390/su9101686 1

Jacob Sohlberg
The Effect of Elite Polarization: A Comparative Perspective on How Party Elites Influence
Attitudes and Behavior on Climate Change in the European Union
Reprinted from: *Sustainability* **2017**, *9*(1), 39; doi: 10.3390/su9010039 6

Michelle Bonera, Elisabetta Corvi, Anna Paola Codini and Ruijing Ma
Does Nationality Matter in Eco-Behaviour?
Reprinted from: *Sustainability* **2017**, *9*(10), 1694; doi: 10.3390/su9101694 19

Kees Vringer, Eline van der Heijden, Daan van Soest, Herman Vollebergh and Frank Dietz
Sustainable Consumption Dilemmas
Reprinted from: *Sustainability* **2017**, *9*(6), 942; doi: 10.3390/su9060942 36

Gerhard Reese and Eva A. Junge
Keep on Rockin' in a (Plastic-)Free World: Collective Efficacy and Pro-Environmental Intentions
as a Function of Task Difficulty
Reprinted from: *Sustainability* **2017**, *9*(2), 200; doi: 10.3390/su9020200 58

Anke Brons and Peter Oosterveer
Making Sense of Sustainability: A Practice Theories Approach to Buying Food
Reprinted from: *Sustainability* **2017**, *9*(3), 467; doi: 10.3390/su9030467 71

Muriel C. D. Verain, Siet J. Sijtsema, Hans Dagevos and Gerrit Antonides
Attribute Segmentation and Communication Effects on Healthy and Sustainable Consumer
Diet Intentions
Reprinted from: *Sustainability* **2017**, *9*(5), 743; doi: 10.3390/su9050743 86

**Sophie de Graaf, Filiep Vanhonacker, Ellen J. Van Loo, Jo Bijttebier, Ludwig Lauwers,
Frank A. M. Tuyttens and Wim Verbeke**
Market Opportunities for Animal-Friendly Milk in Different Consumer Segments
Reprinted from: *Sustainability* **2016**, *8*(12), 1302; doi: 10.3390/su8121302 105

Wencke Gwozdz, Kristian Steensen Nielsen and Tina Müller
An Environmental Perspective on Clothing Consumption: Consumer Segments and Their
Behavioral Patterns
Reprinted from: *Sustainability* **2017**, *9*(5), 762; doi: 10.3390/su9050762 122

Elfriede Penz, Eva Hofmann and Barbara Hartl
Fostering Sustainable Travel Behavior: Role of Sustainability Labels and Goal-Directed Behavior
Regarding Touristic Services
Reprinted from: *Sustainability* **2017**, *9*(6), 1056; doi: 10.3390/su9061056 149

Rouven Doran, Daniel Hanss and Torvald Øgaard
Can Social Comparison Feedback Affect Indicators of Eco-Friendly Travel Choices? Insights
from Two Online Experiments
Reprinted from: *Sustainability* **2017**, *9*(2), 196; doi: 10.3390/su9020196 166

Helena Dall Pizzol, Stefânia Ordovás de Almeida and Mauren do Couto Soares
Collaborative Consumption: A Proposed Scale for Measuring the Construct Applied to a
Carsharing Setting
Reprinted from: *Sustainability* **2017**, *9*(5), 703; doi: 10.3390/su9050703 181

Seo-Hyeon Min, Seul-Ye Lim and Seung-Hoon Yoo
Consumers' Willingness to Pay a Premium for Eco-Labeled LED TVs in Korea: A Contingent
Valuation Study
Reprinted from: *Sustainability* **2017**, *9*(5), 814; doi: 10.3390/su9050814 197

About the Special Issue Editor

Gerrit Antonides is Professor Emeritus of Economics of Consumers and Households at Wageningen University, the Netherlands. He has obtained his PhD at Erasmus University, Rotterdam, in 1988. He has published in the areas of behavioural economics, economic psychology, and consumer behaviour. He has been an editor of the Journal of Economic Psychology, has (co-)authored several textbooks in consumer behaviour and economic psychology and has served as president of the Society for the Advancement of Behavioural Economics (SABE). The behavioural aspects of consumer decision making concerning issues of environment and health, finance, and households, are an important part of his current research activities.

Preface to "Sustainable Consumer Behavior"

Environmental concerns across the globe have led to several large-scale initiatives to protect the environment, most recently the Paris Agreement. The Paris Agreement on global warming—effective from October 2016—includes nationally determined contributions to keeping global temperature rise in this century well below 2 degrees Celsius above pre-industrial levels. Other environmental sustainability initiatives aim for resource efficiency—as, for example, expressed by the European Commission [1]. Key consumption resources, including nutrition, housing and mobility, are mentioned as having the most environmental impacts.

Consumer behavior contributes to a large part of environmental impact. Nobel Prize winner Munasinghe [2] states that the consumption of 1.2 billion richer humans accounts for some 75% of total emissions. Therefore, consumer demand for low-carbon products and services, and greener choices, have to be stimulated [3]. Policy initiatives concerning environmental sustainability often require scientific research to guide and support their implementation. More insight into the drivers and context of consumer decision making should help develop tax incentives, targeted marketing, and consumer empowerment for greater sustainability.

To promote scientific research in the area of sustainable consumer behavior, Sustainability has taken the initiative for a special issue on the topic, now published in book form. As editor of the special issue, I sincerely hope that the scientific contributions will help achieve the sustainability policy goals.

References Gerrit Antonides
Special Issue Editor

1. European Commission. *Roadmap to a Resource Efficient Europe*; Document 52011DC0571; European Commission: Brussels, Belgium, 2011.
2. Munasinghe, M. Can sustainable consumers and producers save the planet? *J. Ind. Ecol.* **2010**, *14*, 4–6.
3. Sustainable Consumption Institute. Consumers 'Key Part of Solution' To Global Warming. *Science Daily*, 24 December 2009.

sustainability

MDPI

Editorial

Sustainable Consumer Behaviour: A Collection of Empirical Studies

Gerrit Antonides

Urban Economics, Wageningen University & Research, P.O. Box 8130, 6700 EW Wageningen, The Netherlands; gerrit.antonides@wur.nl

Received: 18 September 2017; Accepted: 19 September 2017; Published: 21 September 2017

Abstract: We summarise the contributions in this special issue on sustainable consumer behaviour and place them in perspective. Several studies focus on macro- and meso-issues, and others on micro-issues of consumer behaviour. The studies employ a variety of methods, including surveys, field experiments, eye tracking, scale development, and contingent valuation. The 12 contributions from authors of 13 different countries show the wide and varied application of consumer research focused on sustainability issues.

Keywords: eco-behaviour; social dilemma; segmentation; food; travel

1. Introduction

The solution to sustainability issues is often considered as being driven by product innovation. If products and services would become environmentally-friendly, sustainability would no longer be an issue. However, there are several problems with this view. For example, environmental friendliness often requires high levels of investment, political support, consumer acceptance, and willingness to pay. Given the high number of product innovation failures, the study of consumer behaviour seems vital in guiding the direction of product design and policy measures aimed at stimulating sustainable behaviour. Arguments like this underlie the motivation for this special issue on consumer behaviour.

Sustainable consumer behaviour may be approached from different perspectives, including—among others—the policy maker's view, the marketing view, the consumer interest focus, and the ethical focus. Consumer research also applies a variety of different research methodologies. The different angles and methodologies are reflected in the contributions to this special issue, but all of them are empirical, thus providing "flesh to the bones" of consumer theories.

Consumer behaviour research is often an amalgamation of theories and different methodologies, each contributing different pieces to the entire puzzle which is the explanation of consumer behaviour. In this respect, consumer behaviour research is different from economic analysis, which is usually derived from a set of assumptions and leads to a normative framework of consumer decision making. In contrast, students of consumer behaviour often complain about the myriad theories and insights that exist in the field. My answer to their complaints is that consumer behaviour is too complex to be described by one overarching theory, and consumer behaviour researchers should strike a balance between the generality of theory and the set of behaviours that it should explain. For example, we have contributions dealing with social dilemma theory and collective effort, providing some explanation for a particular aspect of sustainable behaviour—namely, social influence. However, such research cannot explain consumer decision making in making trade-offs between price and sustainability, so other research contributions cover this type of decision making. However, decision making research often starts at a higher level of abstraction than the elementary process of perception, for which still other types of research are needed. This special issue reflects this aim for balance.

2. Macro and Meso Views on Sustainable Consumer Behaviour

The Effect of Elite Polarization [1] combines data from EU inhabitants in the Eurobarometer Survey and from the comparative Manifestos Project, including political party positions regarding environmental protection. It appears that the EU citizens' perceived threat of climate change and personal actions to reduce climate change are both negatively influenced by the diversity in political parties' positions regarding the environment. Additionally, perceived threat tends to be positively related to reported personal actions to reduce climate change. The total effect of political party positions thus seems greater than hitherto expected.

In *Does Nationality Matter in Eco-Behaviour?* [2], Italian and Chinese samples are compared on eco-awareness, eco-behaviour, green opinion, a number of different personal values, and a measure of regulatory focus. Although nationality has no significant effect on eco-behaviour in the extended model, a stepwise analysis shows that in addition to the universalism value and regulatory focus, Chinese rather than Italian citizens are more likely to adopt eco-behaviour, despite the fact that Italians are more eco-aware than the Chinese.

Sustainable Consumption Dilemmas [3] considers both the social dilemma and moral dilemma aspects of sustainable consumer behaviour with respect to meat consumption. Unlike most studies, real behaviour has been studied in a large-scale field experiment in which participants received credit which was large enough to cover the extra costs of buying organic meat as compared with conventional meat. Participants in groups of different sizes then voted either in favour of an obligation to use the group members' credit only for buying organic meat, or in favour of freedom to use the credit for organic or non-organic meat. Although the share of votes in favour of the obligation was quite high (around 50%), group size differences were not significantly related to the votes, thus rejecting the social dilemma hypothesis. On the other hand, 76% of the participants were willing to buy organic meat if a certain number of other group members would do the same, thus pointing to a moral dilemma based on a trade-off between individual costs and collective gains.

Collective efforts in reducing waste were studied in *Keep on Rockin' in a (Plastic-)Free World: Collective Efficacy and Pro-Environmental Intentions as a Function of Task Difficulty* [4]. In an innovative experiment, 6000 cards were given out to citizens across Germany. On each of the cards a specific challenge was displayed, which was either easy (I carried my groceries home in either a fabric bag, a backpack, or a basket), moderate (While shopping, I bought all fruits and vegetables without plastic wrapping, and I consequently brought them home in either a fabric bag, a backpack, of a basket), or difficult (I did my entire shopping entirely without plastic. This means that I neither bought plastic bags of any sort nor did I buy any other sort of plastic wrapping). After performing the challenge, participants then completed a questionnaire on the web, including questions about collective efficacy, self-efficacy, and trust in collective performance, among others. As predicted, moderate challenges resulted in higher collective efficacy, whereas task difficulty did not affect self-efficacy. The experiment shows that trust in collective performance of environmental behaviour depends on task difficulty, which may be useful for the way in which collective actions can be stimulated.

The first two papers in this section show that both the political climate and nationality are significant factors in increasing the level of eco-behaviour. However, the actual psychological processes behind these factors need to be understood better in future research. The third paper points to the significance of social influence on consumption without restricting other people's freedom of choice. The fourth paper shows that collective efforts may depend on task difficulty.

3. Micro Views on Sustainable Consumer Behaviour

3.1. Typology and Segmentation Studies

A qualitative study, *Making Sense of Sustainability: A Practice Theories Approach to Buying Food* [5], has explored different typologies of sustainable food consumers. The typology is based on several criteria, one of which is the people and motivations involved in acquiring the practice of buying sustainable food. These might include, for example, parents focusing on healthy diets, friends focusing on environmental concern, or exogenous factors such as living abroad or enrolment in environmental associations. Another criterion concerns the way consumers are engaged in sustainable consumption— for example, by focusing on health, quality of food, or ethics involved in sustainable purchases. The third criterion involves the degree of commitment of sustainable consumers, in knowing, questioning, or pushing their limits. The fourth criterion relates sustainable food consumption to other sustainable consumption, including recycling, saving energy, transportation, etc. The latter criterion seems to be associated with the issue of spillover effects. Since this study is based on a small sample, the typology needs to be confirmed in larger samples in order to be considered in policy making.

Attribute Segmentation and Communication Effects on Healthy and Sustainable Consumer Diet Intentions [6] combines a segmentation of Dutch food consumers with an experiment on communicating dietary guidelines for healthy and/or sustainable food consumption. The segmentation was based on the importance of a range of sustainability aspects, price, taste, and healthiness, and resulted in three segments: pro-self, average, and conscious consumers. Communication concerning sustainability and healthiness of diets was presented to each of four randomly selected parts of the sample in a 2 × 2 (health arguments vs. sustainability arguments) full-factorial between-subjects design. Pro-self and average consumers were thinking most about sustainability due to communication that combined health and sustainability benefits, although no changes in dietary intentions were found in these segments. The combined health and sustainability communication increased the intention to reduce meat consumption for sustainable conscious consumers most. Apparently, communication concerning sustainability and health had differential effects on different consumer segments.

In *Market Opportunities for Animal-Friendly Milk in Different Consumer Segments* [7], a segmentation of Flemish milk consumers is reported, based on purchase intention and perceived evaluation of the current state of dairy cattle welfare. Six consumer segments were found, thus reflecting the high differentiation of the Flemish market for milk. The authors observe that milk market supply does not show a similar differentiation. Hence, they propose to focus on enhanced animal welfare in positioning milk products on the market, including access to pasture, freedom of movement, and absence of diseases. In addition, a star (or equivalent) rating system might serve as a means to increase the market share of animal-friendly milk products, and to encourage farmers to invest in cow welfare.

Rather than studying consumer opinions and intentions, *An Environmental Perspective on Clothing Consumption: Consumer Segments and Their Behavioural Patterns* [8] uses self-reported consumer behaviour as the basis for the segmentation of consumers in four different countries. Based on reported number of clothing items purchased, expenditures, brand, acquisition mode, and sustainable clothing material purchased, five segments were found, ranging from low amount of consumption and purchasing at budget outlets to high-volume consumption and premium outlets. It appears that only the upper two segments, comprising less than 10% of the total population, bought sustainable apparel significantly more often. Although the authors suggest different interventions to promote sustainable clothing consumption, the opportunities seem to be limited.

Apparently, segmentation can be accomplished in different ways on which different interventions for sustainable consumption can be based. As a tentative conclusion of this section, interventions aimed at changing attitudes and opinions may be more successful than those aimed at changing behaviour directly.

3.2. Miscellaneous Topics

Travel behaviour is an important type of consumer behaviour in regard to sustainability. *Fostering Sustainable Travel Behaviour: Role of Sustainability Labels and Goal-Directed Behaviour Regarding Touristic Services* [9] studies the awareness of eco-labels, and the attractiveness of hotel offerings and the preference for certified tour operators in relation to the presence of eco-labels on the web sites of suppliers. The first study used eye tracking to measure the number of fixations and average fixation durations for different stimuli present on the web sites as an indicator of awareness. Clearly, awareness was higher for larger eco-labels than for smaller ones, and was also positively related to attractiveness of the offer. The second study focused on the trustworthiness of sustainability certifications for tour operators, and shows that preference for tour operators was positively influenced by the perceived trustworthiness of certifications. In sum, the research shows that informative labels positively influence consumers' awareness and preferences for sustainable travel.

The second paper on eco-friendly travel choices, *Can Social Comparison Feedback Affect Indicators of Eco-Friendly Travel Choice? Insights from Two Online Experiments* [10], studies the effect of social comparison feedback on the students' ecological footprint on eco-friendly travel intentions. After calculating the students' ecological footprints and the number of Earths needed if everybody would behave like the participant, they were given information about the number of Earths needed if other students had either higher or lower ecological footprints. Additionally, measures were taken regarding the participants' identification with students at their university as a group. It was found that intentions to travel eco-friendly were positively related to negative comparison feedback, but only when group identification was high. A second study was not able to replicate the significant finding from the first study, thus calling for further research on this issue.

Collaborative Consumption: A Proposed Scale for Measuring the Construct Applied to a Car-Sharing Setting [11] reports on the construction of a car-sharing scale in Brazil. Starting with 29 items, 9 items were removed because of their performance in exploratory factor analyses. The remaining items were included in confirmatory factor analysis, resulting in five factors: socio-environmental consciousness, trust, social identity, convenience, and risks. The subscales showed unidimensionality, reliability, and convergent and discriminant validity. Although the scale development was satisfactory, it has not been tested in an independent sample, and is limited to car sharing only.

Since price if often competing with environmental friendliness, it is important to estimate consumers' willingness to pay (WTP) for environmentally-friendly products. *Consumers' Willingness to Pay a Premium for Eco-Labeled LED TVs in Korea: A Contingent Valuation Study* [12] assesses WTP for a popular eco-friendly LED TV by using a sophisticated contingent valuation method. The estimated WTP amounts to about 4% of the price of the TV and is higher for high-income, older, highly-educated, and female consumers with children. Although contingent valuation is not based on actual behaviour, the methodology is directly relevant for suppliers of new eco-friendly products on the consumer market.

The first two papers in this section dealt with the role of information on preferences and behaviour, without focusing on particular segments. The final two papers deal with measurement issues in consumer behaviour (i.e., scale development and WTP measurements). This section touches on the basics of consumer behaviour.

Conflicts of Interest: The author declares no conflicts of interest.

References

1. Sohlberg, J. The Effect of Elite Polarization: A Comparative Perspective on How Party Elites Influence Attitudes and Behavior on Climate Change in the European Union. *Sustainability* **2017**, *9*, 39. Available online: http://www.mdpi.com/2071-1050/9/1/39 (accessed on 28 December 2016). [CrossRef]
2. Bonera, M.; Corvi, E.; Codini, A.P.; Ma, R. Does nationality matter in eco-behaviour? *Sustainability* **2017**, *9*. in press.
3. Vringer, K.; Heijden, E.; Soest, D.; Vollebergh, H.; Dietz, F. Sustainable Consumption Dilemmas. *Sustainability* **2017**, *9*, 942. Available online: http://www.mdpi.com/2071-1050/9/6/942 (accessed on 3 June 2017). [CrossRef]
4. Reese, G.; Junge, E. Keep on Rockin' in a (Plastic-) Free World: Collective Efficacy and Pro-Environmental Intentions as a Function of Task Difficulty. *Sustainability* **2017**, *9*, 200. Available online: http://www.mdpi.com/2071-1050/9/2/200 (accessed on 1 February 2017). [CrossRef]
5. Brons, A.; Oosterveer, P. Making Sense of Sustainability: A Practice Theories Approach to Buying Food. *Sustainability* **2017**, *9*, 467. Available online: http://www.mdpi.com/2071-1050/9/3/467 (accessed on 21 March 2017). [CrossRef]

6. Verain, M.; Sijtsema, S.; Dagevos, H.; Antonides, G. Attribute Segmentation and Communication Effects on Healthy and Sustainable Consumer Diet Intentions. *Sustainability* **2017**, *9*, 743. Available online: http://www.mdpi.com/2071-1050/9/5/743 (accessed on 4 May 2017). [CrossRef]

7. De Graaf, S.; Vanhonacker, F.; Van Loo, E.; Bijttebier, J.; Lauwers, L.; Tuyttens, F.; Verbeke, W. Market Opportunities for Animal-Friendly Milk in Different Consumer Segments. *Sustainability* **2016**, *8*, 1302. Available online: http://www.mdpi.com/2071-1050/8/12/1302 (accessed on 11 December 2016). [CrossRef]

8. Gwozdz, W.; Steensen Nielsen, K.; Müller, T. An Environmental Perspective on Clothing Consumption: Consumer Segments and Their Behavioral Patterns. *Sustainability* **2017**, *9*, 762. Available online: http://www.mdpi.com/2071-1050/9/5/762 (accessed on 6 May 2017). [CrossRef]

9. Penz, E.; Hofmann, E.; Hartl, B. Fostering Sustainable Travel Behavior: Role of Sustainability Labels and Goal-Directed Behavior Regarding Touristic Services. *Sustainability* **2017**, *9*, 1056. Available online: http://www.mdpi.com/2071-1050/9/6/1056 (accessed on 18 June 2017). [CrossRef]

10. Doran, R.; Hanss, D.; Øgaard, T. Can Social Comparison Feedback Affect Indicators of Eco-Friendly Travel Choices? Insights from Two Online Experiments. *Sustainability* **2017**, *9*, 196. Available online: http://www.mdpi.com/2071-1050/9/2/196 (accessed on 29 January 2017). [CrossRef]

11. Dall Pizzol, H.; Ordovás de Almeida, S.; do Couto Soares, M. Collaborative Consumption: A Proposed Scale for Measuring the Construct Applied to a Carsharing Setting. *Sustainability* **2017**, *9*, 703. Available online: http://www.mdpi.com/2071-1050/9/5/703 (accessed on 28 April 2017). [CrossRef]

12. Min, S.; Lim, S.; Yoo, S. Consumers' Willingness to Pay a Premium for Eco-Labeled LED TVs in Korea: A Contingent Valuation Study. *Sustainability* **2017**, *9*, 814. Available online: http://www.mdpi.com/2071-1050/9/5/814 (accessed on 13 May 2017). [CrossRef]

sustainability

MDPI

Article

The Effect of Elite Polarization: A Comparative Perspective on How Party Elites Influence Attitudes and Behavior on Climate Change in the European Union

Jacob Sohlberg

Department of Political Science, University of Gothenburg, Box 711, 405 30 Gothenburg, Sweden;
jacob.sohlberg@gu.se; Tel.: +46-31-786-3553

Academic Editor: Gerrit Antonides
Received: 21 October 2016; Accepted: 23 December 2016; Published: 28 December 2016

Abstract: There is considerable variability in attitudes towards climate change between citizens of different countries. By using individual-level and country-level data, I examine if this variability in public opinion is partially caused by political party elites. The results show that when elites are united in their support for environmental issues, the perceived threat of climate change is higher than in countries where party elites are divided. The results also demonstrate that the perceived threat influences behavior related to climate change, and that threat mediates the effect of party positions. Consequently, the effect of party elites is stronger than previously acknowledged. The models rely on Generalized Method of Moments estimation and instrumental variables with clustering on EU member-states.

Keywords: party cues; elite influence; threat; climate change

---

1. Introduction

Climatologists and other scientists who study climate change have overwhelmingly concluded that the world is going through an unprecedented temperature increase [1,2], yet this information has not uniformly been translated into a public opinion response across countries. Instead, cross-national polls on climate change show that there are substantial differences between countries in how residents view climate change. Residents in many countries view climate change as a very serious problem, whereas citizens in other countries do not think it is a serious problem. Moreover, people differ in the extent to which they have taken personal action in fighting climate change [3]. While there are notable exceptions [4,5], not enough attention has been paid to the major differences that exist between countries in public opinion on climate change and how factors at the national level influence individuals. Furthermore, insufficient focus has been put on how public opinion is translated into behavior, an area that "we need to know far more about" [6] (p. 41). Lastly, there are problematic issues of causality in this field that need to be addressed in more detail than they have been. This multilevel study aims to fill the gaps on what influences cross-national attitudes on climate change and how public opinion is transformed into behavior while at the same time accounting for potential causality problems.

I draw on two different literatures, research on elite influence and research on threat perceptions, to build a model on how (1) political party elites cause changes in the perceived threat of climate change and, how in turn; (2) the perceived threat impacts behavior. As for the first part of the model, elites are important because on issues ranging from foreign policy to attitudes towards the European Union, political party elites have strong effects on the public [7,8]. Therefore, it is plausible that these elites also influence public opinion on climate change. However, there are good reasons to be suspicious of this causal ordering because the direction is sometimes reversed, with public opinion influencing elite opinions [9]. Fortunately, the instrumental variable approach can be used to deal with the problem of endogeneity [7,10]. In the second part of the model, I introduce the concept of perceived threat as a mediating factor between party elites and political behavior. Here, the perceived threat (which is affected by party elites) influences the political behavior of fighting climate change. While previous research on climate change has treated perceived threat as exogenous [11], this paper suggests that the reality is more complicated, with threat serving as a mediator rather than as an exogenous variable. In other words, the effects of political elites have potentially been underestimated in prior research.

I test three predictions on how political party elites and perceived threat influence behaviors and attitudes on climate change. First, I hypothesize that when political elites are divided on environmental issues, people then believe that the threat of climate change is lower. Second, I expect that when the threat of climate change is perceived as higher, individuals are more likely to take personal action to fight climate change. Third, I predict that the effect of elite division on behavior is mediated by perceived threat. That is, the effect of perceived threat on willingness to fight climate change is hypothesized to be partially driven by the effect elites have on the perceived threat of climate change.

2. Elite Influence Explanations and Endogeneity

In *The Nature and Origins of Mass Opinion*, John Zaller [8] finds that when political elites change their opinions, the public changes its attitudes accordingly. A key point in this model is that it distinguishes between when elites send a one-sided message and when they communicate a two-sided message. If elites send a one-sided message on a political issue, the public is persuaded in one direction, and consequently there is little variance in public opinion as they move uniformly. However, if political elites send a two-sided message, the public diverges along political predispositions. Zaller exemplifies with the public opinion dynamic of the Vietnam War. In the early war, political leaders sent out a one-sided message, and consequently the public supported the war. However, later in the war, the elites diverged. With a two-sided elite message on foreign policy, doves among the public became more dovish and hawks became more hawkish [8]. Similarly, public opinion records from World War II and the Iraq War show that if political party elites diverge, this influences regular partisans along party lines. When elites are united in supporting wars, as they were during parts of both wars, the public finds little objection [12,13]. There is also some evidence from U.S. public opinion data that party leaders can influence climate change attitudes of supporters [14,15]. Party cues simplify political decision-making because rather than going through the trouble of finding out information about the issues and then making an informed decision, people can quickly form opinions by adopting the same positions as trusted party politicians. Parties strongly influence a range of attitudes, including the perception of the state of the national economy, an issue that presumably could be objectively verified [7,16–20].

However, there are plausible alternative models to the elite influence approach. One is built around the idea that citizens select candidates and parties that are closest to their own preferences. After all, citizens have stable predispositions such as values that influence political issue positions [21] and vote choice [22]. Since politicians want to get elected or stay in office, they adjust their positions according to the will of the public [23]. Evidence suggests that this is not something politicians do just around elections, but rather that they are continuously trying to follow public opinion [24]. In the case of climate change, it follows that party officials tailor their environmental policies to fit the will of their constituents. If this causal order of model were correct, an analysis based on cross-sectional data that regresses attitudes among the public about climate change on elite opinions would indeed find a relationship. Unfortunately, we might therefore mistakenly conclude that elites influence the public although the reverse is correct. Thus, a traditional ordinary least squares (OLS) regression will produce erroneous results. Another model of the relationship between the public and political elites suggests that they move in unison, i.e., none is leading the other. For example, upon hearing in news media that climate change is a problem, both elites and the public conclude that something needs to be done [25]. Even studies based on time series analysis can be affected by this problem. If elites respond to the public on climate change, even partially, it means that elite positions are endogenous, and coefficient estimates therefore inconsistent. Since it is plausible that political elites adjust their positions on climate change and the environment according to the will of the people, a viable solution is to use instrumental variables to estimate the endogenous variable.

2.1. The Perception of Climate Change as a Threat and the Link to Behavior

A central reason to study how elites influence threat perceptions is that these perceptions tend to strongly influence how people think and behave around climate change. Intuitively, when people sense that an issue poses a serious threat, they want to reduce the threat associated with the issue. With climate change, this is manifested by people taking personal action to reduce their carbon footprint and by their support for policies to reduce greenhouse gas emissions. In contrast, when the threat of climate change is perceived as low, the public tends to be much less supportive of policies and actions aimed at reducing the threat [11,26,27]. In a similar vein, research on American public opinion after the terrorist attacks in 2001 shows that individuals who felt more threatened by the terrorist attacks responded by expressing more support for military action in Afghanistan and a more active role for the U.S. in the world [28]. Likewise, social psychological research on intergroup relations has shown that threat plays a key role in generating anti-immigrant attitudes [29,30]. Faced with threats, people often want take actions to deal with the threats [31].

While prior research on climate change has contributed in identifying the importance of perceived threat, it nonetheless treats it as exogenous. Possibly, this is an oversimplification since research on other types of threat perceptions show that they are caused by a range of factors [28,32,33]. The determinants of climate change threat are presumably different compared to, for example, what affects perceptions about terrorism, but climate change is likely similar in that the perceived threat does not arise on its own. Thus, the statements in the hypotheses below are not as obvious at they might appear; research on climate change attitudes has often treated threat perceptions as exogenous and therefore potentially exaggerated the effect of threat perceptions at the expense of factors such as party elite cues.

2.2. Hypotheses

To summarize, I expect that the more party elites diverge on the environment, the less serious a problem people think that climate change is. It does not matter which parties are skeptical and which ones are pro-environment—what matters is that parties are divided, and that they are sending mixed messages to the public. In contrast, when elites send a more one-sided message on the environment, i.e., they are united in their environmentalism, the public responds by perceiving climate change as a more serious threat.

Hypothesis 1. *The more party elites are divided on the environment, the less likely it is that individuals perceive climate change as a threat.*

Another aspect of the model concerns the effect of climate change threat on climate change-related behavior. The logic here is that if something increases perceived threat, people take actions to reduce the threat. Specifically, when climate change is perceived to pose a serious threat, then people respond by taking personal actions to decrease the threat.

Hypothesis 2. *The more individuals perceive climate change as a threat, the more willing they are to fight climate change.*

The third feature of the model is that the effect of party elites on climate change-related behavior is mediated by the perceived threat of climate change. While the influence of threat perceptions on behavior found in prior research on climate change is not disputed, this model suggests that the conclusion from prior research is incomplete. In other words, the model incorporates the view that threat perceptions are malleable.

Hypothesis 3. *The effect of party elites on individuals' willingness to fight climate change is mediated by the perceived threat of climate change.*

3. Data Description and Methods

3.1. Individual-level Data

Individual-level data comes from a Eurobarometer survey (EB 72.1) that asks appropriate questions on climate change. The questionnaire also includes a number of variables that cover individuals' backgrounds, e.g., age and education. TNS Opinion & Social Network conducted the survey on behalf of the European Commission's Directorate General for Communication, and data collection took place between 28 August and 17 September 2009. Citizens from 27 countries of the European Union were interviewed for a total of 26,719 respondents, all 15 years or older [3].

A central variable in the analysis is the perceived threat of climate change. It serves both as a dependent variable and as a mediating variable. It is measured by the following question: "And how serious a problem do you think climate change is at this moment? Please use a scale from 1 to 10, '1' would mean that it is 'not at all a serious problem' and '10' would mean that it is 'an extremely serious problem'." Like all variables at the individual level except age, it was recoded to range from 0 to 1. Summary statistics of all variables are included in the Table A1.

Willingness to take personal action measures to what extent respondents have taken personal "actions aimed at helping to fight climate change". The indicator is based on a four-point scale with higher values meaning more agreement. It serves as dependent variables in models that estimate the effects of elite division and perceived threat of climate change.

The models also include the individual-level control variables. Female is a dummy variable that is coded one for women and zero for men. Education is also measured with dummy variables; lower education, coded here as 15 years or less of formal education, equals one, higher education, 20 years or more, equals one, and respondents still in school are coded as one. The baseline category is 16–19 years of schooling. Household wealth is a 10-point scale that ranges from zero, very poor, to one, very wealthy. It measures the participants' perception of their own wealth. Age measures how old the respondent is and it ranges from 18 to 98. A dummy variable is included for those participants who were unemployed. Respondents who were manual laborers were also dummy coded. Life satisfaction is a measure of perceived general satisfaction with life. It ranges from zero, very dissatisfied, to one, very satisfied. An indicator for respondents' perceived class, from lowest to highest level in society, ranges from zero to one.

3.2. Country-level Data and Instrumental Variables

Elite positions on the environment are measured with data from the Comparative Manifestos Project. The project, funded by the German Science Foundation, has coded party positions from over 50 countries on a range of issues, including their positions on environmental protection. The parties have not been coded on their policies on climate change specifically, yet rather on their environmental policy platform more generally [34]. Since climate change is an environmental problem, albeit different from many other environmental problems [35,36], this should not pose a serious problem to the analysis. (Climate change is different from other environmental problems in a number of aspects, including the fact that there are a vast number of globally distributed actors responsible for climate change and the consequences are varying and wide-ranging. Moreover, unlike many other environmental problems, the problems associated with climate change do not stop when emissions are reduced, but will most likely remain for centuries [36]. Since climate change is an extraordinary difficult problem, it has been labeled as both a "wicked" [35] and a "super wicked" problem [36].). If anything, by relying on this variable, it becomes harder to reject the null because environmental protection may introduce some noise into the measurement. I match Comparative Manifestos Project data with Eurobarometer survey data for 27 EU countries to create a merged, new dataset.

Elite division is measured by the weighted standard deviation of party positions for each country. In other words, each country receives a score that depends on how much consensus there is. A high consensus indicates that the parties are united and thus produce little variance whereas more elite divergence generates more variance. The positions of parties with higher vote shares were given more weight than those with lower. (The party positions that went into the weighted standard deviation variable came from the date closest in time before the Eurobarometer sample was collected. For example, if the Comparative Manifestos Project had coded party platforms for a country with elections in 2006 and 2010, the party scores were taken from 2006 and not 2010 because the latter date was after the collection of the EB sample.). This indicator is calculated in the same way as Gabel and Scheve [7] although in this paper it is applied to party positions on the environment rather than party positions on EU integration. Moreover, I follow their model in the expectation that parties are either united in their pro-position or that they are divided. In their paper, parties are either uniformly pro-EU or divided. There are no countries where parties are uniformly anti-EU. In the present model, parties are either pro-environment or divided on the environment. I do not expect that parties are uniformly anti-environment.

In identifying valid instruments, I follow the theoretical and empirical strategy of Gabel and Scheve [7] and specify electoral features that are expected to correlate with party elite polarization on issues, but are exogenous to public opinion. The logic behind this is that electoral laws influence the number of political parties [37] and with features that lead to more parties, it also follows that there is more heterogeneity in policy positions [7]. Based on this reasoning, one of the two instrumental variables selected for this study is whether the country relies on proportional representation or a first-past-the-post system. According to Duverger's law, compared to first-past-the-post systems, systems that rely on proportional representation tend to have more parties [38], and consequently, with more parties, there should also be more diversity on issues such as on the environment. (Duverger's law is the notion that electoral systems with single-member districts and plurality rule (i.e., first-past-the-post) tend to lead to two major parties in parliament. The system in the United States is one example of this. There are primarily two reasons for this tendency. First, parties know that they need to get the most votes in order to win any seats, which means that politicians work to form inclusive and big parties. Second, voters are aware that a vote for a smaller party is unlikely to affect the election outcome and therefore tend to vote for the biggest party closest to their preferences. In contrast, electoral systems with proportional representation are likely to produce more parties in parliament because there is less of an incentive for parties to merge and voters are at less of a risk of casting a wasted vote [38].). The data comes from the Quality of Government Social Policy Dataset and Pippa Norris's time-series data [39,40]. The other instrumental variable is an index of electoral fractionalization based on a formula from Rae [41]. Again, with more fractionalization, I expect there to be more diversity in party positions. The data for the variable comes from Comparative Political Data Set III [42].

I also include control variables at the country level such as GDP per capita and inflation rate. Since the study is about attitudes on climate change, the models also include controls related to this issue. The variable of economy energy intensity is an indicator of how much an economy relies on energy. In addition, the models include an indicator of the proportion of electricity that is generated from renewable energy sources. Furthermore, an index of greenhouse gas emissions per capita captures the total sum of CO_2, CH_4, N_2O and fluorinated gas emissions in mg/tons. All control variable data except the climate change risk index have been taken from Eurostat. The data describes the situation in the European Union for the year 2009. The variable climate change risk index is a measure of how exposed countries have been to extreme weather between 1991 and 2009 [43].

3.3. Model Specification

When there is an endogenous relationship between the dependent variable and one or more independent variables, the error distribution is not independent from the distribution of the regressors. Therefore, OLS regression will likely yield inconsistent and biased estimates. It does not matter how many control variables are added to the model. To deal with this problem, two-stage least squares (2SLS) is frequently used. The solution is straightforward; the researcher estimates the endogenous explanatory variable with instrumental variables (IV). Here, instruments should only be related to the dependent variable through the endogenous variable. Given that these two conditions are met, 2SLS will produce consistent estimates, even in the face of endogeneity [44].

However, because of heteroskedasticity, a pervasive problem in empirical studies, the 2SLS approach is often unsound because the standard errors are inconsistent. Robust, or heteroskedasticity-consistent, standard errors can alleviate part of this problem, but the IV estimator is still inefficient because of heteroskedasticity. Fortunately, generalized method of moment estimation leads to efficient estimates despite heteroskedasticity, and therefore solves the problems associated with traditional IV estimation [45–47]. Since its introduction by Hansen [48], generalized method of moments (GMM) estimation has become an increasingly popular method in social sciences. In fact, in economics and finance it is one of the most important statistical tools. GMM estimators are consistent, asymptotically normal and efficient [49].

GMM is also useful when there is clustering. With the present study, based on a sample from several countries, GMM with clustering is ideal, not only because citizens of the same country are correlated, but also because it does not matter what shape the clustering takes from cluster to cluster; it is allowed to vary without it having a negative impact on efficiency or consistency. GMM with clustering produces both consistent standard errors and efficient estimates of coefficients. The benefit with using GMM over random-effects instrumental IV estimators is that GMM relaxes the constraint that correlations within groups are constant [45]. In sum, there are clear advantages with GMM estimation over both traditional 2SLS and random-effects models with instrumental variables, which are estimation methods often used in this type of applied political science research.

Now, GMM or 2SLS estimation should not be the first option for the researcher because there is an inevitable loss of efficiency compared to OLS. The potential nonorthogonality between regressors and errors should be weighed against the efficiency of OLS [50]. In the results section below I examine this issue by calculating the GMM distance, which is an endogeneity test in the GMM context [51].

4. Results

4.1. Elite Influence on the Perceived Threat of Climate Change

Before assessing the support for the hypotheses, a question is whether party elite positions on the environment are endogenous or exogenous. This issue is examined with an endogeneity test, the GMM distance, which is robust to violations of homoskedasticity. The null is that elite division is exogenous and a rejection of the null indicates that the variable must be treated as endogenous. If the variable is exogenous, the GMM-model is unnecessary and a traditional OLS-model preferable. The test statistic, the GMM distance, is distributed as χ^2 with 1 degree of freedom [45]. Table 1 shows that elite positions on climate change are indeed endogenous because the null is rejected ($p = 0.016$). Given these results, OLS-regression would yield inconsistent estimators.

Hypothesis 1 suggests that when party elites in a country express divergent opinions on the environment and climate change, this leads citizens to downplay the threatening nature of climate change. If, on the other hand, parties in a country express similar sentiments in that they are more uniformly pro-environment, this yields less variation, which leads to a heightened perceived threat of climate change. The results support Hypothesis 1 since the coefficient for elite division is statistically significant and negative. The results from the IV-GMM model are presented in Table 1. (The use of the IV-GMM estimation over the traditional 2SLS method is justified also because of the presence of heteroskedasticity. The null hypothesis of homoskedasticity is rejected at $p < 0.001$. Heteroskedasticity is present in all models in this paper.). They show that a one unit change in elite division decreases perceptions of climate change as a serious threat by 0.0635, holding both individual-level and country-level variables constant. In other words, just as predicted, when party elites send a more two-sided message, the public thinks that climate change is less of a threat. Conversely, if party elites send a one-sided message, residents believe that climate change is a more serious threat. To put this in more substantive terms, when the predicted value at one standard deviation above the mean (i.e., in an information environment with a high degree of elite division) the perception of climate change threat is 0.59 (on the 0–1 scale) yet when elite division is low, at one standard deviation below the mean, threat perception is higher at 0.75. (The GMM estimates are clearer compared to the traditional 2SLS approach. The coefficient and standard error for elite division with 2SLS is −0.0460 and 0.0247, respectively ($p = 0.063$). Thus, the 2SLS results also support Hypothesis 1 as it is a directional hypothesis, yet the coefficient is smaller and the standard error larger. Similarly, a GLS random-effects model with instrumental variables also supports Hypothesis 1. According to the estimates based on the random-effects model, elite division decreases perceived threat with 0.0423 (0.0151). The effect is significant ($p = 0.005$).)

Table 1. Determinants of perceived threat of climate change—GMM and OLS estimation.

	Generalized Methods of Moments (Instrumental Variables)		Ordinary Least Squares (No Instruments)	
Female	0.0195	(0.0047) *	0.0213	(0.0048) *
Lower Education	0.0017	(0.0081)	−0.0025	(0.0063)
Higher Education	0.0250	(0.0071) *	0.0137	(0.0067) *
Still Educated	0.0099	(0.0096)	0.0007	(0.0087)
Household Wealth	−0.0142	(0.0142)	−0.0163	(0.0166)
Age	−0.0003	(0.0002)	−0.0003	(0.0002)
Unemployed	−0.0035	(0.0063)	−0.0046	(0.0071)
Manual Laborer	0.0057	(0.0045)	−0.0014	(0.0049)
Life Satisfaction	0.0314	(0.0118) *	0.0189	(0.0133)
Class	−0.0022	(0.0178)	0.0376	(0.0176) *
Elite Division	−0.0635	(0.0188) *	−0.0251	(0.0075) *
GDP/Cap	−0.0038	(0.0019) *	−0.0021	(0.0017)
Inflation	−0.0112	(0.0071)	−0.0119	(0.0062)
Unemployment	−0.0060	(0.0024) *	−0.0067	(0.0034) *
Economy Energy Intensity	−0.0002	(0.0001) *	−0.0001	(0.0001)
Renewable electricity	0.0025	(0.0010) *	0.0009	(0.0006)
Greenhouse Gas Emissions/Cap	0.0072	(0.0061)	0.0009	(0.0053)
Climate Change Risk Index	0.0004	(0.0004)	−0.0001	(0.0002)
Constant	0.8896	(0.0711) *	0.8598	(0.0756) *
Partial R^2	0.178		-	
F Statistic (First Stage)	5.420	0.011	-	-
Hansen's J Statistic	1.187	0.276	-	-
Endogeneity (GMM Distance)	5.802	0.016	-	-
N	24,437		24,437	
Number of clusters	27		27	

Notes: Entries are coefficients with standard errors in parentheses. * $p < 0.05$.

Instrumental variables are effective to the extent that they are related to the endogenous regressor. The partial R-squared from the first-stage regression is 0.178, and the F statistic (2, 26) is 5.42 ($p = 0.011$). Thus, the instruments, the index of electoral fractionalization and the measure of the proportional election system, have a positive and strong effect on party elite division. The Sargan-Hansen test is a test of whether or not the instruments are uncorrelated with the error term. The null hypothesis is that the instruments are valid, so a rejection of the null indicates a validity problem with the instruments. The test statistics is Hansen's J statistic when the GMM estimator is used. As Table 1 shows, the null is not rejected ($\chi^2 = 1.187$, $p = 0.2759$), which suggests that the instruments were excluded correctly.

While OLS-regression yields inconsistent estimates because of endogeneity, for purposes of comparison I nonetheless present these results. Just as in the instrumental variable model, it has clustering based on country. As we can see in Table 1, the coefficients show a similar pattern of results with OLS. Yet while the effect of elite division is significant and in the right direction, −0.0251, it is underestimated compared to the instrumental variable model.

4.2. The Effect of Party Cues and Threat Perceptions

The next steps in the analysis are to examine how the perceived threat of climate change influences climate change-related behavior, and how perceived threat mediates the effect of party elite positions on the environment. Since there are theoretical reasons to suspect an endogenous relationship between elites and climate change attitudes, the subsequent analysis is based on results estimated with IV-GMM.

Hypothesis 2 is supported because the perception of climate change as a serious problem has a statistically significant and substantial effect on personal behavior, as Table 2 demonstrates. A one-unit increase in perceived threat leads to a 0.2127 increase in the likelihood that people take personal action to fight the problem. Since both variables are coded from zero to one, it means that an increase from the lowest to the highest value of perceived threat causes a 21% change in the scale's value. While the effect of elite division is still significant, its effect is reduced (−0.0594) when perceived threat is added to the model.

Table 2. Determinants of personal action to reduce climate change.

Perceived Threat of Climate Change	-	-	0.2127	(0.0245) *
Female	0.0142	(0.0045) *	0.0108	(0.0039) *
Lower Education	−0.0342	(0.0132) *	−0.0329	(0.0121) *
Higher Education	0.0388	(0.0078) *	0.0337	(0.0074) *
Still Educated	−0.0305	(0.0108) *	−0.0294	(0.0107) *
Household Wealth	0.0047	(0.0206)	0.0084	(0.0204)
Age	0.0003	(0.0002)	0.0004	(0.0002) *
Unemployed	−0.0136	(0.0100)	−0.0104	(0.0090)
Manual Laborer	−0.0016	(0.0058)	−0.0033	(0.0057)
Life Satisfaction	0.0670	(0.0156) *	0.0606	(0.0156) *
Class	0.0842	(0.0301) *	0.0792	(0.0276) *
Elite Division	−0.0714	(0.0238)*	−0.0594	(0.0208) *
GDP/Cap	−0.0068	(0.0028) *	−0.0060	(0.0027) *
Inflation	−0.0131	(0.0128)	−0.0108	(0.0120)
Unemployment	−0.0082	(0.0031) *	−0.0066	(0.0029) *
Economy Energy Intensity	−0.0006	(0.0002) *	−0.0005	(0.0002) *
Renewable electricity	0.0037	(0.0013) *	0.0032	(0.0011) *
Greenhouse Gas Emissions/Cap	0.0232	(0.0097) *	0.0219	(0.0094) *
Climate Change Risk Index	0.0006	(0.0004)	0.0006	(0.0004)
Constant	0.6976	(0.1010) *	0.5000	(0.1009) *
Partial R^2	0.181		0.177	
F Statistic (First Stage)	5.63	0.009	5.39	0.011
Hansen's J Statistic	0.154	0.694	0.072	0.789
Endogeneity (GMM Distance)	6.328	0.012	7.056	0.008
N	23,768		23,362	
Number of clusters	27		27	

Notes: Entries are coefficients with standard errors in parentheses. * $p < 0.05$.

Party elite division on climate change reduces the likelihood that residents will take personal action to fight climate change. The left side model of Table 2 shows that a one-unit change in elite division leads to a 0.0714 reduction in personal actions. Thus, not only does a two-sided message on climate change lead to a reduction in perceived threat, it also makes citizens less willing to personally take action on climate change.

As for the instruments, the partial R-squared is similar to the model that uses perceived threat as a dependent variable. This is unsurprising since the instruments are the same. The F statistic is 5.63 and therefore significant ($p = 0.009$) for the relationship between the instruments and the endogenous regressor. Moreover, the use of the GMM-model over OLS is justified because of the endogeneity between personal actions and elite positions on climate change ($\chi^2 = 6.328$, $p = 0.012$). Hansen's J statistic indicates that the instruments are not correlated with personal actions on climate change ($p = 0.694$).

Hypothesis 3 states that the effect of elite positions is mediated by perceived threat. The results show that the four steps of mediation are met [52]. First, elite division (X) is correlated with personal behavior (Y). Second, elite division (X) predicts perceived threat (M). Third, perceived threat (M) significantly affects personal behavior (Y) while controlling for elite division (X). Fourth, the reduction of the effect of elite divisions (X) on personal behavior (Y) when perceived threat (M) is included in the model is statistically significant, as shown by the Sobel test statistic of -2.84 ($p = 0.01$). Consequently, Hypothesis 3 is supported. (Given that IV-GMM is used to estimate the models, the traditional method of assessing mediation is appropriate. The Sobel test can be problematic in small-N situations, but since the dataset includes more than 25,000 observations, it should be acceptable.)

To validate the support for the model, I attempt to replicate the results with another, highly related, dependent variable. Instead of examining the personal actions to fight climate change, I study beliefs about the economic consequences of fighting climate change and anticipate that those who are exposed to polarized party elites are more likely to see negative economic consequences. As shown in the Table A2, this theoretical expectation is confirmed with the alternative outcome variable. Moreover, all four steps of mediation are met, with the Sobel test being statistically significant ($t = 2.45$, $p = 0.005$).

5. Conclusions and Discussion

There are large differences in climate change attitudes between countries. The results presented in this paper suggest that political party elites partially influence these differences in public opinion about climate change. When elites are divided about the importance of environmental problems such as climate change, then people in these countries tend to perceive climate change as less of a threat. In countries where elites are more united in their environmental concern, the perceived threat of climate change is generally higher. That political elites have this causal effect on public opinion can be stated with greater certainty because of the use of instrumental variables. The GMM approach to the endogeneity problem illustrates how this method can deal with the problem without the loss of efficiency that is associated with the traditional 2SLS approach. An advantage with the GMM estimation used in this paper is that the standard errors are not only robust to arbitrary heteroskedasticity, but also to arbitrary intragroup correlation, which is a common feature of cross-national data.

Another finding in the paper is that the perceived threat of climate change has a substantial and significant effect on climate change-related behavior. Individuals who think that climate change is highly threatening are also more likely to have taken personal steps to fight climate change. On the contentious issue of whether or not a fight against climate change helps the economy, an increased perceived threat makes people more likely to believe in the beneficial economic effects. I interpret this as an example of motivated reasoning; people who have been persuaded by the climate change threat also prefer to think that economic growth is compatible with the existence of climate change. The support for the theoretical model indicates that the effect of elites on climate change behaviors and attitudes might have been understated in prior research. While I found a direct effect of party elites on personal behavior, there is also an indirect effect of elites that goes through perceived threat. In other words, perceived threat mediates the effect of elites and party cues thus appear to have a larger effect than previously thought.

Using data from 2009 for the analysis, I look at whether elites drive public opinion on climate change. On the one hand, the observed changes in our climate accumulated over the period of 2009 to the present [1], which could have made the public increasingly aware of the realities associated with climate change. With objective facts available, the possibility of elites affecting public opinion should be reduced. Moreover, other issues, such as the refugee crisis, have gotten a great deal of attention. Thus, even though elites could potentially sway public opinion on climate change, people might currently be paying more attention to other issues. After all, on issues where elite cues are weaker, elite effects should be smaller. On the other hand, political elites may still influence the public. In 2009, the world economy was still reeling from the financial crisis of 2007–2008, which presumably reduced the impact of elites because environmental issues were given less attention than the economy. From this perspective, elite effects on the climate may have been particularly small around this time. Furthermore, while researchers are documenting multiple, tangible changes to the global climate, it may still seem too farfetched for ordinary citizens to conclude that climate change is real based solely on personal experience. Nevertheless, even if ordinary people do conclude that climate change is real, perhaps due to their own experiences, elites may still be able to influence the public simply because of the wickedness of climate change. It is an extraordinarily complex problem to understand and address, which may leave more latitude for elites to affect the public.

An additional caveat to the conclusions drawn in this paper is that they rely on only one method. The cross-national approach with instrumental variables places conclusions of cause and effect on firmer ground, yet experimental techniques could provide additional evidence on causal mechanisms. Moreover, experimental techniques could be used to study factors that moderate the effects of elites. As suggested previously, two factors that may influence the effect of elites are the strength of elite cues and the degree of personal experience, but there are also others. For example, future studies could focus on the interaction between political trust and messages from political elites. It is possible that political elites need to be trusted in order for them to influence their constituents, and with the greater flexibility and internal validity of experimental studies, this could be examined more in-depth.

Acknowledgments: I thank Todd K. Hartman, Catherine de Vries and the anonymous reviewers for their helpful comments. I also thank the Centre for Collective Action Research (CeCAR) at the University of Gothenburg for its financial support to publish in open access.

Conflicts of Interest: The author declares no conflict of interest.

Appendix A

Table A1. Summary statistics.

Variable	Obs	Mean	S.D.	Min.	Max.
Perceived Threat of Climate Change	25,801	0.68	0.25	0	1
Personal Action to Reduce Climate Change	25,078	0.55	0.31	0	1
Belief in Positive Economic Effects of Fighting Climate Change	22,165	0.63	0.27	0	1
Female	26,719	0.55	0.50	0	1
Lower Education	26,234	0.21	0.41	0	1
Higher Education	26,234	0.28	0.45	0	1
Still Educated	26,234	0.08	0.27	0	1
Household Wealth	25,944	0.49	0.18	0	1
Age	26,719	48.12	18.52	15	98
Unemployed	26,719	0.08	0.27	0	1
Manual Laborer	26,719	0.19	0.39	0	1
Life Satisfaction	26,654	0.63	0.25	0	1
Class	26,171	0.51	0.18	0	1
GDP/Cap	26,719	22.05	12.89	4.6	75.2
Inflation	26,719	1.35	1.68	−1.7	5.6
Unemployment	26,719	9.04	3.48	3.7	18
Economy Energy Intensity	26,719	283.63	188.44	108.36	842.54
Renewable electricity	26,719	19.75	16.61	0	66.79
Greenhouse Gas Emissions/Cap	26,719	9.63	3.09	4.74	23.68
Climate Change Risk Index	26,719	77.49	31.31	39	154.5
Elite Division	26,719	2.72	1.31	0.60	5.60
Electoral Fractionalization	26,719	76.89	7.40	51.88	88.94
Proportional Representation	26,719	0.74	0.44	0	1

Table A2. Determinants of Beliefs in Positive Economic Effects of Fighting Climate Change.

Perceived Threat of Climate Change	-	-	0.2265	(0.0199) *
Elite Division	−0.0527	(0.0210) *	−0.0359	(0.0171) *
Partial R^2	0.180		0.175	
F Statistic (First Stage)	5.44	0.011	5.25	0.012
Hansen's J Statistic	3.00	0.083	3.299	0.069
Endogeneity (GMM Distance)	6.05	0.014	5.074	0.024
N	21,083		20,915	
Number of clusters	27		27	

Notes: Entries are coefficients with standard errors in parentheses. * $p < 0.05$. Control variables are excluded from the table for presentational purposes. The dependent variable is measured by asking respondents their agreement or disagreement with, "Fighting climate change can have a positive impact on the European economy", with responses recorded on a four-point scale.

References

1. Intergovernmental Panel on Climate Change (IPCC). *Climate Change 2014: Synthesis Report*; Contribution of Working Groups I, II and III to the Fifth Assessment Report of the Intergovernmental Panel on Climate Change; Pachauri, R.K., Meyer, L.A., Eds.; IPCC: Geneva, Switzerland, 2014; p. 151.
2. Anderegg, W.R.L.; Prall, J.W.; Harold, J.; Schneider, S.H. Expert Credibility in Climate Change. *Proc. Natl. Acad. Sci. USA* **2010**, *107*, 12107–12109. [CrossRef] [PubMed]
3. Eurobarometer. Europeans' Attitudes towards Climate Change. Available online: http://ec.europa.eu/public_opinion/archives/ebs/ebs_300_full_en.pdf (accessed on 19 December 2016).
4. Lo, A.Y.; Chow, A.T. The relationship between climate change concern and national wealth. *Clim. Chang.* **2015**, *131*, 335–348. [CrossRef]
5. Kvaløy, B.; Finseraas, H.; Listhaug, O. The publics' concern for global warming: A cross-national study of 47 countries. *J. Peace Res.* **2012**, *49*, 11–22. [CrossRef]
6. Marquart-Pyatt, S.T.; Shwom, R.L.; Dietz, T.; Dunlap, R.E.; Kaplowitz, S.A.; McCright, A.M.; Zahran, S. Understanding public opinion on climate change: A call for research. *Environ. Sci. Policy Sustain. Dev.* **2011**, *53*, 38–42.
7. Gabel, M.; Scheve, K. Estimating the Effect of Elite Communications on Public Opinion Using Instrumental Variables. *Am. J. Political Sci.* **2007**, *51*, 1013–1028. [CrossRef]
8. Zaller, J. *The Nature and Origins of Mass Opinion*; Cambridge University Press: New York, NY, USA, 1992.
9. Carrubba, C.J. The Electoral Connection in European Union Politics. *J. Politics* **2001**, *63*, 141–158. [CrossRef]
10. Wooldridge, J.M. *Econometric Analysis of Cross Section and Panel Data*, 2nd ed.; The MIT Press: Cambridge, MA, USA, 2010.
11. O'Connor, R.E.; Bord, R.J.; Fisher, A. Risk Perceptions, General Environmental Beliefs, and Willingness to Address Climate Change. *Risk Anal.* **1999**, *19*, 461–471. [CrossRef]
12. Berinsky, A.J. Assuming the Costs of War: Events, elites, and American Public Support for Military Conflict. *J. Politics* **2007**, *69*, 975–997. [CrossRef]
13. Berinsky, A.J. *Time of War: Understanding American Public Opinion from World War II to Iraq*; University of Chicago Press: Chicago, IL, USA, 2009.
14. McCright, A.M.; Dunlap, R.E. The Politicization Of Climate Change And Polarization In The American Public's Views Of Global Warming, 2001–2010. *Sociol. Q.* **2011**, *52*, 155–194. [CrossRef]
15. Brulle, R.J.; Carmichael, J.; Jenkins, J.C. Shifting public opinion on climate change: An empirical assessment of factors influencing concern over climate change in the US, 2002–2010. *Clim. Chang.* **2012**, *114*, 169–188. [CrossRef]
16. Green, D.; Palmquist, B.; Schickler, E. *Partisan Hearts and Minds*; Yale University Press: New Haven, CT, USA, 2002.
17. Campbell, A.; Converse, P.E.; Miller, W.E.; Stokes, D.E. *The American Voter*; University of Chicago Press: Chicago, IL, USA, 1960.
18. Goren, P.; Federico, C.M.; Kittilson, M.C. Source Cues, Partisan Identities, and Political Value Expression. *Am. J. Political Sci.* **2009**, *53*, 805–820. [CrossRef]

19. Bartels, L.M. Beyond the Running Tally: Partisan Bias in Political Perceptions. *Political Behav.* **2002**, *24*, 117–150. [CrossRef]

20. Ray, L. When Parties Matter: The Conditional Influence of Party Positions on Voter Opinions about European Integration. *J. Politics* **2003**, *65*, 978–994. [CrossRef]

21. Jacoby, W.G. Value Choices and American Public Opinion. *Am. J. Political Sci.* **2006**, *50*, 706–723. [CrossRef]

22. Caprara, G.V.; Schwartz, S.; Capanna, C.; Vecchione, M.; Barbaranelli, C. Personality and Politics: Values, Traits, and Political Choice. *Political Psychol.* **2006**, *27*, 1–28. [CrossRef]

23. Downs, A. *An Economic Theory of Democracy*; Harper and Row: New York, NY, USA, 1957.

24. Stimson, J.A.; MacKuen, M.B.; Erikson, R.S. Dynamic Representation. *Am. Political Sci. Rev.* **1995**, *89*, 543–565. [CrossRef]

25. Erikson, R.S.; Tedin, K.L. *American Public Opinion: Its Origins, Content, and Impact*, 8th ed.; Longman: Harlow, UK, 2011.

26. Lubell, M.; Zahran, S.; Vedlitz, A. Collective Action and Citizen Responses to Global Warming. *Political Behav.* **2007**, *29*, 391–413. [CrossRef]

27. Zahran, S.; Brody, S.; Grover, H.; Vedlitz, A. Climate Change Vulnerability and Policy Support. *Soc. Nat. Resour.* **2006**, *19*, 771–789. [CrossRef]

28. Huddy, L.; Feldman, S.; Taber, C.; Lahav, G. Threat, Anxiety, and Support of Antiterrorism Policies. *Am. J. Political Sci.* **2005**, *49*, 593–608. [CrossRef]

29. Stephan, W.G.; Ybarra, O.; Rios Morrison, K. Intergroup threat theory. In *Handbook of Prejudice, Stereotyping, and Discrimination*; Nelson, T.D., Ed.; Lawrence Erlbaum Associates: Mahwah, NJ, USA, 2009.

30. Sniderman, P.M.; Hagendoorn, L.; Prior, M. Predisposing Factors and Situational Triggers: Exclusionary Reactions to Immigrant Minorities. *Am. Political Sci. Rev.* **2004**, *98*, 35–49. [CrossRef]

31. Herrmann, R.K.; Tetlock, P.E.; Visser, P.S. Mass Public Decisions to go to War: A Cognitive-Interactionist Framework. *Am. Political Sci. Rev.* **1999**, *93*, 553–573. [CrossRef]

32. Sjöberg, L. Factors in Risk Perception. *Risk Anal.* **2000**, *20*, 1–12. [CrossRef] [PubMed]

33. Newman, B.J.; Hartman, T.K.; Taber, C.S. Foreign Language Exposure, Cultural Threat, and Opposition to Immigration. *Political Psychol.* **2012**, *33*, 635–657. [CrossRef]

34. Volkens, A.; Lacewell, O.; Lehmann, P.; Regel, S.; Schultze, H.; Werner, A. *The Manifesto Data Collection. Manifesto Project (MRG/CMP/MARPOR)*; Wissenschaftszentrum Berlin für Sozialforschung (WZB): Berlin, Germany, 2011. (In German)

35. Head, B.W. Wicked Problems in Public Policy. *Public Policy* **2008**, *3*, 101–118.

36. Lazarus, R.J. Super Wicked Problems and Climate Change: Restraining the Present to Liberate the Future. *Cornell Law Rev.* **2009**, *94*, 1153–1234.

37. Cox, G.W. *Making Votes Count: Strategic Coordination in the World's Electoral Systems*; Cambridge University Press: New York, NY, USA, 1997.

38. Riker, W.H. The Two-Party System and Duverger's Law: An Essay on the History of Political Science. *Am. Political Sci. Rev.* **1982**, *76*, 753–766. [CrossRef]

39. Teorell, J.; Charron, N.; Samanni, M.; Holmberg, S.; Rothstein, B. *The Quality of Government Dataset*, version 6; University of Gothenburg: Gothenburg, Sweden, 2011.

40. Norris, P. Democracy Time-Series Dataset. Available online: https://www.hks.harvard.edu/fs/pnorris/Data/Data.htm (accessed on 27 December 2016).

41. Rae, D.W. A Note on the Fractionalization of Some European Party Systems. *Comp. Political Stud.* **1968**, *1*, 413–418.

42. Armingeon, K.; Careja, R.; Weisstanner, D.; Engler, S.; Potolidis, P.; Gerber, M.; Leimgruber, P. *Comparative Political Data Set III 1990–2009*; University of Berne: Bern, Switzerland, 2011.

43. Harmeling, S. *Global Climate Change Risk Index 2011: Who Suffers Most from Extreme Weather Events? Weather-related Loss Events in 2009 and 1990 to 2009*; Germanwatch e.V.: Bonn, Germany, 2011; Available online: https://germanwatch.org/en/download/2183.pdf (accessed on 27 December 2016).

44. Wooldridge, J.M. *Introductory Econometrics: A Modern Approach*, 4th ed.; South-Western Colleague Publisher: Mason, OH, USA, 2009.

45. Baum, C.F.; Schaffer, M.E.; Stillman, S. Enhanced Routines for Instrumental Variables/Generalized Method of Moments Estimation and Testing. *Stata J.* **2007**, *7*, 465–506.

46. Baum, C.F.; Schaffer, M.E.; Stillman, S. Instrumental Variables and GMM: Estimation and Testing. *Stata J.* **2003**, *3*, 1–31.

47. Baum, C.F.; Schaffer, M.E.; Stillman, S. IVREG2: Stata Module for Extended Instrumental Variables/2SLS, GMM and AC/HAC, LIML, and k-Class Regression. Available online: http://ideas.repec.org/c/boc/bocode/s425401.html (accessed on 19 December 2016).

48. Hansen, L.P. Large Sample Properties of Generalized Method of Moments Estimators. *Econom. J. Econom. Soc.* **1982**, *50*, 1029–1054. [CrossRef]

49. Hall, A.R. *Generalized Method of Moments*; Oxford University Press: New York, NY, USA, 2005.

50. Bartels, L.M. Instrumental and "Quasi-Instrumental" Variables. *Am. J. Political Sci.* **1991**, *35*, 777–800. [CrossRef]

51. Hayashi, F. *Econometrics*; Princeton University Press: Princeton, NJ, USA, 2000.

52. Baron, R.M.; Kenny, D.A. The Moderator-Mediator Variable Distinction in Social Psychological Research: Conceptual, Strategic, and Statistical Considerations. *J. Personal. Soc. Psychol.* **1986**, *51*, 1173–1182. [CrossRef]

sustainability

MDPI

Article

Does Nationality Matter in Eco-Behaviour?

Michelle Bonera [1],*, Elisabetta Corvi [1], Anna Paola Codini [1] and Ruijing Ma [2]

[1]   Economics and Management, University of Brescia, 25121 Brescia, Italy; elisabetta.corvi@unibs.it (E.C.);
anna.codini@unibs.it (A.P.C.)
[2]   School of Business and Administrations, Zhongnan University of Economics and Law, Wuhan 430073,
China; maruijing38@126.com
*   Correspondence: michelle.bonera@unibs.it; Tel.: +39-030-29885 (ext. 52553)

Received: 15 July 2017; Accepted: 18 September 2017; Published: 22 September 2017

Abstract: Although many authors agree on the role of personal values in explaining the main determinants of eco-behaviour, disagreement about the effects of socio-demographic features exists, particularly about the effect of nationality. In an attempt to fill this gap in the literature, this paper contributes to the debate surrounding the main determinants of eco-behaviour, based on a cross-country analysis. To test the role of nationality and personal values in eco-behaviour, a linear regression model involving 353 Chinese and 333 Italian subjects was performed. A stepwise analysis was then conducted to identify the main significant effects. The explorative and stepwise analyses confirmed that nationality is significant when explaining individual eco-behaviour, for both Italian and Chinese people. Moreover, the linear regression model, as a stepwise analysis, showed that regulatory focus and universalism are the main personal values influencing ecological behaviour. Differences emerging from the analysis show significant differences in terms of eco-behaviour and eco-awareness, for the two countries involved in the analysis, that might lead companies to adopt different marketing strategies when promoting eco-products.

Keywords: eco-behaviour; eco-awareness; eco-responsibility; nationality; personal values; cross-national study

1. Introduction

From a global perspective, the adoption of pro-environmental behaviours by most industrialized countries is not automatic, and requires the joint efforts of all principal stakeholders, including governments, businesses, and individual consumers. As customer adoption of new ideas depends on the media, culture, the legal environment, and other relevant aspects [1], investigating any differences in adopting pro-environmental behaviour has become crucial.

Even given the relevance of this topic, the literature shows that it is difficult to understand and predict pro-environmental behaviour [2]. The numerous definitions for ecological behaviour are sometimes similar, and they depend on the aims of the research itself, the variables used, and the methods adopted, all of which contribute to making this a complex phenomenon.

With the growing focus on environmentally-friendly behaviour, many authors [3–10] have researched its antecedents and determinants. Even though pro-environmental behaviour research has developed in different directions [11], including the socio-demographic or psychological determinants of individual ecological behaviour [12,13], we can still consider the impact of nationality as one of the most challenging topics. Even if nationality differences have been included in many studies [14,15], inter-country analysis is not as common in the pro-environmental behaviour literature, especially involving non-American countries.

Our aim was to identify the main variables affecting ecological behaviour using an inter-country analysis between Italy and China, focusing on the role played by nationality in explaining individual eco-behaviour.

Section 2 is a literature review of the main determinants of eco-behaviour, with a focus on those used in our analysis, including nationality, personal values, regulatory focus, and time. Subsequently, we describe the different eco-constructs used in the analysis. Section 3 reports the methodology used, and in Section 4, the results of the linear regression model and the stepwise analysis is provided. Finally, Section 5 discusses our main conclusions.

2. Literature Review

2.1. Nationality and Eco-Behaviour

Numerous authors have found specific correlations between socio-demographic features and pro-environmental behaviour [13,16–21]. The consumer that has a greater awareness of environmental issues tends to be younger, with a higher level of education, comes from a wealthy family, and has a good employment status. Nevertheless, the literature does give divergent results. Webster [22], while recognizing that socially responsible consumers are usually non-conformist middle class from wealthy families, also argued that demographic characteristics cannot be regarded as predictors of consumer behaviour. Conflicting results have also emerged from green consumer profiling [23,24]. Some authors investigated country-specific demographic variables, as in the case of Jain and Kaur [25] in India and Banyte et al. [26] in Lithuania. Albayrak et al. [27], in agreement with Sandahl and Robertson [28], highlighted that demographic variables are not the most reliable and are not the only determinants of environmental concern and ecological behaviour.

The reason for differences in business ethics across countries may be related to differences in cultures, since culture affects moral orientations such as idealism and relativism [29,30]. In the context of cultural differences, Buller et al. [31] wondered whether a common business ethics core exists across cultures, but also whether widespread differences could be found in the level of ethical standards.

From a theoretical perspective, researchers have attempted to apply Hofstede's [32] cultural constructs of individualism and collectivism in cross-cultural models of ethical decision making in business [33], his constructs of individualism and uncertainty avoidance for social desirability response bias [34], as well as Kohlberg's [35] levels of moral development in explaining cross-cultural differences in business ethics [36]. Within this framework, Tan and Chou [37] tested competing hypotheses based on both cultural and national contexts by comparing groups of Chinese and American respondents together with a "bridging group" of Chinese-Americans. The results of their study showed that culture plays a far more important role in shaping value and ethical orientations than the national background.

Although several empirical comparisons have been completed of ethics of Americans versus non-American business people [38,39], and American versus non-American consumers [40], the most common studies have been of American and non-American business students in cross-national comparisons of business ethics. Indeed, in a comprehensive review of how and why cultural differences arise, Jackson [41] developed and tested a model of ethical decision-making in 10 countries. His results implied that American managers, considered as having individualistic traits and low uncertainty avoidance, put more emphasis on ethical issues that relate to external stakeholders than on issues regarding organizational concerns. On the individualism versus collectivism index, higher scores represent individualistic attitudes, which involve caring for oneself or one's immediate family, with less concern for the wellbeing of one's community. With a score near to 90, many Occidental countries are the most individualistic nations, while many Oriental nations display a collectivist orientation with a score of about 20 [42].

Along similar lines, Tsalikis et al. [43] examined ethical perceptions of two scenarios involving immoral acts in Greece and the U.S.A., finding that gender was not an important factor, while national characteristics had a significant effect. In Sigma-Mugan et al. [14], ethical perceptions of male and female managers were compared in two countries, the U.S.A. and Turkey, that differ in power and in individualism/collectivism dimensions. They showed that ethical sensitivity varies depending upon whether the interests of the principals, agents, or third parties are affected by any given ethical dilemma, and that the nationality and gender of the decision-maker influences ethical sensitivity. Unlike the conclusions of most previous empirical cross-national surveys on business ethics, Peterson et al. [44], conducting studies in 36 different countries involving 6300 business students, suggested that the ethicality scores of American and non-American participants were not significantly different.

If we consider these contributions, nationality may be an important factor when analysing these controversial results. This is why nationality is the base of our first hypothesis when considering environmentally-friendly behaviour:

Hypothesis 1 (H1). *Nationality is a determinant of eco-behaviour.*

2.2. Personal Values and Eco-Behaviour

Shrum et al. [45] noted the features of environmentally friendly consumers that would differentiate them from each other. To better understand green consumers, it is necessary to investigate their characteristics, their personalities, their lifestyle, and their motivations.

Many authors have focused on the influence of individual differences and personal traits on ecological behaviour [4,15,46–53]. Many scholars have shown that socially or ecologically concerned consumers do possess certain psychographic traits, such as motivational factors and human values, that other consumers who rank low in this aspect do not share [16,19,54,55]. Therefore, predictors of environmental behaviour may be, for example, human values, views on sustainability, and concern about sustainability-relevant issues. Values are commonly defined as desirable trans-situational goals that serve as leading principles in life [56]. These values have been proven to be relatively stable and predictive of a broad spectrum of environmentally significant behaviours [57–59].

Unfortunately, the literature has not shown any consensus on ecologically friendly consumers or on the variables that could predict green behaviour [26,60]. Indeed, Roberts [61] even argues for a schizophrenic profile. To investigate the role of nationality in influencing eco-behaviour, we decided to include the main personal values identified as relevant in describing eco-behaviour. Among the various measurements used in the literature to evaluate personal traits [32,42,62,63], those used by Schwartz seemed the most suitable, and have been used to make international comparisons.

In particular, the values used include:

- Power, defined as social status and prestige, controls capabilities and domain toward other people, including social power, authority, wealth, and ability to preserve image.
- Achievement, understood as personal success by proving skills in line with social reference standards. One who possesses a high level of success is a person who can be called clever, ambitious, and influential.
- Hedonism, defined as pleasure and gratification, the ability to experience pleasure, to enjoy life, and to experience self-indulgence.
- Stimulation, defined as excitement, desire to discover the new, and to meet new challenges in life, including courage and the desire to have an exciting life of adventure.
- Self-direction, defined as the ability to be autonomous in the choice of action to be taken and as the ability to create and explore, which includes creativity, freedom, independence, curiosity, and the ability to choose for themselves the targets to be achieved.
- Universalism, defined as understanding, appreciation, tolerance, and the desire to protect the well-being of people in general and nature. A person who has high levels of universalism is a person with extensive views, wise, with a strong sense of justice and equity, animated by the desire to live in a world of peace, in harmony with nature, and in which the environment is respected.

- Benevolence, defined as defending and improving the welfare of people in general, and those who are closest to them. Help, honesty, forgiveness, loyalty, and responsibility are elements that distinguish a person characterized by a strong sense of humanity.
- Tradition, understood as respect and acceptance of the customs and ideas that culture or religion instil including humility, devotion, respect for tradition, balance, and ability to accept life as it comes.
- Conformism, which is the ability to curb instincts and impulses to avoid injury to others, to violate the norms of society, or to counter social expectations, characterized by courtesy, obedience, self-discipline, respect for parents and to older people in general.
- Security, understood as social harmony and stability, confidence and social relationships, involving safety in the home, in your country, in society, with mutual benevolence.

Based on these values and definitions, we defined the second hypothesis as follows:

Hypothesis 2 (H2). *Personal values are determinants of eco-behaviour.*

We further subdivided this hypothesis for each individual value, as follows:

Hypothesis 2a (H2a). *Power values have the largest negative impact on eco-behaviour.*

Hypothesis 2b (H2b). *Achievement values have a negative impact on eco-behaviour.*

Hypothesis 2c (H2c). *Hedonism values have a negative impact on eco-behaviour.*

Hypothesis 2d (H2d). *Stimulation values have both a positive and negative impact on eco-behaviour.*

Hypothesis 2e (H2e). *Self-direction values have a positive impact on eco-behaviour.*

Hypothesis 2f (H2f). *Universalism values have the strongest positive influence on eco-behaviour.*

Hypothesis 2g (H2g). *Benevolence values have a positive impact on eco-behaviour.*

Hypothesis 2h (H2h). *Tradition values have a positive impact on eco-behaviour.*

Hypothesis 2i (H2i). *Conformism values have both a positive and negative impact on eco-behaviour.*

Hypothesis 2j (H2j). *Security values have a negative impact on eco-behaviour.*

2.3. Regulatory Focus and Eco-Behaviour

Although studies have investigated the role of personal characteristics in influencing the behaviour of sustainable consumption in countering the need to integrate with other variables, expression of the personality traits of individuals, such as regulatory focus, remain under-investigated. Considering social values that influence environmentally responsible consumption, some authors [52] have suggested that, as inter-dependence (self-construal) and prevention (regulatory focus) are usually associated with social-oriented values [64], these two constructs could be related to environmentally responsible consumption.

Regulatory focus is defined by Higgins [65] as the set of tools with which individuals self-regulate in pursuit of a goal. Regulatory focus influences how individuals make decisions and determine the ways in which they achieve their goals. This may be due to a particular individual situation or due to a constant individual attitude at the time of the choice [66].

In particular, Higgins [67] defines two fundamental approaches that people take in order to achieve their goals: the promotion approach and the prevention approach. In the former, individuals tend to focus more on responsibilities, tasks, and duties, which they consider necessary to achieve their goals. These are perceived as tasks to be undertaken to make specific strategic decisions while avoiding mistakes and minimizing losses. In the context of purchasing decisions, prevention orientation leads to increased sensitivity to failure or loss of money, which is why individuals seek to fulfil commitments and obligations. However, in the case of a predominantly promotion approach, individuals' choices are guided by their long-term hopes, aspirations, and objectives. These individuals conceive their goals as being ideals, and their strategic choices, including purchasing, are dictated by the desire to maximize profits while minimizing losses. For this reason, their behaviour is oriented toward objectives, such as real progress, success, and growth.

Research in consumer ethics suggests an association between consumers' ethical beliefs and regulatory focus, derived from the definition of regulatory focus itself. In general, promotional goals have been argued to regulate behaviour through positive outcomes, either by maximizing their presence or by minimizing their absence. In contrast, prevention goals act either by minimizing negative outcomes, or maximizing their absence [68,69]. Thus, within a promotional focus, the desired aim is the presence of positive outcomes, while, in the case of a prevention focus, it is the absence of negative outcomes.

With regard to product-related attributes, individuals with a self-regulatory focus on promotion are motivated to pursue such positive outcomes such as "advancement" and "eagerness". This means that they will be more concerned with "getting the job done", will place particular emphasis on "strength" in their choices, and will respond positively to claims that the product is, for example, "powerful" or "effective". On the contrary, those whose focus is prevention, are motivated to pursue "safety" and "vigilance", are more likely to respond favourably to appeals emphasizing the "healthiness" or "gentleness" of the product, even if a cost is incurred in terms of reduced efficiency.

Several converging findings indicate that consumers associate ethics and sustainability with caring, compassion [70,71], gentleness, safety [72], and protectiveness. Because these traits satisfy prevention concerns for security, protection, and responsibility, these findings suggest there is an association between consumer ethics and regulatory focus, and more precisely, prevention focus. Considering this literature, we developed our third hypothesis, as follows: *regulatory focus is a determinant of eco-behaviour (H3)*.

2.4. Time Orientation and Eco-Behaviour

Time orientation is the individual difference that considers the future consequences of a particular choice [73]. Time orientation is a multi-dimensional construct [74] consisting of one's capacity to anticipate, structure, and see the future more clearly [75]. Moreover, time orientation is the customer's willingness to delay or expedite gains, such as obtaining a reward or something of value, and losses, such as giving up something of value [76]. The role that personal time orientation assumes in influencing consumer environmentally friendly attitudes has been emphasized in many studies [77].

The Hofstede [32] definition of a long-term-oriented person is someone who preserves social traditions and adheres to family values, and considers reliability, responsiveness, and empathy to be extremely important. Recent research shows that long-term people tend to develop attitudes pertaining to the protection of the natural environment [78–80]. Indeed, since the long-term person preserves tradition and history, they are also likely to respect and preserve the environment in order to reap benefits for family and friends at a later stage, and maintain sustainable conditions for future generations to prosper [81]. In addition to the cultural dimensions of individualism and collectivism, time orientation scores have different values in Occidental and in Oriental countries. In China, the long-term orientation score is 118; in some Occidental countries, this score is closer to 20 points. Italy's score is 61 [42].

Temporal concerns have received increasing attention in more general pro-environmental literature. For example, several recent studies have demonstrated that individuals who scored high when considering future consequences (CFC), and explicit temporal concerns, are more likely to engage in environmentally conscious consumer behaviour [82,83], more likely to engage in politics [84], and are more inclined to commute by public transportation [78].

The concept of time orientation can be related to the generativity concept [85] which is about the next generation, about bearing, raising, and caring for one's own and others' children. Generativity involves assuming the role of a responsible parent, a mentor, shepherd, guardian, guide, and so on, vis-à-vis those whose development and wellbeing benefit from the care that the role provides [86]. Recently the concept of environmental generativity has been proposed to explain the association between parental status and concern about environmental issues [87]. Because of the similarities between the two concepts of time orientation and generativity, we can assume that both constructs have a positive relationship with environmental issues.

Based on these findings, our fourth hypothesis is as follows:

Hypothesis 4 (H4). *Time orientation is a determinant of eco-behaviour.*

2.5. Eco-Constructs

To define our research hypothesis, we chose an ecological construct representing our dependent variable influenced by the ecological predictors explained above. We adopted a multi-item scale, called Ecoscale [88], used in the literature to measure environmental responsibility and consciousness. To obtain a more specific definition of ecological consumer behaviour, we used three different pieces of information obtained from the original 31 items of the Ecoscale. We created three related constructs: eco-awareness, eco-responsibility, and eco-behaviour, in the same way that the environmental sustainability consciousness (ESC construct) was developed by Diamantopoulos et al. [24], based on the sub-constructs of environmental knowledge, environmental attitude, and environmental behaviour.

2.5.1. Eco-Awareness

Environmental awareness is related to what the consumer knows about ecological problems [89]. The literature has considered customers' environmental awareness [10,24,90]. A correlation has been considered between environmental awareness and environmentally friendly behaviour [10,91,92]. However, empirical results do not always agree [93,94]. Some authors did not find any relevant links between environmental awareness and environmentally friendly behaviour [95]. Most marketers agree, however, that environmental awareness among consumers will eventually grow, and this change in consumers' perception will ultimately affect the market share and marketing activities of green products and companies [96].

2.5.2. Eco-Responsibility

Eco-responsibility is connected to environmental concern or active environmental attention, which includes environmental attitude [55] or social responsibility [97], and it is a complex hypothesis. From the public policy point of view, growing levels of individually perceived environmental responsibility may foster more environmentally friendly attitudes and behaviour, leading to more environmental activism [98]. The more citizens are aware of their own role in problems linked with environmental degradation, the more they are willing to participate in solutions [99].

Environmental or ecological responsibility is considered by many authors to be strictly linked to environmental knowledge and awareness and with conscious environmental intention [100]. Many authors have confirmed the hypothesis that the environmental concern of an individual has a direct and relevant impact on their eco-friendly behaviour [61,90,97]. On the other hand, studies have not agreed on the importance or the impact of environmental concerns on eco-friendly behaviour [23,61].

2.5.3. Eco-Behaviour

Most research has concentrated on the analysis of a particular ecological behaviour, including differentiated waste management [101,102], transportation choice [78,103,104], energy savings [105,106], water consumption [107], littering [108], environmental activism [109], or ecological product purchasing [21,110]. In particular, sustainable consumption is mostly related to the purchase of environment-friendly products and services [7,111–116]. The gap between intention and behaviour has also been widely studied [61,72,93,117,118], giving further evidence that the understanding of environmental problems does not always translate into pro-environmental behaviour.

In relation to these three constructs, our research aimed to test different levels of eco-awareness and eco-responsibility, affecting eco-behaviour. These three hypotheses would test the relationship between the three concepts that have been linked in the literature with conflicting results. Moreover, these results would also outline any differences in a country-specific context.

As a result, our last hypotheses are as follows: Eco-awareness positively affects eco-behaviour for people in both China and Italy (H5); and eco-responsibility positively affects eco-behaviour for people of both Chinese and Italian nationalities (H6).

Figure 1 shows the model, including all of the hypotheses we tested in our empirical analysis.

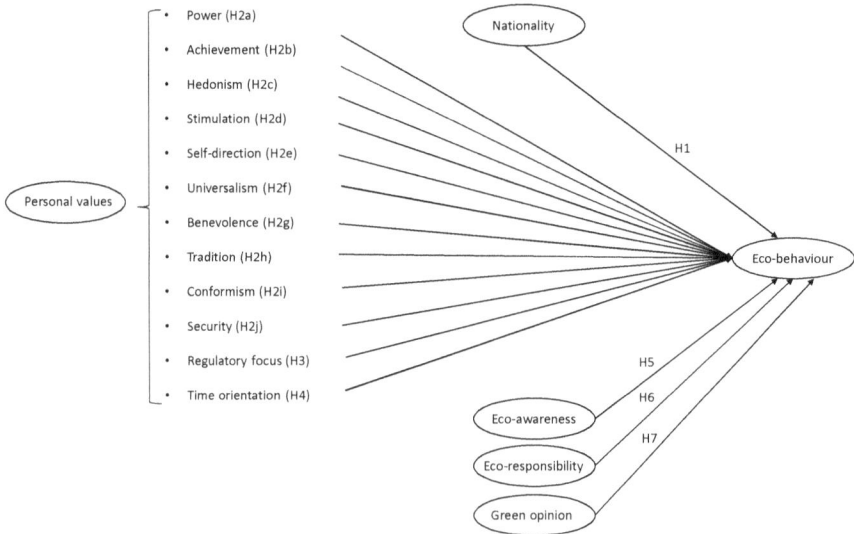

Figure 1. Diagram of the hypotheses tested linking different values to eco-behaviour.

3. Methods

Our empirical research involved 353 Chinese and 333 Italian people, for a total sample size of 686 people. Within this sample, 61.9% were women, while 33.7% were men; the average age was 28.6 years (SD 13.6314). While the Italian sample is quite representative of the Italian population, the Chinese sample is somewhat biased. In the Italian sample, 53.8% were women, while in the Chinese sample the percentage of women was 75.9%, which is not representative of the population. In addition, age distribution reveals some biases. For the Italian group, the average age was 37.1 (SD 15.0887), while for the Chinese sample the average age was 20.18 (SD 0.9730). Data collection in the two countries started in December 2014 and finished in April 2015. The same English version of the questionnaire was submitted directly to Italian and to Chinese respondents. In both countries, some of the respondents were recruited from within a group of university students as part of a course credit. Other participants were directly recruited by the students. A detailed analysis was conducted on the sample in order to determine the main differences between the Italian and in the Chinese groups. The answers to the items used in the survey were analysed in detail and the main differences emerging in the two samples were determined.

We decided to focus our analysis on these two countries due to the cultural differences emerging in these countries, especially for those dimensions we supposed as influencing eco-behaviour. As mentioned before, the two countries mainly differ in term of time orientation scores. Even though there are no studies proving differences between the two countries in terms of regulatory focus orientation, our preliminary analysis on the results of our research (Table S1) showed differences in the prevention scores, being higher for Italian respondents and lower for Chinese respondents.

The questionnaire was composed of 69 questions investigating general pro-environmental beliefs and behaviours using the items included in the Ecoscale [88], and the personal traits included in the Portrait Values Questionnaire (PVQ) [56]. Each of the 10 personal traits included in the PVQ was measured by a different number of items, with an increasing trend, for example, high scores in benevolence were considered as revealing a high level of benevolence in individuals. Reliability scores for PVQ have been established in the existing literature [56]. Other personal traits we considered may have influenced ecological beliefs, specifically regulatory focus and time orientation.

To test regulatory focus, we used the scale used in Higgins et al. [119], which is composed of 11 items, of which 6 measure the promotion state and 5 measure the prevention state. The scale exhibits good internal reliability: an α of 0.73 for the promotion scale and an α of 0.80 for the prevention scale. For the items measuring the promotion state, high scores correspond to a high level of promotion, while for the items measuring the prevention state, high scores correspond to high level of prevention.

Time orientation was measured using the Gjesme scale [75], which is composed of 7 items, and exhibits an alpha coefficient of 0.62. The items measure future time orientation, where high scores in time orientation correspond to future time orientation, and low scores correspond to present time orientation.

In the final part of the questionnaire, we collected socio-demographic information, including sex, age, and nationality.

The linear regression model aimed at testing the impact of nationality and personal values on eco-behaviour. Before starting with this data while considering the items in the Ecoscale, we created new cross-constructs by combining the same items in a different way. Their latent existence was confirmed by the coherent trend assumed by the items defining them.

The general trend assumed by these new constructs showed significant differences in the two samples, giving some insights concerning the role assumed by nationality in influencing eco-behaviour. Moreover, the new eco-constructs gave us the opportunity to focus on the main issues considered relevant for our analysis, including eco-responsibility, eco-attitudes, and eco-behaviour. This allowed us to reduce the eco-scale, which included seven constructs in the original version: opinions and beliefs, awareness, will to act, attitude, actions, ability to act, and knowledge.

Thus, based on these considerations, the new eco-constructs used were as follows:

1. Eco-responsibility: This construct explains the personal sense of responsibility that an individual has toward the environment. The concept we intended to isolate and evaluate expresses how an individual can be considered as being personally responsible for environmental issues, beyond the general declaration of eco-sensitivity. Eco-responsibility, as defined above, is supposed to impact eco-behaviour and therefore we decided to include it in our analysis.

2. Eco-awareness: In this eco-construct, we included all items expressing objective statements that did not require personal opinions, but which were considered to be a good proxy of the level of awareness about environmental issues.

3. Eco-behaviour: This eco-construct is wider than the "actions" construct picked from the Ecoscale to include items picked from "will to act" and "ability to act" constructs in the Ecoscale. We therefore included all statements showing personal and direct action in favour of environment protection.

4. Green-opinion: This eco-construct was created as an average of the ratings assigned to the items on the Ecoscale that were not included in the other eco-constructs. These can be considered as general opinions on green issues.

A list of the items included in each new eco-construct is reported in Table S2. The new constructs were tested and most of the resulting scales exhibited decent internal reliability. The α for eco-responsibility was 0.707, 0.620 for eco-behaviour, and 0.546 for green opinion. Only the reliability of eco-awareness was low, with an α of 0.403.

4. Results

To measure the three constructs, we created three variables called eco-responsibility, eco-awareness, and eco-behaviour, using a 1–5 point scale. People involved in the analysis had a high level of eco-awareness about environmental issues (M = 3.5837; SD = 0.52248). They responded that they had a high sense of responsibility toward the environment (M = 3.9156; SD = 0.68101), but they were not as active in environmental protection (M = 2.8455; SD = 0.56603).

The analysis of the impact of nationality on these three eco-constructs did not show any significant differences within the sample regarding eco-responsibility (M_Chinese = 3.9120; SD = 0.77074; M_Italian = 3.9194; SD = 0.57656). However, Italians were significantly more eco-aware (M_Italian = 3.7928; SD = 0.41073) compared to the Chinese (M_Chinese = 3.3714; SD = 0.53512). Looking at the trend assumed by the eco-behaviour construct, the data revealed a significant difference between Italians (M = 2.7798; SD = 0.57137) and Chinese people (M = 2.9135; SD = 0.55235). In particular, Chinese people were significantly more active in eco-behaviour. As for regulatory focus and time orientation variables, *T*-tests for equality of means of eco-variables are reported in Table S1.

Because the aim of the paper was to investigate the variables influencing eco-behaviour, while paying particular attention to the role assumed by nationality, in this second part of the analysis, we report the results of a linear regression model. In this regression model, eco-behaviour is the dependent variable, while variables related to personal values (benevolence, universalism, self-direction, stimulation, hedonism, achievement, power, security, conformity, tradition, future time orientation, and regulatory focus), demographic features (age, sex, and nationality) and other eco-constructs are included in the model as explanatory variables.

In particular, the eco-constructs included in the model as explanatory variables were eco-responsibility, eco-awareness, and green opinion.

The first regression model we tested, including age, nationality, sex, eco-responsibility, eco-awareness, and green opinion as explanatory variables, had a very poor performance (Adjusted R Squared = 0.030).

Including the personal values as predictors (Table 1), which included benevolence, universalism, self-direction, stimulation, hedonism, achievement, power, security, conformity, tradition, future time orientation, and regulatory focus, the performance of the model increased (Adjusted R Square = 0.056).

The coefficients reported in Table 1 show how a limited number of variables significantly influenced eco-behaviour with different levels of significance: eco-responsibility positively influenced eco-behaviour (B = 0.092), while an increase in eco-awareness decreased eco-behaviour (B = −0.157). This might be due to the high correlation between eco-responsibility and eco-awareness (Pearson correlation index = 0.481). The regulatory focus seems to be, in all models, a good predictor of eco-behaviour (B = 0.188).

Another interesting effect emerging from the coefficient analysis was the effect of nationality. As shown in Table 1, Italian nationality negatively affected eco-behaviour (B = −0.67) but the effect was not significant. We cannot therefore state that this supports our first hypothesis that nationality affects eco-behaviour, even though the exploratory analysis seemed to support the idea that being Italian, rather than Chinese, decreased the likelihood of adopting eco-behaviour, while being Chinese rather than Italian increased the chances of adopting eco-behaviour.

As a result, the model confirmed hypotheses 3, 5, and 6, and consequently, the performance of the model was rather low. This might be due to the complexity of the eco-behaviour construct, which may depend on a higher number of variables than those considered in this model, and to difficulties relating to their measurement. To identify the main variables affecting the eco-behaviour construct and therefore give direction for future research, a stepwise procedure was used to reduce the number of explanatory variables.

Table 1. Coefficients with eco-behaviour mean as the dependent variable.

Model	Unstandardized Coefficients		Standardized Coefficients	T	Sig.
	B	Std. Error	Beta		
(Constant)	1.720	0.326		5.277	0.000
Age	−0.003	0.002	−0.084	−1.462	0.144
Nationality	−0.067	0.073	−0.059	−0.918	0.359
Male	0.083	0.053	0.069	1.562	0.119
Eco-responsibility	0.092	0.050	0.108	1.857	0.064
Eco-awareness	−0.157	0.061	−0.141	−2.553	0.011
Green opinion	0.007	0.055	0.007	0.127	0.899
Benevolence	0.050	0.039	0.070	1.305	0.192
Universalism	0.072	0.044	0.093	1.646	0.100
Self-direction	−0.012	0.039	−0.016	−0.309	0.757
Stimulation	0.030	0.032	0.054	0.953	0.341
Hedonism	−0.010	0.034	−0.017	−0.299	0.765
Achievement	0.028	0.032	0.046	0.883	0.378
Power	−0.002	0.030	−0.004	−0.072	0.943
Security	−0.012	0.037	−0.017	−0.335	0.738
Conformism	−0.022	0.033	−0.033	−0.659	0.510
Tradition	0.037	0.029	0.059	1.278	0.202
Future time orientation	0.058	0.043	0.070	1.364	0.173
Regulatory focus	0.188	0.074	0.124	2.533	0.012

The stepwise analysis allows identification of the best model among all the available regression models derived from the different combinations of the predictors. As a result, the stepwise analysis resulted in a minimal model showing the main effects of the dependent variable used in the regression model. As shown in Table 2 which summarizes the model, the selected model is the best compared to the others shown in the table, even though characterized by a low of R Square value.

Table 2. Model summary of the stepwise analysis.

Model	R	R Square	Adjusted R Square	Std. Error of the Estimates
1	0.191 [a]	0.036	0.035	0.56238
2	0.208 [b]	0.043	0.040	0.56084
3	0.236 [c]	0.056	0.051	0.55768

[a] Predictors: (Constant), universalism_mean; [b] Predictors: (Constant), universalism_mean, regulatory focus_mean;
[c] Predictors: (Constant), universalism_mean, regulatory focus_mean, nationality.

As shown by the coefficients in Table 2, universalism (B = 0.123), regulatory focus (B = 0.196), and nationality (B = −0.140) seem to be the main predictors of eco-behaviour (Table 3). In addition to the regression model, this analysis confirms the effect of regulatory focus as a more important predictor of eco-behaviour than nationality.

Table 3. Coefficients of the stepwise analysis with eco-behaviour mean as the dependent variable.

Model	Unstandardized Coefficients		Standardized Coefficients	T	Sig.
	B	Std. Error	Beta		
(Constant)	1.761	0.234		7.511	0.000
Universalism	0.123	0.033	0.157	3.770	0.000
Regulatory Focus	0.196	0.067	0.130	2.945	0.003
Nationality	−0.140	0.051	−0.122	−2.745	0.006

5. Discussion and Conclusions

This paper contributes to the debate concerning the main determinants of eco-behaviour based on an inter-country analysis. Our aim was to identify the main variables affecting eco-behaviour considered relevant in the literature. Particularly, thanks to a cross-country analysis involving Chinese and Italian subjects, we investigated the role of nationality as a socio-demographic factor, compared to the role of different personal values, including the Schwartz's values with the addition of regulatory focus and time orientation as explanatory variables. In addition, eco-responsibility, eco-awareness, and green opinion were included in the model as variables affecting the eco-behaviour dependent variable.

Firstly, the general trend of the new constructs identified in the regression model, eco-responsibility, eco-awareness, and eco-behaviour, were significantly different in the two samples. Confirming hypothesis 1 and according to the stepwise model, nationality is important in describing eco-behaviour. Furthermore, this effect is stronger than the effect of certain personal values identified as being relevant in the literature. Regarding the role assumed by the Schwartz personal values, our study mostly confirmed the main effects of previous contributions. Our analysis confirmed universalism values as having the highest positive effect on eco-behaviour compared to other personal values.

Nevertheless, some interesting results emerged regarding the other variables included in the model, such as the significant effect of regulatory focus as a personal value influencing eco-behaviour. Looking at the effects of the other eco-constructs, our study mostly supports the defined hypothesis regarding the positive effect of eco-responsibility. However, our analysis shows the negative effect of eco-awareness on eco-behaviour in contrast to the positive effect suggested in the literature.

The results of our research give an interesting contribution to the literature investigating the role of culture in influencing eco-behaviour. With the debate about the role assumed by cultural differences, using nationality as the level of analysis, compared to the role of personal values in influencing eco-behaviour, our paper has controversial results. The first analysis we conducted on the two samples of Chinese and Italian people shows significant differences in terms of eco-awareness and eco-behaviour. On the other hand, the regression analysis shows the significant role of universalism and regulatory focus in predicting eco-behaviour, supporting the hypothesis that personal values have a significant influence on eco-behaviour while nationality does not.

In addition to the theoretical contribution, our study has some interesting managerial implications. Investigating the influence of nationality, as a personal value, on eco-behaviour is particularly interesting for multinationals.

The main results of our research could suggest some guidelines for consumer segmentation. For eco-behaviour, our analysis shows relevant differences in the two countries, recommending country-by-country segmentation as more suitable than transnational segmentation. This means that, when planning marketing strategies for a green product or service in a global context, companies need to differentiate their marketing. Our analysis shows significant differences in terms of eco-behaviour and eco-awareness for the two countries involved that might lead companies to adopt different marketing strategies especially when promoting eco-products.

While Italians were more eco-aware, this did not translate into concrete eco-behaviour. The situation was the opposite for the Chinese sample, who, even with a lower level of eco-awareness, seemed to be more active in terms of eco-behaviour. This would suggest recommending the use of different marketing strategies in these two countries, trying to push Italian people to adopt eco-behaviour, while acting on information available for the Chinese. Based on these results, actions increasing the level of eco-awareness, rather than influencing eco-responsibility to induce eco-behaviour could be an interesting challenge.

Additionally, the results regarding the effect of personal values on eco-behaviour could supply multinational companies with some interesting suggestions on how to define communication strategies encouraging eco-behaviour. Our results show the significant effect of universalism and regulatory focus that needs to be explored in future studies for some practical suggestions on how to define the ecological communication message addressing these personal aspects. If additional analysis confirming these effects, it would be recommended to plan communication messages based on the universalism value in order to stimulate eco-behaviour in a global context. Regarding the effect of regulatory focus, additional analysis is necessary to understand if promotion rather than prevention orientation affect eco-behaviour. After defining this aspect, managers developing communication strategies inducing eco-behaviour would have some guidelines about which kind of message could be effective. The distinction is crucial, considering that the analysis conducted on our sample show that Italian and Chinese are different in terms of regulatory focus orientation. Particularly, the data revealed that Italian respondents have higher scores in prevention than Chinese respondents.

Due to the early stage of this research, our empirical analysis has some limits. For the sample, the analysis of the socio-demographic features of the respondents shows that the sample was not representative of the citizens of both countries, especially for China. However, considering that we are in the explorative step of the research, we think that this limitation could be overcome in the future by sampling other respondents. More precisely, further analysis will be conducted including older respondents and more men in the Chinese sample. Secondly, if the analysis is to contribute to the management of multi-national companies, the analysis should be applied in at least one other country. The United States might be the best benchmark, based on previous studies. Thirdly, because of the interesting results regarding the effect of regulatory focus as the most influential eco-behaviour, this aspect could be supported by other analyses.

Moreover, the empirical analysis, in looking for a correlation between a number of personal values, nationality, eco-awareness, eco-responsibility, and green opinion on eco-behaviour, shows some mixed results. In the first analysis, eco-responsibility, eco-awareness, and regulatory focus were significant, whereas nationality was not. In the second analysis, where eco-responsibility and eco-awareness were excluded, nationality was significant. In addition, nationality showed correlation with regulatory focus and time orientation. These results could call for a more sophisticated model where, for example, personal values and eco-variables influence nationality, and nationality, in turn, influences eco-behaviour. However, before testing a more sophisticated model, the limitation regarding the representativeness of the sample should be addressed. Including older respondents and more men in the Chinese sample, and retesting the regression model we used in this paper, could lead to more significant effects among the tested variables. After this step and according to the results of this analysis, we could design a new and more sophisticated model.

Regarding future lines of research, the conceptual model could be further investigated, using different statistical methodologies in order to comprehend how the suggested relationship between the variables influences the ecological behaviours.

After that, the low Cronbach alpha, assumed by some of the eco-constructs used in the analysis, recommends the use of other scales in order to measure eco-awareness and eco-behaviour. Considering few studies have focused on the development of a measure of eco-behaviour including eco-consumer behaviour, as the decision of effectively buying eco-products, a new scale for measuring eco-behaviour could be developed for our future studies.

Supplementary Materials: The following are available online at www.mdpi.com/2071-1050/9/10/1694/s1, Table S1: *T*-test for equality of means; Table S2: Eco-variables items.

Author Contributions: Michelle Bonera, Elisabetta Corvi and Anna Paola Codini conceived and designed the questionnaire; Michelle Bonera, Elisabetta Corvi and Anna Paola Codini collected data for Italian market; Ruijing Ma collected data for Chinese market; Michelle Bonera, Elisabetta Corvi, Anna Paola Codini and Ruijing Ma analysed the data; and all the Authors contributed to writing the paper.

Conflicts of Interest: The authors declare no conflict of interest.

References

1. Shaw, D.S.; Clarke, I. Culture, consumption and choice: Towards a conceptual relationship. *J. Consum. Stud. Home Econ.* **1998**, *22*, 163–168. [CrossRef]
2. Shrum, L.J.; Lowrey, T.M.; McCarty, J.A. Recycling as a marketing problem: A framework for strategy development. *Psychol. Mark.* **1994**, *11*, 393–416. [CrossRef]
3. Tanner, C.; Kast, S.W. Promoting sustainable consumption: Determinants of green purchases by Swiss Consumers. *Psychol. Mark.* **2003**, *20*, 883–902. [CrossRef]
4. Griskevicius, V.; Tybur, J.M.; Van den Bergh, B. Going green to be seen: Status, reputation, and conspicuous conservation. *J. Personal. Soc. Psychol.* **2010**, *98*, 392–404. [CrossRef] [PubMed]
5. Koller, M.; Floh, A.; Zauner, A. Further insights into perceived value and consumer loyalty: A green perspective. *Psychol. Mark.* **2011**, *28*, 1154–1176. [CrossRef]
6. Pickett-Baker, J.; Ozaki, R. Pro-environmental products: Marketing influence on consumer purchase decision. *J. Consum. Mark.* **2008**, *25*, 281–293. [CrossRef]
7. Paço, A.; Alves, H.; Shiel, C. Development of a green consumer behaviour model. *Int. J. Consum. Stud.* **2013**, *37*, 414–421. [CrossRef]
8. Abeliotis, K.; Koniari, C.; Sardianou, E. The profile of the green consumer in Greece. *Int. J. Consum. Stud.* **2010**, *34*, 153–160. [CrossRef]
9. D'Souza, C.; Taghian, M.; Lamb, P.; Peretiatko, R. Green decisions: Demographics and consumer understanding of environmental labels. *Int. J. Consum. Stud.* **2007**, *31*, 371–376. [CrossRef]
10. Finisterra Do Paço, A.M.; Raposo, M.L.B. Green consumer market segmentation: Empirical findings from Portugal. *Int. J. Consum. Stud.* **2010**, *34*, 429–436. [CrossRef]
11. Bonnes, M.; Passafaro, P.; Carrus, G. *Psicologia Ambientale, Sostenibilità e Comportamenti Ecologici*; Carocci: Rome, Italy, 2006.
12. Gatersleben, B.; Steg, L.; Vlek, C. Measurement and determinants of environmentally significant consumer behavior. *Environ. Behav.* **2002**, *34*, 335–362. [CrossRef]
13. Ukenna, S.; Nkamnebe, A.D.; Nwaizugbo, I.C.; Moguluwa, S.C.; Olise, M.C. Profiling the environmental sustainability-conscious (ESC) consumer: Proposing the S-P-P model. *J. Manag. Sustain.* **2012**, *2*, 197–210. [CrossRef]
14. Simga-Mugan, C.; Daly, B.A.; Onkal, D.; Kavut, L. The Influence of Nationality and Gender on Ethical Sensitivity: An Application of the Issue Contingent Model. *J. Bus. Ethics* **2005**, *57*, 139–159. [CrossRef]
15. Doran, C.J. The role of personal values in fair trade consumption. *J. Bus. Ethics* **2009**, *84*, 549–563. [CrossRef]
16. Anderson, W.T., Jr.; Cunningham, W.H. The Socially Conscious Consumer. *J. Mark.* **1972**, *36*, 23–31. [CrossRef]
17. Anderson, T.W.; Henion, K.E.; Cox, E.P. Socially vs. Ecologically Responsible Consumers. In *1974 Combined Proceedings*; Curhan, R.C., Ed.; American Marketing Association: Chicago, IL, USA, 1974; pp. 304–311.
18. Van Liere, K.D.; Dunlap, R.E. The Social Bases of Environmental Concern: A Review of Hypotheses, Explanations and Empirical Evidence. *Public Opin. Q.* **1980**, *44*, 181–197. [CrossRef]
19. Balderjahn, I. Personality Variables and Environmental Attitudes as Predictors of Ecologically Responsible Consumption Patterns. *J. Bus. Res.* **1988**, *17*, 51–56. [CrossRef]
20. Roper Organization, & Johnson Wax. *The Environment: Public Attitudes and Individual Behaviour*; The Roper Organization, Inc.: New York, NY, USA, 1990.
21. Mohr, M.; Schlich, M. Socio-demographic basic factors of German customers as predictors for sustainable consumerism regarding foodstuffs and meat products. *Int. J. Consum. Stud.* **2016**, *40*, 158–167. [CrossRef]

22. Webster, F.E., Jr. Determining the Characteristics of the Socially Conscious Consumer. *J. Consum. Res.* **1975**, *2*, 188–196. [CrossRef]

23. Straughan, R.D.; Roberts, J.A. Environmental segmentation alternatives: A look at green consumer behaviour in the new millennium. *J. Consum. Mark. [Online]* **1999**, *16*, 558–575. [CrossRef]

24. Diamantopoulos, A.; Schlegelmilch, B.B.; Sinkovics, R.R.; Bohlen, G.M. Can socio-demographics still play a role in profiling green consumers? A review of the evidence and an empirical investigation. *J. Bus. Res.* **2003**, *56*, 465–480. [CrossRef]

25. Jain, S.K.; Kaur, G. Role of socio-demographics in segmenting and profiling green consumers: An exploratory study of consumers in India. *J. Int. Consum. Mark.* **2006**, *18*, 107–146. [CrossRef]

26. Banytė, J.; Brazionienė, L. Agnė Gadeikienė investigation of green consumer profile: A case of lithuanian market of eco-friendly food products. *Econ. Manag.* **2010**, *15*, 374–383.

27. Albayrak, T.; Caber, M.; Aksoy, S. Clustering consumers according to their environmental concerns and skepticisms. *Int. J. Trade Econom. Financ.* **2010**, *1*, 84. [CrossRef]

28. Sandahl, D.M.; Robertson, R. Social determinants of environmental concern: Specification and test of the model. *Environ. Behav.* **1989**, *21*, 57–81. [CrossRef]

29. Srnka, K.J. Culture's role in marketers' ethical decision making: An integrated theoretical framework. *Acad. Mark. Sci. Rev.* **2004**, *1*, 1–32.

30. Swaidan, Z.; Rawwas, M.Y.; Vitell, S.J. Culture and moral ideologies of African Americans. *J. Mark. Theory Pract.* **2008**, *16*, 127–137. [CrossRef]

31. Buller, P.F.; Kohls, J.J.; Anderson, K.S. The challenge of global Ethics. *J. Bus. Ethics* **1991**, *10*, 767–775. [CrossRef]

32. Hofstede, G. *Culture's Consequences: International Differences in Work-Related Values*; Sage: Beverly Hills, CA, USA, 1980.

33. Husted, B.W.; Allen, D.B. Toward a model of cross-cultural business ethics: The impact of individualism and collectivism on the ethical decision-making process. *J. Bus. Ethics* **2008**, *82*, 293–305. [CrossRef]

34. Bernardi, R. Associations between Hofstedes' Cultural Constructs and Social Desirability Response Bias. *J. Bus. Ethics* **2006**, *65*, 43–53. [CrossRef]

35. Kohlberg, L. *Essays on Moral Development: The Psychology of Moral Development*; Harper & Row New\brk: New York, NY, USA, 1984; Volume 2.

36. Kini, R.B.; Ramakrishna, H.V.; Vijayaraman, B.S. Shaping of Moral Intensity Regarding Software Piracy: A Comparison between Thailand and U.S. Students. *J. Bus. Ethics* **2004**, *49*, 91–104. [CrossRef]

37. Tan, J.; Chow, I.H.S. Isolating cultural and national influence on value and ethics: A test of competing hypotheses. *J. Bus. Ethics* **2009**, *88*, 197–210. [CrossRef]

38. Beekun, R.I.; Hamdy, R.; Westerman, J.W.; HassabElnaby, H.R. An exploration of ethical decision-making processes in the United States and Egypt. *J. Bus. Ethics* **2008**, *82*, 587–605. [CrossRef]

39. Singhapakdi, A.; Karande, K.; Rao, C.P.; Vitell, S.J. How important are ethics and social responsibility?—A multinational study of marketing professionals. *Eur. J. Mark.* **2001**, *35*, 133–153. [CrossRef]

40. Vitell, S.J. Consumer ethics research: Review, synthesis and suggestions for the future. *J. Bus. Ethics* **2003**, *43*, 33–47. [CrossRef]

41. Jackson, T. Cultural values and management ethics: A 10-nation study. *Hum. Relat.* **2001**, *54*, 1267–1302. [CrossRef]

42. Hofstede, G. *Cultures and Organizations—Software of the Mind*; McGraw Hill: New York, NY, USA, 1991.

43. Tsalikis, J.; Seaton, B.; Tomaras, P. A new perspective on cross-cultural ethical evaluations: The use of conjoint analysis. *J. Bus. Ethics* **2002**, *35*, 281–292. [CrossRef]

44. Peterson, R.A.; Albaum, G.; Merunka, D.; Munera, J.L.; Smith, S.M. Effects of nationality, gender and religiosity on business-related ethicality. *J. Bus. Ethics* **2010**, *96*, 573–587. [CrossRef]

45. Shrum, L.J.; McCarty, J.A.; Lowerey, T.M. Buyer Characteristics of the Green Consumer and Their Implications for Advertising Strategy. *J. Adv.* **1995**, *24*, 71–90. [CrossRef]

46. Schwartz, S.H. Normative influences on altruism. In *Advances in Experimental Social Psychology*; Berkowitz, L., Ed.; Academic Press: San Diego, CA, USA, 1977; Volume 10, pp. 221–279.

47. Hines, J.M.; Hungerford, H.R.; Tomera, A.N. Analysis and synthesis of research on responsible environmental behaviour: A meta-analysis. *J. Environ. Educ.* **1987**, *18*, 1–8. [CrossRef]

48. Bamberg, S.; Möser, G. Twenty years after Hines, Hungerford, and Tomera: A new meta-analysis of psycho-social determinants of pro-environmental behavior. *J. Environ. Psychol.* **2007**, *27*, 14–25. [CrossRef]

49. Bray, J.; Johns, N.; Kilburn, D. An Exploratory Study into the Factors Impeding Ethical Consumption. *J. Bus. Ethics* **2011**, *98*, 597–608. [CrossRef]

50. Carrington, M.J.; Neville, B.A.; Whitwell, G.J. Why ethical consumers don't walk their talk: Towards a framework for understanding the gap between the ethical purchase intentions and actual buying behaviour of ethically minded consumers. *J. Bus. Ethics* **2010**, *97*, 139–158. [CrossRef]

51. Carrington, M.J.; Neville, B.A.; Whitwell, G.J. Lost in translation: Exploring the ethical consumer intention-behaviour gap. *J. Bus. Ethics* **2014**, *67*, 2759–2767. [CrossRef]

52. Pinto, D.C.; Nique, W.M.; Añaña, E.D.S.; Herter, M.M. Green consumer values: How do personal values influence environmentally responsible water consumption? *Int. J. Consum. Stud.* **2011**, *35*, 122–131. [CrossRef]

53. Miniero, G.; Codini, A.; Bonera, M.; Corvi, E.; Bertoli, G. Being green: From attitude to actual consumption. *Int. J. Consum. Stud.* **2014**, *38*, 521–528. [CrossRef]

54. Kinnear, T.C.; Taylor, J.R.; Ahmed, S.A. Ecologically Concerned Consumers: Who Are They? *J. Mark.* **1974**, *38*, 20–24. [CrossRef]

55. Crosby, L.A.; Gill, J.D.; Taylor, J.R. Consumer/voter behaviour in the passage of the Michigan container law. *J. Mark.* **1981**, *45*, 19–32. [CrossRef]

56. Schwartz, S.H.; Melech, G.; Lehmann, A.; Burgess, S.; Harris, M.; Owens, V. Extending the cross-cultural validity of the theory of basic human values with a different method of measurement. *J. Cross-Cult. Psychol.* **2001**, *32*, 519–542. [CrossRef]

57. Stern, P.C. New environmental theories: Toward a coherent theory of environmentally significant behavior. *J. Soc. Issues* **2000**, *56*, 407–424. [CrossRef]

58. Steg, L.; Bolderdijk, J.W.; Keizer, K.; Perlaviciute, G. An integrated framework for encouraging pro-environmental behaviour: The role of values, situational factors and goals. *J. Environ. Psychol.* **2014**, *38*, 104–115. [CrossRef]

59. Gifford, R.; Nilsson, A. Personal and social factors that influence pro-environmental concern and behaviour: A review. *Int. J. Psychol.* **2014**, *49*, 141–157. [CrossRef] [PubMed]

60. D'Souza, C.; Taghian, M.; Lamb, P. An empirical study on the influence of environmental labels on consumers. *Corp. Commun. Int. J.* **2006**, *11*, 162–173. [CrossRef]

61. Roberts, J.A. Green consumers in the 1990s: Profile and implications for advertising. *J. Bus. Res.* **1996**, *36*, 217–231. [CrossRef]

62. Rokeach, M. Authoritarianism scales and response bias: Comment on Peabody's paper. *Psychol. Bull.* **1967**, *67*, 349–355. [CrossRef] [PubMed]

63. Rokeach, M. *The Nature of Human Values*; Free press: New York, NY, USA, 1973; Volume 438.

64. Homer, P.M.; Kahle, L.R. A structural equation test of the value-attitude-behaviour hierarchy. *J. Personal. Soc. Psychol.* **1988**, *54*, 638–646. [CrossRef]

65. Higgins, E.T. Beyond pleasure and pain. *Am. Psychol.* **1997**, *52*, 1280–1300. [CrossRef] [PubMed]

66. Higgins, E.T.; Roney, C.J.; Crowe, E.; Hymes, C. Ideal versus ought predilections for approach and avoidance distinct self-regulatory systems. *J. Personal. Soc. Psychol.* **1994**, *66*, 276–286. [CrossRef]

67. Higgins, E.T. Self-discrepancy: A theory relating self and affect. *Psychol. Rev.* **1987**, *94*, 319–340. [CrossRef] [PubMed]

68. Freitas, A.L.; Higgins, E.T. Enjoying goal-directed action: The role of regulatory fit. *Psychol. Sci.* **2002**, *13*, 1–6. [CrossRef] [PubMed]

69. Idson, L.C.; Liberman, N.; Higgins, E.T. Distinguishing gains from nonlosses and losses from nongains: A regulatory focus perspective on hedonic intensity. *J. Exp. Soc. Psychol.* **2000**, *36*, 252–274. [CrossRef]

70. Luthans, F.; Youssef, C.M.; Avolio, B.J. *Psychological Capital: Developing the Human Competitive Edge*; Oxford University Press: Oxford, UK, 2007; p. 3.

71. Sisodia, R.; Wolfe, D.; Sheth, J. *Firms of Endearment: How World-Class Companies Profit from Passion and Purpose*; Wharton School Publishing: Philadelphia, PA, USA, 2007.

72. Luchs, M.G.; Naylor, R.W.; Irwin, J.R.; Raghunathan, R. The sustainability liability: Potential negative effects of ethicality on product preference. *J. Mark.* **2010**, *74*, 18–31. [CrossRef]

73. Kees, J. Advertising framing effects and consideration of future consequences. *J. Consum. Aff.* **2011**, *45*, 7–32. [CrossRef]

74. Klineberg, S.L. Future time perspective and the preference for delayed reward. *J. Personal. Soc. Psychol.* **1968**, *8*, 253–257. [CrossRef]
75. Gjesme, T. On the concept of future time orientation: Considerations of some functions' and measurements' implications. *Int. J. Psychol.* **1983**, *18*, 443–461. [CrossRef]
76. Wright, P.; Weitz, B. Time horizon effects on product evaluation strategies. *J. Mark. Res.* **1977**, *14*, 429–443. [CrossRef]
77. Codini, A.; Bonera, M.; Miniero, G. Time horizon and green consumption. *Merc. Comp.* **2016**, *2*, 49–62.
78. Joireman, J.; Van Lange, P.A.M.; Van Vugt, M. Who cares about the environmental impact of cars? Those with an eye toward the future. *Environ. Behav.* **2004**, *36*, 187–206. [CrossRef]
79. Sarigöllü, E. A cross-country exploration of environmental attitudes. *Environ. Behav.* **2009**, *41*, 365–386. [CrossRef]
80. Leonidou, L.C.; Leonidou, C.N.; Kvasova, O. Antecedents and outcomes of consumer environmentally friendly attitudes and behavior. *J. Mark. Manag.* **2010**, *26*, 1319–1344. [CrossRef]
81. Furrer, O.; Liu, B.S.C.; Sudharshan, D. The relationships between culture and service quality perceptions basis for cross-cultural market segmentation and resource allocation. *J. Serv. Res.* **2000**, *2*, 355–371. [CrossRef]
82. Lindsay, J.J.; Strathman, A. Predictors of recycling behaviour: An application of a modified health belief model. *J. Appl. Soc. Psychol.* **1997**, *27*, 1799–1823. [CrossRef]
83. Strathman, A.; Gleicher, F.; Boninger, D.S.; Edwards, C.S. The consideration of future consequences: Weighing immediate and distant outcomes of behavior. *J. Personal. Soc. Psychol.* **1994**, *66*, 742–752. [CrossRef]
84. Joireman, J.A.; Lasane, T.P.; Bennett, J.; Richards, D.; Solaimani, S. Integrating social value orientation and the consideration of future consequences within the extended norm activation model of proenvironmental behavior. *Br. J. Soc. Psychol.* **2001**, *40*, 133–155. [CrossRef] [PubMed]
85. Erikson, E.H. *Childhood and Society*; WW Norton & Company: London, UK, 1993.
86. Keyes, C.L.M.; Ryff, C.D. Generativity in adult lives: Social structural contours and quality of life consequences. In *Generativity and Adult Development: How and Why We Care for the Next Generation*; McAdams, D.P., de St. Aubin, E., Eds.; American Psychological Association: Washington, DC, USA, 1998; pp. 227–263.
87. Milfont, T.L.; Sibley, C.G. Exploring the concept of environmental generativity. *Int. J. Hisp. Psychol.* **2011**, *4*, 21–30.
88. Stone, G.; Barnes, J.H.; Montgomery, C. Ecoscale: A scale for the measurement of environmentally responsible consumers. *Psychol. Mark.* **1995**, *12*, 595–612. [CrossRef]
89. Chan, R.Y. Environmental attitudes and behaviour of consumers in China: Survey findings and implications. *J. Int. Consum. Mark.* **1999**, *11*, 25–52. [CrossRef]
90. Roberts, J.A.; Bacon, D.R. Exploring the Subtle Relationships between Environmental Concern and Ecologically Conscious Consumer Behaviour. *J. Bus. Res.* **1997**, *40*, 79–89. [CrossRef]
91. Synodinos, N.E. Environmental attitudes and knowledge: A comparison of marketing and business students with other groups. *J. Bus. Res.* **1990**, *20*, 161–170. [CrossRef]
92. Vining, J.; Ebreo, A. What makes a recycler? A comparison of recyclers and nonrecyclers. *Environ. Behav.* **1990**, *22*, 55–73. [CrossRef]
93. Chan, R.Y. Determinants of Chinese consumers' green purchase behavior. *Psychol. Mark.* **2001**, *18*, 389–413. [CrossRef]
94. Martin, B.; Simintiras, A.C. The impact of green product lines on the environment: Does what they know affect how they feel? *Market. Intell. Plan.* **1995**, *13*, 16–23. [CrossRef]
95. Geller, E.S. Evaluating energy conservation programs: Is verbal report enough? *J. Consum. Res.* **1981**, *8*, 331–335. [CrossRef]
96. Fitzsimmons, C. Make it Green and Keep them Keen. The Guardian. 21 January 2008. Available online: http://www.guardian.co.uk/media/2008/jan/21/marketingandpr (accessed on 1 June 2016).
97. Liere, K.D.V.; Dunlap, R.E. The social bases of environmental concern: A review of hypotheses, explanations and empirical evidence. *Publ. Opin. Quart.* **1980**, *44*, 181–197. [CrossRef]
98. Paço, A.; Gouveia Rodrigues, R. Environmental activism and consumers' perceived responsibility. *Int. J. Consum. Stud.* **2016**, *40*, 466–474. [CrossRef]
99. Knopman, D.S.; Susman, M.M.; Landy, M.K. Civic environmentalism: Tackling tough land-use problems with innovative governance. *Environ. Sci. Policy Sustain. Dev.* **1999**, *41*, 24–32. [CrossRef]

100. Dunlap, R.E.; Jones, R.E. Environmental concern: Conceptual and measurement issues. In *Handbook of Environmental Sociology*; Dunlap, R.E., Michelson, W., Eds.; Greenwood Press: Westport, CT, USA, 2002.
101. Schultz, P.W.; Oskamp, S.; Mainieri, T. Who recycles and when: A review of personal and situational factors. *J. Environ. Psychol.* **1995**, *15*, 105–121. [CrossRef]
102. Mannetti, L.; Pierro, A.; Livi, S. Recycling: Planned and self- expressive behavior. *J. Environ. Psychol.* **2004**, *24*, 227–236. [CrossRef]
103. Bamberg, S.; Schmidt, S. Incentives, morality or habit? Predicting students' car use for university routes with the models of Ajzen, Schwartz and Triandis. *Environ. Behav.* **2003**, *35*, 264–285. [CrossRef]
104. Heath, Y.; Gifford, R. Extending the theory of planned behaviour: Predicting the use of public transportation. *J. Appl. Soc. Psychol.* **2002**, *32*, 2154–2189. [CrossRef]
105. Poortinga, W.; Steg, L.; Vlek, C.; Wiersma, G. Household preferences for energy-saving measures: A conjoint analysis. *J. Econ. Psychol.* **2003**, *24*, 49–64. [CrossRef]
106. Stern, P.C.; Gardner, G.T. Psychological Research and Energy Policy. *Am. Psychol.* **1981**, *36*, 329–342. [CrossRef]
107. Corral-Verdugo, V.; Bechtel, R.B.; Fraijo-Sing, B. Environmental beliefs and water conservation: An empirical study. *J. Environ. Psychol.* **2003**, *23*, 247–257. [CrossRef]
108. Sibley, C.G.; Liu, J.H. Differentiating Active and Passive Littering A Two-Stage Process Model of Littering Behaviour in Public Spaces. *Environ. Behav.* **2003**, *35*, 415–433. [CrossRef]
109. McFarlane, B.L.; Boxall, P.C. Activism in the forest sector: The role of social psychological and social structural variables. *J. Environ. Psychol.* **2003**, *23*, 79–87. [CrossRef]
110. Tanner, C.; Kaiser, F.G.; Kast, S. Contextual conditions of ecological consumerism: A food-purchasing survey. *Environ. Behav.* **2004**, *36*, 94–111. [CrossRef]
111. Ritter, A.M.; Borchardt, M.; Vaccaro, G.L.R.; Pereira, G.M.; Almeida, F. Motivations for Promoting the Consumption Of Green Products In An Emerging Country: Exploring Attitudes Of Brazilian Consumers. *J. Clean. Prod.* **2015**, *106*, 507–520. [CrossRef]
112. Akenji, L. Consumer scapegoatism and limits to green consumerism. *J. Clean. Prod.* **2014**, *63*, 13–23. [CrossRef]
113. Elliott, R. The taste for green: The possibilities and dynamics of status differentiation through green consumption. *Poetics* **2013**, *41*, 294–322. [CrossRef]
114. Han, H.; Kim, Y. An investigation of green hotel customers' decision formation: Developing an extended model of the theory of planned behavior. *Int. J. Hosp. Manag.* **2010**, *29*, 659–668. [CrossRef]
115. Schaefer, A.; Crane, A. Addressing sustainability and consumption. *J. Macromark.* **2005**, *25*, 76–92. [CrossRef]
116. Mont, O.; Plepys, A. Sustainable consumption progress: Should we be proud or alarmed? *J. Clean. Prod.* **2008**, *16*, 531–537. [CrossRef]
117. Schlossberg, H. Green marketing has been planted-now watch it grow. *Mark. News* **1991**, *4*, 26–30.
118. Laroche, M.; Bergeron, J.; Barbaro-Forleo, G. Targeting consumers who are willing to pay more for environmentally friendly products. *J. Consum. Mark.* **2001**, *18*, 503–520. [CrossRef]
119. Higgins, E.T.; Friedman, R.S.; Harlow, R.E.; Idson, L.C.; Ayduk, O.N.; Taylor, A. Achievement orientations from subjective histories of success: Promotion pride versus prevention pride. *Eur. J. Soc. Psychol.* **2001**, *31*, 3–23. [CrossRef]

sustainability

MDPI

Article

Sustainable Consumption Dilemmas

Kees Vringer [1], Eline van der Heijden [2], Daan van Soest [2,*], Herman Vollebergh [1,2] and Frank Dietz [1]

[1] Netherlands Environmental Assessment Agency (PBL), 2594 AV The Hague, The Netherlands; Kees.Vringer@pbl.nl (K.V.); herman.vollebergh@pbl.nl (H.V.); frank.dietz@pbl.nl (F.D.)
[2] Tilburg Sustainability Centre and Department of Economics, Tilburg University, 5037 AB Tilburg, The Netherlands; Eline.vanderheijden@uvt.nl
* Correspondence: d.p.vansoest@uvt.nl; Tel.: +31-13-466-2072

Academic Editor: Gerrit Antonides
Received: 30 January 2017; Accepted: 25 May 2017; Published: 3 June 2017

Abstract: To examine which considerations play a role when individuals make decisions to purchase sustainable product varieties or not, we have conducted a large scale field experiment with more than 600 participating households. Households can vote on whether the budgets they receive should only be spent on purchasing the sustainable product variety, or whether every household in a group is free to spend their budget on any product variety. By conducting several treatments, we tested whether people tend to view sustainable consumption as a social dilemma or as a moral dilemma. We find little support for the hypothesis that social dilemma considerations are the key drivers of sustainable consumption behaviour. Participants seem to be caught in a moral dilemma in which they not only weigh their individual financial costs with the sustainable benefits but they also consider the consequences of restricting other people's freedom of choice. Complementary survey results further substantiate this claim and show that many people are reluctant to impose restrictions on their peers, but, at the same time, our results also suggest substantial support for the government to regulate the availability of unsustainable product varieties.

Keywords: sustainable consumption; field experiment; social dilemma; moral dilemma

1. Introduction

Problems of sustainability and sustainable development tend to be more wicked: (i) the less consensus there is regarding the (perceived) urgency of the problem; and, not unrelated, (ii) the larger the distance (geographically, or temporally) between beneficiaries of sustainability actions and those who bear the costs of providing them. An example in point is climate change. Future generations, especially those living closest to the equator, will benefit most from climate change mitigation actions, while the costs of these actions need to be incurred by the current generations, and especially those living in the richer countries [1]. That means that considerations such as ethical stance, morality, warm glow and social identity are likely to play an important role in individual decisions whether to (voluntarily) contribute to solving these wicked sustainability problems [2–4]. However, more mundane explanations also exist. (In)action may also be the result of social dilemma considerations [5–7]. Each individual has a negligible impact on solving wicked sustainability problems, and the private costs of taking sustainability actions may be larger than the private returns received by the decision maker. Social dilemmas can be overcome by means of regulations (such as bans) or other inducements (such as subsidies or taxes) that either force all those affected to undertake sustainability actions, or change the cost–benefit ratio such that the sustainability actions become the cheaper actions. When offered the possibility to express one's opinion about the desirability of these regulations or inducements (for example in case of a binding referendum), an individual's support for the regulation

36

would be an increasing function of the number of (other) individuals affected. The larger the number of individuals that can be committed to undertake the sustainable actions, the more likely it is that an individual will vote in favour of such inducements or regulations—because for the same amount of costs incurred by the individual, the impact of collective action will be higher the larger the number of individuals who are contributing too. This holds, for example, for decisions of households to consume the sustainable or conventional variety of a particular product.

In this paper, we explore which of the possible motivations or considerations are the most important drivers of sustainability behaviour—social dilemma considerations, or more personal considerations such as personal morality [8]. We do so by implementing a large scale (semi-)field experiment with more than 600 participating households, which were endowed with a budget that they could spend on either a sustainable or on a conventional product variety. The budgets offered varied with the size and composition of the household, and both product varieties were easily available in (local) shops and supermarkets. The typical procedure was that participating households voted on whether the available budgets had to be spent on purchasing sustainable product varieties or that every household was free to spend it on either product variety. Next, they were informed of the (majority) voting outcome, after which they could purchase the product variety in their preferred shop or supermarket. Finally, they were reimbursed for their purchases up to the amount of money available in their budget—if and only if their purchases were in line with the majority voting outcome.

The key treatments are those in which the voting outcome is binding; if the majority voted in favour of the rule that the available budgets could only be spent on the sustainable product variety, all households in the group are required to do so. Implementing this "binding referendum mechanism" (or "regulation") in groups of different sizes (1 household, 31 households or 61 households) provides a test of whether or not social dilemma considerations are an important driver of sustainable consumption decisions. Because of the public good characteristics of sustainable consumption, agents are expected to derive utility from the sustainability impacts of all sustainable consumption activities—their own, but also those done by the other households in their group. Note that this is fully analogous to the canonical public goods game—also known as the Voluntary Contribution Mechanism; see for example [9]. The amount of money spent on the sustainable product variety in our field experiment can be viewed as the amount of money contributed to the public account in a standard PG —because each individual household cares about the positive sustainability benefits of their group's total consumption, not just about their own. With smaller group sizes, a household may prefer to vote against the group being obliged to purchase the sustainable product variety because the extra costs of sustainable consumption they incur may be larger than the household's perceived welfare benefits obtained if the vote passes, and all households in their group (have to) purchase the sustainable product variety. If the majority voting outcome is in favour of the rule that all households should spend their budgets on purchasing the sustainable product variety, the positive impact is larger if there are 61 households in a group than if there are 31 or just 1 household in a group. For those agents who care about sustainability, the benefits of voting in favour of compulsory purchase of sustainable are larger the larger the size of the group. However, the costs agents face when purchasing the sustainable product variety is the same independent of the size of the group. After all, the price of the product varieties in the shop is fixed, and the extra costs associated with buying the sustainable product variety oneself is just equal to the price difference between the sustainable and the conventional product variety. With larger group size, the environmental benefits of voting in favour of sustainable product consumption are larger while the costs remain constant, and hence the share of votes in favour of sustainable consumption purchases is expected to increase in group size—if and only if social dilemma considerations are an important driver of voting decisions.

The specific product we use in this study is meat, where organic meat is considered the sustainable product variety. As stated before, problems of sustainability and sustainable development tend to be more wicked the less consensus there is regarding the (perceived) urgency of the problem, and—not unrelated—the larger the distance (geographically, or temporally) between beneficiaries of sustainability actions and those who bear the costs of providing them. Climate change is probably the most important sustainability challenge the planet currently faces, but the impact of individual behaviour on climate change outcomes is too small to be amenable for experimentation—and the same holds for other big sustainability issues, such as biodiversity conservation, deforestation and depletion of the high sea fisheries. Given that we want to test whether moral or social dilemma considerations are the most important driver of the (lack of) sustainable consumption behaviour, we needed to choose a consumption product: (i) that would not be too expensive; (ii) where both conventional and sustainable product varieties are readily available in the shops; and (iii) where a coordinated action of reasonably large groups of individuals (groups of 31 households) would result in a considerable improvement of the sustainability problem at hand.

In our search for a suitable product group, we decided to use meat for our experiment. Although there is some debate about the sustainability value of organic food products, we argue that organic meat can be considered to be a (more) sustainable product. The Sustainability Assessment of Food and Agriculture systems (SAFA) Guidelines—developed for assessing the impact of food and agriculture operations on the environment and people—state that food and agriculture systems worldwide can (and should) be evaluated on all four dimensions of sustainability: good governance, environmental integrity, economic resilience and social well-being ([10], p. 2, see also [11]). While little is known about the differential performance on governance criteria, organic meat production tends to outperform conventional meat production on two criteria. Regarding economic resilience organic farming seems to have advantages compared with conventional farming, as it is less reliant on external inputs and has a stronger ability to conserve natural resources [12]. Social well-being includes criteria such as good quality life, animal welfare and the impacts on the welfare of future generation, and organic farming practices score better on these criteria too [13]—and then especially so on animal welfare [14].

Based on a meta-analysis of studies comparing the environmental impacts of organic and conventional meat production in Northern Europe, [15] conclude it is not possible to draw a conclusive picture on the general environmental performance of the different farming systems. While it is difficult to determine with certainty whether the positive sustainability impacts of organic (as compared to conventional) meat production outweigh the negative ones, organic meat production brings clearly more animal welfare than conventional meat production. Taken together, organic meat production tends to be more sustainable than conventional meat production, but, of course, a vegetarian or a vegan life style is likely to be even more sustainable.

Pre-testing revealed that the sustainability consequences of organic meat consumption by a concerted action of 31 households—and then especially the improvements in animal welfare that organic meat production gives rise to, resulting in about 40 chickens having had a better life, as compared to the consumption of conventional meat—was perceived as a sizable impact. In addition, among non-vegetarians, organic meat is perceived as more sustainable than conventional meat, and it is a wicked problem in the sense that the weights people attach to animal welfare differs considerably too. Organic versus conventional meat consumption was thus chosen as the sustainable versus standard product variety. In addition, note that for those households that care about animal welfare, organic meat consumption is a public good. These households value the positive sustainability benefits of their group's total consumption (theirs and those of all other households purchasing organic meat), not just about their own. After all, there is neither rivalry in consumption of the sustainability consequences of purchasing organic meat—the improvement in animal welfare—nor can non-contributors be excluded from enjoying those benefits. As such, the animal welfare consequences of organic meat consumption are a public good. Thus, organic meat has all the necessary characteristics of a social-dilemma consumption good.

Previewing our results, we find only little support for the hypothesis that social dilemma considerations are the key factor driving (the lack of) sustainable consumption behaviour. The share of households voting in favour of the regulation is not an increasing function of the size of the group. Moreover, we do not find substantial differences in shares of households voting in favour of the regulation if it is binding or if it is non-binding. When households have the option to commit themselves conditionally to the share of households that are also willing to do so, we find that the propensity for voluntary commitment does not strongly increase with group size. Interestingly, we do find that the propensity to vote in favour of the regulation is significantly higher if it is framed as a less-restrictive measure—that is, in the form of a subsidy rather than as a ban. We thus do not find substantial experimental evidence that social dilemma considerations are the main drivers of (the lack of) sustainable consumption behaviour, and we offer complementary survey results to further substantiate this claim.

We are not the first to try to identify the key drivers of (in)action in sustainability problems (see for example [16–20]). Previous studies have focused on identifying the relevance of various motivations hampering or fostering sustainable consumption decisions. For example, Moisander [19] and Kurz [21] analyse the role of motivational complexity, and Gupta and Ogden [22] concentrate on the social dilemma aspects of the problem. Rather than using standard survey methods (e.g., [23,24]), we implement a large-scale financially-incentivized field experiment regarding consumption decisions that households make on a daily basis. Furthermore, our participants are a representative sample of the population of Dutch non-vegetarian households, and they make their purchase decisions in the environment where typically these types of decisions are taken—in their homes, and in the supermarket.

The remainder of the paper is organized as follows. In Section 2, we present the theoretical background as well as the experimental design, and in Section 3 we present the results. Section 4 concludes.

2. Theoretical Background and Experimental Design

2.1. Social versus Moral Dilemmas

In the European Union, the share of consumers buying sustainable product varieties is typically quite low [25]. This also applies to the Netherlands, the country in which this study was implemented. The market share of sustainable products in the Netherlands usually does not exceed 5–10% [26–28], yet surveys consistently show that Dutch consumers consider sustainability one of the most pressing societal issues (e.g., [29,30]). Apparently, most Dutch consumers are not willing or able to voluntarily change their consumption patterns to increase sustainability.

To consider sustainability important without acting upon this belief is consistent with a social dilemma. A social dilemma arises if two conditions are met (for classic contributions on the role of social dilemmas in daily life, see for example Olson [5] and Schelling [31], and for an early theoretical analysis, see Sen [32]): (i) collective welfare is maximized if all members of the community undertake a specific action; and (ii) individual members can maximize their private welfare by *not* undertaking this specific action, but this will be at the expense of collective welfare. Indeed, the individual costs of buying sustainable product varieties are relatively high (with price premiums for such products amounting to 10–50% compared to conventional varieties), but society is best off if *everyone* makes this individual contribution. However, individuals are better off free-riding on the investments made by others, than making investments in the collective good (sustainability) themselves. From this reasoning, it is not surprising that consumers support the idea of more far-reaching government measures to promote sustainable consumption—such measures would help to resolve the dilemma. In 2007, as many as 70% of Dutch citizens subscribed the proposition that the government should take the initiative in solving important societal issues [33]. A recent example for this is the strong support of the Dutch population for stricter building regulations to improve their energy efficiency [34].

However, the oftentimes fierce public debates about concrete measures suggest that also something else could be at play. Perhaps it is too easy for survey respondents to say that they consider sustainability important and that government measures are needed, and that this is the case not just in standard surveys (which pose questions on the respondent's opinion, attitudes and behaviours) but also in stated-preference valuation techniques such as contingent valuation and discrete choice experiments. Due to the hypothetical nature of surveys, these studies may overlook the possibility that consumers find sustainable products simply too expensive. Indeed, most studies on preferences related to nonmarket environmental goods employ contingent valuation (CV) and discrete choice experiments (also known as conjoint analysis) techniques [35]. While the literature often assumes that it is in the respondents' own interest to truthfully answer a yes/no preference question ("Are you willing to pay X euros for this project, yes or no?"), it appears that these survey techniques generally lead to an *over*estimation of the true willingness to pay. In the economic literature, this phenomenon is known as *hypothetical bias*, and in the social-psychological literature addressed as *socially desirable answers*. A good overview of the nature and degree of hypothetical bias is provided by the meta-analyses of [36,37], and by the literature reviews of Harrison [38], and Harrison and Rutström [39]. This bias arises because of "yea saying" (stating support for the socially desired project) or because of strategic considerations (when respondents say "yes" to a specific price even though they would not actually be willing to pay that price, just because the project is more likely to be implemented if they answer "yes" rather than "no"). Strategically or socially misrepresenting one's preferences is cheap because the respondent knows that her answers will not have direct financial consequences, as the payment question itself is hypothetical. Clearly, the potential for such hypothetical bias is particularly important for the present research in which we aim to explain the difference between consumers' (stated) support for policies promoting sustainable products, and their much less frequent purchase of such products. An additional or alternative explanation for this observed difference may be that people perceive sustainable consumption as a moral issue, so they take moral motives into consideration. When an individual is purchasing (food) products, he can be motivated by moral concerns as a citizen but also, and at the same time, care about product characteristics as a consumer [40,41]. The phenomenon that individuals' preferences and concerns do not always translate into purchase behaviour may be due to the dual entities that individuals may have, the so-called consumer-citizen duality, or discrepancy. Note that moral concerns may also include (restricting) freedom of choice of others.

2.2. A Field Experiment

To gain insight into whether sustainability issues are viewed as a social or a moral dilemma, we used both standard survey questions as well as an economic semi-field experiment (according to the classification by Harrison and List [42], our study is not a natural field experiment as participants were aware of the fact that they took part in a research project). A key characteristic of economic experiments is that decisions have *real* consequences—financial, or non-financial—for the decision maker herself, but maybe also for others. The participants in our experiment were a representative sample of Dutch consumers responsible for the food shopping in their household. Their households were provided with a budget (or "credit") that they could spend on either the sustainable or the conventional variety of specific product group, and hence decisions had real (financial and sustainability) consequences rather than that decisions were just hypothetical. Compared to standard laboratory experiments (using students as subjects), an important and unique feature of our study is that participants made their decisions in the environment where household decision making with respect to groceries typically takes place—at home, and/or in the supermarket. This way, participants were confronted with the real, tangible consequences of their personal beliefs (and those of others) about abstract values such as "sustainability"—and hence participants are expected to be better able to picture the consequences of their beliefs and actions on abstract values such as sustainability [43]. In addition, we believe that a distinctive and noteworthy aspect of our study is the large sample size: more than 600 household representatives participated in our experiment.

The experiment consisted of a number of stages; the general setup is displayed in Table 1. Before conducting the experiment in its definitive form, we tested the design in qualitative and quantitative pilot studies. Based on the results of these pilot studies, the original design was further optimized [44]. The aim of the qualitative pilot study was to check whether the information provided to the participants on conventional versus sustainable varieties of the product was clear and correctly understood. The quantitative pilot study was done to detect and solve any problems in the design before conducting the final experiment. After having carefully pretested the experimental design, we are confident that participants fully understood the instructions such that confusion can be ruled out as a factor driving our results. All information exchange took place through the Internet, and there was no contact between participants. In Phase 0, we cooperated with an online survey company (TNS-NIPO) to recruit households from their database that would be a representative sample of (non-vegetarian) households in the Netherlands. Our subject pool is a representative sample of the population of non-vegetarian households in the Netherlands because: (i) we started with a representative sample of Dutch households; (ii) we mentioned neither the topic nor the purpose of our study in our contacts with the respondents in the selection phase of the study; and (iii) 93% of the households who were invited for the initial survey, ended up participating in the experiment. For a general analysis of meat consumption in the Netherlands, see Gilsing et al. [45] and also Dagevos and Voordouw [46]. Respondents were asked whether they were willing to participate in a study, and, if so, whether they were available during the entire period in which the study was implemented, whether they ate meat, and who was responsible for the household's groceries shopping. We also collected data such as disposable income, age, household composition and educational level.

Table 1. Overview of the timing of the experiment (2010).

Phase	Time	Name	Activities
0	27 August–12 September	Sample selection	Households were contacted and a sample was selected
1	20 September–29 September	Experiment: Voting	Households received instructions, voted on the proposition, and answered some questions about motivation and expectations
2	29 September–8 October	Purchases	Households were informed about the voting outcome and could spend their credit on (conventional and/or organic) meat
3	8 October–17 October	Survey questions	Households answered questions about how they felt about the voting outcome, motivation to spend their money, some background questions.
4	8 October–28 October	Reimbursement	Participants were reimbursed dependent on whether they complied with the group decision, verified using their receipts

The actual experiment took place in Phase 1, when participants had to decide whether or not to (jointly) address a sustainability problem. They were randomly divided into groups, and each participant was allocated an experimental budget (credit) to be spent on a product of which both a (less expensive) conventional and a (more expensive) sustainable variety were available in the supermarket. To minimize the potential impact of physical differences, the conventional and sustainable product varieties had to be as similar as possible. Furthermore, both varieties had to be widely available and known by most people. The product that we selected for our experiment, meat, meets these criteria. The physical properties such as quality and taste are more or less similar between conventional and organic meat [47–49], and both varieties are widely available and known to most people. However, organic meat is on average about twice as expensive as non-organic meat. If objectively conventional meat and organic meat are very similar in all other respects, this does not mean that people also perceive them as very similar. This holds for the meat's taste, its health consequences, and environmental impact (land use, energy intensity); see for example Gilsing et al. [45]. Note that including or omitting this information is likely to affect the *levels* of support for regulations, but not the treatment *differences*. Similarly, although we cannot rule out the possibility that social desirability "pressure" may have affected the level of support, there is no reason to believe that the perceived social desirability pressure varies between treatments, such that treatment differences are unaffected. Households in a group vote as to whether the budgets they all received can only be spent on purchasing the sustainable product variety, organic meat, or whether every household is free to spend their budget on either organic or conventional meat (see Section 2.3 for details). The budget (credit) received was based on the size and composition of their household—seven euros for every adult in the household, and four euros for every child—and was sufficient to cover the additional costs of buying organic meat for one week.

After the voting (still in Phase 1), we asked the participants a number of questions related to voting motives and their expectations regarding the voting behaviour of other people.

In Phase 2, participants were informed about the outcome of the votes in their group, and the implications for their household, in particular about which type of meat would be reimbursed. Afterwards households had one week to spend their budget on *actual* meat purchase(s).

After the purchases, period Phase 3 started in which we asked participants whether they were happy with the voting outcome in their group, and why they spent the money in a particular way. We also asked them to what extent they thought that the government should take stricter measures to promote sustainable production and consumption, and some other background questions.

Finally, in Phase 4, households submitted the receipts of their meat purchases. After verifying that their behaviour was in line with the group decision, their costs were reimbursed (up the maximum credit available for their household).

2.3. Treatments

In the experiment, households were randomly allocated to six different treatments, which differed in either the rules dictating whether the budgets should be used to buy products of the sustainable variety, or in the number of households involved in the decision making process. Table 2 shows all the treatments as well as the number of participating households in each treatment. Each household participates in only one treatment (a between-subject design). Furthermore, all treatment differences are restricted to Phase 1, such that the procedures, information provided in all phases, etc. are the same across all treatments. Even though people may have different perceptions about potential differences between conventional and organic meat (see discussion in Section 2.2), which may affect the share of participants buying organic meat in our six treatments, this should not affect any treatment *differences*. We rely on randomization combined with sufficiently large numbers of participants in each treatment in order to control for the unobserved characteristics across groups.

Table 2. Overview of the treatments.

Treatment	Group Size	Binding?	Number of Participating Households **
1. Ban, binding	1	Yes	83
2. Ban, binding *	31	Yes	160
3. Ban, binding	61	Yes	111
4. Ban, non-binding	31	No	160
5. Subsidy, binding	31	Yes	124
6. Conditional choice, binding	31	Yes	83
Total number of participating households			721

* This is the main "binding ban" treatment described in Appendix A. ** Note that, in most treatments, the number of participants is not a round multiple of group size. This is due to non-response. To determine the voting outcome in incomplete groups, we randomly assigned participants from intact groups to incomplete groups to cover the missing votes.

We manipulate details of the experimental decision-making environment in four ways. (i) To examine if social dilemma considerations play a role, we vary the group size (from 1 via 31 to 61 households in a group). If social dilemma considerations are the most important factor driving behaviour, we expect the share of households voting in favour of the regulation to increase in the size of the group. In addition, we also explore (ii) whether voting outcomes differ if the voting outcomes are non-binding rather than binding; (iii) if it matters whether the decision problem is framed less restrictively (as a subsidy rather than as a binding regulation); and (iv) how people vote if households can conditionally commit themselves to a particular outcome, depending on the share of households willing to do the same. We will describe the main treatment in most detail, and focus on the difference between this treatment and the other ones when describing the other five treatments. The usage of a between-subjects design brings along the risk of responses being insensitive to variations in "the size of the public good" offered, as is well-documented in the stated preference valuation literature. Reasons why respondents' valuations of a specific project (or policy) may not vary much with the amount of environmental benefits created include, among others, warm glow considerations and the embedding effect [50,51]. However, using a within-subjects design (rather than between-subjects) may also result in biased outcomes because of, among other factors, anchoring and mental accounting bias [52,53]. We are confident that if we find a lack of responsiveness of voting outcomes to, for example, variations in group sizes, this is not due to above the biases for two reasons. First, the information offered regarding group size is salient in our experiment because decisions have real (financial as well as animal welfare) consequences as opposed to hypothetical decision making in stated-preferences studies [54,55]. Second, as stated before, our pre-tests indicated that the difference in sustainability outcomes (including animal welfare consequences) was perceived to be substantial for the different group sizes.

The main treatment, on which all other treatments were based, was the .so-called "binding ban" treatment. In this treatment, a group of a specific size, 31 participants in the basic variant, had to decide, by majority vote, whether to prohibit using the budget for purchasing the conventional variety of the product. The group's decision (voting outcome) was binding. The participants were informed that if the average participating household in their group would decide to spend their budget on buying organic meat for one week, about one chicken would have a better life. However, if the group of 31 participating households decided to vote in favour, the extra costs per household of buying organic meat would be unchanged, while about 40 chickens would have a better life. The instructions also included information about the price difference between the conventional and sustainable variety of the product. The participants were asked to vote as to whether all members of the group should be obliged to use their (experimental) budget only for buying the sustainable alternative, or whether everyone should be free to spend it on the variety of their choice. The question was phrased as follows. The question posed was very similar in all treatments, but the exact formulation was adapted to details of the treatment (e.g., all 61 households when group size was 61). Note that we have not included words such as "prohibit" and "ban" in the experiment.

You are now asked to vote on the following proposition:

"All 31 households shall use their credit only for buying organic meat."

☐ *I vote IN FAVOUR (I think that all 31 households in my group should be obliged to use their credit only for buying organic meat).*

☐ *I vote AGAINST (I think that all 31 households in my group should be free to use their credit for buying organic or non-organic meat).*

The vote was binding, and hence the weakly dominant optimal strategy for a participant is to vote truthfully and according to their (household) preferences [35,56]. After the vote, all participants were informed about the voting outcome in their group (Phase 2). If the majority of the group had voted in favour, then the credit could indeed *only* be used for buying organic meat. Hence, the purchases of meat during the week following the vote were reimbursed only if they complied with the majority decision.

The first treatment variation in the experimental design is the group size. We implemented the binding ban treatment with not just group sizes of 31 participating households, but also with 1 and 61 participants in a group (Treatments 1 and 3 in Table 2). In these treatments, the text in the above-mentioned questions is adjusted as well as the information provided to the participants. In particular, we informed our participants in groups of one (61) household what the "animal welfare" consequences were of their whole group spending their budgets on organic as opposed to conventional meat: about one (80) chicken(s) would have a better life.

A second change involves the type of commitment (binding or advisory). In one treatment, the 31 participants in a group were asked the same question as to whether budgets should be spent on organic meat or not, but where the vote was only advisory (the non-binding ban, Treatment 4 in Table 2). Thus, here, when voting, participants knew that the group decision was not-binding: all meat purchases would be reimbursed, regardless of the type of meat and the voting outcome.

Furthermore, we implemented a binding treatment in which the choice and consequences were similar to those in the binding ban treatment, but in which the situation was framed differently. In this so-called binding subsidy treatment (Treatment 5 in Table 2) the 31 participants of a group could vote as to whether all budgets should be used to *subsidize* the purchase of organic meat only of those who were willing to buy this type of meat rather than voting for or against a ban. If the group majority voted yes in the subsidy treatment, the price *difference* between the organic and the conventional variety was reimbursed. As in the binding ban treatment, the group decision was binding.

Finally, we also implemented a treatment in which we used the so-called strategy method [57] to ask participants as to whether they were willing to commit themselves to buying organic meat conditional on the number of other participants who were willing to do the same (the binding conditional choice treatment, Treatment 6 in Table 2). Here the participants were asked to indicate for six different situations what their decisions were (see Table 4). For example, one question was: "Are you willing to commit yourself to buying organic meat if 9–5 group members will also commit?" As in the main treatment, the outcome was binding.

Before presenting the results, we derive some predictions for expected differences between treatments. The treatments differed as to how (or by whom) it was decided where the budget could be spent on (the sustainable product variety, or the conventional one), but the rules regarding whether or not the credit was disbursed were always the same. If the outcome of the decision process in their group was that no households should spend their budget on the conventional product variety, they were reimbursed for the purchases of organic meat they made in the week in which the experiment took place. If the outcome of the decision process was that no regulations were to be imposed, all meat purchases (up to the allocated budget) were reimbursed independent of whether they purchased organic meat, or not. As organic meat is about twice as expensive as the conventional product variety and the budget per household was large enough for it to cover the *extra* costs of purchasing one week's supply of organic meat, the budget was sufficient to cover the costs of one week of conventional meat or half a week organic meat.

Obviously, the binding ban treatment with just one participant is essentially an individual commitment treatment, where the participant decides to commit her household to buying organic meat, or not. If participants view buying organic meat as a social dilemma, the share of participants voting in favour of the ban should be increasing in group size with 1, 31 or 61 households (Prediction 1). After all, the extra costs of buying organic meat are unchanged but the environmental and/or social consequences of the ban are greater if the ban applies to more households. Similar considerations apply to the binding conditional treatment. Earlier experimental research has documented that a substantial fraction of people are conditional co-operators. For example, Fischbacher et al. [58] report that in a public good experiment half of the people are willing to contribute more to a public good the more others contribute. In our binding conditional treatment, the vote is also a voluntary contribution decision, and if participants are conditional co-operators and view sustainability as a social dilemma, the share of participants willing to commit themselves to purchasing the sustainable product variety can be expected to increase in the share of participants willing to commit themselves (Prediction 2).

Regarding the comparison between the binding ban and non-binding ban treatments one would expect higher shares of people in favour of the proposition when the ban is not binding (Prediction 3). One reason is hypothetical bias—people's tendency to signal their pro-sociality (yea-saying) if the outcome of a poll or question does not have any real consequences. Here one could always express one's support for organic meat consumption in the referendum while deciding to buy conventional meat in the supermarket instead. Another reason is that people may view the non-binding vote as an opportunity to influence other people's opinions and behaviour—expressing their support for organic meat in the referendum in the hope that it will induce other households to (also) buy organic meat.

A final comparison is between the binding ban and the subsidy treatment. These treatments are very similar, but the framing is slightly different. In the subsidy treatment households can vote whether the budget should be used to cover the *extra* costs of purchasing the sustainable product variety whereas in the main treatment they vote whether households should use their credit only for buying organic meat. From a cost–benefit analysis, voting in favour of the subsidy is (weakly) less attractive than voting in favour of the ban and hence, for given sustainability preferences, the participants are expected to be (weakly) less prone to voting in favour of the subsidy than to voting in favour of a ban (Prediction 4). The reason why voting in favour of the subsidy is *weakly* less attractive than voting for the ban is as follows. In the ban treatment, subjects receive compensation for their purchases of organic meat up to the maximum of the budget reserved for them. If they purchase the same amount of organic meat as they would normally do, they pay half of the bill themselves. In this case, the subsidy treatment and the binding ban treatment are identical. However, in the ban treatment, subjects can, in principle, just buy half of the normal quantity they typically consume per week, claim the entire budget, and buy additional meat of the conventional type. In that situation, voting in favour of the "policy" would be less costly to the participant in the binding ban treatment compared to the binding subsidy treatment since in the latter subjects would only receive half of the budget. The experimental results, however, indicate that this "strategy of just spending part of one's budget on organic meat" (rather than 0, or all) is hardly ever used in the binding ban treatment.

3. Results

The results of the most important treatments are shown in Table 3 (for a complete overview of all treatments and results, see [44]), where the top panel presents results for the three binding ban treatments with different group sizes, and the bottom panel displays the results of all treatments with group size 31. We first present some general observations, and next discuss the most important findings in more detail in several subsections, including statistical tests to establish the significance of observed differences.

Table 3. Share of votes in favour of buying organic meat.

Share of Votes in Favour of Buying Organic Meat for Different Group Sizes	
Treatment	Share in Favour of Buying Sustainable Variety
1. Binding ban, group size 1 (N = 83)	0.51
2. Binding ban, group size 31 (N = 160)	0.42
3. Binding ban, group size 61 (N = 111)	0.50
Share of Votes in Favour of Buying Organic Meat, Group Size is 31	
Treatment	Share in Favour of Buying Sustainable Variety
2. Binding ban, group size 31 (N = 160)	0.42
4. Non-binding ban, group size 31 (N = 160)	0.50
5. Binding subsidy, group size 31 (N = 124)	0.57
6. Binding conditional choice, group size 31 (N = 83)	0.76
Share of participants willing to commit themselves	
—if none of the other households does the same	0.43
—if all of the other households do the same	0.57
Overall share of households willing to commit	0.76

The first observation is that the shares of votes in favour of (regulation of) the sustainable variety are remarkably high across all 6 treatments, considering the small market shares of organic meat in the Netherlands (3%; [26]). The second observation from the top panel of Table 3 is that these shares barely vary with group size (Compare 1, 2 and 3). Thirdly, comparing 2 and 4, we do not find a significant difference in the voting shares if the referendum outcome is binding, or not. If the vote is "advisory" only, 50% of the participants vote in favour, which is not much higher than the share of Yes votes in the binding ban treatment with 31 participants (42%). Fourthly, comparing 2 and 5, the percentage of voters in favour of a "subsidy" on organic meat (57%; Group Size 31) is found to be substantially higher than the percentage of voters in favour of a "ban" on buying non-organic meat (42%; Group Size 31). This suggests that people prefer a subsidy over a ban, even though the "subsidy" was financially less attractive. Finally, by far the highest number of voters in favour of a binding ban can be observed in the "binding conditional choice" treatment (see 6 in the top panel of Table 3). As many as 76% of the participants in this treatment were willing to commit to buying organic meat, if a minimum number of other group members would do the same (more details are provided later, in Table 4). The larger the minimum number, the higher the percentage of participants willing to commit. Finally, virtually all participants spend their budgets in line with the voting outcome, and this is irrespective of the treatments. In the next subsections, we discuss these results in more detail.

3.1. Consumers Willing to Buy Sustainable Products, But Up to Some Limit

In our experiment the revealed willingness to commit oneself is considerable higher than what one observes in the real world (see Table 3). Interestingly, this percentage does not differ significantly between treatments with self-commitment (when group size is 1) and those where one could break through the social dilemma by committing others as well (in the treatments with groups of 31 or 61 participants). The same holds for the treatment where individuals were not committed to the group choice (non-binding ban). In the experiment consumers reveal a stronger (conditional or unconditional) willingness to buy more sustainable products than they do in the market place. If we combine our experimental results with self-reported organic meat consumption of participants, the support for the binding ban is not related to the purchase of sustainable product varieties in everyday life. In our experimental environment both groups vote "yes" about equally often. Indeed, over 50% of participants who said to have *never* bought organic meat before still voted in favour of obliging themselves and others to spend their credit only on organic meat.

To check the influence of some other aspects on voting behaviour we checked the relation between voting behaviour on the one hand and gender, household size, income, age, education level and location on the other. Participants aged 70 or older are less likely to vote in favour of organic meat than younger age groups (30% vs. 45% for participants aged between 30 and 40; $p = 0.04$). Similarly, less educated participants are less likely to vote in favour of organic meat than higher educated participants (36% vs. 45%, $p = 0.032$), and participants from the big urban areas are less likely to vote in favour than the other participants (33% vs. 40%, $p = 0.048$). We did not find any significant differences in voting behaviour for income, gender and house size.

3.2. Peer Pressure May Increase Support

To investigate the role of the social dilemma more explicitly, we look at the effect of varying group size. As stated in Prediction 1, if participants view organic meat consumption as a social dilemma one would expect the percentage of Yes voters to increase with group size. As can be observed in Table 3, however, the shares of participants voting in favour of a binding ban are unrelated to group size, and all differences between the three treatments are statistically insignificant: comparing the shares in the standard groups of 31 (i.e., 42%) to those with group sizes 1 (51%) and 61 (50%), the relevant χ^2-tests yield insignificant p-values of 0.20 and 0.16, respectively (the difference between 51% and 50%, comparing groups of 1 and 61, is also not significant ($p = 0.98$)). These findings suggest that participants do not seem to weigh *the size* of the potential collective gains against their individual costs even though they were explicitly informed about the potential size of these collective gains before the vote, which is in contrast to Prediction 1.

Table 4. Percentage of participants willing to commit to buying organic meat, in the conditional choice treatment.

Condition	% of Yes Voters
(1) All other group members will also commit (100%)	57
(2) 22–29 group members will also commit (71–94%)	58
(3) 16–21 group members will also commit (52–68%)	54
(4) 9–15 group members will also commit (29–48%)	42
(5) 1–8 group members will also commit (3–26%)	39
(6) No other group members will commit (0%)	43
Percentage of participants who voted Yes, under *at least one* of the conditions (1–6) above	76

While in this experiment the actual size of collective gains barely seems to matter, *expectations* with respect to the behaviour of others do seem to play a role. Whether people are willing to commit themselves turns out to be a function of other people's willingness to commit, apart from being actual or expected willingness. To substantiate this outcome one has to compare the percentages of Yes voters in the main (unconditional) binding ban treatment with the conditional choice treatment where group size is similar (31). In the unconditional treatment, 42% of the participants vote in favour of the binding agreement, which is virtually identical to the 43% of the participants in the conditional choice treatment reporting that they will commit to buying organic meat even if no other group member would commit (compare Tables 3 and 4). This percentage of 43% is also not significantly different from the 51% of Yes votes in the binding ban treatment with group size 1 (χ^2 test gives $p = 0.53$). However, participants were more willing to commit to buying organic meat if they were sure that at least some other members of their group would do the same. Table 4 shows the larger the number of others willing to commit, the higher the percentage of participants willing to commit as well. Statistically, the percentage of Yes voters is significantly higher if *more* than half of the other group members would also commit (Conditions 1–3; see Table 4), than if *less* than half would also commit (Conditions 4 and 5), or than if *nobody* would commit (Condition 6), This finding is consistent with Prediction 2. (McNemar tests, comparing Conditions 1–3 with 4 and 5: $p = 0.002$–0.008. p-values for the differences between Conditions 1 versus 6, 2 versus 6, and 3 versus 6 are 0.054, 0.038 and 0.093, respectively.) Finally, no less than 76% of the participants in the conditional choice treatment were willing to commit themselves in at least one of the six conditions, a percentage that is significantly larger than in the binding ban treatment ($p < 0.01$, χ^2-test).

Conditionality may have also played a role in the decisions of participants in the *non*-conditional binding ban treatments. Indeed, Figure 1 shows a positive correlation between participants' own votes and their expectations regarding voting behaviour of the other group members: participants who expected more other members of their group to vote in favour of the binding agreement, also voted more in favour themselves, and thus were more willing to commit themselves as well as the other 30 or 60 members of their group to buying only organic meat. In addition, in the individual commitment treatment (i.e., with group size 1, where one's decisions had no consequences for others), this positive correlation between own decision and expectation can be observed. This comparison suggests that conditionality—perhaps unconsciously—also played a role in these non-conditional treatments.

Percentage of participants willing to buy organic meat

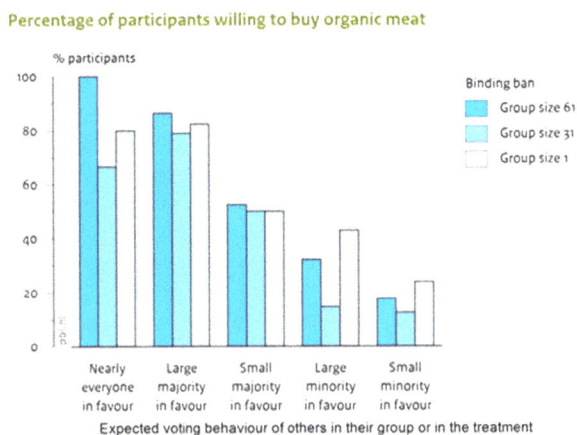

Figure 1. Percentage of participants who voted in favour of the binding agreement to buying only organic meat as a function of their expectations about voting behaviour of others in their group or treatment.

3.3. Freedom of Choice Preferred over Restrictive Regulation

To examine the question what type of policy governments might use we included a non-binding ban and a subsidy treatment, both with group size 31. In the non-binding ban treatment, where participants could only cast an advisory vote, 50% of the participants voted "Yes" versus 42% in the binding ban treatment. The difference between these two treatments is not significant ($p = 0.14$, x^2-test), in contrast to Prediction 3. Thus, it seems that participants were not more prone to yea-saying in the non-binding ban treatment, nor do we observe any evidence that they tried to influence their peers' behaviour (trying to induce them to purchase organic meat, while they themselves spent their budget on conventional meat). Indeed, the participants voted more or less according to their intentions: 55% of the participants in the non-binding treatment actually spend their budget on organic meat, and all participants who voted in favour of spending the budgets on organic meat effectively did so themselves too even though the vote was non-binding (not for others, but also not for oneself).

In the subsidy treatment, participants could vote as to whether the credit should only be used for compensating *the additional costs* of organic meat, or whether all group members should be free to spend their budget. As explained in Section 2, the difference between the binding ban and subsidy treatment is primarily a matter of framing, which should not affect behaviour. However, as stated in Prediction 4, if anything we would expect less Yes votes in the subsidy treatment because voting in favour of the subsidy is weakly less financially attractive than voting in favour of the binding ban (if people would spend only part of their budget on purchasing organic meat and the other part on conventional meat; see footnote 9). However, the results show that subsidies are clearly preferred: a significantly higher percentage of participants voted Yes in the subsidy treatment compared to the binding ban treatment (see bottom panel of Table 3, 57% versus 42%, x^2-test gives $p = 0.01$). Potential explanations include that participants prefer collective measure that leave the freedom of choice intact (such as subsidies) over restrictive regulations (such as a ban on buying non-organic meat), or that the use of the term subsidy triggers more positive responses. This outcome is consistent with earlier experimental evidence showing that participants who could invest in energy-saving technologies did so more often when the technologies were subsidized, even if this investment (including the subsidy) would be against their own interest from a purely financial perspective [59]. A subsidy may be perceived to be less coercive and less inflicting than a binding ban, and therefore may be supported more.

3.4. Additional Results from Survey Questions

Our experimental results imply that individual, moral considerations are more leading in sustainable consumption issues than social dilemma considerations. In this section we present some additional evidence from the post-experimental questionnaire to support our claim.

At the end of the experiment, we invited respondents to fill out a short questionnaire to explain the motivations behind their choices. While the gist of the questions was the same, participants were offered different versions of the survey, depending as to whether they had voted in favour or against the budget being spent on organic meat (see Table 5). If they had voted in favour, we asked whether animal welfare was an important consideration of the decision maker, whether the environment was important, whether the price of meat was *un*important, etc. We asked participants who had voted against the budgets being spent on organic meat more or less the reverse questions—are animal welfare considerations or the environment relatively *un*important in your decision making, is the price of meat important? Both Yes and No voters could choose four options from the list of motives at a maximum. The results of the survey outcomes for the main treatment (binding ban with group size of 31) are shown in Table 5. The outcomes of the other treatments are very similar. For example, in all treatments animal welfare and environment are chosen most frequently by Yes voters, whereas for No voters the price and the averseness to imposing rules on others are most important. Because not all motives are equally valid in all treatments (and the list is not exactly the same for all treatments), the table only shows the results of the main treatment.

Table 5. Motives for voting in favour of or against the proposition and the percentage of participants who have selected the motive in the main treatment.

Motivations of Participants Who Voted in Favour of the Binding Ban	Number of Participants Who Agreed with the Stated Motivation	Motivations of Participants Who Voted Against of the Binding Ban	Number of Participants Who Agreed with the Stated Motivation
animal welfare is important to me	66	animal welfare is less important to me	2
environment is important to me	43	environment is not so important to me	1
organic meat is healthier than non-organic meat	30	non-organic meat is healthier than organic meat	1
organic meat tastes better than non-organic meat	28	non-organic meat tastes better than organic meat	4
I want others to also buy organic meat	28	I do not want to impose on others to buy organic meat	75
organic meat is readily available	24	organic meat is poorly available	19
other considerations	24	other considerations	8
I'm not the only one in buying organic meat	15	n.a.	-
I think there are plenty of others will vote for the proposition	13	I think too few others will vote for the proposition	17
the price of meat is less important to me	10	the price of meat is very important to me	61

Note: Participants could select up to four motives. Results are for the main treatment (binding ban, group size 31).

The table allows for several interesting observations. First, and not surprisingly, those who voted in favour of spending the budgets on organic meat indicated that animal welfare was an important consideration in their decision process, and so was the environment. Two other motivations standing out in this group are taste and health perceptions. The statement that the price of meat was a not so important consideration was not selected very often by the Yes voters. However, cost considerations were important for those who voted against spending the budgets on organic meat (10 vs. 61). Quite surprisingly, however, is that the latter group essentially did not indicate that animal welfare and the environment were *un*important to them (only 1 of the No voters chose this option). The overriding reason for the No voters to vote against the ban on spending the budgets on conventional meat is their unwillingness to impose rules on others—75 of the No voters chose this option. This holds for all relevant treatments (this question was not asked in the individual commitment treatment, with group size 1). Thus, even in the advisory treatment, where the voting outcome was not binding, the reluctance to "force" a rule on others was a frequently mentioned motive, which was chosen more often than the other motives, including the price. Finally, although a substantial share of the Yes voters indicated others should also buy organic meat, this motive is clearly less prevalent than animal welfare and environmental considerations.

These survey results suggest that No voters were motivated not only by concerns about the higher individual cost of sustainable products, but also and to a very large extent by their reluctance to impose rules and regulations on others. Participants who said they did not want to impose a rule on others, may have been driven primarily by their dislike of being bound by rules themselves. One may wonder whether this holds for any type of rules or only for specific ones, for example regulations for which they feel responsible. Participants might indeed be in favour of government intervention because they would not have to impose a rule themselves in that case.

To find out to what extent people think that the *government* should take measures to increase sustainability we also asked participants as to whether the government should impose stricter regulations to improve animal welfare. As part of this question, we explicitly pointed out that such stricter standards would improve the welfare of livestock but would also require significantly higher prices. The results (see Table 6) show that about two-thirds of the participants answered that the government should be stricter and that stricter rules were a very good or good idea, while a minority (7%) strongly disagreed or disagreed. These results are in line with those of a previous study [33], in which participants were asked the (similarly hypothetical) question as to whether they considered sustainability important, and who should take the lead. Not surprisingly, participants who voted in favour of a binding agreement in our experiment are more supportive of stricter government interventions than No voters. However, even among the latter group, only 10% of the participants considered stricter government behaviour or regulations a bad or very bad idea while about half were in favour of stricter regulations.

Table 6. Opinions of participants (%) as to whether the government should impose stricter regulations to improve animal welfare.

	Voting Behaviour in Experiment		
	Against	For	All
Should the Government Be More, or Less, Strict? [a]			
Stricter/Much stricter	47	79	64
Neutral	50	21	35
Less strict/Much less strict	2	0	1
What Would You Think If the Government Imposed Stricter Regulations on Meat Production? [b]			
Good/Very good idea	50	84	68
Neutral	41	14	26
Bad/Very bad idea	9	3	6

[a] The full question was: "Should the government be more, or less, strict in order to improve animal welfare? Compared to the present situation, the government should be....:" (much stricter, stricter, not more strict or less strict, less strict, much less strict); [b] The full question was: "If the government decided to impose stricter regulations on meat production, this would have the following consequences: - Animal welfare would be improved; - Meat in the supermarket would become more expensive; - You would be sure that all the meat you buy comes from animal-friendly production systems. What would you think about this? (very good, good, not good not bad, bad, very bad).

A final interesting (and related) finding is on the participants' ex-post satisfaction with the voting outcome of their group (see Table 7). As expected, participants whose group voting outcome turned out to be different from their own votes were less satisfied than participants who decided similarly as their group. This is clear by comparing Columns 1 and 4 in Table 7 on the one hand and Columns 2 and 3 on the other hand. The *least* satisfied of all participants were those who had voted in favour of a ban on non-organic meat, but whose group decided against it (Column 3 in Table 7). This is somewhat surprising because they at least kept the freedom to buy organic meat, whereas "No voters in Yes groups" (Column 2) lost this freedom of choice. Apparently, it is even more disappointing not to be able to commit yourself and others to buying organic meat, than to be bound by a rule you did not want in the first place. In general, the satisfaction scores are not very sensitive to the treatment.

Table 7. Participants' satisfaction with the voting outcome in their group, conditional on their own vote.*

Voting behaviour	(1)	(2)	(3)	(4)
Majority vote was	Yes	Yes	No	No
Own vote was	Yes	No	Yes	No
Satisfaction scores				
Binding ban	5.8 [a]	4.5 [a]	3.4 [a]	5.8 [b]
Binding subsidy	5.8 [b]	4.3 [b]	-	-

* Satisfaction scores ranging from 1 (very dissatisfied) to 7 (very satisfied); a score of 4 means neither satisfied nor dissatisfied. Standard deviations of the means: [a] = 0.1, [b] = 0.2. No observations because the majority vote in all groups was Yes.

3.5. Discussion

We find that the combination of experimental results and survey outcomes provides little support for the hypothesis that participants view organic meat consumption as a social dilemma. If anything, participants perceive the choice of the type of meat as a decision every household should be free to take. They seem to be caught in a moral dilemma, not only about their individual trade-off in weighing their own (perceived) financial costs and benefits, but also how to take the effects of their decision on others into account, in particular the moral costs of limiting other peoples' room for decision making. As most people are conditionally cooperative as well, participants are significantly more likely to *voluntarily* commit themselves to purchasing organic meat if (all) others *voluntarily* do so as well, than to *force* others (and themselves) to purchasing organic meat by means of voting in favour of a ban on the consumption of conventional meat. Finally, the reluctance to impose rules mainly seems to apply at the level of the individual (i.e., if the individual has to decide), whereas government interventions and regulations are acceptable for a large majority of participants even if those are bans of less sustainable product varieties.

4. Conclusions

In this paper, we have explored whether social dilemma considerations play a role in individual decisions regarding sustainability problems—in addition to more personal considerations such as moral concerns. Wicked sustainability problems are hard to experiment with, and therefore we selected a consumption problem that shares some of the key characteristics of the sustainability challenge society faces: meat consumption and animal welfare. We have conducted a large scale (semi-)field experiment with more than 600 participating households, who received budgets to be spent on either organic or conventional meat. An important characteristic of our experiment is that decisions of participants had financial consequences as well as (potential) consequences at home or in the supermarket, not in a lab.

We have implemented several treatments to test whether people tend to view sustainable consumption as a social dilemma—as typically argued by economists—or as a moral dilemma instead. Our experimental results imply that moral considerations are more leading in sustainable consumption issues than social dilemma considerations. The share of households voting in favour of a binding commitment to only buy organic meat does not systematically change if groups are increased from one household (i.e., individual decision making) to 31 households or 61 households. Nevertheless, participants are significantly more likely to voluntarily commit themselves to purchasing organic meat conditional if many others voluntarily do so as well than if they could force others (and themselves) to purchasing organic meat. This finding suggests that social considerations are not completely absent. Finally, support for subsidies on the consumption of organic meat is larger than the support for the ban on conventional meat, even though the former is financially less attractive. Survey responses indicate that many people are reluctant to restrict the choice set of one's peers, but at the same time also suggest substantial support for the government to regulate unsustainable product varieties. The insights obtained have potentially important consequences for policies aimed at fostering sustainable consumption. Consumers are not opposed to government interventions, albeit that moral considerations are more important for the support for government intervention than social dilemma considerations. In addition, less restrictive policies (such as subsidies) seem to receive larger support than more restrictive ones (such as bans). However, because of the moral dimension, even less invasive instruments—such as nudges [60]—may be very effective too.

Of course, our study has several limitations and the results cannot be translated one-on-one to all sustainability issues we currently face (such as climate change and biodiversity conservation), even though the decision-making process and purchases happened to take place in the participants' natural environments. For instance, the duration and scope of the experiment were limited to one week's meat consumption. Hence, we cannot say much about the implications for a longer period of time or other products. In addition, the support in favour of the sustainable choice would probably be lower if the experiment lasted longer or would have been repeated. Therefore, we might consider our findings as an upper bound for people's longer-term preferences. On the other hand, and in contrast to more traditional techniques such as surveys and contingent valuation studies, the decisions taken by participants in our experiment had real financial consequences, and hence our experiment is likely to have captured their real preferences.

Acknowledgments: We thank Zach Brown, Nick Johnstone and the participants of the SABE/IAREP Conference (Wageningen University, 8–10 July, 2016) and of the NCBEE (BI Norwegian Business School, 30 September–1 October, 2016), and two anonymous reviewers for their very useful comments and suggestions on an earlier version of this paper. The authors gratefully acknowledge financial support by the Netherlands Environmental Assessment Agency (PBL) and the OECD for financial support, and Daan van Soest also thanks the European Commission for funding via the Seventh Framework Program (FP7/2007–2013), grant agreement No. 613420 (Glamurs). All remaining errors are ours.

Author Contributions: All authors were involved in all phases of the project—design, implementation, analysis, interpretation and the write-up of the manuscript.

Conflicts of Interest: The authors declare no conflict of interest.

Appendix A. Setup and instructions of the 'binding ban' treatment—the main treatment.

This appendix describes in detail the treatment in which participants had to vote on banning the purchase of non-organic meat. The instructions for the other treatments are similar (and available upon request). In this treatment, the majority vote was binding: in the week following the poll, participants had to buy meat in compliance with their group's decision (only organic meat; *or* whichever they preferred: organic or non-organic). Before the vote, participants were provided with the following information on organic meat:

Organic meat comes from animals that have had a better life than animals raised in intensive livestock systems (also known as bio-industry or factory farming). Pigs can go outside and root in the mud. Chickens can scratch around. Cows graze in the fields for the greater part of the year. The animal houses have windows, fresh air coming in, and straw bedding. Independent scientific research by Wageningen University has shown that animal welfare on organic farms is higher (animals are less stressed, less anxious, etc.) than on conventional factory farms.

Nowadays organic meat can be bought in most supermarkets. If more people buy organic meat, livestock production in the Netherlands will become more animal-friendly.

However, organic meat is on average about twice as expensive as conventional (non-organic) meat.

At present, the vast majority of Dutch households buy non-organic meat. As a result, animal welfare is hardly improving. If more people switch to buying organic meat, more animals will get a better life.

Next, participants were divided into groups of 31 each. This group size was deemed sufficient for a convincing gain in animal welfare if all group members were to buy organic meat, compared to the effect of just one participant buying organic meat. Before the vote took place, all participants were informed that a certain amount of money had been reserved for each of them, as a kind of shopping credit. This credit roughly covered the additional expenses of buying organic meat instead of non-organic meat, for one week, for one household. These additional costs were estimated at 7 euros for an adult and 4 euros for a child. Daily meat consumption was assumed to be 120 g for adults and 70 g for children. Each participant was informed how much credit was reserved for him or her, based on the size and composition of their household. The remainder of this example is based on a two-adult household, with a credit of $2 \times 7 = 14$ Euros.

Next, the participants were shown the proposition to vote on:

All households shall use their credit only for buying organic meat.

Before the participants could vote on this proposition, the pros and cons of buying organic meat were explained in more detail:

If all 31 households would use their credit for buying organic meat, this would have a greater impact than if only one household would buy organic meat.

If 1 household switches to buying organic chicken breast, then each week 1 chicken will have a better life. If all 31 households switch to buying organic chicken breast, then each week 40 chickens will have a better life.

However, organic meat is on average about twice as expensive as non-organic meat. The table below shows, for three kinds of meat, how much meat you can buy with an average week budget for a household of your size.

Amount of meat that can be bought with 14 euros.

	Non-organic	*Organic*
Minced beef	*2.9 kilos*	*1.3 kilos*
Shoulder chop	*2.5 kilos*	*1.3 kilos*
Chicken breast	*1.8 kilos*	*0.6 kilos*

In the actual poll, the weights in this table were adjusted to the size and composition of the household of the participant in question. This example table is based on a two-adult household. Next, all participants were invited to cast their vote:

You are now invited to cast your vote on the following proposition:
"All 31 households shall use their credit only for buying organic meat."
☐ *I vote IN FAVOUR (I think that all 31 households should use their credit only for buying organic meat).*
☐ *I vote AGAINST (I think that all 31 households should be free to use their credit for buying organic or non-organic meat).*

After everyone had cast their vote, we calculated the results and informed the participants of the voting outcome in their group. The majority decision was binding. Thus, if the majority of the group was of the opinion that the credit should be used only for buying organic meat, then the credit could be spent only on organic meat. In that case, participants were reimbursed only for their purchases of organic meat, up to their credit limit. If the majority had voted *against* the proposition, then participants could decide for themselves whether to buy organic or non-organic meat. In that case they were reimbursed for all their meat purchases, up to their credit limit. We checked the receipts to ensure that participants had made their purchases in compliance with their group's decision. In the case that participants were free to choose between organic and non-organic meat, the receipts allowed us to track their purchasing choices (Note: Although a binding vote is the most accurate method to measure preferences, it may obscure the relation between preferences and ex post behaviour. If the majority is in favour of spending the credit only on organic meat and the vote is binding, then some members of the group will have to buy organic meat while they voted against it. As long as they value animal welfare to some degree, they are better off buying organic meat. Moreover, they might as well buy organic meat because the additional costs are covered by their credit: their expenses are the same whether they buy organic or non-organic meat. Only when the majority is *against* using the credit only for organic meat, we can gain insight into the relation between preferences and purchasing behaviour; in that case, participants are free to choose whether to buy organic or non-organic meat, based on their own preferences. As it happened very rarely that the group majority was against the statement, the number of observations is too low to allow for a proper analysis).

In this 'binding ban' poll, all participants had to comply with the majority decision, and therefore the optimum strategy for each individual was to vote truthfully: the poll question was 'incentive compatible' [35,56]. For the individual participant, the probability of his/her vote being decisive is small. However, in the case that there are already 15 votes in favour and 15 votes against the proposition, the 31st voter who votes a socially desirable 'yes' despite feeling that that the collective benefits are smaller than the individual costs, will afterwards regret his or her untruthful vote. As none of the participants will know beforehand whether their vote will be the decisive one or not, the safest strategy is to vote truthfully.

References

1. Stern, N. *The Economics of Climate Change*; Cabinet Office, HM Treasury: London, UK, 2007.
2. Fornara, F.; Pattitoni, P.; Mura, M.; Strazzera, E. Predicting intention to improve household energy efficiency: The role of value-belief-norm theory, normative and informational influence, and specific attitude. *J. Environ. Psychol.* **2016**, *45*, 1–10. [CrossRef]
3. Belanche, D.; Casaló, L.V.; Flavián, C. Understanding the cognitive, affective and evaluative components of social urban identity: Determinants, measurement, and practical consequences. *J. Environ. Psychol.* **2007**, *50*, 138–153. [CrossRef]
4. Dholakia, U.M.; Bagozzi, R.P.; Pearo, L.K. A social influence model of consumer participation in network-and small-group-based virtual communities. *Int. J. Res. Market.* **2004**, *21*, 241–263. [CrossRef]
5. Olsen, M.C. *The Logic of Collective Action: Public Goods and the Theory of Groups*; Harvard University Press: Cambridge, MA, USA, 1965.
6. Ostrom, E. Collective action and the evolution of social norms. *J. Econ. Perspect.* **2000**, *14*, 137–158. [CrossRef]
7. Vringer, K.; Aalbers, T.G.; Blok, K. Household energy requirement and value patterns. *Energy Policy* **2007**, *25*, 553–566. [CrossRef]
8. Kirchgässner, G. On minimal morals. *Eur. J. Political Econ.* **2010**, *26*, 330–339. [CrossRef]
9. Ledyard, J. Public Goods: A Survey of Experimental Research. Chapter 2. In *Handbook of Experimental Economics*; Kagel, J., Roth, A., Eds.; Princeton University Press: Princeton, NJ, USA, 1995; pp. 111–194.
10. Food and Agriculture Organization of the United Nations (FAO). *SAFA: Sustainability Assessment of Food and Agriculture System. Guideline Version 3.0.*; FAO: Rome, Italy, 2014.
11. Schader, C.; Stolze, M.; Niggli, U. How the organic food system contributes to sustainability. In *Assessing Sustainable Diets within the Sustainability of Food Systems Proceedings of the International Workshop, CREA, Rome, Italy, 15–16 September 2014*; Food and Agriculture Organization of the United Nations (FAO): Rome, Italy, 2015; pp. 27–36.

12. Gattinger, A.; Muller, A.; Haeni, M.; Skinner, C.; Fliessbach, A.; Buchmann, N.; Mäder, P.; Stolze, M.; Smith, P.; Scialabba, N.E.-H. Enhanced top soil carbon stocks under organic farming. *Proc. Natl. Acad. Sci. USA* **2012**, *109*, 18226–18231. [CrossRef] [PubMed]

13. Tuomisto, H.; Hodge, I.; Riordan, P.; Macdonald, D. Does organic farming reduce environmental impacts? A meta-analysis of European research. *J. Environ. Manag.* **2012**, *112*, 309–320. [CrossRef] [PubMed]

14. Netherlands Environmental Assessment Agency (PBL). *De Macht van het Menu. Opgaven en Kansen Voor Duurzaam en Gezond Voedsel; (The Power of the Menu. Challenges and Opportunities for Sustainable and Healthy Food)*; PBL: The Hague, The Netherlands, 2013.

15. Meier, M.S.; Stoessel, F.; Jungbluth, N.; Juraske, R.; Schader, C.; Stolze, M. Environmental impacts of organic and conventional agricultural products—are the differences captured by life cycle assessment? *J. Environ. Manag.* **2015**, *149*, 193–208. [CrossRef] [PubMed]

16. Belk, R.W. Materialism: Trait aspects of living in the material world. *J. Consum. Res.* **1985**, *12*, 265–280. [CrossRef]

17. Borgmann, A. The moral complexion of consumption. *J. Consum. Res.* **2000**, *26*, 418–422. [CrossRef]

18. Cohen, J.; Darian, J. Disposable products and the environment: A consumer behavior perspective. *Res. Consum. Behav.* **2000**, *9*, 227–259.

19. Moisander, J. Motivational complexity of green consumerism. *Int. J. Consum. Stud.* **2007**, *31*, 404–409. [CrossRef]

20. Sheth, J.N.; Sethia, N.K.; Srinivas, S.J. Mindful consumption: A customer-centric approach to sustainability. *J. Acad. Mark. Sci.* **2011**, *39*, 21–39. [CrossRef]

21. Kurz, T. The psychology of environmentally sustainable behavior: Fitting together pieces of the puzzle. *Anal. Soc. Issues Public Policy* **2002**, *2*, 257–278. [CrossRef]

22. Gupta, S.; Ogden, D.T. To buy or not to buy? A social dilemma perspective on green buying. *J. Consum. Mark.* **2009**, *26*, 376–391. [CrossRef]

23. Tanner, C.; Wölfing Kast, S. Promoting Sustainable Consumption: Determinants of Green Purchases by Swiss Consumers. *Psychol. Mark.* **2003**, *20*, 883–902. [CrossRef]

24. Young, W.; Hwang, K.; McDonald, S.; Oates, C.J. Sustainable consumption: Green consumer behaviour when purchasing products. *Sustain. Dev.* **2010**, *18*, 20–31. [CrossRef]

25. Willer, H. *The European Market for Organic Food*; Forschungsinstitut für Biologischen Landbau (FiBL): Frick, Switzerland, 2012.

26. Bionext. Bionext Trendrapport 2015–June 2016, Ontwikkeling Biologische Landbouw en Voeding Nederland. In *Bionext trendreport 2015–June 2016, Development Sustainable Food the Netherlands*; Bionext: Zeist, The Netherlands, 2016.

27. Biomonitor; Monitor Duurzaam Voedsel. Task Force Marktontwikkeling Biologische Landbouw Biologica. In *Biomonitor 2012, Monitor Sustainable Food (2012) Task Force Market Development Organic Agriculture, Biological*; Minsterie van Economische Zaken: The Hague, The Netherlands, 2013.

28. Max Havelaar. *Jaarverslag 2010 Stichting Max Havelaar; Annual Report*; Max Havelaar Foundation: Utrecht, The Netherlands, 2010.

29. Visser, H.; Aalbers, T.G.; Vringer, K.; Verhue, D. *How Dutch Citizens Prioritise the Social Agenda; An Analysis of the 2003, 2005 and 2006 Surveys*; Report 500086002; Netherlands Environmental Assessment Agency: Bilthoven, The Netherlands, 2007.

30. Verbeek, D.; Boelhouwer, J. Milieu van Later, Wiens Zorg Nu? In *Wisseling van de Wacht: Generaties in Nederland. Sociaal en Cultureel Rapport*; van den Broek, A., Bronneman-Helmers, R., Veldheer, V., Eds.; SCP, The Hague. Chapter in report of the Netherlands Institute for Social Research SCP: The Hague, The Netherlands, 2010.

31. Schelling, T.C. *Micromotives and Macrobehavior*; W.W. Norton & Company: New York, NY, USA, 1978.

32. Sen, A. Choice, Orderings and Morality. In *Practical Reason*; Körner, S., Ed.; Blackwell: Oxford, UK, 1974; pp. 54–67.

33. MNP. *Nederland en een Duurzame Wereld. Armoede, Klimaat en Biodiversiteit. Tweede Duurzaamheidsverkenning; (The Netherlands in a Sustainable World. Poverty, Climate and Biodiversity: Second Sustainability Outlook)*; Netherlands Environmental Assessment Agency MNP: Bilthoven, The Netherlands, 2007.

34. Middelkoop, M.; Vringer, K.; Visser, H. Are Dutch residents ready for a more stringent policy to enhance the energy performance of their homes? *Energy Policy* **2017**, *105*, 269–282. [CrossRef]

35. Carson, R.; Groves, T. Incentive and informational properties of preference questions. *Environ. Resour. Econ.* **2007**, *37*, 181–210. [CrossRef]

36. List, J.A.; Gallet, C.A. What Experimental Protocol Influence Disparities between Actual and Hypothetical Stated Values? *Environ. Resour. Econo.* **2001**, *20*, 241–254. [CrossRef]

37. Murphy, J.P.; Allen, P.G.; Stevens, T.H.; Weatherhead, D. A Meta-analysis of Hypothetical Bias in Stated Preference Valuation. *Environ. Resour. Econ.* **2005**, *30*, 313–325. [CrossRef]

38. Harrison, G.W. Experimental evidence on alternative environmental valuation methods. *Environ. Resour. Econ.* **2006**, *34*, 125–162. [CrossRef]

39. Harrison, G.W.; Rutström, E.E. Chaper 81. Experimental Evidence on the Existence of Hypothetical Bias in Value Elicitation Methods. In *Handbook of Experimental Economics Results*; Plott, C., Smith, V.L., Eds.; Elsevier Science: New York, NY, USA, 2008; pp. 752–767.

40. De Graaf, S.; Vanhonacker, F.; Van Loo, E.; Lauwers, J.L.; Tuyttens, F.; Verbeke, W. Market opportunities for animal-friendly milk in different consumer segments. *Sustainability* **2016**, *8*, 1302. [CrossRef]

41. Dagevos, H.; Sterrenberg, L. *Burgers en Consumenten: Tussen Tweedeling en Twee-Eenheid*; Wageningen Pers: Wageningen, The Netherlands, 2003.

42. Harrison, G.W.; List, J.A. Field experiments. *J. Econ. Lit.* **2004**, *42*, 1013–1059. [CrossRef]

43. Levitt, S.D.; List, J.A. What do laboratory experiments measuring social preferences reveal about the real world? *J. Econ. Perspect.* **2007**, *21*, 153–174. [CrossRef]

44. Vringer, K.; Vollebergh, H.; van Soest, D.; van der Heijden, E.; Dietz, F. *Dilemma's Rond Duurzame Consumptie: Een Onderzoek Naar Het Draagvlak Voor Verduurzaming van Consumptie; (Dilemmas Surrounding Sustainable Consumption: A Study on Consumer Support for Increasing the Sustainability of Consumption)*; Netherlands Environmental Assessment Agency PBL: The Hague, The Netherlands, 2013.

45. Gilsing, A.M.; Weijenberg, M.P.; Goldbohm, R.A.; Dagnelie, P.C.; van den Brandt, P.A.; Schouten, L.J. The Netherlands Cohort Study–Meat Investigation Cohort; a population-based cohort over-represented with vegetarians, pescetarians and low meat consumers. *Nutr. J.* **2013**, *12*, 156. [CrossRef] [PubMed]

46. Dagevos, H.; Voordouw, J. Sustainability and meat consumption: Is reduction realistic? *Sustainability* **2013**, *9*, 60–69.

47. Brandt, K. Organic Agriculture and Food Utilisation. In Proceedings of the International Conference on Organic Agriculture and Food Security, Rome, Italy, 3–5 May 2007.

48. Olsson, V.; Andersson, K.; Hansson, I.; Lundström, K. Differences in meat quality between organically and conventionally produced pigs. *Meat Sci.* **2003**, *64*, 287–297. [CrossRef]

49. Wal, P.G.; van der Mateman, G.; de Vries, A.W.; Vonder, G.M.A.; Smulders, F.J.M.; Geesink, G.H.; Engel, B. 'Scharrel' (free range) pigs: Carcass composition, meat quality and taste-panel studies. *Meat Sci.* **1993**, *34*, 27–37. [PubMed]

50. Andreoni, J. Impure Altruism and Donations to Public Goods: A Theory of Warm-Glow Giving. *Econ. J.* **1990**, *100*, 464–477. [CrossRef]

51. Kahneman, D.; Knetsch, J. Valuing public goods: The purchase of moral satisfaction. *J. Environ. Econom. Manag.* **1992**, *22*, 57–70. [CrossRef]

52. Ariely, D.; Loewenstein, G.; Prelec, D. 'Coherent Arbitrariness': Stable Demand Curves without Stable Preferences. *Q. J. Econ.* **2003**, *118*, 73–105. [CrossRef]

53. Bateman, I.J.; Burgess, D.; Hutchinson, W.G.; Matthews, D.I. Learning Design Contingent Valuation (LDCV): NOAA Guidelines, Preference Learning and Coherent Arbitrariness. *J. Environ. Econ. Manag.* **2008**, *55*, 127–141. [CrossRef]

54. Diamond, P.A.; Hausman, J.A. Contingent Valuation: Is Some Number Better than No Number? *J. Econ. Perspect.* **1994**, *8*, 45–64. [CrossRef]

55. Hanemann, W.M. Valuing the Environment through Contingent Valuation. *J. Econ. Perspect.* **1994**, *8*, 19–43. [CrossRef]

56. Cummings, R.G.; Harrison, G.W.; Rutström, E.E. Homegrown values and hypothetical surveys: Is the dichotomous choice approach incentive-compatible? *Am. Econom. Rev.* **1995**, *85*, 260–266.

57. Selten, R. Die Strategiemethode zur Erforschung des Eingeschränkt Rationalen Verhaltens im Rahmen Eines Oligopolexperiments. In *Beiträge zur Experimentellen Wirtschaftsforschung*; Sauermann, H., Ed.; Mohr: Tübingen, Germany, 1967; pp. 136–168.

58. Fischbacher, U.; Gächter, S.; Fehr, E. Are people conditionally cooperative? Evidence from a public goods experiment. *Econ. Lett.* **2001**, *71*, 397–404. [CrossRef]
59. Aalbers, R.F.T.; van der Heijden, E.C.M.; Potters, J.J.M.; van Soest, D.P.; Vollebergh, H.R.J. Technology adoption subsidies: An experiment with managers. *Energy Econ.* **2009**, *31*, 431–442. [CrossRef]
60. Thaler, R.; Sunstein, C.R. *Nudge: Improving Decisions about Health, Wealth, and Happiness*; Yale University Press: New Haven, CT, USA, 2008.

sustainability

MDPI

Article

Keep on Rockin' in a (Plastic-)Free World: Collective Efficacy and Pro-Environmental Intentions as a Function of Task Difficulty

Gerhard Reese [1,*] and Eva A. Junge [2]

1   Environmental Psychology Unit, University of Koblenz-Landau, Fortstr. 7, 76829 Landau, Germany
2   Centre for Sustainability Studies, Lund University, SE 22100 Lund, Sweden; evajunge@posteo.de
*   Correspondence: reese@uni-landau.de; Tel.: +49-6341-2803-1460

Academic Editors: Gerrit Antonides and Marc A. Rosen
Received: 27 October 2016; Accepted: 24 January 2017; Published: 1 February 2017

Abstract: Collective efficacy—the belief that one's group is capable of affecting relevant aspects of its environment—has been highlighted as an important predictor of sustainable behavior. It increases people's collective action tendencies, and is important for fostering environmental behavioral change beyond self-efficacy beliefs. The current study addresses two primary goals. First, we tested whether the difficulty of a task increased collective efficacy, and thereby environmental intentions. Second, we explored how collective and self-efficacy in concert predict such intentions. In a combined field-and-survey study, 165 voluntary participants took part in a plastic reduction challenge that was pretested as easy, moderate, or difficult. After being confronted with the task, participants completed an online questionnaire in which, among other variables, specific and general self-efficacy, collective efficacy, and pro-environmental intentions were measured—both general and plastic-reduction specific. Results revealed that (a) collective efficacy was significantly stronger when task difficulty was moderate rather than easy or difficult; and (b) that through specific collective and self-efficacy perceptions, sustainable intentions were gauged—even when controlling for attitudes and social norms. These findings suggest that collective efficacy beliefs are particularly relevant for attaining environmental goals that are neither too easy nor too difficult, and could thus be valuable for communication and policy strategies.

Keywords: collective efficacy; self-efficacy; sustainable behavior; pro-environmental behavior; plastic use; social norms

1. Introduction

In the face of climatic change and increasingly severe environmental problems, it is evident that humanity needs sustainable solutions to respond to such global challenges. Besides policy measures and transnational cooperative efforts of various stakeholders (e.g., nations in the frame of global climate summits, e.g., [1,2]), one part of the solution is individuals and their compliance with sustainable behavioral options [3]. In fact, various approaches in environmental psychology suggest pathways towards and barriers of pro-environmental action (e.g., [4–6]), and provide compelling evidence for individual psychological processes determining pro-environmental responses. However, it is also apparent that individual contributions, such as avoiding the use of plastic bags during grocery shopping, are limited in their potential to effect change, if they are not carried out by many. Therefore, identifying predictors of collective behavior represents an important endeavor to understand and motivate pro-environmental action. One of these predictors is collective efficacy—the belief that one's group is capable of affecting important aspects of its environment (in the broader sense of the term, not limited to the natural environment; [7]). The current study builds up on this idea that collective efficacy is an important predictor of pro-environmental action ([8–10]). Yet, we extend previous research on the link between collective efficacy and pro-environmental action, testing conditions under which environmental collective efficacy would be increased, and be most predictive of pro-environmental intentions. Specifically, we argue that task difficulty—i.e., the difficulty to perform a specific pro-environmental behavior—affects environmental collective efficacy beliefs, and thereby, pro-environmental intentions. In addition, we draw from recent research that suggests that environmental collective efficacy beliefs raise environmental self-efficacy beliefs, which ultimately predict sustainable behavioral options [11,12]. In the context of plastic-reduction behavior, we developed a combined field-survey-experiment to test these assumptions.

1.1. The Plastic Issue

Production and usage of plastic have been continuously rising since its discovery, reaching a yearly total of about 220 million tons worldwide (of which about a quarter is being consumed in Europe). For its production, high amounts of non-renewable, extremely environmentally-damaging resources such as petroleum, ethylene, and coal are needed [13]. Not only does the extraction-process of these resources yield very harmful consequences, but because of plastic's incapability to decompose, it remains in the environment for up to 500 years (see for example [14]). A huge amount of this gathers in the oceans, where it has an uncountable amount of severe impacts on the environment and its flora and fauna. Apart from the detrimental impacts of plastic(-waste) on the environment and its pollution of rural as well as urban areas, plastic has even been detected in humans and is suspected of causing various health risks [15]. Yet, despite our awareness about the various undesirable consequences plastic already has today, the quantity of plastics produced worldwide in the first decade of this century is equivalent to the total world production in the previous century [16]. Therefore, governments of various states (e.g., Ireland) put a stop on the waste of plastic bags in stores by introducing a fee for each bag, or even completely banning them. While such regulations are a valuable contribution to the effort of global reduction of plastic waste, they force individuals into changing their behavior. Beyond such regulatory approaches, Cherrier [17] has found that voluntary anti-consumption involves environmental consciousness, and that repeatedly taking one's own shopping bag leads to greater reflection on the environmental impact of plastic bag consumption. This underlines the need for tools that facilitate behavioral change complementing political top-down approaches that may evoke reactance.

1.2. Collective Efficacy and Pro-Environmental Action

Human behavior is significantly determined by individuals' belief in their self-efficacy. This personal sense of their own capability to produce and regulate events in their lives is a major incentive to act [18,19]. In fact, a lack of perceived self-efficacy can prevent individuals from becoming active [20], and people even tend to avoid those activities they believe exceed their coping capabilities [21]. In turn, a stronger belief in one's self-efficacy relates to stronger efforts and resilience to adversity [22], better job performance [23], higher satisfaction with relationships [24], and better athletic performance [25]. With such broad effects of self-efficacy on human behavior (but see [25], for a critical analysis of self-efficacy effects), it is plausible and empirically supported that self-efficacy significantly predicts pro-environmental behavior. In fact, the more individuals perceive themselves as self-efficacious, the more prone they are to act in favor of the natural environment [4,12,26]. Specifically, recent evidence shows that self-efficacy beliefs can explain spill-over effects from easy sustainable actions to more difficult ones [26]. Lauren, Fielding, Smith, and Louis [26] showed that previous engagement in a relatively easy pro-environmental task (e.g., turning off water while brushing teeth) was related to increased self-efficacy, which in turn predicted stronger engagement in more difficult tasks nine months later (e.g., actual installment of water-saving devices). In other words: Increasing individuals' belief in their efficacy through acting pro-environmentally could foster future pro-environmental action, even in other contexts.

Yet, it is important to acknowledge that efficacy beliefs are not limited to individuals' personal self, but also connected to their collective self. Individuals can perceive their group as collectively efficacious [19]. The belief that one's own group is capable of affecting important aspects of its environment is particularly relevant for understanding collective action, such as responses to environmental degradation. Evidently, no individual alone will be able to mitigate climate change or combat biodiversity loss. Consequently, it is necessary to understand the social processes that enable individuals to act in concert (see also [27]). Thus, being a member of a group can change our beliefs about which goals we can achieve. While as an individual, using one plastic bag more or less cannot solve the plastic issue, people may feel that as a group, they have the power to make a difference.

Recent studies suggest that this perceived environmental collective efficacy is particularly predictive of pro-environmental action. For example, Barth and colleagues [8] analyzed intentions to use electric vehicles both in a purchasing and sharing scenario. Among other predictors such as descriptive and ingroup norms, personal cost-benefit analyses, knowledge and experience, collective efficacy was assessed and predicted stronger intentions both in the purchasing and the sharing scenario. Similarly, collective efficacy beliefs were more strongly connected to the choice of a more environmentally sustainable travel option than self-efficacy beliefs [10]. These authors also showed environmental collective efficacy beliefs to be a stronger predictor of peoples' willingness to pay for environmental protection than self-efficacy and attitudes [9]. Morton and colleagues [28] assessed collective efficacy as individual's perception of their group being efficacious in mitigating or dealing with the consequences of climate change. Here, collective efficacy was a significant predictor of private-sphere environmental actions (i.e., reducing household waste and non-green energy consumption). Earlier, Homburg and Stolberg [29] found that appraisals of collective efficacy, rather than self-efficacy, predicted pro-environmental intentions (see also [30]). While this evidence suggests that we should focus on collective efficacy in order to promote sustainable behavior, more recent evidence by Jugert and colleagues [12] suggests that a better understanding of the mechanisms linking efficacy perceptions and sustainable behavior is needed. Specifically, these authors argued that collective efficacy exerts its effects on sustainable behavior through raising perceptions of self-efficacy. This process is explained by the model of group-based control that postulates individuals can derive personal benefits (e.g., self-efficacy beliefs) from social groups because groups can make them feel personally capable and in control [31,32]). In fact, Jugert et al. [12] could show that through collective efficacy, individuals came to feel in control of their outcomes: People's intention to act was enhanced through providing a sense of efficacy transferred from the group to the self. Similarly, using a qualitative research approach, Cocking and Drury [11] found that collective efficacy led to a feeling of personal empowerment. Thus, with collective and self-efficacy being strong and closely intertwined predictors of pro-environmental action, the current research seeks to understand under which conditions their effect on sustainable behavior is particularly prominent.

1.3. Task Difficulty and Challenge Framing

Under which conditions do people feel most collectively efficacious to act pro-environmentally? To our knowledge, there is little research specifically addressing this question. However, given that collective efficacy is an important predictor for achieving societal change [7], answering this question could provide insights into a powerful mechanism of sustainable action. Based on the idea that task difficulty affects individuals' performance following an inverted U-shape ([33]; for more recent accounts, see [34,35]), we deem it plausible to assume that similarly, collective and self-efficacy beliefs that precede performance may depend on the difficulty of a task at hand. According to research on the inverted U-model, a moderate level of difficulty would result in strongest motivation to act compared with a task that is too simple or too difficult (cf. [36]). Similarly, we predict that individuals would perceive efficacy particularly for those tasks that are neither too difficult nor too easy. First, people may either expect that fewer others would engage in the behavior when it is too difficult. Supporting this assumption, Van Zomeren et al. [37] found that social action support significantly predicted collective efficacy. Second, behaviors that are easy usually have a weaker environmental impact per se. It is likely that people believe actions that are too easy (e.g., refraining from plastic bags) to be unlikely to make a big difference in environmental issues, even if they are collectively practiced. In other words, when actions are too easy, the (potential) success may not translate into feeling collectively efficacious. In short, this suggests that efficacy beliefs would be strongest for medium difficulty tasks.

1.4. Present Research

The present research thus provides two novel contributions to sustainable behavior: First and foremost, we test whether task difficulty affects efficacy beliefs, and their relation to pro-environmental intentions. Drawing from our reasoning above, we first hypothesize that (a) efficacy—both self-and collective—is highest for tasks perceived to be of medium, rather than low or high, difficulty. In a second step, we (b) hypothesize that collective efficacy is particularly predictive of pro-environmental intentions through raising perceptions of self-efficacy. In statistical terms, we thus expect a serial mediation effect such that medium task difficulty increases collective efficacy, which in turn predicts higher self-efficacy. Ultimately, the higher perceived self-efficacy, the stronger individuals' sustainability intentions. Finally, we test our predictions both with plastic-reduction-specific beliefs and intentions as well as with more general sustainability beliefs and intentions.

The second contribution is our methodological approach. We combine a field experiment—manipulating task difficulty in a playful approach through widely distributed cards presenting "plastic reduction challenges"—with an online survey that assesses our dependent (collective efficacy, pro-environmental intentions) and control variables (see below). This methodology is insofar innovative as it maximizes external validity of the independent variable task difficulty while providing internal validity of our primary dependent variables. Finally, in order to test the unique contribution of our proposed model, we assessed additional constructs that relate to pro-environmental action. Descriptive and injunctive norms (e.g., [38–42]) as well as attitudes (e.g., [5]) were selected for this study.

2. Materials and Methods

2.1. Design and Pretest of the Plastic Challenge Cards

In order to vary task difficulty, we designed playing cards with different challenges. The basic idea was that people receiving the playing cards were challenged to behave in a more sustainable way and after successful completion, sign the card and hand it on to challenge another person. The cards were dark green and had the size of usual playing cards, so that they would easily fit into any purse or pocket. The challenges were printed on the top of the cards, followed by empty fields for participants' signatures. Participants were prompted to sign only once they completed the specific challenge that was displayed on the card. Depending on the degree of challenge difficulty, the following wording was used: "I carried my groceries home in either a fabric bag, a backpack, or a basket" (easy), "While shopping, I bought all fruits and vegetables without plastic wrapping, and I consequently brought them home in either a fabric bag, a backpack, or a basket." (medium), and "I did my entire shopping entirely without plastic. This means, that I neither bought plastic bags of any sorts nor did I buy any other sort of plastic wrapping" (hard). On the flipside of the card, some information about plastic use and its environmental problems was displayed. This information was identical across the conditions. Figure 1 displays the medium condition of the task difficulty (We also manipulated the frame of the wording with the goal of increasing collective efficacy [individual vs. collective wording]. However, this variation had no effect [neither main nor interaction with task difficulty] on any of our dependent variables and is thus not reported on further).

We conducted a pretest to make sure that the challenges we crafted were indeed selective so that participants' evaluation coincided with our proposed task difficulty. A brief questionnaire including the challenges and the question "How difficult do you believe the following challenge is?", rated from 1 (very easy) to 7 (very difficult) was distributed to $N = 60$ passers-by in a public pedestrian area in a German town. In line with our expectations, we found a significant and strong main effect of task difficulty, $F(2, 57) = 86.41$, $p < 0.001$, $\eta^2_p = 0.75$, such that the easy task was rated easiest ($M = 1.56$, $SD = 1.12$), the difficult task as most difficult ($M = 5.02$, $SD = 1.7$), and the moderate task falling in between ($M = 2.54$, $SD = 1.54$). Thus, the pretest shows that the challenges were perceived as differently difficult.

(a) (b)

Figure 1. Back (Panel **a**) and front (Panel **b**) of the "medium difficulty" plastic challenge card. Translation left panel, upper text: "Instructions: 1. Receive card, 2. Accept challenge, 3. Conduct challenge, 4. Enter first name and place, check, 5. Go to website, 6. Hand over card"; Left panel, boxes: "Why less plastic?"; Box 1: "If you and all other people in Germany would use reusable bags, more than 185.000 tons of plastic waste could be prevented", Box 2: "Through reducing plastic, health problems such as coronary diseases, liver problems, diabetes and infertility through hormone dysregulation could be prevented"; Box 3: "In the northern pacific, a waste vortex the size of central Europe has developed over the last decades. By using reusable bags, we can contribute to save our seas"; Right panel, main text: "For our shopping, we bought all our fruits and vegetable without plastic wrapping and consequently brought them home in either a fabric bag, a backpack or a basket"; Right panel, fields: "First name, place"; Right panel, lower text: "Challenge accepted? Go to www.surveymonkey.com/s/geschafft5".

2.2. Research Participants and Procedure

The plastic challenge cards were distributed in various towns and cities across Germany. Altogether, 6000 cards were given out to people directly in face-to-face interactions in May and June 2015. 165 participants (93 female, 58 male, 14 did not indicate gender, $M_{age} = 31.7$, $SD = 12.4$) participated in the online survey after completion of the challenge. Of these, 73 (44%) indicated to be students. If not indicated otherwise, all items in the online questionnaire were administered using 7-point Likert scales reaching from 1 (not true at all) to 7 (completely true) unless otherwise stated, and for each construct, item scores were combined into a single mean score.

2.3. Material

- Collective efficacy. Collective efficacy was measured with two general items "I am optimistic that we as plastic challenge participants can protect the environment together"; "We as plastic challenge participants have the capability to protect the environment"; ($r = 0.90$) and one plastic-specific item ("I think we as plastic challenge participants can collectively protect the environment with reducing plastic usage"). The items were formulated similarly to previous items assessing efficacy beliefs [11,27] to fit the current study design.
- Self-efficacy. We gauged self-efficacy with two general items ("I am optimistic, that I can protect the environment"; "I am capable of protecting the environment"; $r = 0.87$) and one plastic-specific item ("I think that I am capable of protecting the environment by means of my personal plastic reduction"). These were adapted questions from a questionnaire by [5] (In line with other researchers, we measured efficacy perceptions with regard to individuals' confidence in their ability (e.g., [7,8,29]) rather than action-/behavior-directed, as Bandura's conceptualization would suggest. Hanss and colleagues ([43]) provide a comprehensive discussion of different approaches to measure and conceptualize efficacy).
- Behavioral intentions. We tapped behavioral intentions with three general items ("I will try to reduce my eco footprint in the next month"; "I intend to behave more environmentally friendly in the following month"; and "I am planning to waste less of natural resources in the next month"; $\alpha = 0.95$) and one plastic-specific item ("I intend to abstain from plastic while shopping"). These items were taken from the Green Behavior Intention Scale by [44].
- Descriptive norms. We inquired about descriptive norms with four items, adapted from [40]. Participants were asked to estimate the frequency with which "inhabitants of Germany try to reduce plastic while shopping"; "inhabitants of their city try to reduce plastic while shopping"; "friends and family try to reduce plastic while shopping"; and "the person that challenged them tries to reduce plastic while shopping". ($\alpha = 0.79$).
- Injunctive norms. We measured injunctive norms with four items: "If I reduced plastic while shopping, people that matter to me would (disapprove–approve)"; "Most people that matter to me think that consuming less plastic while shopping is (undesirable–desirable)"; "Most people that matter to me think that I should (not at all–very much) advocate for plastic consumption reduction while shopping"; and "The person that challenged me to this card considers plastic reduction while shopping as (irrelevant–very relevant)" ($\alpha = 0.66$).
- Attitudes. In order to measure attitudes towards plastic use, we provided seven bi-polar items on which participants were asked to rate how they perceive plastic consumption while shopping ("good–bad", "foolish–wise", "harmful–useful", uncomfortable—comfortable", "dissatisfactory—satisfactory", "disadvantageous—advantageous", and "negative—positive"). Those items were adapted from [45] ($\alpha = 0.79$).
- Demographics. At the end of the questionnaire, we gauged participants' age, gender, socio-economic status, and education status (student vs. non-student).

3. Results

Means, standard deviations, reliabilities, and bivariate correlations for all measures across conditions are reported in Table 1. Number of participants by condition is depicted in Table 2. As can be seen, the highest number of participants indicated having completed an easy challenge, the lowest number of participants having completed the difficult challenge, and a number of participants in-between completed the moderate challenge. Regarding our hypotheses, we first tested the effect of task difficulty on collective and self-efficacy beliefs, both for plastic-specific and general items. A MANOVA comparing the means of efficacy revealed significant main effects for plastic-specific ($F[2, 156] = 3.26$, $p = 0.041$, $\eta^2_p = 0.04$) and general ($F[2, 156] = 3.82$, $p = 0.024$, $\eta^2_p = 0.05$) collective efficacy. For self-efficacy, there was a tendency for a main effect for plastic-specific ($F[2, 156] = 2.61$, $p = 0.077$, $\eta^2_p = 0.03$) self-efficacy, but no effect for general self-efficacy ($F < 1$).

As can be seen in Table 2, and in line with our predictions, collective efficacy beliefs were most strongly pronounced when the task difficulty of the plastic reduction challenge was moderate. Comparing the moderate condition with both the easy and the difficult condition revealed a significant main effect for both plastic-specific ($F[1, 158] = 6.5$, $p = 0.012$, $\eta^2_p = .04$) as well as general collective efficacy ($F[1, 158] = 7.65$, $p = 0.006$, $\eta^2_p = 0.05$), such that in the moderate condition ($Mplastic = 5.14$, $SDplastic = 1.42$; $Mgeneral = 5.09$, $SDgeneral = 1.48$), collective efficacy was significantly higher than in both other conditions ($Mplastic = 4.44$, $SDplastic = 1.77$; $Mgeneral = 4.34$, $SDgeneral = 1.72$). For self-efficacy, however, there was a tendency for plastic-specific efficacy ($F[1, 158] = 3.81$, $p = 0.053$, $\eta^2_p = 0.02$) such that in the moderate condition ($Mplastic = 6.14$, $SDplastic = 0.97$), plastic-specific efficacy was descriptively higher than in both other conditions ($Mplastic = 5.68$, $SDplastic = 1.63$). There was no effect for general self-efficacy, $F < 1$. These findings suggest that the difficulty of the plastic reduction task affected collective efficacy, but less so self-efficacy.

Table 1. Means, standard deviations, and bivariate correlations for all dependent and control variables, across experimental groups.

	M	*SD*	1.	2.	3.	4.	5.	6.	7.	8.	9.
1. Collective efficacy—plastic	4.69	1.69	—	0.91 *	0.51 *	0.53 *	0.40 *	0.38 *	0.31 *	0.23 *	0.27 *
2. Collective efficacy—general	4.61	1.67		—	0.43 *	0.58 *	0.33 *	0.40 *	0.31 *	0.16 *	0.25 *
3. Self-efficacy—plastic	5.84	1.44			—	0.60 *	0.48 *	0.24 *	0.50 *	0.13	0.19 *
4. Self-efficacy—general	5.36	1.51				—	0.33 *	0.32 *	0.45 *	0.08 *	0.09 *
5. Sustainable intentions—plastic	6.03	1.21					—	0.65 *	0.51 *	0.28 *	0.34 *
6. Sustainable intentions—general	5.42	1.3						—	0.33 *	0.23 *	0.33 *
7. Attitudes	6.15	0.78							—	0.23 *	0.29 *
8. Descriptive norms	3.91	0.99								—	0.37 *
9. Injunctive norms	5.98	0.72									—

Note: $N = 156$–160, due to missing values. * $p < 0.05$, two-tailed.

Table 2. Means and standard deviations for collective and self-efficacy as a function of task difficulty.

	Task Difficulty		
Measure	**Easy**	**Medium**	**Difficulty**
	M (SD)	*M (SD)*	*M (SD)*
Collective efficacy—plastic	4.40 (1.76)	5.14 (1.42)	4.58 (1.84)
Collective efficacy—general	4.31 (1.72)	5.1 (1.48)	4.46 (1.75)
Self-efficacy—plastic	5.77 (1.55)	6.14 (0.97)	5.42 (1.86)
Self-efficacy—general	5.29 (1.6)	5.46 (1.26)	5.33 (1.77)
N (participants)	78	58	29

Note: A higher score indicates higher efficacy, except for last line. Chi^2-Analysis shows that cases are not equally distributed between levels of task difficulty, $X^2 (2,165) = 22.07$, $p < 0.001$.

In a second step, we tested our serial mediation hypothesis. Specifically, we predicted an indirect effect of task difficulty on sustainable intentions via collective and self-efficacy. To test this assumption, we ran two statistical models, one each for plastic-specific and general efficacy beliefs and sustainable intentions. We conducted analyses of the assumed indirect effects with bootstrapping resamples, computing confidence intervals of an indirect effect—a method preferred to the normal theory approach, which assumes the often violated assumption of normality of the sampling distribution of the indirect effect [46]. An indirect effect as the one we propose here is deemed significant with 95% confidence if "0" is not within the 95% confidence interval. To test our indirect effects, we used the SPSS process macro (Model 6; [46]) with 5000 bootstrapping resamples. Task difficulty was recoded so that the moderate condition could be compared with both the easy and the medium conditions that were collapsed into one group (1 = moderate task difficulty, 0 = otherwise) before analyses.

In line with our expectations, there was a significant sequential indirect effect of task difficulty via plastic-specific collective and self-efficacy on plastic reduction intentions, $B = 0.10$, $SE = 0.06$, bias-corrected 95% CI [0.02; 0.24]. This effect remained significant even after controlling for covariates (injunctive and descriptive norms, attitudes), $B = 0.04$, $SE = 0.03$, bias-corrected 95% CI [0.003; 0.11]. Thus, a moderate task difficulty—compared with an easy or difficult task—increased sustainable intentions through a process of increased collective efficacy and subsequently increased self-efficacy (see Figure 2). To gauge additional evidence of this proposed process, we also tested the reverse pathway that task difficulty first increased self-efficacy, which in turn increased collective efficacy to predict sustainable intentions. This model, however, was substantially weaker, $B = 0.04$, $SE = 0.03$, bias-corrected 95% CI [0.005; 124], and non-significant when controlling for the covariates above, $B = 0.01$, $SE = 0.01$, bias-corrected 95% CI [−0.003; 0.06], supporting our suggested sequence.

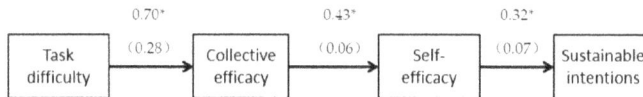

Figure 2. Indirect effect of task difficulty via collective and self-efficacy for plastic-specific efficacy and intentions. Note: $N = 155$, due to missing values. Coefficients are unstandardized, with standard errors in brackets. Model without controlling for the covariates.

We also tested the model for general collective and self-efficacy on general sustainable intentions. For these, there was no significant sequential indirect effect, $B = 0.05$, $SE = 0.04$, bias-corrected 95% CI [−0.001; 0.15]. Controlling for the covariates did not improve the indirect effect, $B = 0.02$, $SE = 0.03$, bias-corrected 95% CI [−0.02; 0.10]. Also, there was no reverse mediation with self-efficacy first, followed by collective efficacy, $B = 0.03$, $SE = 0.04$, bias-corrected 95% CI [−0.04; 0.13]. Note, however, that there was an indirect effect of task difficulty via collective efficacy alone, $B = 0.19$, $SE = 0.09$, bias-corrected 95% CI [0.06; 0.42], suggesting that collective efficacy may indeed play a more important role for such collective tasks than self-efficacy.

The separate steps of the serial mediation were also significant: There was an indirect effect of task difficulty on self-efficacy via collective efficacy for plastic specific efficacy, $B = 0.15$, $SE = 0.06$, bias-corrected 95% CI [0.04; 0.30], as well as for general sustainable efficacy, $B = 0.20$, $SE = 0.08$, bias-corrected 95% CI [0.06; 0.37].

For intentions, there was an indirect effect of collective efficacy on plastic specific intentions via self-efficacy, $B = 0.14$, $SE = 0.05$, bias-corrected 95% CI [0.06; 0.25], but not for general sustainable intentions, $B = 0.06$, $SE = 0.04$, bias-corrected 95% CI [−0.02; 0.15], resembling the non-significant full sequential model above.

4. Discussion

Responding to climate and environmental crises requires the collective efforts of many. It is therefore necessary to understand the conditions under which people perceive a collective to be effective in reaching its goal [7,19]. The current study contributes significantly to this understanding, showing that collective efficacy beliefs depend on the perceived difficulty of a particular task. When the task difficulty was medium, rather than low or high, collective efficacy beliefs were strongest, and in turn, most predictive of pro-environmental intentions. In addition, this experiment suggests that collective efficacy beliefs can influence self-efficacy beliefs that in turn result in sustainable behavior (see also [12]). Thus, even without a direct effect of the task difficulty manipulation on sustainability, it did indirectly make a difference via increasing participants' collective and self-efficacy perceptions. This evidence is both theoretically as well as practically relevant.

First, the current study suggests that collective efficacy is not always such a powerful predictor as suggested in previous research. Apparently, a task that is perceived to be of moderate difficulty seems appropriate to induce a maximum of collective efficacy beliefs. Our findings thus parallel previous research on the effects of task difficulty on performance (e.g., [34–36]), suggesting that task-related changes in performance may be due to changes in collective efficacy beliefs. This is relevant for research on collective and pro-environmental action as it shows that depending on how difficult societal challenges are, different feelings of what people can achieve emerge. Thus, this study may provide a starting point for more rigorously assessing the conditions that make people trust (or not trust) in their capabilities to foster change, and thus has clear implications for sustainability policy making (see below).

Second, the sequential model we propose here suggests that effects of collective efficacy should be understood as depending on changes in self-efficacy. As Jugert et al. [12] suggest, self-efficacy seems a necessary ingredient that drives the effects of collective efficacy on behavioral outcomes. Importantly, in our experiment, this sequential indirect effect was only statistically significant for plastic-specific behaviors—not surprisingly, given that the challenge we asked participants to perform dealt with the reduction of plastic use. However, for research on spillover effects (for a review, see [47]), it is helpful to know that task difficulty of a topic-specific challenge (as in our case, a plastic reduction task) can also increase general collective efficacy beliefs that might in turn enhance pro-environmental behavior in other domains—a finding in line with [26], who show that self-efficacy beliefs mediate between less difficult and more difficult behaviors. Our findings nicely complement this research, suggesting that such spill-over can also be mediated via collective efficacy beliefs.

Interestingly, while our model received support such that strongest efficacy was reported for a medium task, most participants who took part in the survey completed the easy task. This is not surprising, given that this task, compared with the medium and difficult task, was the least time consuming task. Participants could just do this casually, without extended planning of grocery shopping. In other words, an easy task may result in stronger response rates but lower efficacy beliefs and a moderate task in lower response rates but higher efficacy beliefs—that in turn predict future intentions and behavior. This information may be particularly relevant to policy makers and practitioners working in sustainability campaigning.

- Policy implications. The trade-off between responses to more or less difficult tasks and perceived (collective) efficacy is informative for policy making as it shows that people may more easily engage in behaviors that cost little but feel more efficacious through performing somewhat more difficult behaviors. The latter, however, may be performed by fewer individuals. Thus, it is important to identify sustainable actions that are moderately difficult but at the same time appealing enough on other dimensions (e.g., time efficient) in order to result in stronger response rates. We thus believe that the current experiment suggests applications in the field of policy communication and campaigning. Based on the current findings, it seems helpful to craft policy measures—or at least their way of communication—in a way that enables individuals to collectively address issues through moderate "behavioral challenges". For example, providing a community with information about moderate behaviors needed to achieve energy autonomy could increase their collective efficacy to actually engage in such an endeavor, increasing people's self-efficacy to ultimately act. Focus groups or representative surveys could help in identifying broad concepts of difficulty in the public. Of course, such policy measures need to be flanked by additional psychological concepts such as subjects of justice [48], intergenerational and ecological justice appraisals [49], as well as others. Yet, gaining knowledge about possibilities to directly encourage individuals through raising their efficacy beliefs represent an encouraging path to take. Specifically, it could be a fruitful step to investigate the underlying dimensions of difficulty (e.g., economic cost, psychological cost, time, effort, etc.) to understand the difficulty—efficacy trade-off described above.

- Limitations. The limitations of this work also deserve comment. It is in the nature of field experiments that we cannot control every potential confounding variable. First of all, cards were handed out to participants in public spaces with the plea to fill out the online survey (link and QR-Code given at the bottom of the cards) after completing the challenge. Consequently, there was no direct means of ensuring that participants in the different conditions participated to equal extents. This implies that we do not know about the individual reasons of why participants did or did not fill out the survey. Additionally, we do not know how much time passed between participants' receiving their card and engaging in the challenge neither do we know the time lag between completion of the task and survey participation. These points notwithstanding, it is even more intriguing that the difficulty of the task influenced beliefs and intentions in the subsequent online questionnaire. A second issue that needs clarification is the perceived difficulty of the task. While our pretest was successful in showing that our manipulation resulted in the expected difficulty ratings (yet, with the medium difficulty being statistically somewhat closer to the easy than the difficult task), future studies should implement a methodology that allows participants to select their preferred task difficulty. In our study, participants were confronted with one of the three difficulties at random so that it is likely that "moderate difficulty" could be easy for some, and hard for others. In this line, it is important to mention that the different tasks yielded differing environmental impacts depending on consumption patterns and specific products that participants would purchase while completing the challenge (e.g., glass containers might, under certain circumstances, yield worse environmental impact than the equivalent plastic container). We assume that the great majority of participants did not possess the necessary background knowledge to take this into consideration when consequently rating one's own efficacy beliefs concerning the behavior change. It is also possible that people from various socio-structural backgrounds (e.g., students vs. non-students) perceive task difficulty differently. Unfortunately, our pretest data did not include such a ratio.

- Future research. Finally, we encourage future researchers to link self- and collective efficacy more strongly to the issue of private vs. public sphere behavior [3]. While it is quite plausible to assume that private sphere behavior (i.e., personal practice) may be less influenced by collective efficacy beliefs than public sphere behavior (i.e., civic action), some empirical evidence suggests otherwise. For example, Morton and colleagues [29] showed that collective efficacy predicted private sphere behavior (specifically, reducing household waste and non-green energy consumption); similarly, Lubell and colleagues [50], using a rational choice framework, came to similar conclusions (see also [30,31]). These findings show that collective efficacy is also important in private sphere settings—a view researchers have just begun to acknowledge (see also [11]). Yet, it would be informative and important to understand whether different aspects of efficacy relate to different private or public behaviors (see [51,52])—and whether such efficacy beliefs could be gauged by identification with groups that support sustainability causes.

5. Conclusions

To conclude, we believe that this study sheds a light on the boundary conditions of a potentially powerful route to sustainable intentions. Convincing individuals of their collective ability to achieve change could ultimately lead to collective efforts for attaining environmental goals, and it seems that one way to trigger these collective beliefs is through providing and developing moderately challenging goals.

Acknowledgments: We are thankful to Karen Hamann and Josephine Troeger for valuable comments on an earlier version of our manuscript. This research was partly funded by the Melton Foundation with a grant to the second author.

Author Contributions: G.R. and E.A.J. conceived and designed the experiment; E.A.J. performed the experiments; G.R. and E.A.J. analyzed the data; G.R. wrote most parts of the paper.

Conflicts of Interest: The authors declare no conflict of interest.

References

1. Batalha, L.; Reynolds, K. ASPIRing to mitigate climate change: Superordinate identity in global climate negotiations. *Polit. Psychol.* **2012**, *33*, 743–760. [CrossRef]
2. Reese, G. Common human identity and the path to global climate justice. *Clim. Chang.* **2016**, *134*, 521–531. [CrossRef]
3. Stern, P. Toward a coherent theory of environmentally significant behavior. *J. Soc. Issues* **2000**, *56*, 407–424. [CrossRef]
4. Bamberg, S.; Möser, G. Twenty years after Hines, Hungerford, and Tomera: A new meta-analysis of psycho-social determinants of pro-environmental behavior. *J. Environ. Psychol.* **2007**, *27*, 14–25. [CrossRef]
5. Fielding, K.S.; McDonald, R.; Louis, W.R. Theory of planned behavior, identity and intentions to engage in environmental activism. *J. Environ. Psychol.* **2008**, *28*, 318–326. [CrossRef]
6. Schultz, P.W. The structure of environmental concern: Concern for self, other people, and the biosphere. *J. Environ. Psychol.* **2001**, *21*, 327–339. [CrossRef]
7. Van Zomeren, M.; Postmes, T.; Spears, R. Toward an integrative social identity model of collective action: A quantitative research synthesis of three socio-psychological perspectives. *Psychol. Bull.* **2008**, *134*, 504–535. [CrossRef] [PubMed]
8. Barth, M.; Jugert, P.; Fritsche, I. Still underdetected—Social norms and collective efficacy predict the acceptance of electric vehicles in Germany. *Transp. Res. F* **2016**, *37*, 64–77. [CrossRef]
9. Doran, R.; Hanss, D.; Larsen, S. Attitudes, efficacy beliefs, and willingness to pay for environmental protection when travelling. *Tour. Hosp. Res.* **2015**, *15*, 281–292. [CrossRef]
10. Doran, R.; Hanss, D.; Larsen, S. Intentions to make sustainable tourism choices: Do value orientations, time perspective, and efficacy beliefs explain individual differences? *Scand. J. Hosp. Tour.* **2016**, 1–16. [CrossRef]
11. Cocking, C.; Drury, J. Generalization of Efficacy as a Function of Collective Action and Intergroup Relations: Involvement in an Anti-Roads Struggle. *J. Appl. Soc. Psychol.* **2004**, *34*, 417–444. [CrossRef]
12. Jugert, P.; Barth, M.; Greenaway, K.; Buechner, R.; Eisentraut, S.; Fritsche, I. Collective efficacy increases pro-environmental intentions through increasing personal efficacy. *J. Environ. Psychol.* **2016**, *48*, 12–23. [CrossRef]
13. Environment Protection and Heritage Council. *Plastic Shopping Bags in Australia: National Plastic Bags Working Group Report to the National Packing Covenant Council*; Environment Protection and Heritage Council: Adelaide, Australia, 2002. Available online: http://www.nepc.gov.au/system/files/resources/0c513e54-d968-ac04-758b-3b7613af0d07/files/ps-pbag-rpt-npbwg-report-npcc-200212.pdf (accessed on 27 January 2017).
14. Steinmetz, Z.; Wollmann, C.; Schaefer, M.; Buchmann, C.; David, J.; Tröger, J.; Schaumann, G.E. Plastic mulching in agriculture. Trading short-term agronomic benefits for long-term soil degradation? *Sci. Total Environ.* **2016**, *550*, 690–705. [CrossRef] [PubMed]
15. Halden, R.U. Plastics and Health Risks. *Annu. Rev. Public Health* **2010**, *31*, 179–194. [CrossRef] [PubMed]
16. Thompson, R.; Moore, C.; vom Saal, F.; Swan, S. Plastics, the environment and human health: Current consensus and future trends. *Philos. Trans. R. Soc. Lond. Ser. B* **2009**, *364*, 2153–2166. [CrossRef] [PubMed]
17. Cherrier, H. Consumer identity and moral obligations in non-plastic bag consumption: A dialectical perspective. *Int. J. Consum. Stud.* **2006**, *30*, 515–523. [CrossRef]
18. Bandura, A. Self-efficacy mechanism in human agency. *Am. Psychol.* **1982**, *37*, 122–147. [CrossRef]
19. Bandura, A. Exercise of Human Agency through Collective Efficacy. *Curr. Dir. Psychol. Sci.* **2000**, *9*, 75–78. [CrossRef]
20. Ajzen, I. Perceived behavioral control, self-efficacy, locus of control, and the theory of planned behavior. *J. Appl. Soc. Psychol.* **2002**, *32*, 665–683. [CrossRef]
21. Bandura, A. *Self-Efficacy: The Exercise of Control*; Freeman: New York, NY, USA, 1997.
22. Tims, M.; Bakker, A.B.; Derks, D. Daily job crafting and the self-efficacy—Performance relationship. *J. Manag. Psychol.* **2014**, *29*, 490–507. [CrossRef]

23. Riggio, H.R.; Weiser, D.A.; Valenzuela, A.M.; Lui, P.P.; Montes, R.; Heuer, J. Self-efficacy in romantic relationships: Prediction of relationship attitudes and outcomes. *J. Soc. Psychol.* **2013**, *153*, 629–650. [CrossRef] [PubMed]

24. LaForge-MacKenzie, K.; Sullivan, P.J.; Hansen, S.; Marini, M. The effect of attentional focus on the self-efficacy-performance relationship in a continuous running task: A pilot study. *J. Exerc. Mov. Sport* **2013**, *45*, 1.

25. Sitzmann, T.; Yeo, G. A Meta-Analytic Investigation of the Within-Person Self-Efficacy Domain: Is Self-Efficacy a Product of Past Performance or a Driver of Future Performance? *Personal. Psychol.* **2013**, *66*, 531–568. [CrossRef]

26. Lauren, N.; Fielding, K.S.; Smith, L.; Louis, W.R. You did, so you can and you will: Self-efficacy as a mediator of spillover from easy to more difficult pro-environmental behavior. *J. Environ. Psychol.* **2016**, *48*, 191–199. [CrossRef]

27. Fielding, K.S.; Hornsey, M.J. A social identity analysis of climate change and environmental attitudes and behaviors: Insights and opportunities. *Front. Psychol.* **2016**, *7*. [CrossRef] [PubMed]

28. Morton, T.A.; Rabinovich, A.; Marshall, D.; Bretschneider, P. The future that may (or may not) come: How framing changes responses to uncertainty in climate change communications. *Glob. Environ. Chang.* **2011**, *21*, 103–109. [CrossRef]

29. Homburg, A.; Stolberg, A. Explaining pro-environmental behavior with a cognitive theory of stress. *J. Environ. Psychol.* **2006**, *26*, 1–14. [CrossRef]

30. Chen, M.-F. Self-efficacy or collective efficacy within the cognitive theory of stress model: Which more effectively explains people's self-reported proenvironmental behavior. *J. Environ. Psychol.* **2015**, *42*, 66–75. [CrossRef]

31. Fritsche, I.; Jonas, E.; Ablasser, C.; Beyer, M.; Kuban, J.; Manger, A.-M.; Schultz, M. The power of we: Evidence for group-based control. *J. Exp. Soc. Psychol.* **2013**, *49*, 19–32. [CrossRef]

32. Greenaway, K.H.; Haslam, S.A.; Cruwys, T.; Branscombe, N.R.; Ysseldyk, R.; Heldreth, C. From "we" to "me": Group identification enhances perceived personal control with consequences for health and well-being. *J. Personal. Soc. Psychol.* **2015**, *109*, 53–74. [CrossRef] [PubMed]

33. Atkinson, J.W. Motivational determinants of risk-taking behavior. *Psychol. Rev.* **1957**, *64*, 359–372. [CrossRef] [PubMed]

34. Baron, R.A.; Mueller, B.A.; Wolfe, M.T. Self-efficacy and entrepreneurs' adoption of unattainable goals: The restraining effects of self-control. *J. Bus. Ventur.* **2016**, *31*, 55–71. [CrossRef]

35. Kanfer, R.; Ackerman, P.L. Aging, adult development, and work motivation. *Acad. Manag. Rev.* **2004**, *29*, 440–458.

36. Vancouver, J.B.; More, K.M.; Yoder, R.J. Self-efficacy and resource allocation: Support for a nonmonotonic, discontinuous model. *J. Appl. Psychol.* **2008**, *93*, 35. [CrossRef] [PubMed]

37. Van Zomeren, M.; Spears, R.; Fischer, A.H.; Leach, C.W. Put your money where your mouth is! Explaining collective action tendencies through group-based anger and group efficacy. *J. Personal. Soc. Psychol.* **2004**, *87*, 649–664. [CrossRef] [PubMed]

38. Bator, R.J.; Tabanico, J.J.; Walton, M.L.; Schultz, P.W. Promoting energy conservation with implied norms and explicit messages. *Soc. Influ.* **2014**, *9*, 69–82. [CrossRef]

39. Goldstein, N.J.; Cialdini, R.B.; Griskevicius, V. A room with a viewpoint: Using social norms to motivate environmental conservation in hotels. *J. Consum. Res.* **2008**, *35*, 472–482. [CrossRef]

40. Hamann, K.R.; Reese, G.; Seewald, D.; Loeschinger, D.C. Affixing the theory of normative conduct (to your mailbox): Injunctive and descriptive norms as predictors of anti-ads sticker use. *J. Environ. Psychol.* **2015**, *44*, 1–9. [CrossRef]

41. Nolan, J.M.; Schultz, P.W.; Cialdini, R.B.; Goldstein, N.J.; Griskevicius, V. Normative social influence is underdetected. *Personal. Soc. Psychol. Bull.* **2008**, *34*, 913–923. [CrossRef] [PubMed]

42. Reese, G.; Loew, K.; Steffgen, G. A towel less: Social norms enhance pro-environmental behavior in hotels. *J. Soc. Psychol.* **2014**, *154*, 97–100. [CrossRef] [PubMed]

43. Hanss, D.; Böhm, G.; Doran, R.; Homburg, A. Sustainable consumption of groceries: The importance of believing that one can contribute to sustainable development. *Sustain. Dev.* **2016**, *24*, 357–370. [CrossRef]

44. Mancha, R.; Muniz, K.; Yoder, C. Studying Executives' Green Behaviors: An Environmental Theory of Planned Behavior. Unpublished Manuscript. 2014. Available online: http://aisel.aisnet.org/cgi/viewcontent.cgi?article=1574&context=amcis2014 (accessed on 27 January 2017).

45. Han, H.; Hsu, L.; Sheu, C. Application of the Theory of Planned Behavior to green hotel choice: Testing the effect of environmental friendly activities. *Tour. Manag.* **2010**, *31*, 325–334. [CrossRef]

46. Hayes, A.F. *Introduction to Mediation, Moderation, and Conditional Process Analysis*; Guildford Press: New York, NY, USA, 2013.

47. Truelove, H.B.; Carrico, A.R.; Weber, E.U.; Raimi, K.T.; Vandenbergh, M.P. Positive and negative spillover of pro-environmental behavior: an integrative review and theoretical framework. *Glob. Environ. Chang.* **2014**, *29*, 127–138. [CrossRef]

48. Sikor, T.; Martin, A.; Fisher, J.; He, J. Toward an empirical analysis of justice in ecosystem governance. *Conserv. Lett.* **2014**, *7*, 524–532. [CrossRef]

49. Reese, G.; Jacob, L. Principles of environmental justice and pro-environmental action: A two-step process model of moral anger and responsibility to act. *Environ. Sci. Policy* **2015**, *51*, 88–94. [CrossRef]

50. Lubell, M.; Zahran, S.; Vedlitz, A. Collective action and citizen responses to global warming. *Polit. Behav.* **2007**, *29*, 391–413. [CrossRef]

51. Alisat, S.; Riemer, M. The environmental action scale: Development and psychometric evaluation. *J. Environ. Psychol.* **2015**, *43*, 13–23. [CrossRef]

52. Dono, J.; Webb, J.; Richardson, B. The relationship between environmental activism, pro-environmental behavior and social identity. *J. Environ. Psychol.* **2010**, *30*, 178–186. [CrossRef]

sustainability

MDPI

Article

Making Sense of Sustainability: A Practice Theories Approach to Buying Food

Anke Brons * and Peter Oosterveer

Environmental Policy Group, Wageningen University, 6706 KN Wageningen, The Netherlands;
peter.oosterveer@wur.nl
* Correspondence: anke.brons@wur.nl; Tel.: +31-6-1115-5827

Academic Editor: Marc A. Rosen
Received: 8 December 2016; Accepted: 17 March 2017; Published: 21 March 2017

Abstract: In light of global climate change the relevance of sustainable food consumption is growing, yet access to it has not correspondingly developed. This paper addresses the issue of accessing sustainable food from a practice theories perspective. The case of students in Paris is examined by means of interviews and participant observation. Four indicators serve to structure the results, i.e., mode of recruitment, mode of engagement, degree of commitment, and bundles of practices. Based on this analysis, three types are constructed, each with distinct access issues. We conclude that access to sustainable food is not necessarily determined by financial means only, nor by individual attitudes, but should be analysed as embedded in the complex dynamics of multiple social practices. Building on these insights means that more attention for the actual practice of accessing sustainable food, the different elements, and bundles involved is needed when looking for ways to increase access to sustainable food.

Keywords: sustainable consumption; food access; practice theories

---

1. Introduction

A call for the consumption of more sustainable food is increasingly heard [1,2]. To achieve this aim, a crucial element is how to advance access to sustainable food in order to make buying sustainable food more feasible. Some scholars argue that improved information provision about the sustainability of food will enhance access (see e.g., [3]). Behind this approach lies the assumption of a conscious consumer who makes rational decisions based on information and price. Yet, this expectation fails to address the so-called attitude-behaviour gap, or knowledge-to-action gap [4,5]. This means that consumers do not always straightforwardly act upon the knowledge on sustainability provided to them, but rather are also guided by other issues, including material, mental, and social barriers. Other literature primarily emphasizes the role of the supply side and the physical environment in accessing healthy and sustainable food (see [6,7] for an overview). Financial circumstances of consumers are also frequently flagged as a major factor determining access to sustainable food [7,8].

Critics of all of these interpretations of access instead call for more attention to the role of the broader "food environment" and consumers' interactions with it [4–6]. These authors argue that understanding access as dictated by information, financial circumstances, or supply-side dynamics only, overlooks crucial factors, like the social and cultural environment, as well as personal preferences. Rather, access should be explained within the context of people's "lived experiences" [7]. Such an approach warrants a qualitative study from a consumers' perspective, to complement the existing primarily quantitative research focussed on consumer values and attitudes (see e.g., [2,9,10]).

In order to conduct such a study, the body of practice theories offers insightful theoretical and analytical tools (see [8–11]). With their focus on social practice as the basic unit of analysis instead of overstating either individual actors or social structures, practice theories start from daily routines and habits to explain social reality. When applied to the question of access to sustainable food, a practice theoretical outlook can provide an analytical framework that moves beyond deterministic explanations. This paper shows how access is embedded in practices and how this conceptualization contributes to identifying what relevant elements enable access to sustainable food and to the embedded understanding of what sustainable food actually entails.

The main aim of this paper is to provide a theoretical contribution to the debate on sustainable food consumption by illustrating how a practice theoretical approach serves particularly well to explain the dynamics of consumption and access. In light of this aim, a case study is selected to inform our analysis as much as possible [11], guided by the following question: what are the practices of buying sustainable food and which access issues are prevalent in them? The case of students in Paris was chosen to study buying practices and access dynamics for several reasons. Firstly, students are going through a transitional phase. Having recently left their parents' home with its meanings, habits, and lifestyle, students enter a stage where they are faced with the challenge of developing their own perspectives and routines, in a context of significant budgetary and space constraints. Secondly, in Paris the supply of sustainable food is rather diverse, leading to a broad variety of potential buying practices. Thirdly, students provide for an interesting population in terms of financial circumstances, as they often have to live on a tight budget, especially challenging in Paris, which is characterized by high costs of living and expensive groceries. Typically, students will have expensive and small rooms in which they may not have fridges, freezers, or ovens at their disposal. Students in Paris may not be the average food consumer, but through the in-depth study of the dynamics in their daily practices we may generate more insights into the ways in which consumers more generally deal with sustainability when accessing food.

This paper deals with "sustainable" food, but it is less concerned with the actual sustainability of food choices. Instead, its main interest is how consumers make sense of sustainability in their food buying-practices, as public perception of what constitutes environmentally-sustainable food varies significantly. This study is, thus, specifically interested in the ways in which consumers themselves understand sustainable food. Admittedly, "sustainability" is a broad term, which is commonly conceptualized as consisting of three pillars: economic development, social development, and environmental protection (see [9] for a recent consumption study using all three dimensions, [12] for a more elaborate account). In French, however, this general concept of sustainability is difficult to translate. We, therefore, chose to opt for the equivalent of "environmentally-friendly food" in the interviews, thereby establishing a clear focus on the environmental dimension of sustainability. Beyond this delimitation, however, interviewees were free to interpret the concept, leading to insights in what consumers themselves considered as sustainable food.

The results of the case study are analysed based on a novel theoretical framework derived from practice theories, serving to distinguish between people on the basis of their modes of recruitment, modes of engagement, degrees of commitment, and bundles of practice. Our results indicate how actual buying patterns differ between practitioners, how access is contingent and how mismatches can occur between supply and demand. We conclude that access cannot, and should not, be considered as the outcome of a singular practice, but that interactions between materials and infrastructure, on the one hand, and consumer lifestyles with their temporalities and preferences, on the other, play a crucial role.

The remainder of this paper is structured as follows. The next section introduces the theoretical framework of practice theories, followed by an outline of the applied methodology in Section 3. In the fourth section, the case study on students in Paris will be presented, and the closing section contains the discussion and conclusion.

2. Theoretical Framework

The growing body of literature on practice theories (see i.e., [13–19]) contains rich insights for consumption research, mainly due to their appreciation of routines and habits. Research on sustainable food consumption is particularly well served by these notions, as a large share of consumption takes place on an non-deliberate level; "we consume in a state of distraction" (after [20]). At the same time, routines can also be disrupted and change can come about, instigated for instance by developments in the social and/or physical environment. This practice theoretical vocabulary is then particularly insightful when considering the case of students, who go through a transitory phase during which habits from the parental home are translated into a new environment and whereby routines are challenged. These changes have consequences for both buying practices and access issues.

When operationalizing this practice theoretical literature into a conceptual framework four indicators were selected. These indicators were drawn up inductively when interpreting the data in order to analyse both performance and the entity of the practice [14]; i.e., to understand how the actual "doings and sayings" in the practice are linked through meanings, ends, connections, etc. [21]. The indicators chosen to uncover this entity and consequently differentiate between access issues are: mode of recruitment, mode of engagement, degree of commitment, and bundles of practice. First of all, "mode of recruitment" into the practice [22] refers to the way in which practitioners were enrolled in the practice of buying sustainable food. This indicator was chosen to underline the relevance of considering social trajectories [14] and to shed more light on change: what are some of the elements of practices that play a role in people changing their buying patterns to become a participant in the practice of buying sustainable food?

The next two indicators ("mode of engagement" and "degree of commitment") are borrowed from Southerton [18], and elaborated further by Plessz and Gojard [23]. A practice contains multiple "modes of engagement", referring to the way in which practitioners engage in a practice, or in Halkier [15] terms to the "emotional and normative orientations related to what and how to do something" (p. 361). This indicator reflects the different ways in which practitioners make sense of their own performances, particularly with regard to the status and place of their concerns with sustainability.

"Degree of commitment" to a practice, then, is "the value a practitioner attaches to the practice" [23] (p. 174), or the extent to which practitioners are willing to "go out of their way": going beyond convenience and adapting their habits more fundamentally. This indicator can be used to reflect on the viability of the practice in the face of change: how far does a practitioner's commitment go and which access obstacles will prove too much?

Finally, the last indicator is "bundle of practices", which refers to other practices linked to buying sustainable food. Such bundling can occur, for instance, when, in Schatzki [24] terms, "their [the practices'] organizations contain the same element, i.e., the same end, rule, task or understanding" (p. 12). The present study is interested in the practices that are linked by their sharing of the aim of environmental sustainability. Identifying bundles of practices can show typical combinations of practices, illuminate the relative place the practice of buying sustainable food occupies in practitioners' lives, and demonstrate the consequences for access of this position.

3. Methods

3.1. Case Study Background

The general attitude among French consumers is positive towards buying more environmentally-friendly food, provided that the prices of these foods are equal to their conventional variants and that a larger offer of sustainable food is available [25]. In France, the home consumer market for organic food is growing, for instance, between 2014 and 2015 by almost 15% [26]. Nevertheless, organic food is estimated to make up only 2.5% of the total food market. Organic food in France is mostly offered through four food providers: (1) supermarkets (46% of total organic food purchase); (2) specialized organic stores (36%); (3) direct sales (fresh market or farm; 13%); and (4) independent shopkeepers (5%) [26]. Consumers tend to buy organic food through more than one of these means of provision. An additional option for buying local, often organic fruits and vegetables, is through box schemes or AMAPs ("Associations pour le Maintien d'une Agriculture Paysanne" or "Associations for the maintenance of a peasant agriculture"), which are increasingly becoming popular in France [27]. These AMAPs, a form of consumer-supported agriculture [28], consist of a local farmer and a group of individuals who form an alliance in which the growers and consumers share the risks and benefits of food production, and whereby consumers have products delivered from the farm every week. In 2012, over 1600 of such AMAP networks had been set up all over France, of which 260 were in the Ile-de-France region, where Paris is located [29].

3.2. Methods

Parisian students engaging in the practice of buying sustainable food were recruited as participants in various ways. First of all, they were approached through personal contacts at INRA's ALISS research unit (Alimentation et Sciences Sociales, where the main researcher was based during the research); through student AMAP networks; through REFEDD (Réseau Français des Etudiants pour le Développement Durable, a pro-environmental association across French universities, with a Paris-based branch); and, finally, through snowballing. The main sources of qualitative data were semi-structured interviews with these students. As our main theoretical interest was in mapping practices, the interview guide was based on the operationalization of central concepts from practice theories, mostly based on Gram-Hanssen [30] overview of general elements of a practice. A total of 19 interviews were conducted over a period of two months (January–February 2016). Each of the interviews was transcribed in their original language (French)—translations into English of the quotes used in this paper were made by the main researcher and corrected by a French native at INRA. The interviews were consequently uploaded into Weft QDA (an open source software package for the analysis of qualitative data; Fenton, London, UK) and coded. Some codes were drawn up a priori, i.e., general practice theoretical concepts based on Gram-Hanssen [30] overview. These were complemented by more exact inductive codes grounded in the data, such as specific access issues and strategies students employed to address these challenges.

To complement the interviews, participant observation through "shopping along" was done, accompanying two students in their shopping routes through their usual location for doing groceries. These observation moments were supplemented by attendance of the distribution of vegetable boxes at one of the AMAPs (Leg'Ulm, the AMAP of the École Normale Supérieure). Lastly, the main researcher's own trips to organic stores and supermarkets during her stay in Paris also served as observation material, in which her foreigner's (Dutch) viewpoint allowed for a specifically perceptive outlook.

4. Results

4.1. General

Of the 19 students that were interviewed, 13 were female and six male. Most of them ($n = 17$) studied at so-called "grandes écoles". These are relatively elite higher education establishments with selective admittance procedures, and include AgroParisTech ($n = 5$; no fees), the École Normale Supérieure ($n = 3$; pays its students a stipend) and Sciences Po ($n = 3$; has an income-based fee scale). The ages of the interviewees ranged from 18 to 26, with an average of 22 years, and most students were in the Master's phase of their studies. Their study programs were diverse, with ecology being the most common study orientation ($n = 5$), followed by a rather splintered field including business management, marketing techniques, sociology and environmental politics (all $n = 2$). The average monthly income of the interviewees was 974 euro (min. 400, max. 1600). To compare this average to national French statistics: the minimum wage for 2016 was 1467 euro, and the poverty line set at 734 euro, with six interviewees falling under this line [31].

Concerning what constitutes "sustainable food consumption", the various elements that were brought up by the participants were buying organic, local, seasonal, fresh/unprocessed food, eating less meat, vegetarianism, veganism, and buying products with less or no packaging. To clarify, when interviewees indicated they were a member of an AMAP, they checked the boxes of "organic", "local", and "seasonal", as AMAP products are all of these. Both organic and local were highlighted as important criteria for sustainable food by every single interviewee. Seasonality was also taken into account by almost everyone ($n = 17$), followed by eating less meat ($n = 15$). The number of actual vegetarians was much lower ($n = 5$), and only one interviewee indicated she was a vegan, with another one expressing a leaning towards veganism. Packaging was referred to by about half of the interviewees.

The various locations for buying sustainable food that were mentioned were supermarkets, (online) organic stores, AMAPs and fresh markets. The most commonly used food provider was the supermarket; because organic stores are very expensive, many students resorted to shopping at the organic aisle in (large) supermarkets, where organic products are less costly and clearly displayed. However, other interviewees stated their dislike of supermarkets, because of the sheer amount of choice, the atmosphere, and/or the lacking offer of unpackaged products.

By contrast, the option to buy unpackaged products is amply available in the numerous organic stores in Paris. 12 out of 19 students indicated they went to organic stores to buy at least a share of their food products. At the same time, this option to buy loose products also withheld some students from shopping at organic stores, as practical issues like having to bring boxes and jars to the store when doing groceries did not match very well with the often impromptu nature of their shopping trips.

The AMAP or vegetable box scheme turned out to be popular. About half ($n = 9$) of the participants were members of an AMAP. These AMAPs are tailored to the rhythm of student life. Whereas conventional AMAPs are usually paid for a whole year in advance, in Paris specific student-oriented AMAPs are well available which could be paid for per month or even per week. Quantities are also flexible: there is usually the option of sharing a box with another AMAP member, or paying per item. Lastly, fresh markets were also used for sustainable shopping, although only by a minority ($n = 6$). Fresh markets have limited "opening hours" (often only on Sunday morning), which seemed a bad fit with the temporality of student life.

4.2. Typology

To map the practice of buying sustainable food and related access issues, a typology was drawn up to do justice to the variation in the sample and allow for an accurate description of access problems (see Table 1 below). This typology is based on the four indicators from practice theories that were elaborated above in Section 2, and constructs three types: the food environmentalist, the balancing environmentalist, and the comprehensive environmentalist. Essentially, each of the types in the typology represents a different answer to the question: To what extent do you take the environment into account in buying food and beyond?

Table 1. Typology.

	(1) The Food Environmentalist	(2) The Balancing Environmentalist	(3) The Comprehensive Environmentalist
Mode of recruitment	Continuation	Modification	Transformation
Mode of engagement	Concerns with environment, health, quality and ethics in food only	Concerns with environment, health, quality, ethics and social equality in food and other domains	Concerns with environment in food and other domains
Degree of commitment	Know their limits	Question their limits	Push their limits
Bundles of practice	Recycling, buying second-hand	Transportation, recycling, saving energy, buying second-hand, activism	Transportation, recycling, saving energy, buying second-hand, activism

Below, we will first provide a brief introduction to each type by presenting an exemplary member of each category and sketch out the type's general understanding of sustainable food and their buying practices. Consequently, we will further distinguish between the types and their participation in the practice of buying sustainable food by addressing each of the four indicators individually, and finally discuss the resulting access issues that characterize each type.

4.2.1. Introducing the Types

To start with the food environmentalists (*n* = 4), Sarah (23) is in the second year of her Master's program in business management. Her father is a farmer and sensitized her to the importance of animal well-being. Eggs, fruits, and vegetables are the most important products Sarah almost always buys organically. Seasonality of products is something she also learned at home. She does indicate the problem of high prices for organic products. For Sarah, buying sustainable food does not mean a large overturning of her habits. Rather, it is routine for her to take the environment into account through her shopping: "Actually, I kind of do the same things as at home, when I do my groceries. I've sort of followed the habits from home. This coincides with a limited extension of her environmental concern to other domains".

For all food environmentalists, "sustainable food" means at least organic, local, and seasonal food. Three also mention eating less meat, with one being a vegetarian, and one person pays attention to the aspect of packaging. As for their buying patterns: the supermarket is the most popular provider of sustainable food, where choices for or against environmentally friendly food are sometimes made based on the mood and budget of the moment. One food environmentalist is also member of an AMAP and half of all food environmentalists go to the fresh market, but only one indicated to also shopping at an organic store. This group hardly pays attention to the environment when eating out.

Turning to the second type, Arthur (21) is a typical balancing environmentalist (*n* = 9). He is a first year Master's student in environmental politics and economics. At home, he was not particularly taught to care for the environment. Over the course of his studies, Arthur began to develop an interest in the environment and became a member of pro-environmental associations. He pays attention to seasonality, eating less meat, and for half a year he also subscribes to his university's AMAP. For the remainder of his food products he shops at the next door supermarket—which he describes as not necessarily sustainable, but where he does look at the origin of products and buys organic products when possible. Arthur's concern with the environment is also extended to other domains, such as transportation, recycling, and energy consumption. He is willing to pay a bit more, and to travel somewhat further to buy organic products, but he also states that "if it [i.e., sustainable food] is really inaccessible, that is to say, if I have to travel for half an hour for something I can also find just across the street, I will stop".

Balancing environmentalists' interpretation of what constitutes "sustainable food" includes a sensitivity to food being local, organic, and seasonal for almost all of its members (except for two who do not refer to seasonality). There is more attention to the packaging of food (*n* = 5) than among food environmentalists, and six out of nine balancing environmentalists also refer to eating less meat as important, with one actual vegetarian. Buying patterns are more structured and consistent than among food environmentalists. Although like the latter, balancing environmentalists shop at supermarkets for organic food, organic stores are also visited more often. Likewise, AMAP membership is higher, allowing for more constancy in buying sustainable food. Moreover, balancing environmentalists buy more products in their sustainable versions and some also take the environment into account when eating out.

Lastly, Lea (22) is an exemplary comprehensive environmentalist (*n* = 6). She is in the second year of her Master's in agroecology. For Lea, taking the environment into account has meant a huge change in many aspects of her life. Growing up, she was not particularly sensitized to taking care of the environment. Her motivation for buying sustainable food primarily comes from friends she regularly had discussions and watched documentaries with on environmental issues. This trajectory was sped up during her time abroad studying and working at organic farms. Lea says about herself that she has "completely changed her diet". She is now a vegetarian with vegan tendencies, and purchases all of her groceries at an organic store, clearly expressing a strong dislike of supermarkets: "I can't even go in anymore". In addition, she extends her concern with the environment to a large number of other practices: next to the more frequently mentioned practices such as transportation and recycling, Lea also changed to a greener bank.

Comprehensive environmentalists check the most boxes in answering what "sustainable food" comprises. All of them mention organic, local, seasonal, eating less meat, and all–minus one—also refer to packaging. Moreover, half of them are vegetarians, of whom two are vegan or inclining towards veganism. Regarding buying patterns, comprehensive environmentalists tend to buy almost all of their food products in their organic versions. All comprehensive environmentalists shop in organic stores, and some even exclusively do their groceries there. Supermarkets are also visited, but limitedly so, and only to complement. Four out of six comprehensive environmentalists also subscribe to an AMAP. This group is also the only group to categorically include eating out in the scope of their environmental concerns.

4.2.2. Indicator 1: Mode of Recruitment

The recruitment of food environmentalists to the practice of buying sustainable food is the logical extension of a previously existing concern with food and is labelled "continuation". All members of this category were sensitized by their parents to pay attention to eating well and having a healthy, high-quality diet. Like Sarah, all food environmentalists referred to growing up in the countryside to explain their motivation for buying sustainable food. Due to this mode of recruitment, for food environmentalists buying sustainable food is not a drastically new practice demanding the invention and application of new routines. Their "routinized (…) behaviour" [14] or "doings and sayings" [32] are not significantly challenged.

Balancing environmentalists' mode of recruitment into the practice of buying sustainable food is characterized as "modification". Balancing environmentalists were recruited into the practice through studies or friends or both, and by a concern for the environment rather than for food. Their trigger for turning to this practice has come later in life, induced by exogenous factors in their changing (social) environment. As such, participation in the practice is not in continuity with their trajectory but rather "confronts" ["brings to the front", from practical to discursive consciousness, [33]] their habits and routines. Still, these changes are not as transformative as for the comprehensive environmentalists, but only present a modification to people's overall habits.

Comprehensive environmentalists entered the practice of buying sustainable food through a mode of recruitment called "transformation". Except for one, none of the comprehensive environmentalists were sensitized to respecting the environment by their parents. Rather, their motivations for participating in the practice of buying sustainable food can be found in more profoundly disruptive factors. Three out of six mention living abroad for an exchange semester or internship as contributing to their changing views, marking clear moments of disruption. The other three refer to frequent encounters with environmentally minded friends or enrolment in environmental associations as sources for transformation. For comprehensive environmentalists, these exogenous factors fundamentally altered existing routines and generated an altogether different "logic of practice" [34].

4.2.3. Indicator 2: Mode of Engagement

Food environmentalists' mode of engagement with the practice of buying sustainable food is characterized by two "orientations" [15]. Firstly, a concern with the environment is not exclusive: it has to compete with other criteria for food. Three out of four group members indicate a concern with health, quality and/or ethics, when it comes to deciding which food to buy. Secondly, this engagement is limited to the practice of buying sustainable food and does not abundantly expand into other practices.

Balancing environmentalists have a more elaborate mode of engagement which includes an extension of environmental concern into other domains, such as mobility, recycling, saving energy, buying second-hand, and participation in pro-environment associations. However, like for the food environmentalists, a concern for the environment has to compete with other food criteria, such as health, quality, and ethics. Shopping along with Tisha provided a neat illustration of these concerns with health and quality, as she repeatedly indicated the better quality and taste of specific organic products when verbalizing her choices of products. For instance, she explains her choice for the cheapest organic label jam:

> "Those are too expensive [points at the jams from a specific organic label]. And this one costs one euro [points at and takes the jam from the supermarket's private organic label]. In fact it's the same price as the non-organic jam. So well, you don't know whether "organic", whether that means something. But it's true that it's better, well, you normally have less sugar. Anyway, the quality is considerably better, and it's the same price."

Clearly, in this case, quality and health are more important to Tisha than the precise philosophy or (environmental) values underlying organic labels.

Finally, comprehensive environmentalists' mode of engagement is characterized by a concern with the environment in buying food and in other domains. What mainly distinguishes comprehensive from balancing environmentalists here is the environment being the main criterion in buying food, rather than having to compete with health or quality.

4.2.4. Indicator 3: Degree of Commitment

Food environmentalists' degree of commitment is restricted: they "know their limits". To illustrate: Chloe repeatedly stresses her apprehension of supermarkets, but still opts for the easiest way and always goes there for her sustainable shopping. Buying sustainable food in the supermarket is not very demanding: it does not require a major rearrangement of shopping routes or routines, and is the most popular food provider among this category of consumers.

Balancing environmentalists' have a higher degree of commitment which is best described as "questioning their limits". An example can be found in Brenda, a 23 year old student in business management, for whom the environment is "something I have in the back of my mind often when I make choices in my daily life", but who does distinguish herself from the extremely committed people: "There are these people who are super engaged and all, for me it's just occasionally some small things". Yet, these "small things" do cover quite a few practices, i.e., mobility, recycling, saving energy, buying second-hand, and activism. Brenda also buys a lot of organic products, in the supermarket, organic stores, and at the fresh market. Evidently, she is committed to the environment beyond just food. Brenda does, however, acknowledge limits, although she simultaneously challenges these: she is aware that she could do more.

Comprehensive environmentalists' degree of commitment, then, can be characterized as "pushing their limits". The considerable willingness of this type to change their food routines can be seen, for instance, in the fact that half of them are vegetarians or vegans, which requires a substantial change of diet. In addition, comprehensive environmentalists push their limits as almost all indicate a drive to further expand their concern for the environment, each in their own way. For Bruno, pushing his limits means having his own garden at some point, for Lea it means moving towards veganism, Christian and Agathe talk about taking packaging into account and Agathe also mentions further reducing her meat consumption.

4.2.5. Indicator 4: Bundles of Practices

Among food environmentalists, bundling buying sustainable food with other practices is very limited, with only recycling ($n = 2$) and buying second-hand products ($n = 1$) being mentioned. As such, taking the environment into account is not the central end providing pivotal meaning to food environmentalists' self-narrative. In other words, for these practitioners, participation in the practice of buying sustainable food is not a basic identity determiner.

Balancing environmentalists include a larger range of practices in the scope of their environmental concern, as the abovementioned case of Brenda exemplifies who also considers the environment in the realms of mobility, recycling, energy management, buying second-hand and activism. For the balancing environmentalist it is more important to make their wider set of practices comply with their environmental convictions. To put it in the words of Arthur, "you adapt in order to be coherent with what you say, what you do, you adopt more responsible practices".

Lastly, comprehensive environmentalists have similar bundles of practice as balancing environmentalists, but with a slightly higher average of connected practices ($n = 5$ vs. $n = 3$ for balancing environmentalists). Additionally, almost all comprehensive environmentalists include eating out in their environmental concern, and are also more advanced in arriving at eating out sustainably. They do so for instance by discussing organic restaurants within their social circle or by having phone applications with overviews of environmentally friendly dinner options. Comprehensive environmentalists' basic narrative seems to be based on their concern with environmental sustainability. It is this conviction that serves as a core around which other practices are integrated and their lives are shaped. To speak with Shove, Pantzar and Watson [22], "[a]s people become committed to the practices they carry, their status changes sometimes to the point that they become that which they do" (p. 70).

4.2.6. Implications for Understanding Access

Having detailed each of the types with their respective modes of recruitment, modes of engagement, degrees of commitment and bundles of practice, we will now show how these indicators and the types they construct help understanding access. We will do so by first elaborating the shared access issues of housing and finances and detailing the response of each type to the financial challenge. Next, more particular access issues encountered by each type will be discussed, i.e., convenience among food environmentalists and social bonds for comprehensive environmentalists. Finally, a brief outline will be given of our conclusions from this case study.

In general, the amount of access issues is not significantly higher or lower for any of the three types, but their nature differs. One exception is the issue of housing, which is a similar challenge for each type. Problems encountered in this domain include the absence of ovens or freezers, the latter of which prevents storing left-over meals. Living together with other people also influences access to sustainable food, in two different ways. When fellow residents show a similar concern with the environment, access increases due to the exchange of for instance recipes and tips for good stores and restaurants. On the other hand, when housemates do not care as much for the environment, this sometimes presents difficulties because budgetary priorities will, for instance, differ between environmentalists and their housemates. In general, then, interviewees express that living alone is easier because it allows them to make their own choices—although it does come with other problems, such as struggling with quantities of food.

Turning to finances, for all interviewees monthly budgets are restricted, with an average total budget of 975 euros and an average food budget of 218 euros—two interviewees (both "comprehensive environmentalists") are excluded from the calculations regarding food budgets because they were unaware of how much money they spent on food, reiterating the profile of the comprehensive environmentalist as someone who does not feel too much hindered by finances when buying (sustainable) food. Indeed, examining the way in which students respond to the challenge of balancing finances with convictions reveals differences between the three types and significantly makes finances more of an issue for some than for others. To start with food environmentalists, these students spend 25% of their budgets on food, which is average. Their most important response to the higher costs of sustainable food is a resorting to shopping at the organic aisle of the supermarket. Moreover, they are also more selective in the products they buy sustainably. They tend to buy only some products in their environmentally-friendly version, mostly dairy, fruits, and vegetables. Although food environmentalists do express a willingness to pay a bit more for sustainable food, they envisage this as something to develop and expand in the future, when they will have a higher and steadier income. In short, finances substantially impede food environmentalists' access to sustainable food.

Balancing environmentalists have the lowest overall budgets (865 euros) but the highest food budgets (235 euros). They also show a readiness to pay more for sustainable food. Nevertheless, the tension between budgetary constraints and a commitment to sustainability is still quite strongly felt in this group, in which the latter typically loses out. Like food environmentalists, this type is also selective about the food products they buy sustainable. Similarly, balancing environmentalists generally consider organic stores too expensive for doing all groceries and they, therefore, also shop at the supermarket's organic aisle. However, at the same time among this type there is a stronger awareness of the limits of buying sustainable food at the supermarket. As Tisha puts it, "I prefer buying organic [food] that is not so expensive. It's a bit better. But I know that sometimes it's not great either". Finances, thus, present a smaller, but still reasonable, access issue for balancing environmentalists.

Comprehensive environmentalists do have slightly higher overall budgets than the other types (1150 euros), but neither their average food budgets nor the percentage of their budgets spent on food are significantly high (200 euros; 16%). Rather, in weighing prices against principles comprehensive environmentalists go further in favouring the latter, which translates into a larger willingness to adapt in the face of the financial challenge. For instance, comprehensive environmentalists are more ready to prioritize food in their budgeting, as Bruno illustrates:

> "I figured that if I try to minimize eating out in restaurants, that really makes a significant price difference, I figured that on that condition I could afford almost any organic product I want. Rather than saying, I'm going out, and afterwards I'll restrict my budget and buy poor quality stuff, I prefer to try to limit outings, or in any case to restaurants for example, to continue being able to afford buying organic."

Financial considerations are thus not entirely absent among this last type, but they do not constitute an insuperable obstruction to accessing sustainable food: strategies can be employed to circumvent the challenge.

Moving on to more specific access issues, then, food environmentalists recurrently show a tendency to let "convenience" determine access to sustainable food. For instance, if the store closest to one's home is a shop that neither has an extensive variety of organic products nor offers products without packaging, then food environmentalists will typically still go to this store and end up buying less environmentally friendly products, simply because it is easiest and least time-consuming to go there. Another illustration can be found in Sadia, who avoids going to the Biocoop (an organic chain store) across the street from where she lives, because of their extensive offer of loose products. She finds this too demanding because it obliges her to always bring her own bags and jars, so she ends up going to another store. Sadia is also never actually going to the fresh market despite planning to do so, because it opens only on Sunday mornings and she likes to party on the weekend and sleep in.

Among comprehensive environmentalists, in turn, the issue of convenience in access is nearly absent. Instead, these practitioners have conformed themselves to the rhythm and temporality of the practice and are willing to adjust their routines to arrive at buying sustainable food. They are ready to adapt other practices to better accommodate the practice of buying sustainable food (whereas, for food environmentalists, this priority is reversed). Rather, comprehensive environmentalists' most significant and distinctive access issue is the role of social ties. All category members refer to having, at some point, felt hindered by their social environment in choosing for environmentally-friendly food. For instance, Stephanie, who is a vegan, has felt socially obliged to discard her vegan principles when offered home-made cake containing dairy products, feeling it would be socially unacceptable or rude to refuse when someone had put in so much effort.

From another perspective, the social environment can also advance access. Most comprehensive environmentalists have likeminded social circles: a concern with the environment seems to be an important factor for them in choosing a social group. Finding access then becomes easier within this social circle, and awareness grows through it. Nevertheless, perhaps due to this increasing sensitivity which goes hand in hand with higher levels of engagement, commitment and bundles of practice, the social does become more of an obstacle *outside* of the comprehensive environmentalists' circle of friends. Comprehensive environmentalists' interpretation of what constitutes sustainable food also includes more aspects than that of the other types, meaning they will more frequently be confronted with and challenged on their principles in everyday life as their convictions simply cover a larger domain.

Finally, despite the variations in access issues elaborated above, a more general conclusion can already be drawn. Looking from a practice perspective has helped explain the success of some and the failure of other food distribution channels in providing access. When comparing the AMAPs with the fresh markets, attention is drawn to the different temporalities these practices produce and to the extent to which these are in agreement with those of student life. With time in student life being a rather unpredictable element, the fixed and limited "opening hours" of fresh markets present a problem of access. On the other hand, the AMAP is a means of food provision that has successfully evolved itself to fit the rhythms of student life. As the original annual, one-size AMAPs were too rigid for students, special student AMAPs were installed that were specifically tailored to student lifestyles. Moreover, AMAP membership only requires a small effort, i.e., picking up the vegetable box each week. Since distribution usually takes place at the university, this does not require large detours and can easily be combined with going to classes.

What matters most, then, is enabling access by better aligning the various practices associated with buying sustainable food and their temporalities and rhythms with the lifestyle of students, in order to also include those who are less committed. Concretely, this is already happening by accommodating shoppers through making organic products available in supermarkets, which only requires a slight change of course, and by adapting the AMAP to better fit the rhythm of student life. Alternatively, efforts could respond to students' habits of eating in university canteens and aim for offering sustainable food options there, which again demands no grand gestures but anticipates well people's propensity for convenience. Moreover, there is also potential in the increase of the use of digital applications such as OptiMiam (an anti-food waste app with an overview of the local offer of leftover fresh products) and YesWeGreen (an app with information on local eco-friendly projects such as restaurants, second-hand stores, AMAPs and community gardens). Together with AMAP Facebook groups and online food blogs for recipes, these digital technologies correspond well with student lifestyle and contain promises for increasing access to buying sustainable food.

5. Discussion and Conclusions

This reflection starts with an evaluation of the indicators used above, then moves to assessing the typology as a whole, and finally concludes with some insights for theorizing on and researching access to sustainable food.

5.1. Evaluating the Indicators

In evaluating the indicators used above, it is important to note that it is jointly, as a portfolio, which serves to illustrate this paper's central argument that access is embedded in a network of socially-shared tastes and meanings, knowledge and skills, and materials and infrastructure. Each indicator highlights one particular aspect of this embeddedness. The first indicator, *mode of recruitment*, proves useful for its insights into practice trajectories, which are significant towards understanding the extent of people's concern with sustainability and/or food, and as such towards explaining people's actual buying practices. The distinctions between continuation, modification, and transformation also aid further understanding of successes and failures, stability and change, and directions of practices' development. Secondly, the indicator *mode of engagement* does not differentiate as strongly between the three types, but does illustrate how people's motivations for participating in the practice of buying sustainable food need not necessarily stem from a concern with sustainability, but can also come from other considerations, such as health worries. Thirdly, the indicator *degree of commitment* distinguishes more clearly and is important in light of understanding and evaluating dynamics and change within the practice. In order for the practice to persist and even expand, it seems important to continue recruiting practitioners, like the comprehensive environmentalists, with high degrees of commitment and willingness to push their own limits and the limits of the practice. This indicator is also useful for its insights into which access issues would prove to be insurmountable for some practitioners, for instance when buying sustainable food would mean travelling twice as long as for normal food shopping or when social ties compete with principles. Lastly, the indicator *bundles of practices* most clearly separates between the first and third types and serves to explain the extent to which meaning is attached to sustainability and, consequently, the place of the practice in a practitioner's lifestyle.

5.2. Reflecting on the Typology

What distinguishes one practice from another, or "[w]hat is it that allows one to say that many performances which are not identical are all part of the same practice"? [14] (p. 146). This central query of practice theories arises upon reflecting on the typology used in this paper. What exactly does this typology describe: are the three types of environmentalists just distinct participants in one and the same practice (a typology of practitioners) or do the types represent different practices altogether (a typology of practices)? To answer this question, Dobernig, et al. [35] propose a two-fold assessment: (1) comparing the internal components of the practices at stake—i.e., Shove, Pantzar and Watson [22] materials, competences, and meanings; and (2) applying a diachronic approach to see how the practice of interest connects with other practices. Analysing the typology based on the first criterion suggest that materials, competences and meanings do not differ fundamentally between the types, but only gradually. The second criterion does however show considerable differences as shown above under indicator "bundles of practice".

Thus, differences between practitioners are the outcome of practitioners' varying portfolios—of which bundles of practice constitute one element. More committed practitioners will, accordingly, carry larger bundles of practices than less committed ones, but do still populate the same practice. Conceived of in this way, our typology of practitioners is in fact compatible with Dobernig et al.'s second criterion and its outcomes.

A final point on the relationship between the types: they should not be considered as three stages on a progressive scale, but rather as three different possible pathways within the practice. The various modes of recruitment correspond with significantly distinct motivations, commitments, and bundles of practices. These do not necessarily succeed one another: being a food environmentalist does not imply that one will ever become a comprehensive environmentalist. Rather, the types represent distinct routes through the practice.

5.3. Theorizing on Access

Finally, the findings of this study bear consequences for the conceptualization of access and for how to research and address it. When doing this we need to acknowledge the limits of our empirical study as it covers a limited group of students in Paris. Nevertheless, we can claim that, as our analysis has demonstrated, accessing sustainable food is characterized by plurality, containing different modes of recruitment and engagement, degrees of commitment, and bundles of practice. To understand access, it is crucial to dig deeper than the observable behaviour that is performed, and to disclose underlying meanings, ends, connections, etc. First, this makes clear that access cannot, and should not, be considered as the outcome of a singular practice. Rather, buying sustainable food is connected to numerous other practices in many different ways. Sometimes a link is established through shared meanings or ends, bundling several practices through a shared aim for more sustainability. At other times a connection is formed through competition, for instance when buying sustainable food competes for time with practices of working and studying. How these linkages develop and how strong they are differs between practitioners and depends on interactions within and between the different elements of practices, materials, meanings, and competences, resulting in various access outcomes. Like the effect of production on consumption, also access is moderated by the nexus of practices [14]. Crucially, this means that efforts to improve access cannot and should not address one single aspect only, but rather should build on understanding and addressing the continuous negotiations between and dynamics within practices and their elements. Thus, uniform strategies to promote sustainable food consumption are likely to be ineffective as they ignore these differences and dynamics. Designing more effective strategies to promote sustainable food consumption should, therefore, build on in-depth understanding of these practices of access and accept that no one singular strategy will suffice to reach all consumers.

Secondly, this also calls for a sensitivity for the interactions between materials and infrastructure, on the one hand, and practitioners' lifestyles with their temporalities and preferences, on the other. Access is not solely determined by material components, but rather is a result of the interplay between the food on offer and people's trajectories, knowledge, meanings, narratives, and networks. This study's example of the success of the AMAP in aligning well with the rhythm of a student lifestyle versus the failure of fresh markets to achieve this, serves as an illustration of such an embedded understanding of access. Research should, therefore, focus on interactions rather than statically assessing material and infrastructural circumstances and deducing access issues from these. Nevertheless, the physical environment should not be discarded altogether, as materials clearly do provide an important background against which dynamics of access unfold.

Thirdly, this research also aimed to critically assess the decisive role that finances play in buying practices. Examination of the ways in which practitioners negotiate the question of money with their convictions leads to the conclusion that finances matter, but that limited resources are not insuperable in finding access to sustainable food. Even a "low-income" group like students manages to arrive more or less at their desired pattern of buying sustainable food. Assuming that this and similar groups are automatically excluded from accessing sustainable food due to their financial circumstances, therefore, seems unfounded. Rather, to account for the myriad strategies in which practitioners' resourcefulness in finding access becomes apparent, research should open up to include trade-offs between buying sustainable food and other practices, such as the adaptation of cooking preferences or habits and budgetary priorities in the face of financial challenges. Zooming out from the moment of buying sustainable food in this way allows for a more nuanced view of the role finances play in access.

Lastly, the above analysis has mostly focused on a consumer perspective, showing how actual buying patterns differ between practitioners, how consumption is contingent, and how mismatches can occur between supply and demand. By also studying more extensively the precise dynamics of production at play in the practice of buying sustainable food, production and consumption can be even better coordinated and access further improved.

Acknowledgments: The authors would like express their gratitude towards INRA, the French National Institute for Agricultural Research, for material and other support, with special thanks to Marie Plessz for her valuable insights and expertise during the data collection and analysis stage.

Author Contributions: Anke Brons and Peter Oosterveer conceived and designed the experiments; Anke Brons collected and analyzed the data; and Anke Brons and Peter Oosterveer wrote the paper.

Conflicts of Interest: The authors declare no conflict of interest.

References

1. Reisch, L.; Eberle, U.; Lorek, S. Sustainable food consumption: An overview of contemporary issues and policies. *Sustain. Sci. Pract. Policy* **2013**, *9*, 7–25.
2. Verain, M.C.; Bartels, J.; Dagevos, H.; Sijtsema, S.J.; Onwezen, M.C.; Antonides, G. Segments of sustainable food consumers: A literature review. *Int. J. Consum. Stud.* **2012**, *36*, 123–132. [CrossRef]
3. MacRae, R.; Szabo, M.; Anderson, K.; Louden, F.; Trillo, S. Empowering the citizen-consumer: Re-regulating consumer information to support the transition to sustainable and health promoting food systems in Canada. *Sustainability* **2012**, *4*, 2146–2175. [CrossRef]
4. Kollmuss, A.; Agyeman, J. Mind the gap: Why do people act environmentally and what are the barriers to pro-environmental behavior? *Environ. Educ. Res.* **2002**, *8*, 239–260. [CrossRef]

5.   Gorgitano, M.T.; Sodano, V. Sustainable food consumption: Concept and policies. *Calitatea* **2014**, *15*, 207.
6.   Lucan, S.C.; Maroko, A.R.; Sanon, O.; Frias, R.; Schechter, C.B. Urban farmers' markets: Accessibility, offerings, and produce variety, quality, and price compared to nearby stores. *Appetite* **2015**, *90*, 23–30. [CrossRef] [PubMed]
7.   Walker, R.E.; Keane, C.R.; Burke, J.G. Disparities and access to healthy food in the United States: A review of food deserts literature. *Health Place* **2010**, *16*, 876–884. [CrossRef] [PubMed]
8.   Rose, D.; Richards, R. Food store access and household fruit and vegetable use among participants in the US Food Stamp Program. *Public Health Nutr.* **2004**, *7*, 1081–1088. [CrossRef] [PubMed]
9.   Giampietri, E.; Koemle, D.; Yu, X.; Finco, A. Consumers' Sense of Farmers' Markets: Tasting Sustainability or Just Purchasing Food? *Sustainability* **2016**, *8*, 1157. [CrossRef]
10. Vittersø, G.; Tangeland, T. The role of consumers in transitions towards sustainable food consumption. The case of organic food in Norway. *J. Clean. Prod.* **2015**, *92*, 91–99. [CrossRef]
11. Goodland, R. The concept of environmental sustainability. *Annu. Rev. Ecol. Syst.* **1995**, *26*, 1–24. [CrossRef]
12. Flyvbjerg, B. Five Minsunderstandings about Case-Study Research. *Qual. Inq.* **2006**, *12*, 219–245. [CrossRef]
13. Dubuisson-Quellier, S.; Gojard, S. Why are food practices not (more) environmentally friendly in France? The role of collective standards and symbolic boundaries in food practices. *Environ. Policy Gov.* **2016**, *26*, 89–100. [CrossRef]
14. Warde, A. Consumption and theories of practice. *J. Consum. Cult.* **2005**, *5*, 131–153. [CrossRef]
15. Halkier, B. A practice theoretical perspective on everyday dealings with environmental challenges of food consumption. *Anthropol. Food* **2009**. Available online: http://aof.revues.org/6405 (accessed on 20 March 2017).
16. Røpke, I. Theories of practice—New inspiration for ecological economic studies on consumption. *Ecol. Econ.* **2009**, *68*, 2490–2497. [CrossRef]
17. Shove, E. *Comfort, Cleanliness and Convenience: The Social Organization of Normality*; Berg: Oxford, UK, 2003; Volume 810.
18. Southerton, D. Analysing the temporal organization of daily life: Social constraints, practices and their allocation. *Sociology* **2006**, *40*, 435–454. [CrossRef]
19. Spaargaren, G.; Van Vliet, B. Lifestyles, consumption and the environment: The ecological modernization of domestic consumption. *Environ. Politics* **2000**, *9*, 50–76.
20. Warde, A. *The Practice of Eating*; Polity Press: Cambridge, UK, 2016.
21. Schatzki, T.R. *Social Practices: A Wittgensteinian Approach to Human Activity and the Social*; Cambridge University Press: Cambridge, UK, 1996.
22. Shove, E.; Pantzar, M.; Watson, M. *The Dynamics of Social Practice: Everyday Life and How It Changes*; Sage Publications: Thousand Oaks, CA, USA, 2012.
23. Plessz, M.; Gojard, S. Fresh is best? Social position, cooking, and vegetable consumption in France. *Sociology* **2012**, *49*, 172–190. [CrossRef]
24. Schatzki, T.R. *Where the Action Is (On Large Social Phenomena Such as Sociotechnical Regimes)*; Working Paper; Sustainable Practices Research Group, University of Manchester: Manchester, UK, 2011.
25. Hoibian, S. *Enquête sur les Attitudes et Comportements des Français en Matière d'Environnement: Edition 2011*; CRÉDOC: Paris, France, 2012.
26. AgenceBio. Les Chiffres-clés de la Bio—La Bio en France: De la Production a la Consommation. Available online: http://www.agencebio.org/sites/default/files/upload/documents/4_Chiffres/BrochureCC/cc2016_france_1.pdf (accessed on 20 March 2017).
27. Cavard, P.; Baros, C. *Neighbourhood Proximity of Commerce. Distribution Concepts and Consumer Lifestyles*; Centre Technique Interprofessionnel des Fruits et Légumes: Paris, France, 2005.
28. Seyfang, G. Cultivating carrots and community: Local organic food and sustainable consumption. *Environ. Values* **2007**, *16*, 105–123. [CrossRef]
29. MIRAMAP. Les AMAP. Available online: http://miramap.org/-Les-AMAP-.html (accessed on 20 March 2017).
30. Gram-Hanssen, K. Standby consumption in households analyzed with a practice theory approach. *J. Ind. Ecol.* **2010**, *14*, 150–165. [CrossRef]
31. INSEE. Nomenclature des Professions et Catégories Socioprofessionnelles (PCS). Available online: https://www.insee.fr/fr/information/2497952 (accessed on 20 March 2017).
32. Schatzki, T.R. *The Site of the Social: A Philosophical Account of the Constitution of Social Life and Change*; Pennsylvania State University Press: University Park, PA, USA, 2002.

33. Giddens, A. *The Constitution of Society: Outline of the Theory of Structuration*; University of California Press: Oakland, CA, USA, 1984.

34. Bourdieu, P. *The Logic of Practice*; Stanford University Press: Redwood City, CA, USA, 1990.

35. Dobernig, K.; Veen, E.J.; Oosterveer, P. Growing urban food as an emerging social practice. In *Practice Theory and Research: Exploring the Dynamics of Social Life*; Spaargaren, G., Weenink, D., Lamers, M., Eds.; Routledge: London, UK; New York, NY, USA, 2016.

sustainability

MDPI

Article

Attribute Segmentation and Communication Effects on Healthy and Sustainable Consumer Diet Intentions

Muriel C. D. Verain [1,*], Siet J. Sijtsema [1], Hans Dagevos [2] and Gerrit Antonides [3]

[1] Wageningen Economic Research, Wageningen University & Research, P.O. Box 35, 6700 AA Wageningen, The Netherlands; siet.sijtsema@wur.nl

[2] Wageningen Economic Research, Wageningen University & Research, P.O. Box 29703, 2502 LS The Hague, The Netherlands; hans.dagevos@wur.nl

[3] Urban Economics, Wageningen University & Research, P.O. Box 8130, 6700 EW Wageningen, The Netherlands; gerrit.antonides@wur.nl

* Correspondence: muriel.verain@wur.nl; Tel: +31-(0)70-335-831

Academic Editor: Marc A. Rosen
Received: 29 January 2017; Accepted: 28 April 2017; Published: 4 May 2017

Abstract: A shift towards more sustainable consumer diets is urgently needed. Dietary guidelines state that changes towards less animal-based and more plant-based diets are beneficial in terms of sustainability and, in addition, will have a positive effect on public health. Communication on these guidelines should be most effective when tailored to the motivations of specific consumer segments. Therefore, the current study (1) segments consumers based on the importance they attach to sustainability, health, taste and price of food in several food categories; and (2) tests different ways (with health arguments, sustainability arguments, or both) of communicating the dietary guideline. Three segments have been identified: pro-self, average, and sustainable conscious consumers. For pro-self and average consumers, the communication of both health and sustainability benefits made them think most about sustainability, although communication did not result in changes in dietary intentions in these segments. For sustainable conscious consumers, intention to reduce their meat consumption increased when both health and sustainability benefits were communicated. These research outcomes indicate the importance of segmentation research in the development of dietary messages. In addition, the findings show the importance of taking product category differences into account in studying consumer food motivations and intentions.

Keywords: communication; consumer segmentation; attributes; food; sustainability; health; experiment; dietary guidelines

---

1. Introduction

Food consumption patterns are increasingly related to health (e.g., obesity) and sustainability (e.g., environmental pollution and animal welfare issues) challenges [1–5]. Sustainability of food consumption includes a reduction of the ecological footprint related to carbon emission, water and energy use in production and transportation of food, animal welfare and fair trade. A shift towards more sustainable and healthy diets is urgently needed and therefore synergies between sustainability and health are important [3,6–8]. Many countries provide national dietary guidelines to inform their citizens and advise them on their food consumption. Currently, nutritional guidelines are focused on the healthiness of a diet, but debates on whether these guidelines should consider health and sustainability aspects of diets simultaneously are emerging. While Lang and colleagues [9] already pled for the integration of human health and environment ("planetary health") in the field of food, even more specifically Hoek and colleagues [10] recommended that health should remain the overarching principle for policies and actions concerned with shifting consumer behaviors, as this personal benefit appears to have a greater potential to support behavior change.

Recently, the Live Well for LIFE project funded by the EU and WWF formulated the following policy recommendation: "National governments should develop policies to give more balanced, integrated dietary recommendations on healthy and sustainable diets" [11]. In 2011, the Health Council of the Netherlands published a pioneering report in which guidelines for a healthy diet were evaluated from an ecological perspective [12]. This report concludes that the use of less animal-based and more plant-based diets would lead to health and ecological gains simultaneously. In the US, a governmental advisory report with similar conclusions has been published recently [13]. Changes towards more plant-based and less animal-based diets have been widely acknowledged in the scientific literature as benefiting both healthiness and sustainability of present-day diets [5,7,12,14–16]. A less animal-based diet would significantly reduce emissions, is beneficial in terms of animal welfare, and can improve public health [3,16]. In addition, increased consumption of fruits and vegetables would promote public health [17–21]. Currently, adherence to nutritional guidelines is low. Current intake levels of fruits and vegetables are far below recommendations in most European regions as well as in the US [17,18,21–23], and meat intake is too high in many affluent countries [3,14,24] despite nutritional campaigns.

Consumers have an important role to play in the desired shift towards more healthy and sustainable diets [6,25–29]. In order to achieve a change in consumers' dietary patterns, a whole range of interventions can be used. Rothschild [30] developed a conceptual framework for interventions in the public health domain. He poses that motivation, opportunity (a supporting environment) and ability (knowledge and skills) are prerequisites for behavior change. Education (information), marketing (environmental incentives) and law are identified as the three main categories of interventions. The expected effectiveness of these three categories of interventions depend on the level of motivation, opportunity and ability. For example, when consumers are motivated but lack ability, education can help to develop the ability to behave. Which of the three aspects is most important to a person also depends on his or her stage of change towards more healthy and/or sustainable diets [31]. First, awareness should be created that something needs to be changed, which may result in increased motivation. Education can help to create awareness. When a person is motivated to change, the person should be able and have the opportunity to conduct the desired behavior [31].

Information campaigns and educational measures are by far the most used interventions in Europe that aim to achieve behavior change towards more healthy diets. The effectiveness of such campaigns on awareness and attitudes seems quite strong; but so far, nutritional campaigns have had limited success in changing behavior [32–35]. Also, in the domain of sustainable behavior, information has not proven very successful in achieving behavior change [36]. A possible reason for the ineffectiveness of food campaigns can be the "one-size-fits-all approach" [37]. As an antidote to this approach, the essential role of audience segmentation in developing effective communication is widely acknowledged [37–42]. Consumer populations are heterogeneous and should be segmented into more homogenous subgroups with regard to key characteristics [43]. Consumers can differ, for example, in their food choice motives, which are important determinants of food choices [24,44–49] and are food-category specific [47]. Because consumers differ in the importance they attach to food choice motives, they may also differ in the arguments and information that appeal to them most. Nutrition campaigns may benefit from developing tailored messages that fit the motives of the receiver, because motivation is an important determinant of the way in which a message is cognitively processed and perceived [50]. Therefore, it might not be advisable to communicate dietary guidelines as either guidelines for a healthy diet, or guidelines for a healthy and sustainable diet. The most effective communication in terms of behavior change might depend on the motivations of the audience.

Intuitively, it seems favorable to focus on more than one motive in nutrition interventions, in order to ensure that arguments appeal to different consumers. In addition, a dietary change might be perceived as more attractive when multiple goals can be simultaneously satisfied by

Sustainability **2017**, *9*, 743

performing a single act. Kareklas, Carlson and Muehling [51] show that promoting organic meat with both health arguments and environmental arguments is more effective in stimulating organic purchases as compared to an ad providing only health arguments. On the other hand, there are several reasons to believe that it might not always be beneficial to combine arguments within the same communication [52]. Motives can sometimes be conflicting or be perceived as conflicting [6,53,54]. In this context, it is useful to note two important distinctions in food choice motives. First, some motives relate to present-based benefits (e.g., price), whereas other motives relate to future-based benefits (e.g., health and sustainability) [55]. Second, some motives are related to individual benefits (e.g., price or health) whereas other motives are related to social benefits (e.g., sustainability) [6,56]. Consumers differ in whether they focus more on current or future benefits [57] and whether they attach more importance to egoistic or altruistic/biospheric values [58,59]. A mismatch between a message and the audience can undermine the credibility and the persuasiveness of the message [39].

The literature does not provide a decisive answer on whether nutritional guidelines can best be communicated as healthy, sustainable or both. Our first hypothesis is that the optimal communication differs across motive-based population subgroups, because we expect a message to be most effective when it matches the motives of the audience. Second, we hypothesize that the effect of such an informational intervention on behavioral intentions will differ across motive-based segments, as providing information is probably not sufficient when motivation is low. In short, the current study aims to identify and characterize motive-based consumer segments and to explore how the nutritional guideline should best be communicated to the identified segments in order to increase their intention to consume according to this guideline.

2. Materials and Methods

An online consumer survey was used to gather cross-sectional data in the Netherlands. A research agency collected the data in spring 2014. The sample was representative for the Dutch adult population in terms of age, gender and education. Selection criteria were used to exclude consumers who never or seldom make dinner choices and/or never or seldom shop for groceries. The survey consisted of two parts. The second part was filled out approximately one week after the first part. In the first part, the segmentation variables, the profiling variables and socio-demographic variables were assessed. In the second part, the respondents were randomly assigned to one of four experimental conditions. After the experiment, respondents were asked to fill out the manipulation checks and the dependent measures. In total, 1308 respondents filled out the first survey. Of these 1308 respondents, 829 also participated in the experiment; 46.1% of whom were male and 53.9% were female. The respondents' age ranged from 18 to 90 years with a mean of 50.1 years (the total Dutch population in 2014 consisted of 50.5% females, with a mean age of 41.0 years).

The study consists of three aspects. First, segmentation variables that measure food choice motives are used to identify motive-based consumer segment. Second, profiling variables are used to gain insights into the characteristics of these segments that are important to consider in the development of effective (information) interventions. Third, the experiment will be used to test the hypothesis that (1) the optimal way of communicating the guideline differs across the identified segments; and (2) the effectiveness of such an informational intervention on behavioral intentions differs across the identified segments.

Segmentation variables: The identification of consumer segments was based on the importance consumers attached to a range of food-category specific motives. Price, taste, healthiness and a range of sustainability aspects were included. The perceived importance of these aspects was assessed for each of four product categories, as previous research showed that importance of motives is category specific [47]. Motives were measured with the following question: "I think it is important that [food category] is [motive]". An example item is: "I think it is important that dairy is animal friendly". The items were rated on seven-point Likert scales (1 = Totally disagree, 7 = Totally agree) [41]. In total, 55 items were included (see Figure 1). Data reduction was applied by conducting an exploratory factor analysis (EFA) with oblique rotation on the 13 or 14 ratings for each of the product categories separately to estimate the underlying factors. Though a detailed explanation of the procedure is beyond the scope of this article (for more information, see [47]), eight factors emerged from the analysis: one pro-self factor including price, taste and health; and one pro-social factor including all sustainability attributes for each of the four product categories. The total variance explained was 74.7% for dairy, 75.4% for meat, 76.8% for fish and 71.1% for vegetables. The resulting factor scores were mean centered per respondent, in order to cancel out response tendencies [60]. The correlations between the pairs of mean-centered factor scores were -0.353 for dairy, -0.362 for meat, -0.135 for fish and -0.404 for vegetables (all $p < 0.01$). The reliability scores (Cronbach's alpha) for the eight factors ranged from 0.793 to 0.968. Data reduction was checked with a confirmatory factor analysis (CFA) for each food category, each with two factors. Each of these models yielded comparable factor loadings and satisfactory fit (a Root Mean Square Error (RMSE) below 0.07 [61] and a Standardized Root Mean Square Residual (SRMR) below 0.08 indicate satisfactory model fit [62]. Comparative Fit Index (CFI), Non-Normed Fit Index (NNFI) and Goodness of Fit Index (GFI) of at least 0.90 indicate a satisfactory model fit [62,63]. Dairy: RMSE = 0.09, NNFI = 0.98, CFI = 0.98, SRMR = 0.03, GFI = 0.93; Meat: RMSE = 0.09, NNFI = 0.98, CFI = 0.98, SRMR = 0.02, GFI = 0.93; Fish: RMSE = 0.11, NNFI = 0.98, CFI = 0.98, SRMR = 0.03, GFI = 0.91; Vegetables: RMSE = 0.13, NNFI = 0.96, CFI = 0.97, SRMR = 0.04, GFI = 0.88), except for RMSE and, for vegetables, GFI.

To me it is important that dairy	To me it is important that meat	To me it is important that fish	To me it is important that vegetables
...is sustainable	...is sustainable	... is sustainable	...are sustainable
...is healthy	...is healthy	...is healthy	...are healthy
...is environmental friendly	...is environmental friendly	...is environmental friendly	...are environmental friendly
...gives little waste	...gives little waste	...gives little waste	...give little waste
...comes from the Netherlands	...comes from the Netherlands	...comes from the sea close to the Netherlands	...come from the Netherlands
...has a short transportation distance	...has a short transportation distance	...has a short transportation distance	...have a short transportation distance
...is animal friendly	...is animal friendly	...is caught in a sustainable way	...are seasonal
... comes from cows that walked outside	... comes from animals that walked outside	... is stated on the 'sustainable fish index'.	
...that I eat/drink is sustainable	...that I eat is sustainable	...that I eat is sustainable	...that I eat are sustainable
...has a sustainability logo	...has a sustainability logo	...has a sustainability logo	...have a sustainability logo
...comes from cows with a low usage of antibiotics	...comes from animals with a low usage of antibiotics	...comes from animals with a low usage of antibiotics	...have a low usage of pesticides
...is tasty	...is tasty	...is tasty	...are tasty
...is affordable	...is affordable	...is affordable	...are affordable
...is healthy and sustainable	...is healthy and sustainable	...is healthy and sustainable	...are healthy and sustainable

Figure 1. Segmentation variables.

The mean-centered factor scores on the importance of product-category attributes were used as segmentation variables in a two-step cluster analysis, performed in the Statistical Package for Social Sciences (SPSS 22). In the first step, a hierarchical agglomerative clustering procedure determined the number of clusters [64]. Log-likelihood was used as distance measure [65]. Cluster centroids were determined to be used as initial starting points in the second step [64,66]. In the second step, K-means clustering was used to group respondents into the final clusters [65]. Merging of clusters may depend on the input order of the cases [65] and therefore, analyses were run 10 times with randomly ordered cases [44,67]. Based on a combination of the lowest Bayesian Information Criterion (BIC) in the 10 runs, the agglomeration schedule and interpretability, the final cluster solution was chosen.

Profiling variables: A range of profiling variables was included to gain more insight into the characteristics of the segments. Food intake and behavior regarding the dietary guideline were included to evaluate how the identified segments currently perform in terms of sustainable food behavior. Life values, time orientation, agreement regarding the dietary guideline, stage in the transition towards more healthy and towards more sustainable eating, and socio-demographic and background characteristics were used as profiling variables, because these are important determinants of food intake and can give insights in how the segments can best be targeted.

Life values have been measured with a short version of Schwartz's value scale, developed by [59]. The scale included egoistic, altruistic and biospheric values measured with 13 items. Respondents were asked to rate the importance of the 13 values "as guiding principles in their lives" on a seven-point scale (1 = "Very unimportant", 7 = "Very important"). The 13 items were included in a factor analysis with oblique rotation. Three underlying factors were identified. The first factor included all biospheric values and explained 37.8% of the item variance. Cronbach's alpha of the four items was high (α = 0.90). The second factor included all egoistic values and explained 20.7% of the item variance. Cronbach's alpha could be improved by deleting "ambition". The remaining four items had a Cronbach's alpha of 0.78. The third factor included all altruistic values and explained 7.8% of the item variance. Cronbach's alpha of the four items was 0.84. The three constructs have been computed by averaging the items.

Time orientation has been measured with a short version of the Consideration of Future Consequences scale (CFC) [68]. Four items have been selected (items 1, 2, 10 and 11 of the original scale): the two items that scored highest on the consideration of future consequences factor and the two items that scored highest on the consideration of immediate consequences factor in a previous study [69]. The items were measured on a 7-point scale (1 = "Totally disagree", 7 = "Totally agree"). The four items were captured by two factors (CFC-future and CFC-immediate), explaining 41.5% and 34.4% of the variance, respectively. Cronbach's alpha of the scales were 0.69 and 0.67, respectively. The two constructs have been computed by averaging the items.

Agreement with and general behavior related to the dietary guideline stating the advice to eat less animal-based and more plant-based diets has been measured with two items. The items were: "A less animal-based (e.g., meat and dairy) and more plant-based (e.g., vegetables) diet is healthy and sustainable" and "While grocery shopping, I always consider the healthiness and the sustainability of the meal". The respondents were asked to indicate on a 7-point scale (1 = "Totally not", 7 = "Totally") whether they agreed with the statements.

Stage of change has been measured with four statements about health and four statements about sustainability. These statements reflected the respondents' commitment to purchase healthy or sustainable food. The stages are based on the transtheoretical model [31] and represent a pre-contemplation stage, a contemplation stage, a preparation stage and an action and maintenance stage. The statements were adapted for healthy food and sustainable food from Gwozdz, Netter, Biartmarz and Reisch [70]. Respondents were asked to think about how important sustainability, respectively healthiness, are when they buy food. Subsequently they were asked to choose one of the four health statements and one of the four sustainability statements that best matched their considerations. The four statements were: "I base my food purchase decisions on price, taste, quality and/or convenience. I am not concerned with sustainability [health] issues and I don't think about them when I purchase food," "I believe that sustainability [health] is important, but it is too difficult and time-consuming to base my food purchase decisions on them," "When it is easy to do, I use sustainability [health] information on these issues in my purchase decisions," and "I make an effort to learn about sustainability [health], and I am willing to pay more or sacrifice on product quality in order to use sustainability [health] in my food purchases".

Food intake has been measured with thirteen items. The respondents were asked to indicate how many days a week (0 to 7) they ate a range of products or meals. The included items were: (1) organic meat, organic fruits and vegetables, organic dairy, organic eggs, free range meat, products with a sustainability logo; (2) small portions of meat, small portions of dairy, small portions, seasonal vegetables; (3) vegetarian burgers, no meat; and (4) no dairy. Four underlying factors were identified. The first factor included consumption of sustainable products and explained 32.0% of the item variance. Cronbach's alpha of the six items was high (α = 0.85). The second factor included items concerning the consumption of small portions of food products and seasonable food and explained 13.4% of the item variance. Cronbach's alpha of the four items was 0.64. The third factor included consumption of vegetarian meals and explained 10.4% of the item variance. Cronbach's alpha of the remaining two items was 0.52. The last factor consisted of only one item, dairy-free meals, and explained 8.5% of the item variance. The constructs have been computed by averaging the items, thus indicating the average frequency of consuming a particular food category. Finally, questions on gender, age, education, income, and family composition were included in the survey. Differences between the resulting segments on the profiling variables were investigated through ANOVA and Chi-square tests, depending on the measurement scale of the variable.

Experimental design: The experiment was a 2 × 2 (health arguments vs. sustainability arguments) full-factorial between-subjects design in which participants were randomly assigned to one of four conditions: (1) a health condition received information on health benefits of having a less animal-based and more plant-based diet; (2) a sustainability condition received information on sustainability benefits of having a less animal-based and more plant-based diet; (3) a health and sustainability condition received combined information; and (4) a control condition received neutral information on eating behavior (without health or sustainability arguments) (see Appendix A). After having read the information, the participants were asked to note a few words (one to five) that came to their mind when they thought about healthy eating, sustainable eating, healthy and sustainable eating, and eating in general, respectively in the four conditions, in order to force them to think of these aspects. In addition, they were asked to give an example of a healthy, a sustainable, a healthy and sustainable, or general food choice, respectively in the four conditions, again to force them to think of these aspects.

As a manipulation check, respondents were asked on a 7-point scale (1 = "Very little", 7 = "Very much") to indicate to what extent the text they had just read made them think about healthiness, sustainability, price, taste and convenience of food. A second manipulation check was conducted by counting the number of times certain words were associated with the information texts in the four conditions. To assess the impact of the experimental manipulation, one-way between-subjects ANOVAs were carried out on the first manipulation check. The same analyses were repeated per identified segment, in order to see whether the manipulation differed in effectiveness across segments. For the second manipulation check, two researchers recoded the words that were mentioned into broader categories. Frequencies of categories with more than 20 counts were compared across conditions using Chi-squared tests.

For the main analyses, a general linear model was used to test the main effect of experimental manipulation, the main effect of segment, and the interaction effect between manipulation and segment. The dependent variables included a range of sustainable and unsustainable food choice intentions related to dinner options. Respondents were asked to indicate, for each of 26 dinner components, the number of days (0–7) in the following week they intended to choose that component for their dinner. The options differed in quantities of unsustainable food (meat and dairy) as well as in sustainability of the production method (e.g., organic and animal friendly) and components were related to one of four product categories: vegetables, dairy, meat and "other". Five underlying factors were identified with a total explained variance of 67.0%. The first factor included consumption intentions of sustainable products and explained 38.1% of the item variance. One item, consumption of small portions of meat, has been removed from the scale in order to improve its reliability. The remaining six items had a Cronbach's alpha of 0.92. The second factor included items concerning intentions to consume meals with (regular and large amounts of) meat and explained 12.9% of the item variance. Removing the item concerning consumption of large amounts of meat improved the reliability of the scale. Cronbach's alpha of the remaining three items was 0.84. The third factor included items concerning intentions to consume meals with (regular) dairy and explained 6.7% of the item variance. Deletion of the item concerning the intention to consume small amounts of dairy improved the reliability of the scale leading to a Cronbach's alpha of 0.86 for the remaining three items. The fourth factor included items concerning intentions to consume meals with vegetables and regular products and explained 5.1% of the item variance. Cronbach's alpha of the four items was 0.75. The final factor included consumption intentions of large amounts of meat, large amounts of vegetables and products that could be used as meat replacers (nuts, fish, meat replacers, legumes) and explained 4.2% of item variance. Cronbach's alpha of the eight items was 0.88. The factors were moderately correlated, with values ranging from 0.11 to 0.52. The constructs have been computed by averaging the items.

3. Results

3.1. Segmentation on Food Category Attribute Importance

The first step in the data analysis was the classification of respondents into homogenous consumer segments. The cluster analysis resulted in three segments with relatively homogenous importance ratings of the food category specific attributes:

1. Pro-selves
2. Average consumers
3. Conscious consumers

The cluster centroids are shown in Table 1.

Table 1. Cluster centroids.

Segmentation Variable	Pro-Self [1]	Average	Conscious
	Mean (sd)	Mean (sd)	Mean (sd)
Dairy_Sustainable	−0.80 [a] (0.68) [2]	−0.19 [b] (0.32)	0.31 [c] (0.32)
Dairy_Healthy/Tasty/Affordable	0.75 [a] (1.14)	0.22 [b] (0.43)	−0.31 [c] (0.46)
Meat_Sustainable	−0.70 [a] (0.79)	−0.18 [b] (0.35)	0.27 [c] (0.37)
Meat_Healthy/Taste/Affordable	0.90 [a] (1.00)	0.26 [b] (0.38)	−0.37 [c] (0.58)
Fish_Sustainable	−0.84 [a] (0.84)	−0.18 [b] (0.32)	0.31 [c] (0.31)
Fish_Healthy/Tasty/Affordable	0.27 [a] (1.52)	0.24 [a] (0.38)	−0.20 [b] (0.42)
Vegetables_Sustainable	−0.63 [a] (1.026)	−0.31 [b] (0.40)	0.33 [c] (0.31)
Vegetables_Healthy/Tasty/Affordable	1.04 [a] (0.50)	0.14 [b] (0.42)	−0.34 [c] (0.51)

[1] The pro-self cluster included 116 respondents (14.0%), the average cluster included 253 respondents (30.5%), and the conscious cluster included 460 respondents (55.5%). [2] Different superscripts indicate significantly different means in each row following ANOVA post-hoc Tukey test at $p < 0.05$.

Cluster 1 was the smallest segment, including 14.0% of the respondents. This cluster scored relatively high on all pro-self factors and relatively low on all sustainability factors. Apparently, the relative importance of pro-self attributes (price, taste and health) was higher in this cluster compared to the other clusters. Therefore, this cluster was labeled the pro-self cluster. The pro-self cluster consisted of 53% males and the mean age was 47 years.

Cluster 2 represented 30.5% of the respondents. Respondents in this cluster attached about average importance to pro-self factors and sustainability factors for all product categories. Therefore, this cluster was labelled "average consumers". The average cluster consisted of 50% males, and the mean age was 50 years. This segment had the highest number of respondents in the youngest age group (18–29 years).

Cluster 3 was the largest cluster, representing 55.5% (N = 460) of the sample. This cluster attached relatively high importance to the sustainability attributes compared to pro-self attributes. Therefore, this cluster was labelled "sustainable conscious consumers" (or "conscious consumers" in short). Cluster 3 consisted of 58% females and had the highest mean age of 53 years, and the highest percentage of people over 65 years of age.

The segments did not show any significant differences in education, income and household composition. In addition, the segments did not differ in the number of times per week the respondents cooked a hot meal, went grocery shopping, or decided what would be served for dinner.

3.1.1. Life Values and Time Orientation

Both egoistic motives ($F(2826) = 4.39$, $p < 0.05$) and biospheric motives ($F(2826) = 34.60$, $p < 0.001$) differed significantly between segments. Pro-selves had a significant lower mean score ($M = 3.11$) on egoistic motives than average consumers ($M = 3.42$) and conscious consumers ($M = 3.45$). Altruistic values showed no significant differences. Biospheric values were lowest for pro-selves ($M = 4.60$), followed by average consumers ($M = 5.21$) and conscious consumers had the highest mean score on biospheric values ($M = 5.58$). Peace, equality and justice were the most important values for pro-selves as well as for average consumers. Conscious consumers also valued peace and equality most, but protection of nature scored on the third place for this segment.

Consideration of future consequences differed significantly between the segments ($F(2826) = 21.86$, $p < 0.001$) with conscious consumers ($M = 4.43$) considering future consequences more than the pro-selves ($M = 3.71$) and average consumers ($M = 3.98$). Consideration of immediate consequences did not differ significantly across segments ($M = 3.78$ for pro-selves, $M = 3.72$ for average consumers, and $M = 3.56$ for conscious consumers).

3.1.2. Agreement with the Dietary Guideline and Related Behavior

Agreement with the dietary guideline ($F(2826) = 37.29$, $p < 0.001$) and the consideration of healthiness and sustainability in food purchasing ($F(2826) = 80.57$, $p < 0.001$) both differed significantly across segments. Pro-selves ($M = 4.08$) and average consumers ($M = 4.38$) agreed to a lesser degree that eating less animal-based and more plant-based food provides health and sustainability benefits than conscious consumers ($M = 5.15$). Pro-selves also considered health and sustainability least while grocery shopping ($M = 3.09$), followed by average consumers ($M = 3.86$), and conscious consumers considered health and sustainability most ($M = 4.77$).

3.1.3. Transition Stage

A large majority (69.8%) of pro-selves were beginning to make the transition towards sustainable food choices and towards health (42.2%). About half of the average consumers were beginning to make the transition towards sustainable consumption, but they were equally divided over the transition stages towards healthy food consumption. Conscious consumers were about equally divided over the transition stages towards sustainable consumption, but more than a third (36.5%) were in the most progressed stage towards healthy food consumption, indicating that health was important in their food purchases.

3.1.4. Food Intake

Intake of sustainable food products ($F(2826) = 86.15$, $p < 0.001$), small portions ($F(2826) = 7.19$, $p < 0.01$), and vegetarian meals ($F(2826) = 12.30$, $p < 0.001$) all differed significantly between the segments. Pro-selves consumed sustainable products the least frequently ($M = 0.51$), followed by average consumers ($M = 1.04$), and conscious consumers consumed sustainable products the most frequently ($M = 1.98$). Regarding the intake of small portions, pro-selves scored significantly lower ($M = 2.84$) as compared to average consumers ($M = 3.19$) and conscious consumers ($M = 3.41$). Vegetarian intake was significantly more frequent for conscious consumers ($M = 1.24$) than for pro-selves ($M = 0.74$) and average consumers ($M = 0.81$).

3.2. Effect of Communication on Thoughts and Meal Intentions

Overall, the manipulation checks showed that respondents in both the sustainability condition and the combined condition had started to think more about sustainability than those in the health and control conditions ($F(3825) = 12.37$, $p < 0.001$). In addition, respondents in the control condition thought more about taste than those in the other conditions ($F(3825) = 12.598$, $p < 0.001$) (see Table 2). No differences were found across conditions in the extent to which the provided information made the respondents think of healthiness, convenience and price.

Concerning differences between segments in the amount of thoughts after the manipulations, several significant differences were found (see Table 2). Respondents in the pro-self segment who received health and sustainability arguments indicated that the information made them think more about sustainability, compared to pro-selves in the control group ($F(3112) = 3.31$, $p < 0.05$). In addition, taste showed a significant result ($F(3112) = 3.17$, $p < 0.05$), but no significance between the four conditions have been found in a post-hoc test. For average consumers, differences across conditions were found for sustainability thoughts ($F(3249) = 3.02$, $p < 0.05$) and taste thoughts ($F(3249) = 5.43$, $p < 0.01$). Respondents in the health and sustainability condition thought more about sustainability than respondents in the healthy condition. In addition, respondents in the control condition thought more about taste compared to those in the healthy and sustainable, and sustainable conditions. For conscious consumers, thoughts about sustainability ($F(3456) = 4.46$, $p < 0.01$) and taste ($F(3456) = 6.17$, $p < 0.001$) also differed across conditions, but the pattern of differences between conditions differed slightly from what had been found for the average consumers (see Table 2). Those in the sustainable condition thought more about sustainability than those in the control and healthy conditions. In addition, those in the control condition thought more about taste compared to the other conditions.

Table 2. Manipulation check. [1]

Communication Type	N	Attributes				
		Health	Sustainability	Price	Taste	Convenience
Total sample						
Control	209	4.90 [a,2]	3.98 [a]	4.68 [a]	5.74 [a]	4.64 [a]
Healthy	205	5.02 [a]	4.04 [a]	4.37 [a]	5.16 [b]	4.49 [a]
Sustainable	210	4.91 [a]	4.65 [b]	4.70 [a]	5.02 [b]	4.32 [a]
Healthy & sustainable	205	5.00 [a]	4.71 [b]	4.68 [a]	5.01 [b]	4.46 [a]
Pro-self consumers						
Control	35	4.09 [a]	2.51 [a]	4.26 [a]	5.60 [a]	4.20 [a]
Healthy	33	5.03 [a]	2.97 [a,b]	4.64 [a]	5.24 [a]	4.61 [a]
Sustainable	29	4.07 [a]	3.55 [a,b]	4.66 [a]	4.45 [a]	3.76 [a]
Healthy & sustainable	19	4.26 [a]	3.79 [b]	3.79 [a]	4.37 [a]	3.74 [a]
Average consumers						
Control	73	4.90 [a]	3.81 [a,b]	4.66 [a]	5.71 [a]	4.63 [a]
Healthy	63	4.92 [a]	3.71 [a]	4.19 [a]	5.10 [a,b]	4.19 [a]
Sustainable	64	4.67 [a]	4.23 [a,b]	4.52 [a]	4.95 [b]	4.05 [a]
Healthy & sustainable	53	5.04 [a]	4.40 [b]	4.62 [a]	4.85 [b]	4.43 [a]
Conscious consumers						
Control	101	5.18 [a]	4.61 [a]	4.85 [a]	5.80 [a]	4.79 [a]
Healthy	109	5.08 [a]	4.56 [a]	4.39 [a]	5.17 [b]	4.63 [a]
Sustainable	117	5.26 [a]	5.15 [b]	4.80 [a]	5.20 [b]	4.61 [a]
Healthy & sustainable	133	5.09 [a]	4.97 [a,b]	4.83 [a]	5.17 [b]	4.57 [a]

[1] "To what extent did the text above make you think of the following aspects of food?" (1 = very little, 7 = very much). [2] Different superscripts in each column (per cluster) indicate significantly different means following ANOVA post-hoc Tukey test at $p < 0.05$.

The results of the open-ended question in which respondents were asked to mention a few words that came up after they read the manipulation confirmed the manipulations (see Appendix B). Those in the control condition mentioned taste most often. In addition, product groups such as meat, bread, potatoes, pasta and rice were often mentioned, as were general food aspects such as hunger, grocery shopping and cooking. Respondents in the sustainable, and the healthy and sustainable condition, most often thought about all kinds of sustainability aspects such as environmentally friendly, Fair Trade, animal friendly, regional, ecological, seasonal and vegetarian, but also expensiveness was mentioned frequently in these conditions. Respondents in the health condition mentioned fruits and vegetables most often, but also respondents in the health and sustainable condition mentioned fruits and vegetables frequently. In addition, calories, dairy, vitamins and minerals, fibers and variety of food were often mentioned in the health condition. Calories were also mentioned frequently in the combined condition. Finally, respondents in the health, sustainable and combined conditions thought of natural production and pureness more often than those in the control condition.

A multivariate ANOVA shows that the main effect of experimental manipulation condition was not significant for any of the intentions. The main effect of segment was significant for intentions to consume sustainable products ($F(2817) = 72.27$, $p < 0.001$), intentions to consume regular meat ($F(2817) = 14.62$, $p < 0.001$) and intentions to consume vegetarian meals ($F(2817) = 21.08$, $p < 0.001$). Pro-selves intended to eat less sustainable products compared to average consumers, and conscious consumers intend to eat more. Conscious consumers also intended to eat more products that can replace meat in the meal than the other two segments. In addition, conscious consumers intended to eat meat less regularly (see Table 3). In addition, there was a significant interaction between the manipulation condition and segment for regular meat intentions ($F(6817) = 2.18$, $p = 0.043$). A subsequent one-way between-subjects ANOVA with post-hoc Tukey test per segment shows that for sustainable conscious consumers, intentions to consume regular types and portions of meat were significantly lower in the combined condition ($M = 4.01$) than in the control condition ($M = 4.89$) ($F(3456) = 3.89$, $p < 0.01$).

Table 3. Consumption intention (in number of days of the following week).

Cluster	Sustainable Products	Regular Meat	Regular Dairy	Vegetables and Regular Products	Meat Replacers, and Large Amounts of Vegetables and Meat
Pro-self consumers	0.68 [a, 1] (1.08)	4.36 [a] (1.83)	2.95 [a] (2.42)	4.45 [a] (1.67)	1.43 [a] (1.40)
Average consumers	1.31 [b] (1.58)	3.96 [a] (1.75)	2.99 [a] (2.16)	4.39 [a] (1.51)	1.55 [a] (1.40)
Conscious consumers	2.56 [c] (1.93)	3.38 [b] (1.99)	3.15 [a] (2.21)	4.25 [a] (1.58)	2.21 [b] (1.64)

[1] Different superscripts within one column indicate significantly different intentions following ANOVA post-hoc Tukey test at $p < 0.05$.

No significant differences were found in attitudes towards the food consumption guideline (to eat less animal-based and more plant-based diets) between conditions within the clusters. The only significant difference was that, overall, those in the combined condition scored higher than those in the healthy condition on the question whether the information that they had read made them think about the amount of animal-based and plant-based products that they ate.

4. Discussion

This study revealed the potential of targeting dietary messages to motive-based consumer segments. Segmentation may allow nutritional campaigns to reach specific audiences with the most effective message, tailored to their motivations. This study shows the importance of consumer segmentation, as well as the focus on the product-category level, in the development of effective dietary communication. Implications of the findings will be considered in more detail below.

This study has proposed to segment consumers based on food category specific motives. Three consumer segments have been identified: "pro-selves", "average consumers" and "sustainable conscious consumers". For the identification of the segments, this study used a domain-specific segmentation base. The identification of homogeneous subgroups was based on people's reasons and motivations behind their food choices instead of more general descriptive variables (e.g., socio-demographics) that are commonly used as segmentation base [71]. Food-related motivations are more closely related to behavior and are therefore preferred to more abstract variables in identifying segments [72]. The current study adds to the literature by considering food-category differences in domain-specific motivations (see also [47]) as well as the relation with effective dietary communication.

This study replicated and extended an earlier motive-based segmentation study [47]. The replication of the segmentation procedure almost three years after the initial study showed similar results, indicating the stability of the segments. Segment sizes slightly changed with an increase of just over ten percent of the sustainable conscious segment, mainly at the expense of the size of the average consumer segment. This finding looks promising, as it shows that the proportion of the population for whom sustainability attributes are relatively important has increased. The factor analysis also replicated the underlying factor structure of a pro-self factor (capturing taste, price and healthiness) and a sustainability factor (capturing a range of sustainability aspects such as animal welfare and environmental welfare) for each of the food categories (dairy, meat, fish and vegetables). This replication again underpins the significance of considering food category differences in attribute importance. In addition, this replication confirms that sustainability can be used as a container construct, because several sustainability aspects such as environmental aspects and animal welfare aspects loaded on one dimension.

The main added value of this study as compared to the previous study is twofold. First of all, the current study extends previous findings by gaining deeper insights into the segment profiles. The segments differed in food consumption, personal characteristics and food-related lifestyle aspects; elements which should be taken into consideration in the development of nutritional campaigns. Second, the current study provides insights into communication strategies towards the segments. Implications for the development of dietary communication will be discussed next.

The main aim of this study was to show how nutritional messages on healthy and sustainable diets should be tailored to different segments. The domain-specific lifestyle and personal characteristics of the three segments identified here imply some strategies for communicating dietary guidelines to each of the groups. The results show, however, that the same option—the strategy in which health and sustainability messages were combined—can best be used for all three segments. In other words, against our expectations, there was no strategy that showed to be significantly more effective than the health and sustainability condition in any of the segments. This is an unexpected result because we assumed that segments needed different communication strategies, adapted to their motivations. Apart from being unexpected, it is an interesting result. It shows that even those consumers who are less motivated to make healthy and sustainable food choices may benefit from information on healthy and sustainable diets. Although the information may not result in changing meal intentions, it makes them think more of sustainability and less of taste. This finding is in line with the literature, stating that the effectiveness of information campaigns on awareness is quite strong, but does not often result in behavior change [32–34,36]. In addition, based on our results, no negative effects are expected in any of the segments from communicating health and sustainability benefits of less animal-based and more plant-based diets.

Although we found that the most effective communication strategy is the same for all segments, results do indicate the relevance of motive-based consumer segmentation, as the effect of the communication on behavioral intentions differs across segments. A positive effect of the communication on sustainable dietary intentions has been found for sustainable conscious consumers only. The other two segments may need other issues addressed in their strategies to stimulate them to shift their diets towards more sustainable consumption levels or other pathways—next to providing information—are needed in order for behavior change to occur in these segments. An option might be to consider the addition of pro-self motives in the formulation of and communication on dietary guidelines. In accordance with a flood of food studies, this study shows the importance of taste, price and convenience to food consumers. The lack of consideration of these attributes may be a reason why communication of dietary guidelines shows limited effectiveness in the real world. Synergies between pro-self short-term motives (e.g., price and taste), and healthy and sustainable choices should be communicated. An example could be the stimulation of seasonal fruit and vegetable consumption by emphasizing their low price and good taste, next to their possible health and sustainability gains.

However, the provision of information might also be insufficient. Literature shows that the effectiveness of information is limited, especially in terms of behavioral intentions, which is in line with our results. This research has focused on educational interventions adapted to the motivations of consumers. Results show that communicating the guideline only results in improved intentions for the segment that is already motivated. Agreement with the guideline does not differ across conditions within segments, indicating that communicating the guideline has no effect on agreement with it. Therefore, it is likely that for pro-self and average consumers, dietary communications that can increase knowledge or awareness will not result in behavior change. General agreement exists that knowledge is necessary but insufficient to change (health) behaviors [73]. Therefore, other pathways must be considered, such as marketing and legal interventions to help create the necessary motivation, ability and opportunity for behavior change [30]. Nudges or labelling could help to make the healthy and sustainable choice the easy choice and taxes, subsidies or prohibitions of certain products can create a supporting environment. A combination of different types of interventions is likely to be needed to achieve a sufficient level of motivation and ability and the right opportunity. This implies that several actors are needed to achieve a dietary shift. Actors communicating about dietary guidelines, such as governmental organizations, dieticians, retail and food industries should work together to communicate about nutritional guidelines in an effective and unambiguous way, combining health and sustainability arguments. In addition, supermarkets could use nudging and labelling strategies, governments could provide regulations and food industries could get involved in regulation and labeling, for example.

Our insights into personal characteristics of the segments can be used in developing effective strategies for each of the segments. It may be beneficial, for example, to make pro-self and average consumers more future oriented. This study has shown that pro-selves differ from sustainable conscious consumers on this aspect. In addition, messages can be adapted to the transition phase in which a consumer is positioned. For instance, in the pre-contemplation phase, it is important to raise consumers' awareness of health and sustainability problems. In the contemplation stage, one's self image is crucial and can be influenced by providing role models, for example. In the preparation stage, it is important to make consumers believe that they can change, for instance by providing a range of practical options. Consumers in the action and maintenance stage can be helped by prompting healthy and sustainable choices [31]. The finding that the segments differ in their transition stages suggests that different types of messages best fit these segments. Prompting health and sustainable choices, as has been done in this study by the provided information, best fits consumers in the maintenance stage. It is therefore not surprising that the effect on intentions was only found for the sustainable conscious consumers, the segment with the largest number of consumers in the maintenance stage.

The results underpin the importance to take product-category differences into account. First of all, the communication of the dietary guideline seems to have an effect on intentions, if only for the product-category of meat. The specific character of meat is also shown in a study about vegetarian diets [74], which showed that although these diets are generally perceived as positive, the consumption of such a diet is still hampered by health concerns, unwillingness to make dietary changes or enjoyment of eating meat.

Second, the factor analysis on intentions shows that consumption of regular portions and regular variants of meat, dairy and vegetables load on different underlying factors. This implies that the guideline to consume less animal-based products might be too general. Motivational differences exist concerning meat and dairy, and it might be better not to lump these product categories together in the same message.

Furthermore, the results show that the effect of communicating the guideline is only found for the curtailment of meat, and not for the purchase of sustainably produced meat products (e.g., organic or animal friendly variants) [49]. This finding is not surprising, as the guideline is focused on curtailment behavior, and not on stimulating the purchase of sustainably produced products, but it shows that the effect does not lead to spillovers to other types of sustainable behavior. This implies that communication aimed at stimulating sustainably produced products may have additional beneficial effects on stimulating sustainable diets.

In short, we can conclude that it is not so much the nature of the message (healthiness and/or sustainability argument) that is key in differentiating between segments, but the relation between message, segment and product category. Those involved in communicating dietary guidelines could choose to use a mix of pro-self and pro-social arguments for all consumer segments, as including both types of arguments might appeal to a larger audience. The current study did not find any negative effects on either thoughts or meal intentions of a frame that combines health and sustainability in any of the segments. Therefore, we propose to place dietary guidelines in a context of both healthiness and sustainability, and to combine both health and sustainability arguments. In other words, sustainability should become part of the criteria on which dietary guidelines are formulated and communicated, like Lang and colleagues [9] already pled for in 2009. This study underpins the ongoing debates on the shift in focus of nutritional guidelines to include sustainability considerations.

Overall, the results imply that in the development of dietary messages:

- Product-category differences should be taken into account.
- Differences between motive-based segments should be taken into account.
- The type of sustainability that is targeted—curtailment versus sustainable products—should be taken into account.
- Communication strategies seem insufficient to shift diets, especially among pro-self and average consumers, and therefore additional strategies should be considered.

Although this research has some important implications, it also faces some limitations and raises some important issues for future research. First, the health manipulation did not result in more health thoughts. A possible explanation is that, at the baseline level (regardless of any communication), health is more salient in the consumer's mind than sustainability. Therefore, it is much harder (and maybe unnecessary) to increase health thoughts through communication. We do not perceive it as a problem that the health manipulation check did not show significant differences between conditions, because the open-ended question on association words show that the manipulation has been read and understood, because respondents mentioned health-related words (those in the health manipulation mention 'health' least often. This is a logical result of the way we framed the question, as we asked them to mention words that came to their mind when thinking of healthy food).

Future research should include a broader range of communication conditions to check the effect of combining short-term pro-self motives (e.g., taste, price and convenience) with long-term pro-social motives (sustainability) and/or long-term pro-self motives (health). All segments, specifically the pro-self segment, could be attracted with messages including those pro-self short-term motives. Such additional communication strategies may result in larger differences in effectiveness between segments. Furthermore, additional attribute combinations may give insights into whether a combination of two attributes is more effective than focusing on a single attribute. The current study is not conclusive on whether the health and sustainability condition shows the best results, because of the synergy of the two arguments or because of the fact that two arguments are included in this condition as compared to one argument in the other conditions. We did, however, keep the information comparable in length by shortening the length of both arguments in the combined condition, and therefore it is most likely that the effect occurs because of synergy. Another argument to support this reasoning is that, from previous research [47], we know that sustainable conscious consumers perceive the most synergy and pro-selves perceive the least synergy between health and sustainability of food products. If the effect of the health and sustainability condition was due to the number of arguments, than the largest effect would be expected to occur for pro-selves, whereas if it were the synergy perception, the largest effect would be expected to occur for conscious consumers (which is the case). A final interesting direction for future research can be found in the spillover literature [75]. Based on the current study it can be concluded that the best communication strategy is to include a combination of health and sustainability arguments. It seems intuitive to persuade people that sustainable behavior is in their own interest, for example by stressing the health or price benefits that come along with certain sustainable behaviors. Previous research showed, however, that making self-interest motivations salient may counteract prosocial motivations and therefore it may prevent positive spillover from one prosocial behavior to other prosocial behaviors [75,76]. Future research should provide more insights into positive or negative spillover effects resulting from communication strategies.

5. Conclusions

This study puts forth a preliminary segmentation based on food-category specific food motivations that may help develop effective dietary communication strategies motivating consumers towards more healthy and sustainable diets. We can conclude that communicating both health and sustainability benefits of eating less animal-based and more plant-based products is advisable for all motive-based consumer segments. Effects on behavioral intention differ across motive-based segments and additional ways of stimulating sustainable food consumption beyond informing are needed, especially for pro-self and average consumers. The effectiveness of the communication in terms of sustainable food intentions not only depends on the segment, but also on the product category. Future research is needed to study the generalizability of the findings to other guidelines, in other food categories, with other product attributes and considering the entire diet, but this study leads to useful insights for those who are involved in communicating healthy and sustainable dietary guidelines. Thereby this study contributes to a more healthy and sustainable food consumption pattern.

Acknowledgments: This research was part of the doctoral thesis of the first author. The research work has received financial support from both Wageningen University and Wageningen Economic Research, which is greatly acknowledged.

Author Contributions: All authors conceived and designed the experiment together; Muriel C. D. Verain analysed the data and wrote the paper, which had then been checked and revised by all authors.

Conflicts of Interest: The authors declare no conflict of interest. The founding sponsors had no role in the design of the study; in the collection, analyses, or interpretation of data; in the writing of the manuscript, and in the decision to publish the results.

Appendix A

The following manipulations have been used in the experiment (original Dutch text followed by the English translation).

Control condition:

Deze vragenlijst gaat over eten. Hiermee bedoelen we eetgedrag dat bijdraagt aan uw totale voedselinname gedurende de hele dag. U kunt hierbij bijvoorbeeld denken aan wat voor soort producten u eet en hoeveel u ervan eet. Het eten van drie hoofdmaaltijden en (eventueel) een aantal tussendoortjes bepaalt uw voedselinname. Het gaat om hoe u uw maaltijden samenstelt.

English translation: This questionnaire focusses on food. With this we mean dietary behavior that contributes to your total food intake during the entire day. You could think of the type of products you eat and the amount you eat of it. The intake of three main meals and (potentially) a number of snacks determines your food intake. It entails the way you compose your meals.

Health condition:

Deze vragenlijst gaat over gezond eten. Hiermee bedoelen we eetgedrag dat bijdraagt aan een goede gezondheid met een goede weerstand, weinig ziekte en een fit en energiek gevoel. U kunt hierbij bijvoorbeeld denken aan de verhouding dierlijke en plantaardige producten die u eet. Het eten van weinig dierlijke producten (zoals vlees en zuivel) en veel plantaardige producten (zoals groente) is gezond. Het gaat er om hoe gezond de maaltijden zijn die u samenstelt.

English translation: This questionnaire focusses on healthy eating. With this we mean dietary behavior that contributes to a good health with a good resistance, little illness and a fit and energetic feeling. You could think of the proportion of animal-based and plant-based products that you eat. The intake of few animal-based products (such as meat and dairy) and many plant-based products (such as vegetables) is healthy. It entails the healthiness of the meals you compose.

Sustainability condition:

Deze vragenlijst gaat over duurzaam eten. Hiermee bedoelen we eetgedrag dat bijdraagt aan een duurzame wereld met respect voor het milieu, de dieren en de mensen om ons heen. U kunt hierbij bijvoorbeeld denken aan de verhouding dierlijke en plantaardige producten die u eet. Het eten van weinig dierlijke producten (zoals vlees en zuivel) en veel plantaardige producten (zoals groente) is duurzaam. Het gaat er om hoe duurzaam de maaltijden zijn die u samenstelt.

English translation: This questionnaire focusses on sustainable eating. With this we mean dietary behavior that constitutes to a sustainable world, with respect for the environment, the animals and the people surrounding us. You could think of the proportion of animal-based and plant-based products that you eat. The intake of few animal-based products (such as meat and dairy) and many plant-based products (such as vegetables) is sustainable. It entails the sustainability of the meals you compose.

Combined condition:

Deze vragenlijst gaat over gezond en tegelijk duurzaam eten. Hiermee bedoelen we eetgedrag dat bijdraagt aan een goede gezondheid en een duurzame wereld met respect voor het milieu, de dieren en de mensen om ons heen. U kunt hierbij bijvoorbeeld denken aan de verhouding dierlijke en plantaardige producten die u eet. Het eten van weinig dierlijke producten (zoals vlees en zuivel) en veel plantaardige producten (zoals groente) is gezond én duurzaam. Het gaat er om hoe gezond en duurzaam de maaltijden zijn die u samenstelt.

English translation: This questionnaire focusses on healthy and simultaneously sustainable eating. With this we mean dietary behavior that contributes to a good health and a sustainable world, with respect for the environment, the animals and the people surrounding us. You could think of the proportion of animal-based and plant-based products that you eat. The intake of few animal-based products (such as meat and dairy) and many plant-based products (such as vegetables) is healthy AND sustainable. It entails the healthiness and sustainability of the meals you compose.

Appendix B

Table A1. Number of times words in certain categories were mentioned in the four conditions.

	Control	Health	Sustainable	Health & Sustainable	F-Value
Tasty	140 [a]	13 [b]	10 [b]	13 [b]	287.961 ***
Fruit and vegetables	70 [a]	263 [b]	30 [c]	86 [a]	327.226 ***
Healthy	47 [a]	5 [b]	40 [a,c]	21 [c]	38.152 ***
Meat	43 [a]	21 [b]	7 [c]	4 [c]	50.929 ***
Sociable	37 [a]	0 [b]	1 [b]	0 [b]	105.974 ***
Bread	34 [a]	11 [b]	1 [c]	6 [b,c]	49.080 ***

Table A1. *Cont.*

	Control	Health	Sustainable	Health & Sustainable	F-Value
Cooking	28 [a]	0 [b]	0 [b]	0 [b]	83.627 ***
Potatoes	27 [a]	3 [b]	5 [b]	2 [b]	45.647 ***
Good	25 [a]	3 [b]	6 [b]	7 [b]	28.938 ***
Calories	24 [a]	86 [b]	4 [c]	27 [a]	112.505 ***
Pasta	18 [a]	1 [b]	1 [b]	0 [b]	44.874 ***
Hungry	15 [a]	0 [b]	0 [b]	1 [b]	40.187 ***
Fish	13 [a]	18 [a]	9 [a]	9 [a]	4.686
Grocery shopping	12 [a]	0 [b]	0 [b]	0 [b]	35.701 ***
Dairy	11 [a,b,c]	25 [c]	2 [b]	13 [a,c]	21.948 ***
Rice	10 [a]	1 [b]	0 [b]	0 [b]	25.494 ***
Nutritious	8 [a]	2 [a]	2 [a]	1 [a]	9.327 *
Variety	6 [a,b]	16 [b]	0 [a]	1 [a]	28.553 ***
Vitamins & minerals	5 [a,b]	21 [c]	1 [b]	10 [a,c]	25.140 ***
Fresh	4 [a]	20 [b]	1 [a]	23 [b]	32.042 ***
Expensive	3 [a]	8 [a]	29 [b]	26 [b]	30.672 ***
Organic	2 [a]	29 [b]	73 [c]	81 [c]	94.831 ***
Vegetarian	2 [a]	1 [a]	6 [a,b]	13 [b]	16.517 **
Natural	1 [a]	5 [a]	2 [a]	4 [a]	3.473
Water	1 [a,b]	8 [b]	0 [a]	3 [a,b]	12.968 **
Animal friendly	1 [a]	1 [a]	21 [b]	14 [b]	31.975 ***
Nutrition guideline	1 [a,b]	9 [b]	0 [a]	1 [a,b]	19.558 ***
Wasting	1 [a,b]	0 [b]	9 [a]	1 [a,b]	18.847 ***
Regional	1 [a]	0 [a]	14 [b]	15 [b]	26.444 ***
Fiber	1 [a]	20 [b]	0 [a]	3 [a]	45.343 ***
No additives	1 [a]	7 [a]	7 [a]	6 [a]	4.792
Environmentally friendly	0 [a]	0 [a]	27 [b]	19 [b]	48.839 ***
Fair Trade	0 [a]	0 [a]	23 [b]	21 [b]	44.464 ***
Natural production	0 [a]	7 [b]	13 [b]	20 [b]	22.287 ***
Ecological	0 [a]	2 [a,b]	11 [b]	11 [b]	17.063 **
Seasonal	0 [a]	3 [a,b]	11 [b]	9 [b]	13.668 **
Pure	0 [a]	8 [b]	4 [a,b]	8 [b]	9.083 *
Responsible	0 [a]	0 [a,b]	7 [b]	6 [a,b]	13.119 *
Don't know	0 [a]	3 [a]	30 [b]	23 [b]	46.928 ***

[1] Control includes 1045 words, health includes 1025 words, sustainable includes 1050 words and health & sustainable includes 1025 words. [2] Different superscripts within one row indicate significant differences following ANOVA post-hoc Tukey test at $p < 0.05$. [3] * $p < 0.05$, ** $p < 0.01$, *** $p < 0.001$.

References

1. Caballero, B. The global epidemic of obesity: An overview. *Epidemiol. Rev.* **2007**, *29*, 1–5. [CrossRef] [PubMed]
2. Garnett, T. Where are the best opportunities for reducing greenhouse gas emissions in the food system (including the food chain)? *Food Policy* **2011**, *36*, S23–S32. [CrossRef]
3. McMichael, A.J.; Powles, J.W.; Butler, C.D.; Uauy, R. Food, livestock production, energy, climate change, and health. *Lancet* **2007**, *370*, 1253–1263. [CrossRef]
4. Ng, M.; Fleming, T.; Robinson, M.; Thomson, B.; Graetz, N.; Margono, C.; Mullany, E.C.; Biryukov, S.; Abbafati, C.; Abera, S.F.; et al. Global, regional, and national prevalence of overweight and obesity in children and adults during 1980–2013: A systematic analysis for the global burden of disease study 2013. *Lancet* **2014**, *384*, 766–781. [CrossRef]
5. Reisch, L.; Eberie, U.; Lorek, S. Sustainable food consumption: An overview of contemporary issues and policies. *Sustain. Sci. Pract. Police* **2013**, *9*, 7–25.
6. Aschemann-Witzel, J. Consumer perception and trends about health and sustainability: Trade-offs and synergies of two pivotal issues. *Curr. Opin. Food Sci.* **2015**, *3*, 6–10. [CrossRef]
7. Carlsson-Kanyama, A.; González, A.D. Potential contributions of food consumption patterns to climate change. *Am. J. Clin. Nutr.* **2009**, *89*, S1704–S1709. [CrossRef] [PubMed]

8. De Boer, J.; Schösler, H.; Boersema, J.J. Motivational differences in food orientation and the choice of snacks made from lentils, locusts, seaweed or "hybrid" meat. *Food Qual. Preference* **2013**, *28*, 32–35. [CrossRef]

9. Lang, T.; Barling, D.; Caraher, M. *Food Policy: Integrating Health, Environment and Society*; Oxford University Press: Oxford, UK, 2009.

10. Hoek, A.C.; Pearson, D.; James, S.W.; Lawrence, M.A.; Friel, S. Shrinking the food-print: A qualitative study into consumer perceptions, experiences and attitudes towards healthy and environmentally friendly food behaviours. *Appetite* **2017**, *108*, 117–131. [CrossRef] [PubMed]

11. Alarcon, B.; Gerritsen, E. On Our Plate Today: Healthy, Sustainable Food Choices. LiveWell for LIFE, 2014. Available online: http://www.wwf.eu/what_we_do/eu_forests/publications_forest.cfm?uNewsID=238793 (accessed on 5 January 2017).

12. Health Council of The Netherlands. *Guidelines for a Healthy Diet: The Ecological Perspective*; Health Council of The Netherlands: The Hague, The Netherlands, 2011.

13. Department of Health and Human Services; Department of Agriculture. *Scientific Report of the 2015 Dietary Guidelines Advisory Committee*; HHS: Washington, DC, USA; USDA: Washington, DC, USA, 2015.

14. Raphaely, T.; Marinova, D. (Eds.) *Impact of Meat Consumption on Health and Environmental Sustainability*; IGI Global: Hershey, PA, USA, 2016.

15. Van Dooren, C.; Marinussen, M.; Blonk, H.; Aiking, H.; Vellinga, P. Exploring dietary guidelines based on ecological and nutritional values: A comparison of six dietary patterns. *Food Policy* **2014**, *44*, 36–46. [CrossRef]

16. Westhoek, H.; Lesschen, J.P.; Rood, T.; Wagner, S.; De Marco, A.; Murphy-Bokern, D.; Leip, A.; van Grinsven, H.; Sutton, M.A.; Oenema, O. Food choices, health and environment: Effects of cutting Europe's meat and dairy intake. *Glob. Environ. Chang.* **2014**, *26*, 196–205. [CrossRef]

17. Naska, A.; Vasdekis, V.G.S.; Trichopoulou, A.; Friel, S.; Leonhäuser, I.U.; Moreiras, O.; Nelson, M.; Remaut, A.M.; Schmitt, A.; Sekula, W.; et al. Fruit and vegetable availability among ten European countries: How does it compare with the 'five-a-day' recommendation? *Br. J. Nutr.* **2000**, *84*, 549–556. [PubMed]

18. Pomerleau, J.; Lock, K.; McKee, M.; Altmann, D.R. The challenge of measuring global fruit and vegetable intake. *J. Nutr.* **2004**, *134*, 1175–1180. [PubMed]

19. Trichopoulou, A.; Naska, A.; Antoniou, A.; Friel, S.; Trygg, K.; Turrini, A. Vegetable and fruit: The evidence in their favour and the public health perspective. *Int. J. Vitam. Nutr. Res.* **2003**, *73*, 63–69. [CrossRef] [PubMed]

20. Van't Veer, P.; Jansen, M.C.; Klerk, M.; Kok, F.J. Fruits and vegetables in the prevention of cancer and cardiovascular disease. *Public Health Nutr.* **2000**, *3*, 103–107. [CrossRef] [PubMed]

21. Van Rossum, C.T.M.; Fransen, H.P.; Verkaik-Kloosterman, J.; Buurma-Rethans, E.J.M.; Ocké, M.C. *Dutch National Food Consumption Survey 2007–2010*; National Institute for Public Health and the Environment: Bilthoven, The Netherlands, 2011.

22. Haack, S.A.; Byker, C.J. Recent population adherence to and knowledge of United States federal nutrition guides, 1992–2013: A systematic review. *Nutr. Rev.* **2014**, *72*, 613–626. [CrossRef] [PubMed]

23. Joffe, M.; Robertson, A. The potential contribution of increased vegetable and fruit consumption to health gain in the European Union. *Public Health Nutr.* **2001**, *4*, 893–901. [CrossRef] [PubMed]

24. Henchion, M.; McCarthy, M.; Resconi, V.C.; Troy, D. Meat consumption: Trends and quality matters. *Meat Sci.* **2014**, *98*, 561–568. [CrossRef] [PubMed]

25. Dagevos, H. Exploring flexitarianism: Meat reduction in a meat-centred food culture. In *Impact of Meat Consumption on Health and Environmental Sustainability*; Raphaely, T., Marinova, D., Eds.; IGI Global: Hershey, PA, USA, 2016; pp. 233–243.

26. Dagevos, H.; Voordouw, J. Sustainability and meat consumption: Is reduction realistic? *Sustain. Sci. Pract. Policy* **2013**, *9*, 60–69.

27. Grunert, K.G. Sustainability in the food sector: A consumer behaviour perspective. *Int. J. Food Syst. Dyn.* **2011**, *2*, 207–218.

28. Heller, M.C.; Keoleian, G.A.; Willett, W.C. Toward a life cycle-based, diet-level framework for food environmental impact and nutritional quality assessment: A critical review. *Environ. Sci. Technol.* **2013**, *47*, 12632–12647. [CrossRef] [PubMed]

29. Spaargaren, G.; Oosterveer, P. Citizen-Consumers as Agents of Change in Globalizing Modernity: The Case of Sustainable Consumption. *Sustainability* **2010**, *2*, 1887–1908. [CrossRef]

30. Rothschild, M.L. Carrots, sticks, and promises: A conceptual framework for the management of public health and social issue behaviors. *J. Mark.* **1999**, *63*, 24–37. [CrossRef]
31. Prochaska, J.O.; Velicer, W.F. The transtheoretical model of health behavior change. *Am. J. Health Promot.* **1997**, *12*, 38–48. [CrossRef] [PubMed]
32. Boles, M.; Adams, A.; Gredler, A.; Manhas, S. Ability of a mass media campaign to influence knowledge, attitudes, and behaviors about sugary drinks and obesity. *Prev. Med.* **2014**, *67*, S40–S45. [CrossRef] [PubMed]
33. Brambila-Macias, J.; Shankar, B.; Capacci, S.; Mazzocchi, M.; Perez-Cueto, F.J.A.; Verbeke, W.; Trail, W.B. Policy interventions to promote healthy eating: A review of what works, what does not, and what is promising. *Food Nutr. Bull.* **2011**, *32*, 365–375. [CrossRef] [PubMed]
34. Capacci, S.; Mazzocchi, M.; Shankar, B.; Macias, J.B.; Verbeke, W.; Perez-Cueto, F.J.A.; Koziol-Kozakowska, A.; Piorecka, B.; Niedzwiedzka, B.; D'Addesa, D.; et al. Policies to promote healthy eating in Europe: A structured review of policies and their effectiveness. *Nutr. Rev.* **2012**, *70*, 188–200. [CrossRef] [PubMed]
35. Geeroms, N.; Verbeke, W.; Kenhove, P.V. Health advertising to promote fruit and vegetable intake: Application of health-related motive segmentation. *Food Qual. Preference* **2008**, *19*, 481–497. [CrossRef]
36. Ölander, F.; Thøgersen, J. Informing versus nudging in environmental policy. *J. Consum. Policy* **2014**, *37*, 341–356. [CrossRef]
37. Kazbare, L.; van Trijp, H.C.M.; Eskildsen, J.K. A-priori and post-hoc segmentation in the design of healthy eating campaigns. *J. Mark. Commun.* **2010**, *16*, 21–45. [CrossRef]
38. Hine, D.W.; Reser, J.P.; Morrison, M.; Phillips, W.J.; Nunn, P.; Cooksey, R. Audience segmentation and climate change communication: Conceptual and methodological considerations. *WIREs Clim. Chang.* **2014**, *5*, 441–459. [CrossRef]
39. Moser, S.C. Communicating climate change: History, challenges, process and future directions. *WIREs Clim. Chang.* **2010**, *1*, 31–53. [CrossRef]
40. Noar, S.M.; Benac, C.N.; Harris, M.S. Does tailoring matter? Meta-analytic review of tailored print health behavior change interventions. *Psychol. Bull.* **2007**, *133*, 673–693. [CrossRef] [PubMed]
41. Slater, M.D. Theory and method in health audience segmentation. *J. Health Commun.* **1996**, *1*, 267–283. [CrossRef] [PubMed]
42. Wilson, B.J. Designing media messages about health and nutrition: What strategies are most effective? *J. Nutr. Educ. Behav.* **2007**, *39*, S13–S19. [CrossRef] [PubMed]
43. Wedel, M.; Kamakura, W. *Market Segmentation: Conceptual and Methodological Foundations*, 2nd ed.; Kluwer Academic Publishers: Boston, MA, USA, 2000.
44. Onwezen, M.C.; Reinders, M.J.; van der Lans, I.A.; Sijtsema, S.J.; Jasiulewicz, A.; Dolors Guardia, M.; Guerrero, L. A cross-national consumer segmentation based on food benefits: The link with consumption situations and food perceptions. *Food Qual. Preference* **2012**, *24*, 276–286. [CrossRef]
45. Realini, C.E.; Kallas, Z.; Pérez-Juan, M.; Gómez, I.; Olleta, J.L.; Beriain, M.J.; Albertí, P.; Sañudo, C. Relative importance of cues underlying spanish consumers' beef choice and segmentation, and consumer liking of beef enriched with n-3 and cla fatty acids. *Food Qual. Preference* **2014**, *33*, 74–85. [CrossRef]
46. Steptoe, A.; Pollard, T.M.; Wardle, J. Development of a measure of the motives underlying the selection of food: The food choice questionnaire. *Appetite* **1995**, *25*, 267–284. [CrossRef] [PubMed]
47. Verain, M.C.D.; Sijtsema, S.J.; Antonides, G. Consumer segmentation based on food-category attribute importance: The relation with healthiness and sustainability perceptions. *Food Qual. Preference* **2016**, *48*, 99–106. [CrossRef]
48. Pollard, T.M.; Steptoe, A.; Wardle, J. Motives underlying healthy eating: Using the food choice questionnaire to explain variation in dietary intake. *J. Biosoc. Sci.* **1998**, *30*, 165–179. [CrossRef] [PubMed]
49. Verain, M.C.D.; Dagevos, H.; Antonides, G. Sustainable food consumption. Product choice or curtailment? *Appetite* **2015**, *91*, 375–384. [CrossRef] [PubMed]
50. Petty, R.E.; Cacioppo, J.T. The effects of involvement on responses to argument quantity and quality: Central and peripheral routes to persuasion. *J. Personal. Soc. Psychol.* **1984**, *46*, 69–81. [CrossRef]
51. Kareklas, I.; Carlson, J.; Muehling, D.D. 'I eat organic for my benefit and yours': Egoistic and altruistic considerations for purchasing organic food and their implications for advertising strategists. *J. Advert.* **2014**, *43*, 18–32. [CrossRef]
52. Feiler, D.C.; Tost, L.P.; Grant, A.M. Mixed reasons, missed givings: The costs of blending egoistic and altruistic reasons in donation requests. *J. Exp. Soc. Psychol.* **2012**, *48*, 1322–1328. [CrossRef]

53. Raghunathan, R.; Naylor, R.W.; Hoyer, W.D. The unhealthy = tasty intuition and its effects on taste inferences, enjoyment, and choice of food products. *J. Mark.* **2006**, *70*, 170–184. [CrossRef]

54. Newman, G.E.; Gorlin, M.; Dhar, R. When going green backfires: How firm intentions shape the evaluation of socially beneficial product enhancements. *J. Consum. Res.* **2014**, *41*, 823–839. [CrossRef]

55. Gad Mohsen, M.; Dacko, S. An extension of the benefit segmentation base for the consumption of organic foods: A time perspective. *J. Mark. Manag.* **2013**, *29*, 1701–1728. [CrossRef]

56. Chryssohoidis, G.M.; Krystallis, A. Organic consumers' personal values research: Testing and validating the list of values (lov) scale and implementing a value-based segmentation task. *Food Qual. Preference* **2005**, *16*, 585–599. [CrossRef]

57. Van Lange, P.A.M.; Joireman, J.; Parks, C.D.; van Dijk, E. The psychology of social dilemmas: A review. *Organ. Behav. Hum. Decis. Process.* **2013**, *120*, 125–141. [CrossRef]

58. Messick, D.M.; McClintock, C.G. Motivational bases of choice in experimental games. *J. Exp. Soc. Psychol.* **1968**, *4*, 1–25. [CrossRef]

59. De Groot, J.I.M.; Steg, L. Value orientations to explain beliefs related to environmental significant behavior: How to measure egoistic, altruistic, and biospheric value orientations. *Environ. Behav.* **2008**, *40*, 330–354. [CrossRef]

60. Fischer, R.; Milfont, T.L. Standardization in psychological research. *Int. J. Psychol. Res.* **2010**, *3*, 88–96.

61. Steiger, J.H. Understanding the limitations of global fit assessment in structural equation modelling. *Personal. Individ. Differ.* **2007**, *42*, 893–899. [CrossRef]

62. Hu, L.; Bentler, P.M. Cut-off criteria for fit indexes in covariance matrix analysis: Conventional criteria versus new alternatives. *Struct. Equ. Model.* **1999**, *6*, 1–55. [CrossRef]

63. Baumgartner, H.; Homburg, C. Applications of structural equation modeling in marketing and consumer research: A review. *Int. J. Res. Mark.* **1996**, *13*, 139–161. [CrossRef]

64. Ketchen, D.J., Jr.; Shook, C.L. The application of cluster analysis in strategic management research: An analysis and critique. *Strateg. Manag. J.* **1996**, *17*, 441–458. [CrossRef]

65. SPSS Inc. *SPSS User Manual*; IBM: Armonk, NY, USA, 2010.

66. Hair, J.F.; Black, W.C.; Babin, B.J.; Anderson, R.E.; Tatham, R.L. *Multivariate Data Analysis*; Pearson Prentice Hall: Upper Saddle River, NJ, USA, 2006.

67. Wedel, M.; Desarbo, W.S. Market segment derivation and profiling via a finite mixture model framework. *Mark. Lett.* **2002**, *13*, 17–25. [CrossRef]

68. Joireman, J.; Shaffer, M.J.; Balliet, D.; Strathman, A. Promotion orientation explains why future-oriented people exercise and eat healthy: Evidence from the two-factor consideration of future consequences-14 scale. *Personal. Soc. Psychol. Bull.* **2012**, *38*, 1272–1287. [CrossRef] [PubMed]

69. Antonides, G.; Nyhus, E.K. Time preference and household financial capability. (in preparation)

70. Gwozdz, W.; Netter, S.; Biartmarz, T.; Reisch, L.A. *Survey Results on Fashion Consumption and Sustainability among Young Swedes*; Mistra Future Fashion: Borås, Sweden, 2013.

71. Verain, M.C.D.; Bartels, J.; Dagevos, H.; Sijtsema, S.J.; Onwezen, M.C.; Antonides, G. Segments of sustainable food consumers: A literature review. *Int. J. Consum. Stud.* **2012**, *36*, 123–132. [CrossRef]

72. Van Raaij, W.F.; Verhallen, T.M.M. Domain-specific market segmentation. *Eur. J. Mark.* **1994**, *28*, 49–66. [CrossRef]

73. Bersma, L.; Ferris, E. The impact of health-promoting media-literacy education on nutrition and diet behavior. In *Handbook of Behavior, Food and Nutrition*; Preedy, V.R., Watson, R.R., Martin, C.R., Eds.; Springer: New York, NY, USA, 2011.

74. Corrin, T.; Papadopoulos, A. Understanding the attitudes and perceptions of vegetarian and plant-based diets to shape future health promotion programs. *Appetite* **2017**, *109*, 40–47. [CrossRef] [PubMed]

75. Thøgersen, J.; Crompton, T. Simple and painless? The limitations of spillover in environmental campaiging. *J. Consum. Policy* **2009**, *32*, 141–163. [CrossRef]

76. Evans, L.; Maio, G.R.; Corner, A.; Hodgetts, C.J.; Ahmed, S.; Hahn, U. Self-interest and pro-environmental behaviour. *Nat. Clim. Chang.* **2013**, *3*, 122–125. [CrossRef]

sustainability

MDPI

Article

Market Opportunities for Animal-Friendly Milk in Different Consumer Segments

Sophie de Graaf [1,2,3,*], **Filiep Vanhonacker** [1,4], **Ellen J. Van Loo** [1], **Jo Bijttebier** [2], **Ludwig Lauwers** [1,2], **Frank A. M. Tuyttens** [3] **and Wim Verbeke** [1]

1   Department of Agricultural Economics, Faculty of Bioscience Engineering, Ghent University, 9000 Ghent, Belgium; Filiep.Vanhonacker@ugent.be (F.V.); Ellen.VanLoo@ugent.be (E.J.V.L.); Ludwig.lauwers@ilvo.vlaanderen.be (L.L.); Wim.Verbeke@ugent.be (W.V.)
2   Social Sciences Unit, Institute for Agricultural and Fisheries Research (ILVO), 9820 Merelbeke, Belgium; Jo.Bijttebier@ilvo.vlaanderen.be
3   Animal Sciences Unit, Institute for Agricultural and Fisheries Research (ILVO), 9090 Melle-Gontrode, Belgium; Frank.Tuyttens@ilvo.vlaanderen.be
4   Department of Applied Biosciences, Faculty of Bioscience Engineering, Ghent University, 9000 Ghent, Belgium
*   Correspondence: sophie.degraaf@ugent.be; Tel.: +32-9-272-2609

Academic Editor: Gerrit Antonides
Received: 29 September 2016; Accepted: 7 December 2016; Published: 11 December 2016

Abstract: Consumers have increasing, but highly variable, interest in sustainability attributes of food, including ethical aspects, such as animal welfare. We explored market opportunities for animal-friendly cow's milk based on segmentation (cluster) analysis. Flemish survey participants (n = 787) were clustered (n = 6) based on their intention to purchase (IP) animal-friendly milk, and their evaluation of cows' welfare state (EV). Three market opportunity segments were derived from clusters and labelled as "high", "moderate" and "limited". Only 8% of the participants belong to the "high market opportunities" segment, characterized by a high IP and a low EV. The "limited" segment (44%) indicated a neutral to low IP and a positive EV. The "moderate" segment (48%) had a moderately positive IP and positive/negative EV. Reported willingness to pay, interest in information about the state of animal welfare and importance of the product attribute "animal welfare" differed among segments and were strongly related to IP. Most promising selling propositions about animal-friendly milk were related to pasture access. The high degree of differentiation within the Flemish milk market reveals market opportunities for animal-friendly milk, but for an effective market share increase supply of animal-friendly products needs to get more aligned with the heterogeneous demand.

Keywords: animal welfare; consumers; dairy cattle; ethical consumption; market segmentation; milk; survey

---

1. Introduction

The public is increasingly interested in sustainability aspects of food consumption, including the various characteristics of the production process and of the final food products themselves. For the livestock production, these concerns also imply the more ethical dimension such as animal welfare [1,2]. However, although European citizens report high levels of concern in relation to farm animal welfare [3], the market for animal-friendly products—or of products that are commonly perceived as such—is small. For example, the market share of organic milk, which is associated with higher levels of animal welfare by consumers [4–6], was 2.7% in Belgium in 2015 [7]. This may illustrate that concerns do not always translate into purchase behaviour [8,9], called the "consumer-citizen-duality". While citizens are driven by moral concerns, consumers are driven by the product characteristics involved in their food purchasing decision process [10]. To account for this duality, it is important to take both consumer-related and citizen-oriented measures into consideration when studying this topic.

The European food market for premium animal welfare products is currently a niche market where differentiation levels in the products vary according to the farm animal species. Eggs, for example, have moderate differentiation (i.e., cage, barn eggs, free range, and organic), whereas cow's milk shows little differentiation in terms of animal welfare with the exception of welfare-related options such as "organic" (following EU Council Regulation No. 834/2007) and "access to pasture". The current market for animal-friendly products mostly attracts consumers with only one specific profile, while previous studies [11–14] demonstrated a more heterogeneous interest in farm animal welfare. Whilst some consumer clusters are highly interested in animal-friendly products, other clusters may consider animal welfare to be an important product attribute but not dominant to other product attributes such as price, taste or quality. For these consumers, products that compromise between animal welfare and price, termed "compromise products", "mildly sustainable products" or "medium welfare products" in different papers, may be an attractive alternative [14–17]. However, knowledge about market opportunities in different consumer clusters for specific types of animal(-derived) products is currently lacking.

Societal concern about animal welfare varies among species of farm animals [17] along with the degree of "feeling well-informed about welfare" [18]. In response, the current study focuses on dairy cattle with cow's milk as product, for several reasons. First, consumers do not want to be reminded of the living animal when it had to be killed for the product while purchasing meat (so-called "strategic ignorance" [19–21]). Hence, it is expectedly easier to communicate about the animal and its welfare for products, such as milk, that do not require the animal to be killed. A second advantage is that dairy farms strongly differ in the housing and management factors affecting cow welfare [22,23]. This makes it possible to differentiate the milk based on animal welfare status. Third, the dairy sector represents a significant proportion (15%) of the EU agricultural output [24], and market differentiation might be a welcome strategy for this sector, which regularly faces economic crises and searches for overall sustainability.

The overall objective of this study is therefore, to explore market opportunities for animal-friendly milk by clustering individuals based on a consumer- and a citizen-oriented measure. The overall objective is further specified into three research goals. First, this study will identify consumer segments for animal-friendly milk. Second, it will be examined to what extent market opportunities exist within different consumer segments for animal-friendly milk in Flanders, Belgium. The specific focus on the region Flanders is motivated by the significance of the dairy sector in the study area itself and for milk production in Belgium. Third, the resulting segments will be profiled in terms of perceived attribute importance and interest in information as basis for the development of marketing and communication strategies for animal-friendly milk. These insights can support a targeted marketing approach, relevant to seize market opportunities.

2. Materials and Methods

A web-based questionnaire was completed in May 2014 by 827 consumers living in Flanders, the northern region of Belgium. Participants were recruited by a subcontracted professional market research agency. The sample was representative for the Flemish population in terms of age, regional distribution and gender (Table 1). As 44% of the participants had a university college or university degree, the sample was slightly biased towards higher educated people (which was ±30% in the Flemish population in 2014), which is common in online surveys [25]. All respondents were involved in food purchasing (not necessarily the main person responsible).

Table 1. Socio-demographic profile of the sample and the Flemish population.

	Characteristics	Sample (%)	Population [a] (%)
	21–29	17.5	18.3
	30–39	23.1	24.3
Age	40–49	24.7	25.8
	50–59	21.9	21.7
	60–65	12.9	10.0
	Antwerp	28.4	27.6
	East Flanders	23.9	22.9
Regional distribution	West Flanders	18.1	18.5
	Flemish Brabant	15.2	17.1
	Limburg	14.4	13.8
Gender	Female	52.4	49.5
	Male	47.6	50.5
	Elementary education (6 years of schooling)	4.6	15.7
Education	Secondary education (12 years of schooling)	51.8	54.9
	University college (Bachelor's degree)	33.1	14.8
	University degree (Master's degree)	10.5	14.5

[a] Based on Belgian Federal Government Statistics for the Flemish population, 2012.

The survey consisted of four tiers of variables: (1) segmentation variables; (2) variables aimed to form a socio-demographic profile of the clusters; (3) variables used to examine market opportunities of the different clusters; and (4) measures aimed to support the market positioning of animal-friendly milk, mainly in terms of communication.

2.1. Segmentation Variables

The consumer-related measures used as segmentation variables were the intention to try and the intention to effectively purchase animal-friendly milk. These were measured with the statements "I am willing to buy animal-friendly milk from now on, instead of the milk I usually buy", and "I am willing to buy animal-friendly milk to try it" using a 5-point Likert scale ranging from "totally disagree" to "totally agree". The citizen-oriented measure was the perceived evaluation of the current state of dairy cattle welfare (EV), which was measured using the question "How would you rate the welfare of dairy cattle in Flanders?" on a 7-point scale ranging from "very bad" to "very good". The term "dairy cattle welfare" was not defined in the survey because there are varying definitions of animal welfare, among consumers [13] and even among animal scientists [26]. We wanted respondents to use their own perception of animal welfare, as they would do so as a consumer too.

2.2. Socio-Demographics

Age, regional distribution (Flemish provinces), gender and education were probed using categorical scales. Rural or urban living conditions, familiarity with agriculture and livestock were scored on 5-point semantic differential scales. The bipolar adjectives were "rural"/"urban", "not familiar at all with agriculture"/"very familiar with agriculture" and "not familiar at all with livestock"/"very familiar with livestock".

2.3. Market Opportunities

To determine market opportunities in Flanders, Belgium for animal-friendly milk among different consumer segments, we examined the different segments' milk consumption pattern, general attitudes towards milk and the milk processing industry, and willingness to pay for animal-friendly milk.

2.3.1. Milk Consumption

Participants were asked about their milk consumption frequency and about the type of milk they usually buy. Options for frequency of milk consumption were: "multiple times per day", "every day", "multiple times per week", "once per week" or "less than once per week". For the type of milk, the main types present in the Belgian market were listed, including "organic" (following Council Regulation (EC) No. 834/2007), "fair trade" (indicates that farmers received a fair and higher price for their milk), "farm milk" (i.e., the whole process, from milking the cow to packaging the milk, is performed by the farmer), "AA-milk" (a Belgian quality label with specific hygiene requirements for farmers and milk processors), and "conventional milk" (defined as none of the above). Participants could also indicate "our family does not purchase milk", in which case they ($n = 40$) were excluded from the analysis (see inclusion criteria), resulting in 787 usable responses.

2.3.2. General Attitudes towards Milk and Milk Processing Industry

General attitudes towards milk and the milk industry were scored on 5-point semantic differential scales. For attitude towards milk, the bipolar adjectives were "unhealthy"/"healthy", "not essential"/"essential", "not tasty"/"tasty", "expensive"/"cheap", "old-fashioned"/"modern", and "negative"/"positive". For attitude towards the milk industry, the bipolar adjectives were "unjust"/"just", "negative"/"positive", "unsustainable"/"sustainable" and "not transparent"/"transparent".

2.3.3. Willingness to Pay (WTP)

WTP was measured using contingent valuation [27] using the question: "suppose that a label came onto the market that you trust which guarantees animal-friendly production of the milk. To which degree would you be willing to buy this product instead of a product without such a label?" This is a widely used method in consumer studies that is easily understood by participants. Despite limitations, e.g., relating to hypothetical bias, the contingent valuation method can yield valuable insight into eventual differences between consumer segments regarding WTP. Respondents were provided with a reference price of the current average conventional milk price in Belgian supermarkets (based on an online consultation of five Belgian supermarkets, €1.10 per litre). WTP for animal-friendly label milk was probed for different price points, including no change in price (€1.10 per litre) and for price increases of 5% (€1.16 per litre), 10% (€1.21 per litre), 20% (€1.32 per litre), 50% (€1.65 per litre) and 100% (€2.20 per litre). Answers were on a 5-point scale ranging from "very unlikely" to "very likely".

2.4. Communication about Animal-Friendly Milk

To form the basis for development of marketing and communication strategies about animal-friendly milk, segments were profiled in terms of perceived attribute importance, trust in information sources, preferred format of information on dairy cattle welfare, and interest in information about dairy cattle welfare.

2.4.1. Perceived Attribute Importance

The perceived attribute importance was measured using the question: "When buying milk, how important are the following product attributes for you?" on a 5-point interval scale ranging from "1 = totally unimportant" to "5 = very important". Based on Vanhonacker et al. [13], attributes included were: "quality", "food safety", "freshness", "health", "price", "packaging", "taste", "sustainability", "production method", "animal welfare", "local production", "country of origin", "environmental friendliness" and "fair trade").

2.4.2. Trust in Information Sources and Preferred Format of Information on Dairy Cattle Welfare

Respondents were asked to indicate their level of trust in different information sources in relation to dairy cattle welfare on a 5-point scale ranging from "a complete lack of trust" to "a great deal of trust". Sources were "government", "animal welfare organization", "supermarket", "milk processing sector", "farmer", "consumer organization", "science" and "veterinarian". Additionally, respondents were asked to indicate their preference towards five possible welfare labels on a 5-point scale ranging from "absolutely no preference" to "strong preference". Options were chosen to allow comparison between: (1) a general animal welfare label versus a specific animal welfare label; (2) a tangible animal welfare issue versus an intangible animal welfare issue (i.e., more difficult to imagine without having specific knowledge on dairy cattle) from the consumer point of view; and (3) a product label with a broader scope including animal welfare versus an animal welfare label. Therefore, options were "a general cow welfare label" (general animal welfare label), "a cow welfare label with a focus on access to pasture" (specific animal welfare label, tangible issue), "a cow welfare label with a focus on welfare problems such as udder infection and lameness" (specific animal welfare label, intangible issue), "a label with focus on sustainability, where higher animal welfare requirements are one aspect" (product label with a broader scope, including animal welfare) and "a label with a focus on local production, where higher animal welfare requirements is only one of the aspects" (product label with a broader scope, including animal welfare).

2.4.3. Interest in Information about Dairy Cattle Welfare

Respondents were probed about their interest in information about dairy cattle welfare using measures and criteria derived from the Welfare Quality® (WQ) protocol for dairy cattle [28]. This protocol describes methods to integrate dairy cattle welfare measures into 12 criteria, four principles and an overall welfare category. All 26 welfare measures and 11 of the 12 criteria were used in the current study (Appendix). In dairy cattle, the criterion "Thermal comfort" is not measured and was thus not included in the survey. The full WQ protocol for dairy cattle can be found at http://www.welfarequalitynetwork.net/.

To measure interest in information, the following question was used for each WQ measure and criterion: "Several aspects that can influence the welfare of dairy cows are listed below. To what degree do you wish to be informed about each of these aspects in order to make the right choice when buying cow's milk?" Answers were on a 100-point scale ranging from "I do not want to be informed about this at all when I am buying cow's milk" to "This is very interesting information for me when I am buying cow's milk". Measures and criteria were shown separately and in random order to prohibit the respondents from scoring the measures purely based on the criteria they belong to.

2.5. Statistical Analysis

Factor Analysis using principal components was performed for both attitude measures. Items were excluded using backwards selection when factor scores were lower than 0.6 and when the item loaded high (greater than half of the highest) on two or more factors, as recommended by Field [29]. Internal consistency (using Cronbach's alpha's) was checked and deemed acceptable when higher than 0.7 following Nunnally [30]. Factor Analysis revealed that all descriptors for attitude towards milk loaded on one factor (total variance explained: 70.2%, $\alpha = 0.85$), except for the items "expensive versus cheap" and "old fashioned versus modern", which were removed because factor loadings were not high enough (0.43 and 0.57). The items of attitude towards the milk industry could all be fit into one factor (total variance explained: 73.2%, $\alpha = 0.88$). Because of the high Cronbach's alphas, a mean attitude score towards milk and the milk processing industry was calculated, by summating and averaging the respondents scores for the individual adjectives, and used in further analyses (bivariate analysis using one-way ANOVA).

Data were analysed using SPSS 22 (Chicago, IL, USA). For the cluster analysis, first hierarchical clusters were developed using Ward's method. Subsequently, K-means cluster analyses were performed to obtain clusters (following [31]). Z-scores were used for all segmentation variables to get a better view of the relative position of the clusters. Bivariate analysis using one-way ANOVA with Dunnett's T3 post hoc comparison of mean scores and cross-tabulation with χ^2–statistics were used to profile the clusters.

3. Results

3.1. Cluster Analysis

The evaluation of the current state of dairy cattle welfare (EV) was neutral on average (not poor and not good, mean 4.1 ± 1.3 on a scale of 1–7). EV was perceived as very negative–rather negative by 29% of respondents, as neutral by 31% and as rather good–very good by 40%. With regard to the questions dealing with intention, mean intention to try was rather positive (3.9 ± 0.8 on a scale of 1–5) and intention to purchase from now on neutral–rather positive (3.6 ± 0.9). Most respondents (72%) (strongly) stated to be willing to try animal-friendly milk, while only 4% (strongly) disagreed. For more than half of the respondents this resulted in a positive intention to purchase animal-friendly milk from now on (53%). As IT and IP were highly correlated ($r = 0.73$, $p < 0.001$), we will discuss them together under the term "intention to purchase" (IP) from here on.

The clustering procedure resulted in six clusters (Table 2, Figure 1). The existence of multiple consumer segments is in accordance with previous studies showing heterogeneity in interest in farm animal welfare [11,12,32,33]. We divided the clusters into three segments based on market opportunities. The first segment, with "high market opportunities", consists of cluster 2 (CL2) which is characterized by a high IP and a low EV. The second segment, referred to as "limited market opportunities", consists of three clusters (CL4, CL5 and CL6) and is characterized by a more positive perception of the current state of dairy cattle welfare and a neutral to low IP. The third segment, referred to as "moderate market opportunities", consists of two clusters (CL1 and CL3). Whereas CL1 does not seem concerned about dairy cattle welfare, they do have a positive IP, while CL3 does seem to be concerned about animal welfare (negative EV) with a neutral–rather positive IP. As some important nuances did exist between clusters in these three segments, further analysis was performed using all clusters, but results are mainly discussed using the three segments. However, where differences between clusters within segments are present, these will be discussed.

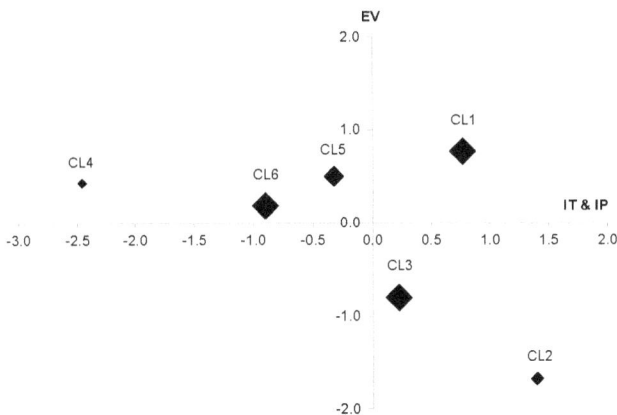

Figure 1. Mapping of the cluster centres (CL1-CL6) according to the evaluation of welfare (EV z-score) and intention to purchase welfare friendly milk (IT and IP z-score, mean of intention to try and intention to purchase from now on). The size of the marks reflects the relative size of the clusters (total $n = 787$).

Table 2. Segmentation variables, percentages of the sample and market opportunities for each cluster (CL) (Mean ($\pm$ Standard Deviation), $n = 787$).

Cluster Code	CL1	CL2	CL3	CL4	CL5	CL6
Market opportunities [1]	Moderate	High	Moderate	Limited	Limited	Limited
% of sample	24.4	8.1	23.8	3.6	16.0	24.1
Evaluation dairy cattle welfare (EV, z-score)	0.8	−1.7	−0.8	0.4	0.5	0.2
Evaluation dairy cattle welfare [2]	5.1 ± 0.7	1.8 ± 0.8	3.0 ± 0.9	4.6 ± 1.3	4.7 ± 0.9	4.3 ± 0.9
Intention to try (IT, z-score)	0.7	1.3	0.2	−2.7	0.2	−1.1
Intention to try [3]	4.5 ± 0.5	5.0 ± 0.0	4.1 ± 0.4	1.6 ± 0.6	4.1 ± 0.9	3.0 ± 0.9
Intention to purchase from now on (IP, z-score)	0.8	1.5	0.2	−2.2	−0.9	−0.7
Intention to purchase from now on [2]	4.3 ± 0.5	4.9 ± 0.3	3.8 ± 0.4	1.7 ± 0.5	2.8 ± 0.4	3.0 ± 0.3

[1] As derived from the segmentation variables; [2] 7-point scale from "very bad" to "very good"; [3] 5-point scale from "strongly disagree" to "fully agree".

3.2. Socio-Demographics

Fewer male respondents were found in the high market opportunities segment (20% versus 49%–59% for moderate market opportunities and limited market opportunities, $p < 0.001$). This is in accordance with previous studies where females were more interested/concerned about animal welfare [32,34,35]. The high market opportunities segment also contained more respondents with a higher education (54.7%), while there were fewer in the limited market opportunities segment (specifically, CL4: 32.1%, CL6: 34.9%, CL1: 45.8%, CL3: 44.9%, and CL5: 50.0%, $p < 0.001$). The profile of the high market opportunities segment corresponds to the "ethical consumers" that Vermeir and Verbeke [1] characterize as being more educated and better informed than average.

In CL4, more respondents indicated that they were familiar with livestock compared to the other clusters (39.3% versus 15%–25% for the high market opportunities and moderate market opportunities segments, $p < 0.001$). This is in line with a study by Boogaard et al. [36] among Dutch citizens who found that respondents with more stated familiarity with farming were more content with dairy farming practices. Vanhonacker et al. [32] found a similar cluster in their study and argued that the respondents were involved with animal production more on a socio-economical level than on a moral and ethical level.

As segments did not differ with respect to province, rural versus urban living conditions, familiarity with agriculture and age of the respondents, EV and IP appeared to be influenced by the respondents' attitudes, knowledge and opinions rather than by their socio-demographics. This is in accordance with earlier studies that question the usefulness of socio-demographic factors in studies involving ethical concerns [37–39].

3.3. Market Opportunities

3.3.1. Milk Consumption

Self-reported frequency of milk consumption did not differ between segments, which is in contrast with earlier studies concerning meat, where different clusters were found to indicate a different consumption pattern [38]. Regarding type of milk, respondents in the high market opportunities segment purchased significantly more organic milk compared to consumers of the other clusters ($p < 0.001$, 10.9% for CL2 and 7.1% for CL4, versus 3.1%, 4.3%, 1.6% and 0.0% for CL1, CL3, CL5 and CL6, respectively). This is in line with expectations for this segment given their very positive intention to purchase animal-friendly milk.

3.3.2. General Attitudes towards Milk and the Milk-Processing Industry

Generally, the mean attitude towards milk score was positive (4.0 ± 0.8), and the attitude towards the milk-processing industry was neutral (3.0 ± 0.8). Both attitudes differed among clusters

($p < 0.001$). Attitude towards the milk-processing industry was more negative among the high market opportunities segment (2.1 ± 1.0) than for all other clusters. This is very likely related to their negative EV, which reflects poorly on the milk-processing industry.

3.3.3. Willingness to Pay

The WTP differed for each price-increase category between clusters ($p < 0.001$ for all). As measuring WTP using contingent valuation may be subject to hypothetical bias, we here use the results of this measure only to compare between segments, not to determine thresholds for maximum prices of animal-friendly milk. The pattern followed the IP indicated by the three segments. The high market opportunities segment indicated a higher WTP for all price-increases. Most clusters with limited market opportunities (CL4 and CL6) indicated a lower WTP for 0% increase, 5% and 10% (neutral and rather unlikely, respectively, Figure 2), and no majority indicated a positive WTP at any price level (i.e., maximum of 35% and 39% for a 0% price increase). The majority of respondents indicated a positive (likely or very likely) WTP up to a price increase of 20% for CL2, 10% for CL1 and CL3 and 5% for CL5.

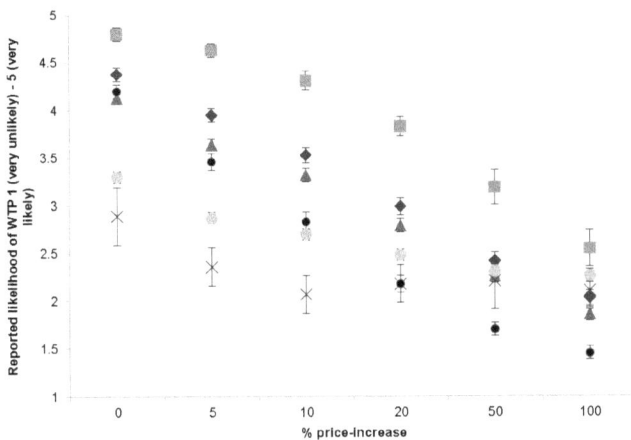

Figure 2. Mean willingness-to-pay scores $\pm$ SEM for CL1-CL6, per % of price-increase.

3.3.4. Considerations—Market Opportunities

The most pronounced differences between segments were found for the WTP, where the segment that indicated a higher IT and IP (high market opportunities) also showed a higher WTP. This segment would likely purchase products with the highest level of animal welfare, with a matching price (currently organic milk in the Flemish market). Attitudes towards milk as a product were positive, with generally neutral attitudes towards the dairy industry. Along with the finding that milk consumption frequency did not differ between clusters, these findings indicate the existence of market opportunities for animal-friendly milk, both for the highest level of animal welfare and for more intermediate products.

3.4. Communication about Animal-Friendly Milk

3.4.1. Perceived Importance of Product Attributes

The perceived importance of all milk attributes differed among clusters ($p < 0.001$, Table 3), in a somewhat different pattern than the segments. Generally, CL1 and CL2 indicated the highest importance for most attributes (all rather important to very important), CL3 and CL5 mostly indicated "neutral"–"rather interested" and the CL4 and CL6 most often indicated "neutral". An exception was the attribute "price", which CL1 and CL5 scored highest (both "very important"). These findings indicate that although CL1 might be a more conscious consumer than CL3, they do value price a lot, which causes lower market opportunities than for CL2.

The absolute importance scores for the product attribute "animal welfare" ranged from "neutral" for CL4 and CL6, to "rather important" for CL3 and CL5 clusters and "very important" for CL1 and CL2. However, when viewing the product attribute "animal welfare" relative to other product attributes, the high market opportunities and moderate market opportunities segments scored animal welfare among the more important product attributes, and the limited market opportunities segment among the less important product attributes (paired samples t-test, $p < 0.001$).

Table 3. Perceived importance of product attributes (Mean $\pm$ Standard Deviation, $n = 787$).

	Sample	CL1	CL2	CL3	CL4	CL5	CL6	*p*-Value
Packaging	3.2 ± 1.0	3.5 ± 1.0 [b]	3.2 ± 1.3 [a,b]	3.2 ± 1.0 [a,b]	3.1 ± 1.1 [a]	3.1 ± 1.0 [a]	3.1 ± 0.8 [a]	<0.001
Country of origin	3.5 ± 1.0	3.9 ± 0.9 [b]	4.0 ± 1.1 [b]	3.4 ± 1.0 [a]	3.0 ± 1.1 [a]	3.3 ± 1.0 [a]	3.2 ± 0.8 [a]	<0.001
Fair trade	3.5 ± 1.0	3.9 ± 0.9 [c]	4.2 ± 1.1 [c]	3.6 ± 0.8 [b]	3.0 ± 1.2 [a,b]	3.2 ± 1.0 [a]	3.2 ± 0.7 [a]	<0.001
Local production	3.6 ± 0.9	4.0 ± 0.8 [b]	4.1 ± 1.0 [b]	3.5 ± 0.9 [a]	3.0 ± 1.1 [a]	3.3 ± 1.0 [a]	3.2 ± 0.7 [a]	<0.001
Method of production	3.7 ± 0.9	4.0 ± 0.7 [c]	4.6 ± 0.6 [d]	3.8 ± 0.8 [b]	3.0 ± 1.0 [a]	3.4 ± 0.9 [a]	3.3 ± 0.7 [a]	<0.001
Sustainability	3.8 ± 0.8	4.1 ± 0.7 [d]	4.3 ± 0.7 [d]	3.8 ± 0.7 [c]	3.1 ± 1.1 [a,b]	3.6 ± 0.9 [b,c]	3.4 ± 0.7 [a]	<0.001
Environmental friendliness	3.8 ± 0.8	4.1 ± 0.7 [c]	4.5 ± 0.8 [d]	3.9 ± 0.6 [b]	3.1 ± 0.9 [a]	3.5 ± 0.9 [a]	3.3 ± 0.7 [a]	<0.001
Price	3.9 ± 0.8	4.1 ± 0.8 [b,c]	3.7 ± 1.0 [a,b]	3.9 ± 0.8 [b]	3.8 ± 1.1 [a,b,c]	4.2 ± 0.7 [c]	3.6 ± 0.8 [a]	<0.001
Animal welfare	4.0 ± 0.9	4.3 ± 0.7 [c]	4.9 ± 0.3 [d]	4.2 ± 0.6 [c]	3.3 ± 1.0 [a,b]	3.7 ± 0.8 [b]	3.4 ± 0.8 [a]	<0.001
Taste	4.1 ± 0.7	4.4 ± 0.6 [c]	4.6 ± 0.5 [d]	4.1 ± 0.6 [b]	3.5 ± 0.7 [a]	4.1 ± 0.6 [b]	3.6 ± 0.8 [a]	<0.001
Health	4.1 ± 0.8	4.4 ± 0.6 [d]	4.8 ± 0.4 [e]	4.2 ± 0.7 [c]	3.5 ± 0.9 [a,b,c]	4.0 ± 0.7 [b]	3.6 ± 0.8 [a]	<0.001
Quality	4.1 ± 0.7	4.5 ± 0.6 [c]	4.7 ± 0.5 [c]	4.2 ± 0.6 [a,b]	3.6 ± 1.1 [a]	4.2 ± 0.6 [b]	3.6 ± 0.8 [a]	<0.001
Food safety	4.2 ± 0.8	4.5 ± 0.6 [c]	4.8 ± 0.4 [d]	4.2 ± 0.6 [b]	3.5 ± 1.1 [a]	4.3 ± 0.7 [b]	3.6 ± 0.8 [a]	<0.001
Freshness	4.2 ± 0.7	4.5 ± 0.6 [c]	4.7 ± 0.7 [c]	4.2 ± 0.6 [b]	3.9 ± 0.8 [a,b]	4.3 ± 0.7 [b,c]	3.7 ± 0.8 [a]	<0.001

[a–e] Means $\pm$ SD within a row without common superscript differ significantly ($p < 0.05$, one-way ANOVA with Dunnett's T3 post hoc comparison of mean scores).

3.4.2. Information Sources and Preferred Format of Information on Dairy Cattle Welfare

All clusters indicated a neutral to rather negative score for "the dairy processing industry" regarding trust as a source of animal welfare information (Table 4). Possibly, this is caused by the industries vested interests in milk, which potentially biases towards creating a positive image. Besides a negative score for "the dairy processing industry", the high market opportunities segment indicated rather negative scores for trust in "government", "supermarket", and "farmer" as well. This is likely related to their low EV-score, which reflects poorly on these stakeholders. The most trusted sources of an animal-friendly milk label were veterinarians and animal welfare organizations, as all clusters indicated a neutral to positive trust in these segments.

Content of the label for all categories (i.e., "general cow welfare", "focus on access to pasture", "focus on specific welfare problems", "sustainability" and "local production") was least preferred by CL4 and CL6 (scored neutral to rather uninteresting, Table 3). The high market opportunities segment showed the highest preference for all suggested label content (scored rather to very interesting). The same goes for the type of label. None of the segments indicated a clear preference for any of the label contents.

Regarding the type of dairy cattle welfare label, preference was given to a label with a star rating system by the high market opportunities and moderate market opportunities segments. The limited segments' scores did not differ significantly between the options. These results are in line with the "extremeness aversion" theory [40], meaning that when a wider range of products is provided, consumers are less likely to choose the cheapest product. In animal welfare products, a similar construct has been examined studies [14,15], who found a smaller share of respondents choosing for the product lowest in price and animal welfare when products at intermediate levels of animal welfare and price were offered. An example of a similar and rather successful labelling scheme (representing approximately 22% of the egg market share) can be found in The Netherlands, where an animal welfare organization (Dierenbescherming) developed a label with star rating system to indicate different levels of animal welfare for various farm animal species. In addition, the recently established state-controlled animal welfare label in Denmark (Bedre Dyrevelfærd) that will enter the market in 2017 distinguishes between three levels of improved welfare following similar principles, though using hearts instead of stars.

Table 4. Preferred source, content of a label and type of label (Mean ± Standard Deviation, $n = 787$, between-segments p-value < 0.001 for all).

		Sample	CL1	CL2	CL3	CL4	CL5	CL6
Source	Veterinarian	3.7 ± 0.8	4.0 ± 0.8 [c]	3.7 ± 1.1 [b,c]	3.7 ± 0.8 [b]	3.8 ± 1.0 [b,c]	3.8 ± 0.7 [b,c]	3.2 ± 0.6 [a]
	Animal welfare organization	3.7 ± 0.8	4.0 ± 0.8 [c]	4.2 ± 0.9 [c]	3.7 ± 0.7 [b]	3.3 ± 1.1 [a,b]	3.6 ± 0.8 [b]	3.2 ± 0.7 [a]
	Science	3.5 ± 0.8	3.8 ± 0.8 [b]	3.7 ± 0.8 [b]	3.6 ± 0.8 [b]	3.1 ± 1.1 [a]	3.7 ± 0.7 [b]	3.3 ± 0.6 [a]
	Consumer organization	3.5 ± 0.8	3.9 ± 0.7 [c]	3.5 ± 1.0 [b]	3.5 ± 0.8 [b]	3.4 ± 0.9 [a,b]	3.6 ± 0.7 [c,b]	3.2 ± 0.5 [a]
	Farmer	3.1 ± 0.8	3.3 ± 0.9 [c]	2.3 ± 1.1 [a]	3.0 ± 0.9 [b]	3.3 ± 0.9 [b,c]	3.5 ± 0.8 [c]	3.1 ± 0.6 [b]
	Supermarket	3.1 ± 0.7	3.2 ± 0.8 [b]	2.6 ± 0.9 [a]	3.0 ± 0.7 [b]	3.2 ± 0.8 [b]	3.3 ± 0.7 [b]	3.2 ± 0.5 [b]
	Government	3.1 ± 0.9	3.3 ± 1.0 [b]	2.5 ± 1.0 [a]	3.0 ± 0.9 [b]	3.2 ± 1.1 [b]	3.1 ± 0.8 [b]	3.1 ± 0.6 [b]
	Dairy processing sector	3.0 ± 0.9	3.3 ± 0.9 [c,d]	2.4 ± 1.1 [a]	3.0 ± 0.9 [b]	3.1 ± 1.0 [b,c,d]	3.3 ± 0.9 [d]	3.0 ± 0.5 [b,c]
Content	General cow welfare	3.7 ± 0.9	4.3 ± 0.9 [c]	4.4 ± 0.7 [c]	3.9 ± 0.7 [b]	2.9 ± 1.1 [a]	3.8 ± 0.8 [b]	3.1 ± 0.7 [a]
	Focus on access to pasture	3.6 ± 0.9	4.2 ± 0.8 [c]	4.3 ± 0.7 [c]	3.8 ± 0.7 [b]	2.8 ± 0.8 [a]	3.6 ± 0.8 [b]	3.1 ± 0.7 [a]
	Focus on specific welfare problems	3.6 ± 0.9	4.2 ± 0.9 [d]	4.4 ± 0.8 [d]	3.7 ± 0.7 [c]	2.6 ± 1.0 [a]	3.7 ± 0.9 [c]	3.1 ± 0.7 [b]
	Sustainability	3.6 ± 0.9	4.2 ± 0.8 [c]	4.0 ± 0.7 [c]	3.7 ± 0.7 [b]	2.7 ± 1.2 [a]	3.6 ± 0.8 [b]	3.1 ± 0.7 [a]
	Local production	3.5 ± 0.9	4.0 ± 0.8 [c]	4.3 ± 1.0 [c]	3.6 ± 0.8 [b]	2.7 ± 1.1 [a]	3.3 ± 0.8 [b]	3.0 ± 0.7 [a]
Type	A label with a star rating system	3.7 ± 1.0	4.4 ± 0.9 [d]	4.3 ± 1.0 [d]	3.8 ± 1.0 [c]	2.5 ± 1.0 [a]	3.6 ± 1.0 [c]	3.2 ± 0.8 [b]
	A label without star rating system	3.2 ± 1.0	3.4 ± 1.1 [b]	3.3 ± 1.3 [a,b]	3.2 ± 1.0 [a,b]	2.7 ± 1.1 [a]	3.3 ± 1.0 [b]	3.1 ± 0.8 [a,b]

[a–d] Means within a row without common superscript differ significantly (p < 0.05, one-way ANOVA with Dunnett's T3 post hoc comparison of mean scores).

3.4.3. Interest in Information about WQ Measures and Criteria

Two findings were most apparent from the respondents' interest in information about WQ measures and criteria. First, for all measures and criteria, interest in information between clusters differed significantly (p < 0.001 for all; interest scores for all measures and criteria can be found in the Appendix). Post-hoc tests showed a clear pattern: interest in information in measures and criteria was lowest for the "limited market opportunities" segment (mean scores ranged from 27.1–35.9 for CL4, 27.9–58.6 for CL5, and 32.8–45.2 for CL6), followed by the "moderate" segment (CL1: 44.3–78.4 and CL3: 43.9–72.9) and highest for the segment with "high market opportunities" (CL2: 66.1–93.6) (p < 0.05 for all differences). Second, even though interest in all measures differed, generally the same criteria and measures received the highest importance score for all clusters. This is not in accordance with previous studies where heterogeneity in perceived important factors for farm animal welfare was found (e.g., for broiler chickens [11]). However, in these studies respondents were not given a list of (WQ) welfare impairments, but were asked to think of them themselves. When a predetermined list was given to respondents, (as done by Tuyttens et al. [41] using WQ criteria), the same criteria were found among the most and least important scores.

Both the high and moderate segments indicated most interest in "freedom of movement", whereas the limited opportunities segment attached most interest to "absence of diseases" (all p-values < 0.05). The moderate market opportunities segment and CL5 indicated the second-to most interest in absence of diseases, although moderate clusters indicated as much interest for "absence of injuries" (CL5), "comfort around resting" (CL3), "good human-animal relationship" (CL3) and "positive emotional state" (CL3). The high market opportunities and moderate market opportunities segments, and CL6, generally indicated least interest for the criteria "expression of other normal behaviour" and "expression of social behaviour". Both CL4 and CL5 did not score any of the criteria as lower than most other criteria. Regarding measures, highest scores (all $p < 0.05$) by the moderate market opportunities segment and CL5 and CL6 were attributed to "access to pasture", but some scored "expression of positive behaviour" (CL1, CL3, CL5, and CL6), "expression of negative behaviour" (CL1, CL3, CL5, and CL6), dehorning method (CL3), tail docking method, "number of drinking points, cleanliness and functioning of the drinking points" (CL3) and "tied housing" (CL3, CL5, and CL6) equally high. CL2 scored all the aforementioned measures equally high, and CL4 scored all equally low.

While most segments attributed lowest scores to the criterion measured using "access to pasture" (criterion "expression of normal behaviour"), this measure was given the highest importance score by the majority of segments. Possibly, freedom of movement was associated with access to pasture by the respondents (which actually is a measure of the criterion "expression of normal behaviour") which explains this discrepancy. Access to pasture is consistently mentioned in literature as being highly important to citizens [8,42,43]. Additionally, although the criterion "absence of diseases" was scored high by many clusters, none of the measures for diseases were among the highest scores for most clusters. It is likely that a high level of knowledge or familiarity is needed to understand the importance of these specific welfare measures, while a general lack of knowledge about farming practices and specific welfare problems among consumers has been shown [44]. Besides a lack of knowledge, respondents also seemed to not prefer specific information, given that the least preferred content for an animal-friendly label was "specific welfare problems". The latter is in accordance with previous studies which found that too detailed information (or information overload) could have a detrimental effect on the intention to purchase [33,45,46].

3.4.4. Considerations—Communication Targeted to the Various Segments

Generally, animal welfare was scored as a neutral to a very important product attribute, but less important than taste, health, quality, food safety and freshness. This is in accordance with earlier studies, which report that consumers generally give higher priority to primary product attributes like quality, health and safety than to aspects related to moral issues and/or sustainability such as fair trade, local production and animal welfare [14,47,48]. By underlining the product attributes that are considered most important in milk, consumers who are negative or neutral in their intention to purchase might see benefits of the animal-friendly products. Perceived benefits from animal-friendly milk (e.g., healthier and better quality) have previously been found to be related to intention to purchase previously [49] and could change consumers' purchase behaviour. Naturally, these benefits would have to actually exist in order to make such claims about animal-friendly milk. A study has already shown a positive relationship between milk quality and animal welfare [50], but more research on this subject is still needed.

The most trusted sources for information on cow welfare were veterinarians and animal welfare organizations. Regarding type of dairy cattle welfare label, general preference was given to a label with a star rating. Regarding interest in information about the current state of animal welfare, the measure "access to pasture" and criterion "freedom of movement" were considered to be most interesting. Although the WQ criterion "absence of diseases" was among the highest scores as well, using individual diseases or injuries like lameness or mastitis as attributes to communicate does not seem a promising route, because no preference was given to this type of welfare label, nor to the WQ measures of disease.

4. Conclusions

The objective of this paper was to explore market opportunities for sustainable products, specifically animal-friendly milk, by identifying and profiling market segments based on a consumer- and a citizen-oriented segmentation variable (IP and EV, respectively). A high degree of differentiation within the Flemish market for milk was shown (six consumer clusters), with identification of market opportunities for animal-friendly milk, while the market supply does not show a similar differentiation.

Intention to purchase and, to a lesser degree, WTP were strongly linked to interest in information about animal welfare. The consumer segment with the highest IP and WTP is believed to be most interested in the products with the highest level of animal welfare (e.g., organic and high market opportunities segment). In addition, this segment was most negative regarding the state of animal welfare and the dairy industry. Milk with the highest level of both price and animal welfare could be positioned in the market by primarily focusing on enhanced welfare as this appears to be a dominant selection criterion for the segment with high market opportunities. This study lays the foundation for future research, which could focus on examining consumer segments with moderate and/or limited market opportunities, where communication could highlight specific benefits (e.g., healthier and better quality) at an intermediate level of animal welfare and price to change these consumers' purchase behaviour.

Although, in this paper, we collated clusters based on market opportunities to form three segments, some crucial differences between clusters within segments were apparent. While CL5 was identified as having "limited" market opportunities, this cluster did seem somewhat more interested in animal-friendly milk than CL4 and CL6 within the same segment. Since age was not associated with the clusters, a transition of individuals from one segment to another, e.g., from limited to moderate, or from moderate to high, is unlikely to happen automatically over time as the simple result of people's ageing. Specific efforts that aim at stimulating such a transition will be needed, and the fact that gender is associated with clusters indicates that extra efforts targeting male consumers might be required. The use of informational approaches emerges as a potential strategy. The finding that education is associated with clusters suggests that better and more easily accessible information may be effective in moving people from one to another segment. Such informational approaches could focus on the state of animal welfare or on the precise characteristics of animal-friendly products.

Promising selling propositions in future communication about animal-friendly milk were found to be "access to pasture" and the related criterion (according to respondents) "freedom of movement", and the criterion "absence of diseases". Our results reveal an information need that confirms actual practices as foreseen in operational labelling systems, such as a star rating system differentiating between diverse levels of animal welfare at different price levels. Marketing effort that underlines access to pasture and the healthiness of cows would play into the publics' interests regarding dairy cattle welfare. To position products with the highest level of price and animal welfare, enhanced welfare could be the main focus, whereas intermediate products could be positioned based on benefits of increased cow welfare for milk. When the market supply would be better aligned with the heterogeneous demand, for instance by using a star (or equivalent) rating system, the market share of animal-friendly products could increase. Additionally, such a rating system could encourage farmers to invest in improved cow welfare as a higher rating could translate into a higher price for their dairy products.

The results obtained in the present study are specific for milk in Flanders, Belgium. Nevertheless, it is likely that the finding of a high degree of differentiation in the market based on consumers' intention to purchase and their evaluation of the state of animal welfare as an attribute of livestock products, as well as the existence of related market opportunities, can be extrapolated to other livestock products, animal species, and regions. Further research into this domain is recommended.

Acknowledgments: The authors thank Miriam Levenson for language editing. We also thank the ILVO personnel of Social Sciences and Animal Sciences for pre-testing the questionnaire.

Author Contributions: Sophie de Graaf, Filiep Vanhonacker, Jo Bijttebier, Ludwig Lauwers, Frank A. M. Tuyttens and Wim Verbeke conceived and designed the study; Sophie de Graaf analysed the data; Sophie de Graaf wrote the paper; and Filiep Vanhonacker, Jo Bijttebier, Ludwig Lauwers, Ellen Van Loo, Frank A. M. Tuyttens and Wim Verbeke provided necessary feedback during the research process, and proofread the paper.

Conflicts of Interest: The authors declare no conflict of interest.

Appendix A

Table A1. Mean scores of the interest in information about WQ measures and criteria for the entire sample ($p < 0.001$ for all) and per cluster.

WQ Criteria and WQ Measures	Sample	CL1	CL2	CL3	CL4	CL5	CL6
Absence of prolonged hunger	57.58	68.70 [c]	91.73 [d]	63.83 [c]	27.21 [a]	46.02 [b]	40.74 [a,b]
The number of cows on a farm that are too thin	50.95	59.71 [b]	84.23 [c]	57.50 [b]	25.64 [a]	36.38 [a]	37.74 [a]
Absence of prolonged thirst	57.80	68.82 [b]	90.23 [c]	64.89 [b]	29.82 [a]	46.33 [a]	40.40 [a]
Number of drinking points, cleanliness and functioning of the drinking points	56.40	66.51 [b]	89.41 [c]	62.68 [b]	27.64 [a]	44.84 [a]	40.69 [a]
Comfort around resting	58.56	70.19 [c]	90.53 [d]	66.10 [c]	25.82 [a]	45.94 [b]	41.66 [b]
Number of cows on a farm colliding with housing equipment when they lie down	43.22	46.96 [b]	79.53 [c]	48.57 [b]	23.64 [a]	31.17 [a]	32.77 [a]
The number of cows on a farm that lie down on places that are not meant for lying (indication of a dirty or unsuitable lying area)	50.90	58.76 [b]	88.28 [c]	56.43 [b]	25.14 [a]	38.44 [a]	36.90 [a]
The number of cows on the farm with dirty legs, udder or flanks	48.32	54.91 [b]	78.61 [c]	55.13 [b]	23.64 [a]	34.03 [a]	37.83 [a]
The time that it takes for a cow to lie down as indicator of pain or fear of colliding with housing equipment	47.77	54.11 [b]	83.59 [c]	53.41 [b]	27.61 [a]	33.85 [a]	35.87 [a]
Freedom of movement	65.22	78.43 [c]	93.44 [d]	72.89 [c]	33.25 [a]	58.62 [b]	43.78 [a]
Housing where the cows are tied instead of able to walk around freely	57.93	67.11 [b]	92.23 [c]	64.72 [b]	32.32 [a]	47.31 [a]	41.13 [a]
Absence of injuries	57.88	68.27 [c]	86.97 [d]	64.89 [c]	27.43 [a]	47.25 [b]	42.29 [a,b]
The number of lame cows on the farm	53.11	60.05 [b]	88.67 [c]	59.37 [b]	32.43 [a]	39.90 [a]	39.69 [a]
The number of cows on a farm with hairless patches. cuts and/or swellings	54.23	62.09 [b]	88.59 [c]	61.14 [b]	32.71 [a]	41.59 [a]	39.37 [a]
Absence of diseases	63.00	73.99 [c]	89.36 [d]	68.64 [c]	35.93 [a,b]	57.17 [b]	45.24 [a]
The number of cows on a farm that cough and sneeze	51.99	59.80 [b]	84.69 [c]	57.58 [b]	29.50 [a]	41.96 [a]	37.49 [a]
The number of cows on a farm with a runny nose or runny eye (symptom of an infection)	53.97	62.85 [b]	87.50 [c]	58.08 [b]	33.39 [a]	42.35 [a]	40.33 [a]
The number of cows on a farm that have difficulty breathing	54.19	62.10 [b]	88.86 [c]	59.70 [b]	32.00 [a]	44.22 [a]	38.90 [a]
The number of cows on a farm with diarrhoea	54.24	61.46 [b]	87.77 [c]	59.23 [b]	33.86 [a]	42.34 [a]	41.56 [a]
The number of cows on a farm with a vaginal or uterine infection	53.39	62.75 [b]	88.83 [c]	57.81 [b]	27.54 [a]	40.94 [a]	39.63 [a]
The number of cows on a farm with an udder infection	57.77	66.86 [b]	89.33 [c]	63.07 [b]	34.71 [a]	48.05 [a]	42.52 [a]
The number of cows on a farm that have died	50.98	59.22 [b]	84.67 [c]	54.64 [b]	31.46 [a]	40.75 [a]	37.29 [a]
The number of difficult calvings	39.86	44.32 [b]	66.08 [c]	43.88 [b]	24.32 [a]	27.86 [a]	32.78 [a]
The number of cows on a farm that could not stand upright anymore	52.09	60.35 [b]	87.31 [c]	57.93 [b]	25.43 [a]	41.45 [a]	37.02 [a]

Table 1. *Cont.*

WQ Criteria and WQ Measures	Sample	CL1	CL2	CL3	CL4	CL5	CL6
Absence of pain induced by management procedures	56.99	67.53 [c]	89.50 [d]	63.98 [c]	27.11 [a]	45.64 [b]	40.35 [a,b]
The number of cows on a farm where the horns are removed using a caustic paste in comparison to a soldering iron and whether anaesthesia or pain medication is used during this procedure	54.17	61.44 [b]	90.81 [c]	62.05 [b]	28.07 [a]	43.25 [a]	37.72 [a]
The number of cows on a farm whose tail has been removed using a rubber band instead of an operation and whether anaesthesia or pain medication was used during this procedure	54.18	61.55 [b]	90.30 [c]	61.23 [b]	26.71 [a]	43.16 [a]	38.92 [a]
Expression of social behaviour	55.44	64.72 [b]	83.75 [c]	63.04 [b]	32.68 [a]	45.98 [a]	38.58 [a]
Cows butting heads or showing other aggressive behaviour among themselves	43.77	48.79 [b]	76.56 [c]	49.34 [b]	27.21 [a]	29.75 [a]	33.86 [a]
Expression of other normal behaviour	55.03	65.39 [c]	84.89 [d]	62.11 [c]	25.18 [a]	45.00 [b]	38.51 [a,b]
The number of days per year that the cows have access to a pasture for more than 6 h per day	60.31	72.18 [c]	89.27 [d]	65.78 [c]	29.46 [a]	51.79 [b]	43.30 [a,b]
Good human-animal relationship	60.60	71.86 [b]	91.17 [c]	68.64 [b]	33.14 [a]	48.37 [a]	43.07 [a]
Number of cows that are not approachable by people (indicates cows' fear of people)	50.25	57.84 [b]	83.66 [a]	56.71 [b]	25.75 [a]	37.76 [a]	36.78 [a]
Positive emotional state	57.34	68.18 [b]	89.25 [c]	66.39 [b]	26.57 [a]	44.67 [a]	39.57 [a]
Showing positive behaviour (active, relaxed, calm, content, friendly, playful, positively occupied, lively, curious, social and happy)	60.10	72.82 [b]	92.45 [c]	67.50 [b]	30.32 [a]	48.45 [a]	41.08 [a]
Showing negative behaviour (fearful, irritated, indifferent, frustrated, bored, agitated, nervous, apathetic and stressed)	60.92	72.48 [b]	93.59 [c]	68.48 [b]	35.71 [a]	49.41 [a]	42.03 [a]

[a–d] Means within a row without common superscript differ significantly ($p < 0.05$, one-way ANOVA with Dunnett's T3 post hoc comparison of mean scores).

References

1. Vermeir, I.; Verbeke, W. Sustainable food consumption: Exploring the consumer attitude–behavioral intention. *J. Agric. Environ. Ethics* **2006**, *19*, 169–194. [CrossRef]
2. Briggeman, B.C.; Lusk, J.L. Preferences for fairness and equity in the food system. *Eur. Rev. Agric. Econ.* **2010**. [CrossRef]
3. European Commission. *Attitudes of Europeans towards Animal Welfare*; Special Eurobarometer 442; European Commission: Brussels, Belgium, 2016.
4. Harper, G.C.; Makatouni, A. Consumer perception of organic food production and farm animal welfare. *Br. Food J.* **2002**, *104*, 287–299. [CrossRef]
5. Van Loo, E.J.; Caputo, V.; Nayga, R.M.; Meullenet, J.-F.; Crandall, P.G.; Ricke, S.C. Effect of organic poultry purchase frequency on consumer attitudes toward organic poultry meat. *J. Food Sci.* **2010**, *75*, S384–S397. [CrossRef] [PubMed]
6. Van Loo, E.J.; Caputo, V.; Nayga, R.M.; Verbeke, W. Consumers' valuation of sustainability labels on meat. *Food Policy* **2014**, *49*, 137–150. [CrossRef]
7. Samborski, V.; Van Bellegem, L. *De Biologische Landbouw in Vlaanderen: Stand van Zaken 2014*; Departement Landbouw en Visserij: Brussels, Belgium, 2014; p. 15.
8. Harvey, D.; Hubbard, C. Reconsidering the political economy of farm animal welfare: An anatomy of market failure. *Food Policy* **2013**, *38*, 105–114. [CrossRef]
9. Toma, L.; McVittie, A.; Hubbard, C.; Stott, A.W. A structural equation model of the factors influencing British consumers' behaviour toward animal welfare. *J. Food Prod. Mark.* **2011**, *17*, 261–278. [CrossRef]
10. Dagevos, H.; Sterrenberg, L. *Burgers en Consumenten: Tussen Tweedeling en Twee-Eenheid*; Wageningen Academic Publishers: Wageningen, The Netherlands, 2003.
11. Hall, C.; Sandilands, V. Public attitudes to the welfare of broiler chickens. *Anim. Welf.* **2007**, *16*, 499–512.
12. Liljenstolpe, C. Evaluating animal welfare with choice experiments: An application to Swedish pig production. *Agribusiness* **2008**, *24*, 67–84. [CrossRef]
13. Vanhonacker, F.; Van Poucke, E.; Tuyttens, F.; Verbeke, W. Citizens' views on farm animal welfare and related information provision: Exploratory insights from Flanders, Belgium. *J. Agric. Environ. Ethics* **2010**, *23*, 551–569. [CrossRef]
14. De Jonge, J.; van der Lans, I.A.; van Trijp, H.C. Different shades of grey: Compromise products to encourage animal friendly consumption. *Food Qual. Preference* **2015**, *45*, 87–99. [CrossRef]
15. Van Herpen, E.; Fischer, A.R.; van Trijp, H.C. How to position 'mildly sustainable' products: The joint impact of assortment display and price setting. *Food Qual. Preference* **2015**, *46*, 26–32. [CrossRef]
16. Weinrich, R.; Spiller, A. Developing food labeling strategies: Multi-level labeling. *J. Clean. Prod.* **2016**, *137*, 1138–1148. [CrossRef]
17. Eurobarometer, S. *Attitudes of EU Citizens towards Animal Welfare*; European Commission: Brussels, Belgium, 2007.
18. Harper, G.; Henson, S. *Consumer Concerns about Animal Welfare and the Impact on Food Choice*; EU FAIR CT98-3678; Centre for Food Economics Research, The University of Reading: Reading, UK, 2001.
19. Holm, L.; Möhl, M. The role of meat in everyday food culture: An analysis of an interview study in Copenhagen. *Appetite* **2000**, *34*, 277–283. [CrossRef] [PubMed]
20. Kennedy, O.B.; Stewart-Knox, B.J.; Mitchell, P.C.; Thurnham, D.I. Consumer perceptions of poultry meat: A qualitative analysis. *Nutr. Food Sci.* **2004**, *34*, 122–129. [CrossRef]
21. Onwezen, M.C.; van der Weele, C.N. When indifference is ambivalence: Strategic ignorance about meat consumption. *Food Qual. Preference* **2016**, *52*, 96–105. [CrossRef]
22. de Vries, M.; Bokkers, E.A.M.; Van Reenen, C.G.; Engel, B.; van Schaik, G.; Dijkstra, T.; de Boer, I.J.M. Housing and management factors associated with indicators of dairy cattle welfare. *Prev. Vet. Med.* **2015**, *118*, 80–92. [CrossRef] [PubMed]
23. Von Keyserlingk, M.A.G.; Barrientos, A.; Ito, K.; Galo, E.; Weary, D.M. Benchmarking cow comfort on North American freestall dairies: Lameness, leg injuries, lying time, facility design, and management for high-producing Holstein dairy cows. *J. Dairy Sci.* **2012**, *95*, 7399–7408. [CrossRef] [PubMed]

24. Europea Commission. *Overview of Cap Reform 2014–2020. Agricultural Policy Perspectives Brief*; Europea Commission: Brussels, Belgium, 2013.

25. Granello, D.H.; Wheaton, J.E. Online data collection: Strategies for research. *J. Couns. Dev.* **2004**, *82*, 387–393. [CrossRef]

26. Fraser, D. Understanding animal welfare. *Acta Vet. Scand.* **2008**, *50*. [CrossRef]

27. Vossler, C.A.; Kerkvliet, J. A criterion validity test of the contingent valuation method: Comparing hypothetical and actual voting behavior for a public referendum. *J. Environ. Econ. Manag.* **2003**, *45*, 631–649. [CrossRef]

28. Welfare Quality® Consortium. *Welfare Quality® Assessment Protocol for Cattle*; Welfare Quality®Consortium: Lelystad, The Netherlands, 2009; p. 182.

29. Field, A. *Discovering Statistics Using SPSS*; Sage Publications: Thousand Oaks, CA, USA, 2009.

30. Nunnally, J.C. *Psychometric Theory*, 2nd ed.; McGraw-Hill: New York, NY, USA, 1987.

31. Kuo, R.J.; Ho, L.M.; Hu, C.M. Integration of self-organizing feature map and K-means algorithm for market segmentation. *Comput. Oper. Res.* **2002**, *29*, 1475–1493. [CrossRef]

32. Vanhonacker, F.; Verbeke, W.; Van Poucke, E.; Tuyttens, F.A. Segmentation based on consumers' perceived importance and attitude toward farm animal welfare. *Int. J. Sociol. Agric. Food* **2007**, *15*, 91–107.

33. Pouta, E.; Heikkilä, J.; Forsman-Hugg, S.; Isoniemi, M.; Mäkelä, J. Consumer choice of broiler meat: The effects of country of origin and production methods. *Food Qual. Preference* **2010**, *21*, 539–546. [CrossRef]

34. Phillips, C.; Izmirli, S.; Aldavood, J.; Alonso, M.; Choe, B.I.; Hanlon, A.; Handziska, A.; Illmann, G.; Keeling, L.; Kennedy, M. An international comparison of female and male students' attitudes to the use of animals. *Animals* **2010**, *1*, 7–26. [CrossRef] [PubMed]

35. Kendall, H.A.; Lobao, L.M.; Sharp, J.S. Public Concern with Animal Well-Being: Place, Social Structural Location, and Individual Experience. *Rural Sociol.* **2006**, *71*, 399–428. [CrossRef]

36. Boogaard, B.K.; Bock, B.B.; Oosting, S.J.; Krogh, E. Visiting a farm: An exploratory study of the social construction of animal farming in Norway and the Netherlands based on sensory perception. *Int. J. Sociol. Agric. Food* **2010**, *17*, 24–50.

37. Diamantopoulos, A.; Schlegelmilch, B.B.; Sinkovics, R.R.; Bohlen, G.M. Can socio-demographics still play a role in profiling green consumers? A review of the evidence and an empirical investigation. *J. Bus. Res.* **2003**, *56*, 465–480. [CrossRef]

38. Vanhonacker, F.; Verbeke, W. Buying higher welfare poultry products? Profiling Flemish consumers who do and do not. *Poult. Sci.* **2009**, *88*, 2702–2711. [CrossRef] [PubMed]

39. Verbeke, W.; Vackier, I. Profile and effects of consumer involvement in fresh meat. *Meat Sci.* **2004**, *67*, 159–168. [CrossRef] [PubMed]

40. Simonson, I.; Tversky, A. Choice in context: Tradeoff contrast and extremeness aversion. *J. Mark. Res.* **1992**, *29*, 281–295. [CrossRef]

41. Tuyttens, F.A.; Vanhonacker, F.; Van Poucke, E.; Verbeke, W. Quantitative verification of the correspondence between the Welfare Quality® operational definition of farm animal welfare and the opinion of Flemish farmers, citizens and vegetarians. *Livest. Sci.* **2010**, *131*, 108–114. [CrossRef]

42. Boogaard, B.K.; Oosting, S.J.; Bock, B.B. Defining sustainability as a socio-cultural concept: Citizen panels visiting dairy farms in the Netherlands. *Livest. Sci.* **2008**, *117*, 24–33. [CrossRef]

43. Schuppli, C.A.; Von Keyserlingk, M.A.G.; Weary, D.M. Access to pasture for dairy cows: Responses from an online engagement. *J. Anim. Sci.* **2014**, *92*, 5185–5192. [CrossRef] [PubMed]

44. Miele, M. *Report Concerning Consumer Perceptions and Attitudes towards Farm Animal Welfare*; European Animal Welfare Platform: Brussels, Belgium, 2010.

45. Kolodinsky, J. Persistence of health labeling information asymmetry in the United States: Historical perspectives and twenty-first century realities. *J. Macromark.* **2012**, *32*, 193–207. [CrossRef]

46. Van Kleef, E.; Van Trijp, H.; Paeps, F.; Fernandez-Celemin, L. Consumer preferences for front-of-pack calories labeling. *Public Health Nutr.* **2008**, *11*, 203–213. [CrossRef] [PubMed]

47. Heleski, C.R.; Mertig, A.G.; Zanella, A.J. Assessing attitudes toward farm animal welfare: A national survey of animal science faculty members. *J. Anim. Sci.* **2004**, *82*, 2806–2814. [CrossRef] [PubMed]

48. Ingenbleek, P.T.M.; Binnekamp, M.H.A.; van Trijp, J.C.M. *Betalen Voor Dierenwelzijn: Barrieres en Oplossingsrichtingen in Consumentenmarkten en Business-to-Business Markten*; Landbouw Economisch Instituut (LEI): Den Haag, the Netherlands, 2006.

49. De Graaf, S.; Van Loo, E.J.; Bijttebier, J.; Vanhonacker, F.; Lauwers, L.; Tuyttens, F.A.; Verbeke, W. Determinants of consumer intention to purchase animal-friendly milk. *J. Dairy Sci.* **2016**, *99*, 8304–8313. [CrossRef] [PubMed]

50. Müller-Lindenlauf, M.; Deittert, C.; Köpke, U. Assessment of environmental effects, animal welfare and milk quality among organic dairy farms. *Livest. Sci.* **2010**, *128*, 140–148. [CrossRef]

sustainability

MDPI

Article

An Environmental Perspective on Clothing Consumption: Consumer Segments and Their Behavioral Patterns

Wencke Gwozdz *, Kristian Steensen Nielsen and Tina Müller

Department of Management, Copenhagen Business School, Society & Communication, CBS Centre for Corporate Social Responsibility (cbsCSR), Porcelænshaven 18A, DK-2000 Frederiksberg, Denmark; ksn.msc@cbs.dk (K.S.N.); tm.msc@cbs.dk (T.M.)
* Correspondence: wg.msc@cbs.dk; Tel.: +45-3815-3391

Academic Editor: Gerrit Antonides
Received: 15 February 2017; Accepted: 2 May 2017; Published: 6 May 2017

Abstract: Efforts to decrease the environmental impact of today's clothing industry across the entire process of production, purchase, maintenance, and disposal can be driven by either suppliers or consumers. Changing the behavior of the latter, however, requires an understanding of current clothing consumption patterns—a currently under-researched area. We therefore shed more light on these patterns in the purchase, use and maintenance, and discard phases by analyzing unique data on 4617 adult consumers (aged 18–65) from Germany, Poland, Sweden, and the U.S., who we divide into five segments based on clothing consumption behavior. At the low end of the spectrum is a consumer segment that earns the least, consumes mostly budget brand clothing, and is the least open to alternative more environmentally friendly business models such as fashion leasing or clothing libraries. At the other extreme lies a small segment that earns the most, engages in high consumption of medium or premium brand clothing, and is most open to alternative business models. Lying between these two is a primarily female segment that purchases an above average amount of clothing from budget brands. In addition to the segments' different reported purchase behavior and a varying openness to alternative business models, we identify differences in willingness to pay for clothing made of material that is more environmentally friendly than conventional fabrics. These observations suggest several promising directions for environmental interventions tailored toward specific consumer segments.

Keywords: clothing consumption; consumer segmentation; environmental impact; Western countries

1. Introduction

In addition to meeting the basic human need for protection against weather variations, clothing functions as a means of personal communication by which individuals express themselves through their clothing choices. Because this practice has persisted over recorded human history, it might be regarded as an acquired human need [1]. Nonetheless, the clothing industry of today has moved well beyond merely satisfying basic physiological and psychological needs, and the rise of fast fashion, especially, has greatly altered clothing's societal and cultural significance. In particular, fast fashion has drastically shortened the clothing life cycle, with new styles swiftly superseding the old. Not only do many fast fashion retailers (e.g., H&M or Forever 21) introduce new merchandise on an almost weekly basis and deliberately manipulate the supply to create "must have" items targeted primarily at young consumers [2,3], but fast fashion products also tend to have a short lifespan [4]. This brevity is not necessarily a result of the clothing's intrinsic quality but rather may stem from a reduction in the products' symbolic value (e.g., being outdated by newer trends). Overall, therefore, the fast fashion industry is characterized by short-term use, symbolic obsolescence, and increasing waste generation [5], meaning that its rise has had detrimental consequences for the environment. In fact, the clothing industry is currently one of the world's most polluting industries [6], heavily impacting the environment through its immense use of water and chemicals during production (e.g., for growing cotton or dying textiles), as well as ecosystem pollution, and textile waste generation [6,7]. However, even though much environmental degradation can be attributed to the clothing industry, an equal part of the responsibility is borne by consumers, who, rather than being mindless market actors with no control over clothing's environmental impact, are instrumental in determining the number, frequency, and type of clothing items purchased, how these items are used and maintained, and the means of disposal once items are worn out or no longer wanted. All these consumer-related aspects have implications for clothing's final impact on the environment (see, e.g., [1]).

The purpose of the present study, therefore, is to assess consumer behavior as it relates to each of these aspects—with particular attention to current clothing consumption patterns through the purchase, use and maintenance, and disposal phases—as well as this behavior's implications for environmental sustainability. We do so using a consumer segmentation analysis that not only addresses consumer heterogeneity but, instead of characterizing the segments demographically as is common in previous research, differentiates them by purchase behavior. Such segmentation contributes to a better understanding of clothing consumption, one that can inform the development of targeted behavior change interventions. Our analysis also contrasts with previous empirical work in environmentally friendly and unfriendly clothing consumption in that rather than using small-scale or one-country samples to focus on one of the three consumption phases, it employs large diverse samples from four countries (Germany, Poland, Sweden, and the U.S.) to trace behavior patterns across all three phrases. It thus makes a unique contribution to this literature stream in both scope and analytical approach. Before reporting our results, however, we present an overview of the primary environmental concerns related to the clothing life cycle and then describe our sample and methodology.

2. Background

Because the evolution of fast fashion and the subsequent globalized mass consumption of clothing have greatly influenced the state of the environment, we begin our discussion with an explanation of how production and purchase, use and maintenance, and the eventual disposal of clothing each creates different environmental concerns. Although a lack of supply chain transparency and traceability from clothing retailers makes it impossible to attribute some of these concerns directly to consumers, other problems could be directly alleviated or accommodated by changes in consumer purchase and post-purchase behavior patterns.

2.1. Production and Purchase

The high resource intensity of clothing production makes it the primary source of environmental degradation in the clothing life cycle [1], with particularly heavy environmental impacts from voluminous use of energy, water, and chemicals. The production of one pair of jeans, for instance, requires 3625 liters of water, 3 kilograms of chemicals, 400 MJ of energy, and 16 m^2 of harvested land [8]. The clothing industry is thus high on energy consumption but low on energy use efficiency [9], with most energy in clothing production consumed during weaving, spinning, and chemical processing [6]. During 2008, for example, textile and clothing production used 1074 billion kWh of electricity (or 132 million tons of coal) [10].

Clothing production also consumes vast amounts of water, a resource that is becoming increasingly scarce across the globe because of climate change, pollution, and overuse. The primary source of water usage is in the production of cotton, a water-intensive crop that may need as much as 8.5 tons per kilogram [11]. The fabric preparation process of desizing, scouring, and bleaching also depends on water throughout, and nearly all textile dying and application of specialty or finishing chemicals occurs in water baths. Even worse, following each process, the fabrics are washed to remove used chemicals and the water is returned to the ecosystem, often without any purification efforts, which leads to water pollution [12]. Hence, in addition to an estimated nine trillion liters of water per year [12], textile processing also uses about 25% of the chemicals employed in production globally [13]. Even synthetic fibers, such as polyester, although developed in factories independent of water, have a negative impact because of their derivation from fossil hydrocarbons [14].

Naturally, the environmental concerns arising from the production phase are highly interconnected with those from the purchase phase, although in this latter phase, consumers, through their purchasing power, have the volitional capacity to choose items made of more environmentally friendly and higher quality materials (e.g., lyocell fibers such as Tencel®) than are conventional. Consumers also decide when new clothing items are needed and how many should be purchased. Hence, the purchase phase is critically important to clothing's environmental impact through its strong interaction with the other life cycle phases. For example, whereas garment quality inherently influences maintenance and eventual necessity for disposal, the sheer volume of clothing items sold has profound implications for the environmental impact of the production phase. Over recent decades, this volume has been rising, with private consumption of clothing and shoes in Sweden increasing by 53% from 1999 to 2009 [15], including an average purchase of nine t-shirts per year [16]. In America, as of 2013, the average consumer purchased 64 clothing items per year with an associated expenditure of $907 [17], approximately $14.17 per item. However, most consumers still do not link their clothing consumption patterns with environmental degradation [18,19].

In fact, this increasing consumption comes at a high environmental cost, one that Roos et al. [20] suggested can be most efficiently reduced by increasing the service life of clothing items whenever feasible to lower overall consumption rates. Another possible solution is to use more environmentally friendly materials, which, although increasingly more available in clothing stores, still represent only a niche on the global market. Even when such materials are relatively plentiful—for example, organic cotton with a market value of $15.7 billion for an annual production of 112,488 tons of fiber [21]—it is unclear to what extent consumers are willing to pay an additional cost for clothing made from these materials. The empirical evidence on this issue is inconclusive: whereas over half of Ha-Brookshire and Norum's respondents were willing to pay a premium for t-shirts made from U.S.-grown organic cotton [22], participants in a study by Ellis et al. reported that when purchasing clothes for themselves, they were unwilling to pay a premium for an organic cotton t-shirt [23].

Another important aspect is clothing acquisition, alternative forms of which have slowly become more popular (particularly in urban areas) in the form of clothing libraries, swap markets, fashion rentals, and second-hand stores. Although these alternative business models may represent a more environmentally friendly approach to clothing acquisition, their ability to lower clothing's environmental impact may be highly dependent on the consumer's transportation mode to and from the store [15]. That is, if using alternative models involves increased consumer transportation (e.g., more driving), the environmental benefits are likely to evaporate.

2.2. Use and Maintenance

Clothing can be costly to maintain both from a monetary and environmental perspective; especially as most maintenance practices are strongly influenced by social norms of high level hygiene and cleanliness. Adherence to these social norms, however, often involves an environmental burden of energy, water, and detergent use [24]. Europeans, for example, wash their clothes at an average temperature of 45.8 °C [25], a practice whose environmental impact is dependent on geographic and demographic context, including specific energy source [1]. When the energy source is renewable, wash temperature has a lower environmental impact, but when the energy comes from fossil fuels, the impact rises significantly. In addition to the associated environmental impact, how often clothing is washed may also have implications for product life because laundering contributes to wear and tear [26]. Among young Swedish consumers, for example, the average number of wearings before washing is two to three times for t-shirts, shirts, and tops but four or more times for trousers and skirts [27]. Although

38% of these young consumers use eco-labeled detergents, reflecting the increasing replacement of harmful chemicals with bio-based, degradable ingredients [28], consumers typically experience difficulties fully understanding dosing instructions, which may lead to overuse [29].

The environmental burden increases if laundering includes tumble drying, which consumes 3–4 times more energy than washing at 40 °C [1] but is used after around 20% of washing cycles [30]. Admittedly, such statistics should be interpreted with caution because dryer ownership varies greatly from 16% of all households in Poland to 83.4% in the U.S. [31,32]. Nevertheless, lowering washing temperatures and eliminating tumble drying and ironing would reduce a clothing product's energy consumption by 50% [33].

2.3. Discarding

The excessive consumption of clothing items generates an overflow of discarded clothing, a throw-away culture that is particularly evident in developed economies. According to the U.S. Environmental Protection Agency (EPA), in 2014, the U.S. generated 16 million tons of textile and clothing waste, 64.5% of which was sent to landfills with only 16.2% recycled [34]. In the U.K., although the average lifetime of a clothing item is 2.2 years, approximately 30% of these owned clothes have probably not been worn for a year, leading to an estimated £140 million worth of used clothing (350,000 tons) being sent to landfills each year [35].

Although clothing disposal takes many forms, including binning, reselling, recycling, donating to charity, and using unwanted clothes as rags, the European Commission's 2008 Waste Framework Directive provides clear guidance on the most environmentally significant methods [36]. This directive outlines a waste hierarchy based on environmental impact, with prevention (e.g., using fewer materials or keeping products longer) being the lowest, followed by (preparation for) reuse and recycling. The highest impact methods are recovery (e.g., incineration with energy recovery) and binning (e.g., landfilling or incineration without energy recovery). Although the directive applies to all waste handling, it is especially valid in a clothing context [37,38], in which the greatest energy and carbon emissions savings are achieved by increasing clothing longevity and direct reuse, and the next greatest by reuse through charity donation and material recycling [37–39]. However, even though many consumers discard their clothing by passing it on to family members, donating it to charity, or using it as rags [26,40], binning unwanted clothing (i.e., sending it to landfills or incineration) is still common, leading to much clothing ending up in landfills or incinerators that could have been reused, recycled, or otherwise down-cycled. This widespread disposal carries a heavy environmental burden [34,35], especially given that the synthetic materials widely used in fast fashion do not decompose, while clothes made from natural fibers such as wool, although decomposable, produce the highly potent greenhouse gas, methane.

3. Data and Methods

To gain new insights into consumer clothing consumption behavior, we administered an online survey in Germany, Poland, Sweden, and the U.S., countries selected to provide a broad but representative spectrum of clothing markets within the Western world. Whereas Sweden has a modern and increasingly sustainability oriented fashion market, Germany is the largest economy in Europe with a major clothing market similar to that of the U.S., which is also included because of its cultural and political distinction from continental Europe. Poland, on the other hand, is representative of Eastern Europe and thus a post-communist regime, but one that largely accepts materialistic values. Because the survey questionnaire addressed not only demographics and consumer behavior throughout the three consumption phases but also concepts beyond the focus of this current study, it was split into two parts to avoid participant fatigue.

3.1. Data Collection

The survey was administered between October 2016 and January 2017 by the private research software company, Qualtrics, which was responsible for contacting potential participants and collecting data in collaboration with its local panel partners. The questionnaire was first developed in English and then translated into German, Polish, and Swedish by ISO17100 certified translators. These translations were proofread by native speakers and all ambiguities resolved in collaboration with the translators before the survey was implemented online. The survey employed numerous quality measures to maximize data quality and screen out careless responses, including instruction-based attention filters ("Please select strongly agree"), bogus items ("I always sleep less than one hour per night"), response pattern indicators (e.g., straight-lining), time filters, and self-reported data quality checks (e.g., "I gave this study enough attention") [41,42]. Participants failing the instruction-based attention filters were eliminated automatically while those failing multiple quality checks were replaced. All participants received an incentive for taking part in the study in the form of points redeemable for rewards such as airline miles or gift cards.

3.2. The Sample

The sample for Part I of the survey, taken from the target consumer population aged 18 to 65, is representative on age, gender, region, and education. Although participants themselves made the decision of whether to return for Part II, subjecting the process to a self-selection bias, we also strove for representativeness in this second sample. The final sample consists of respondents who participated in both survey parts for a total of around 1000 participants for each country ($N = 4617$), with 1174 from Germany, 1116 from Poland, 1182 from Sweden, and 1145 from the U.S. The mean participant age is 42.21 years ($SD = 13.59$), and females are slightly overrepresented at 56.70%.

3.3. Measurements

To the best of our knowledge, most of our survey items on clothing consumption behavior are totally new, meaning no pre-existing standard item formulations or tested scales. Hence, all items and answer categories were developed based on an extensive review of the literature, previous survey experience, and results from consumer focus groups (also aged 18 to 65). Before survey administration, all items were proofread and tested for comprehension and validity using a small-scale face-to-face pilot. Each of the three main clothing consumption phases (purchase, use and maintenance, discard/disposal) is captured by different measures that cover both general clothing consumption and product category-specific consumption of jeans and t-shirts. Introducing this product category level alongside the domain level helps to validate questions that rely on self-reported behavior. This practice is supported in prior pilot tests in which respondents tended to recall their behavior more precisely when given a concrete clothing category. We chose jeans and t-shirts because these two categories are well known across sexes and cultures and widely purchased in the countries surveyed (e.g., in Sweden, t-shirts and jeans make up 24% and 19% of clothing consumption, respectively [1]).

For the purchase phase, the survey includes questions about the number of items bought in the past 3 months and how much was spent on clothing in general or jeans and t-shirts in particular. Because we know of no representative spending data for all four countries based on which to develop categories, the questions on expenditure for all clothing items (general, jeans, and t-shirt) during the past 3 months were open ended. The responses were then harmonized for cross-country comparability by conversion into euros and adjustment based on the Harmonized Index of Consumer Prices (HCIP) [43]. Using 2015 as the index reference period, set to 100 across all European countries, each respondent's spending was then adjusted using the average HCIP value of the corresponding country from July to September 2016. The survey also asked which brands of clothing the respondents typically purchased, whether budget, casual/medium, or premium (based on [44]); which materials (new, conventional; new, organic; reused, recycled; reused, second-hand); and through which acquisition modes.

Information collected for the use and maintenance phase included how many clothing items the respondents possessed at that time, how long they usually keep and wear their clothing, and how often they wear clothes before washing and other laundry related behaviors. Because no general behavior patterns are observable for all clothing product categories in this phase (e.g., laundry behavior differs strongly for a t-shirt vs. a jacket), these items focused on the product category rather than the general fashion domain level (see Table 1, for all clothing consumption related questions and the corresponding answer categories). Lastly, respondents were asked where they discard their unwanted clothes.

Table 1. Measurements by consumption phase.

Question	Items	Answer Categories
Purchase Behavior		
How many items of clothing did you acquire during the last 3 months?		• None • 1–4 • 5–9 • 10–15 • 16–20 • 21–25 • 26 or more
How many of items of the following did you acquire during the last 3 months? (number) ▪ Jeans ▪ T-shirt		• Free answer field
How much money did you spend on clothes/the following within the last 3 months? ▪ General ▪ Jeans ▪ T-shirt		• Free answer field in relevant currency
At which stores do you typically acquire your clothes? *Indicate a total sum of 100%* ▪ General ▪ Jeans ▪ T-shirt	• Premium (e.g., Hugo Boss or Gucci) • Casual/middle (e.g., Levi's, Esprit, or Gap) • Budget (e.g., H&M or Forever 21)	• 0%–100%
Of which material is the clothing you acquire typically made? *Indicate a total sum of 100%*	• New—conventional material • New—organic material • Reused—recycled material • Reused—second-hand material	• 0%–100%
In the last 3 months, approximately how frequently did you use the listed modes to acquire new clothes?	• High street • Shopping mall • Online shopping • Mail-order • Small boutiques • Second-hand (e.g., shop, flea market, eBay) • Supermarket • Swap (i.e., exchange/barter of clothes) • Other: (Please indicate)	• Never • 1–2 times • 3–5 times • 6–10 times • 11–15 times • More than 15 times

Table 1. *Cont.*

Question	Items	Answer Categories
Use and Maintenance Behavior		
How many items do you have of the following? (number) ▪ Jeans ▪ T-shirt		• Free answer field for each jeans and t-shirt
How long do you usually keep the following clothing items before discarding (disposing) it? ▪ Jeans ▪ T-shirt		• Less than 6 months • Less than a year • 1–2 years • 3–4 years • 5 years or more
How many times do you wear an average pair of jeans or t-shirt from your wardrobe? ▪ Jeans ▪ T-shirt		• Very rarely (once a year or less) • Rarely (less than once every 3 months) • Sometimes (at least once every other month) • Often (at least once a month) • Very often (at least once a week)
How many times do you wear the following clothing items on average before washing?		• Free answer field for each jeans and t-shirt
At which temperature do you wash? ▪ Jeans ▪ T-shirt		• 20 °C • 30 °C • 40 °C • 50 °C • 60 °C
Do you use detergent when washing? Do you use softener when washing? ▪ Jeans ▪ T-shirt		• No • Yes, non-eco • Yes, eco
Do you use the dryer after washing?		• Yes • No
Discard Behavior		
How do you typically discard your unwanted clothing? *Indicate a total sum of 100%* ▪ General ▪ Jeans ▪ T-shirt	• Second-life (e.g., donating, recycling programs, flea-market, passing on to family) • Down-cycling (e.g., use as rags) • Trash	• 0%–100%

The survey also included a set of questions relating to *environmentally friendly clothing consumption behaviors*, measured on the environmental apparel consumption (EAC) scale [45], which assesses the frequency of such behaviors as purchasing recycled or second-hand apparel or purposely selecting energy efficient or less polluting clothing products (see Table 2). The EAC measure is a mean score calculated over all eight scale items. The survey also asked, again on the product category-specific level (jeans and t-shirts), how much the respondents value second-hand clothing items or those made from recycled or organic materials compared to new products made of conventional materials. Lastly, it recorded respondents' past and future intended use of alternative business models (developed in collaboration with industry experts), such as clothes leasing, libraries, or in-store repair services.

Table 2. Measurements of environmentally friendly clothing consumption behavior.

Question	Items	Answer Categories
Environmental Apparel Consumption (EAC) In the following, please indicate what applies to you. When acquiring clothing items, I ...	• Buy clothes with environmentally friendly labeling or packaging techniques • Buy clothing made from organically grown natural fibers • Buy second-hand clothes • Buy clothes with low impact or no dye processing • Select clothes that you can wear over a longer term compared to trendy clothes that go out of style quickly • Purposely select fabrics that require cooler washing temperature, shorter drying time, or less ironing • Avoid clothes products because of environmental concerns • Buy clothes made from recycled material	• Very rarely or never • Rarely • Sometimes • Often • Very often or always
If a pair of new conventional jeans/a new conventional t-shirt is 100%, how much would you pay for exactly the same pair of *Indicate by a slider a higher or lower value compared to the conventional product*	• Recycled jeans/t-shirt • Second-hand jeans/t-shirt • New organic material jeans/t-shirt	• Low (0%)–High (200%)
Have you previously used the following ...	• Fashion leasing (e.g., similar to car leasing) • Traditional repair services (e.g., mending clothes yourself, tailor) • Reselling clothes online (e.g., eBay) • Swap markets (swapping clothes without payment) • Repair services in-store (e.g., Nudie Jeans) • Fashion rental (e.g., special occasion like weddings or carnival) • Clothing libraries (e.g., similar to book libraries) • Incentivized take back services (e.g., leaving clothing for recycling in exchange for a voucher or a buy-back program)	• Yes • No
Could you imagine using the following in the future: *Indicate on a percentile slider from 0–100*	• Fashion leasing (e.g., similar to car leasing) • Traditional repair services (e.g., mending clothes yourself, tailor) • Reselling clothes online (e.g., eBay) • Swapping markets (swapping clothes without payment) • Repair services in-store (e.g., Nudie Jeans) • Fashion rental (e.g., special occasion like weddings or carnival) • Clothing libraries (e.g., similar to book libraries) • Incentivized take back services (e.g., leaving clothing for recycling in exchange for a voucher or a buy-back program)	• Very unlikely (0) • Neutral (50) • Very likely (100)

The final section of the survey collected *sociodemographic data* such as sex, age in years, country, and income, which later we divide for comparability into 11 categories based on corresponding national statistics (Eurostat for Germany, Poland and Sweden; U.S. Census Bureau for the U.S.). The income calculation algorithm, which uses the 2014 statistic for the monthly net income of the 18–64 age group in each country, ensures cross-country comparability through the following four-step process: (1) identifying the median income per country and using this as the lower boundary of the middle-income category; (2) defining the upper boundary of the lowest category as the poverty line for singles (i.e., 60% of the median income of a single household); (3) defining the lower boundary of the upper level as approximately 2.5 times the median income; and (4) spreading the intervals for the 11 categories evenly.

3.4. Analytic Strategy

To assess current clothing consumption behavior, we created artificial consumer segments by employing a cluster analysis. However, because sociodemographics seemed to have lost their predictive power through consumer fragmentation [46], we achieved our main aim of identifying consumption patterns and their potential relations to different related environmental aspects by eschewing the socioeconomic clustering variables common in segmentation strategies, as well as values or attitudes toward a product domain, general lifestyle, or actual reported behavior. Rather, we defined our segments based on purchasing behavior, building the different segments to sort the heterogeneous sample into more homogenous subgroups whose members resemble each other on the clustering variables. At the same time, to account for as many intergroup differences as possible, we identified our consumer groups based on the amount and type of clothing bought and then compared them based on both purchasing and environmentally related behaviors across the consumption phases. This process enabled us to compare, for example, high volume and budget brand buying consumers with low volume premium buying consumers with regard to discard behavior.

To achieve our aim, we combined domain specific (general fashion) and product category-specific (jeans and t-shirts) variables [47]. As the segmentation base, we included on the domain-specific level only the following purchase characteristics: material purchased (new, conventional; new, organic; recycled; and second-hand) and acquisition mode, divided into first market acquisitions, including high street, shopping mall, online shopping, mail order, small boutiques, and supermarket; and second market acquisitions, including second-hand purchases and swapping (see also Table 1). We then assessed the type of brands purchased (budget, casual/medium and premium), the number of purchased items, and spending over the last 3 months on both the domain- and product category-specific levels. To determine the number of clusters, we employed a hierarchical cluster analysis with the squared Euclidean distance as the distance measure and then used Ward's algorithm to link consumers. In line with the Duda–Hart stopping rule, we created five clusters by running a k-means clustering analysis on a 3984 respondent sample determined by missing values in the segmentation base variables (n = 633) and case-wise deletion. The resulting segments are: (1) low consumption—budget brands; (2) low consumption—casual/medium brands; (3) medium consumption—budget brands; (4) medium consumption—casual/medium brands; and (5) high consumption—casual/medium and premium brands.

We then compared these five consumer segments on sociodemographics, use and maintenance behavior, discard behavior, and environmentally related behavior employing either ANOVA or Kruskal–Wallis equality-of-populations rank tests dependent on the measurement level and variable distribution across segments. In presenting the results, instead of p-values, we report only the differences that are statistically significant (the group comparison results are available from the authors upon request). After first describing the consumer segments' demographic characteristics and reported purchase behaviors, which serve as the segmentation base, we compare their use and maintenance, and discard behaviors. We then investigate intersegmental differences in environmentally friendly clothing consumption behavior.

4. Results

4.1. Consumer Segments and their Purchasing Behavior

The descriptive statistics for the purchasing behavior of the overall sample and consumer segments are presented in Table 3, which also gives the size of the individual segments. Over the course of three months, the average consumer purchases an average 5.9 clothing items, of which 2.1 are t-shirts (costing an average of 29 euro for two) and 0.9 is a pair of jeans (around 33 euro), for an overall cost of approximately 153 euro (column 1). Purchasing occurs about twice in the three-month period, mostly in shopping malls and online, followed by second-hand (1.4 times) and high street (1.1 times) shops, with swapping as the least used acquisition mode (column 1). Approximately 58.7% of these clothes are from budget brands, 33.5% from casual/medium brands, and only 7.8% from premium brands. The most purchased clothing material, at 61.1%, is new conventional fabric, followed by new organic at 17.8%, second-hand clothing at 13.2%, and recycled materials at only 7.8%.

This purchasing behavior, however, differs significantly across consumer segments: whereas Segments 1 and 2 buy only a little clothing, Segments 3 and 4 purchase an above average number of items, and Segment 5 engages in heavy clothing consumption of luxury items. At the low end of this spectrum, Segment 1 (1712 respondents) consumes little and prefers budget outlets, meaning that a large share of consumers (over 43.0% of the full sample) purchase only a limited amount of clothing for relatively little money. At the other extreme, Segment 5 (100 respondents) has a high clothing purchase profile with high spending on mainly casual/medium and premium clothing; however, this segment accounts for only 2.5% of the full sample. In the more moderate range, Segment 3, comprising around 20.8% of the full sample (828 respondents), engages in relatively high clothing consumption segment but buys from budget outlets.

Although the number of items purchased is very similar for the two lowest consumer segments (see Table 3, columns 2 and 3), they differ significantly in their spending habits and brand selection. Whereas Segment 1 spends around 58 euro on 4.4 clothing items, Segment 2 spends around 78 euro on 4.3 items. Similarly, whereas Segment 3 purchases around 8.4 items, Segment 4 buys around 10.9 items at a significantly higher per item price for a higher total outlay. These differences in money spent are mirrored in brands chosen, with Segments 2 and 4 purchasing less from budget brands and significantly more from casual/medium brands (columns 2 and 4). In fact, Segment 4 consumers have a high consumption of casual/medium and premium brands, buying about 13.6 clothing items for 950 euro over the three-month period, about 41.0% from casual/medium brands and 36.4% from premium brands. Segment 5 also reported the highest usage frequencies for all acquisition modes, over five times each in three months for shopping malls and online shopping, three times for mail order (by far the highest) and 2.4 times for second-hand outlets. As regards acquisition modes, whereas Segments 4 and 5 account for a higher share of small boutiques, the middle consumer segments engage in a higher share of online shopping. Second-hand outlets, however, have the relatively highest share among Segment 1 consumers, the low consumption budget buyers, which might explain their low expenditure on clothing purchases. As a result, Segment 1 buys the highest proportion of second-hand material, at 16.2%, while Segments 4 and 5 purchase the highest share of clothing made of new organic material, at 23.5% and 22.1%, respectively (see Table 3). Conventional material is dominant in all consumer segments.

The segments also differ in their demographics, especially country of residence (see Figure 1). Polish consumers account for the highest share of Segment 1 (35.2%) but lowest share of Segment 5 (4.0%), perhaps because of their limited purchasing power compared to consumers from the other participating countries. Germans make up around 19.9% of Segment 1 but account for 27.7% or above of the other segments. Together with Germans, Swedes, at over 30%, make up the highest share of the Segment 3 medium consumption budget consumers. U.S. consumers, in contrast, make up only 21.4% of the Segment 3 budget shoppers but account for a relatively high share (37.0%) of the high consumption purchasers of casual/medium and premium brands. Hence, even after expenditures are harmonized, the consumer segments are substantially differentiated by nationality.

Table 3. Descriptive statistics for segmentation variables.

	All		Segment 1 Low-Budget		Segment 2 Low-Casual		Segment 3 Medium-Budget		Segment 4 Medium-Casual		Segment 5 High-Premium	
	Mean	(SD)	Mean	(SD)	Mean	(SD)	Mean	(SD)	Mean	(SD)	Mean	(SD)
Items purchased last 3 months (number)												
General fashion	5.86	(5.14)	4.38	(4.01)	4.25	(3.63)	8.39	(5.23)	10.90	(6.37)	13.63	(7.24)
Jeans	0.87	(1.29)	0.58	(0.98)	0.75	(1.18)	1.17	(1.38)	1.72	(1.67)	2.42	(2.28)
T-shirts	2.12	(2.72)	1.59	(2.35)	1.87	(2.35)	2.65	(2.81)	3.97	(3.77)	4.33	(3.90)
Expenditures last 3 months (€, harmonized HCIP)[1]												
General fashion	153.43	(182.84)	57.87	(44.28)	78.38	(47.63)	244.45	(57.52)	481.90	(97.86)	950.83	(83.17)
Jeans	33.38	(77.93)	10.58	(20.12)	23.28	(39.38)	45.90	(63.00)	114.08	(140.20)	209.53	(270.57)
T-shirts	29.14	(63.09)	10.59	(16.24)	22.06	(33.50)	39.56	(46.73)	96.32	(117.00)	154.39	(228.64)
Brand (%, accumulates to 100%)												
General fashion: premium	7.81	(15.85)	1.81	(6.01)	9.51	(16.55)	10.57	(17.81)	20.00	(21.89)	36.36	(24.86)
General fashion: casual/medium	33.49	(29.78)	13.94	(19.23)	54.78	(27.56)	41.01	(28.01)	47.00	(23.98)	40.97	(19.63)
General fashion: budget	58.70	(34.52)	84.26	(21.05)	35.72	(27.88)	48.41	(32.21)	33.00	(26.09)	22.67	(17.69)
Jeans: premium	7.26	(17.45)	0.97	(4.11)	9.36	(18.64)	9.80	(19.84)	20.54	(26.41)	35.57	(30.54)
Jeans: casual/medium	36.82	(36.09)	10.27	(17.55)	69.68	(27.89)	43.89	(34.62)	50.32	(32.54)	43.67	(29.81)
Jeans: budget	55.91	(39.68)	88.76	(18.66)	20.95	(23.68)	46.31	(37.78)	29.14	(32.01)	20.76	(25.39)
T-shirt: premium	6.30	(15.73)	0.91	(5.53)	7.88	(16.26)	8.57	(17.93)	18.06	(23.13)	30.88	(29.27)
T-shirt: casual/medium	31.95	(33.61)	8.09	(14.31)	60.72	(30.41)	38.49	(32.31)	46.21	(30.68)	39.02	(28.45)
T-shirt: budget	61.75	(37.66)	91.00	(15.82)	31.40	(29.67)	52.95	(36.41)	35.73	(32.46)	30.10	(31.00)
Acquisition mode[2]												
High street	1.10	(2.00)	0.71	(1.32)	0.84	(1.67)	1.44	(2.09)	2.49	(3.30)	3.96	(4.00)
Shopping mall	2.09	(2.79)	1.65	(2.40)	1.74	(2.34)	2.48	(2.70)	3.92	(4.28)	5.01	(4.47)
Online shopping	2.10	(3.02)	1.39	(2.33)	1.74	(2.44)	3.03	(3.47)	4.07	(4.36)	4.97	(4.55)
Mail order	0.84	(2.03)	0.58	(1.43)	0.61	(1.51)	1.18	(2.49)	1.63	(3.21)	2.82	(4.28)
Small boutiques	0.72	(1.73)	0.44	(1.18)	0.61	(1.55)	0.93	(1.99)	1.56	(2.45)	2.82	(3.64)
Second-hand	1.41	(2.90)	1.61	(3.07)	1.21	(2.78)	1.14	(2.44)	1.49	(2.87)	2.24	(3.96)
Supermarket	0.84	(2.12)	0.80	(1.78)	0.75	(2.24)	0.75	(1.86)	1.40	(3.20)	1.91	(3.63)
Swapping	0.36	(1.58)	0.23	(1.20)	0.38	(1.72)	0.33	(1.33)	0.78	(2.32)	1.53	(3.46)
Material purchased (%, accumulates to 100%)												
New conventional	61.13	(32.70)	62.03	(34.31)	60.13	(32.69)	61.93	(30.12)	57.70	(30.81)	59.16	(29.37)
New organic	17.81	(20.52)	14.14	(19.70)	19.39	(20.69)	20.77	(20.62)	24.04	(21.19)	22.14	(19.10)
Reused—recycled	7.82	(12.65)	6.73	(12.73)	8.48	(13.36)	8.53	(11.88)	9.52	(11.64)	9.03	(10.82)
Reused—secondhand	13.24	(22.35)	17.10	(26.44)	12.00	(20.63)	8.78	(15.55)	8.74	(15.04)	9.67	(16.04)
Observations	3984		1712		1073		828		271		100	

[1] The expenditures, which are from September 2016, are converted into euro exchange rates and harmonized on clothing prizes across countries using the Harmonized Index of Consumer Prices (HCIP). The baseline is the averaged HCIP for the period June-August 2016 with the average clothing prices in Europe in 2015 as the reference (100);[2] Acquisition mode is measured in times over the last three months.

Country by consumer segment

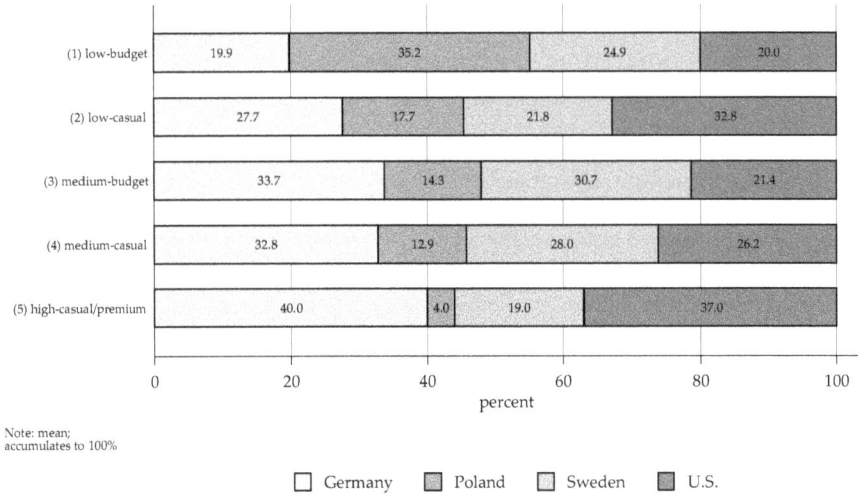

Note: mean;
accumulates to 100%

☐ Germany   ▨ Poland   ☐ Sweden   ■ U.S.

Figure 1. Country by consumer segment.

Although the age distribution is similar across all five segments, one gender difference is notable: whereas female consumers make up over 60% of the largest segment (the budget buyers in Segment 1), male consumers account for the majority (57%) of the 100 (medium and premium) consumers in Segment 5. As regards the final sociodemographic variable of monthly net income, (see Figure 2), Segment 1 buyers have the lowest median income of all consumer segments, while the median income of Segment 2 and 3 consumers fall into category 5. This latter observation is interesting given that although consumers in both Segments (2 and 3) spend similar amounts, Segment 3 consumers buy twice as many clothing items for the money as Segment 2 buyers: 214 euro for 8.4 budget brand items versus 93 euro for 4.2 casual/medium brand items, respectively (see Appendix A Table A1 for the descriptive statistics for all sociodemographic variables).

Sex by consumer segment

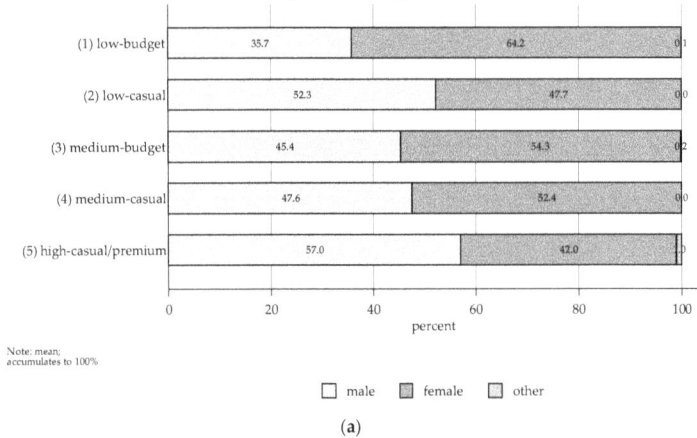

Note: mean;
accumulates to 100%

☐ male   ▨ female   ☐ other

(a)

Figure 2. *Cont.*

133

Income by consumer segment

(monthly net income)

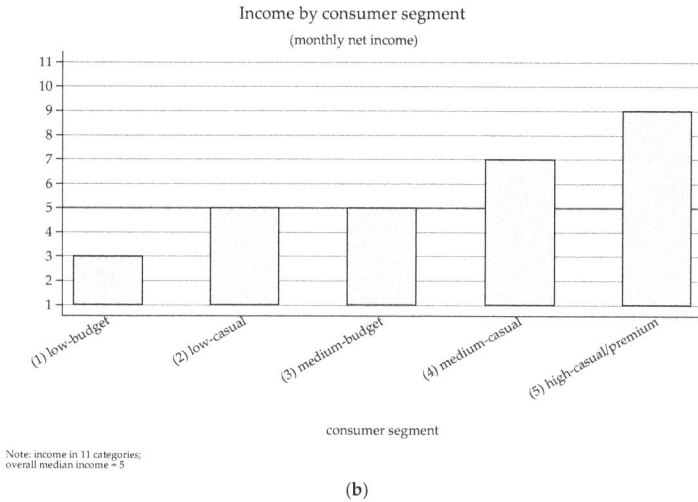

Note: income in 11 categories;
overall median income = 5

(b)

Figure 2. Demographics by consumer segment. (a) Sex by consumer segment (b) Income by consumer segment.

4.2. Use and Maintenance Behavior

Based on our survey participant responses, the average consumer possesses 18.6 t-shirts (SD = 12.72) and six pairs of jeans (SD = 4.90) intended for wear at least monthly for 3–4 years. In fact, as Figure 3 shows, Segments 4 and 5 own significantly more than any other segment—about 22.9 and 24.4 t-shirts, and 8.5 and 11 pairs of jeans, respectively—which is not surprising given their high consumption during the purchasing phase. The segments exhibit no differences, however, in the time clothes are kept before being discarded and/or the frequency of wearing each clothing item, which violates our expectations of differences based on different purchasing behaviors (e.g., the likelihood that Segment 5 consumers, having purchased so many clothing items, would wear them less often).

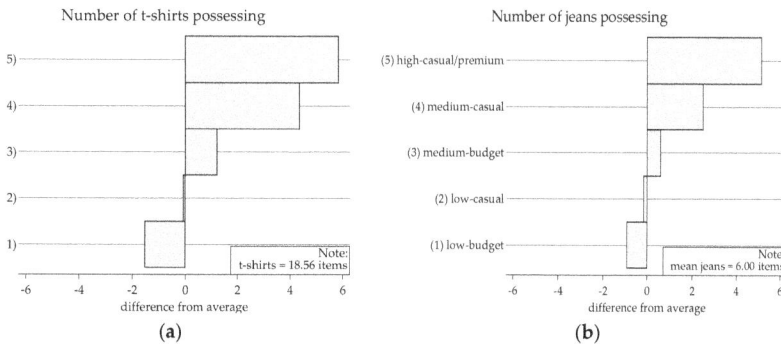

Figure 3. Number of jeans and t-shirts owned by consumer segment. (a) Number of t-shirts processing; (b) Number of jeans processing.

Although the average consumer wears a pair of jeans about 8.2 times and a t-shirt about 2.3 times before washing, we find one significant difference in this number of wears: Segment 1 wears jeans and t-shirts more often (at 8.7 and 2.5 times, respectively) before washing than Segments 4 and 5 (at 7.3 and 2.0 times, and 6.4 and 1.9 times, respectively). All consumer segments, however, exhibit similar

134

washing behavior, using an average temperature of 40 °C, regardless of whether jeans or t-shirt, with a small number (3.2%) using no detergent, the majority (65.4%) using a non-eco detergent, and just under a third (31.3%) using an eco-detergent. Around 50% of the consumers use softener, about 14% of which is eco-softener, but only about 30% use a dryer. No intersegmental differences are observable, however, in washing and drying behavior (see Appendix A Table 2 for all descriptive statistics for this phase).

4.3. Discard Behavior

Our survey respondents reported giving about 70.7% of their discarded clothes a second life by donating, recycling, selling at flea markets, or passing them on to family members. Disposal of the remaining 30% is equally distributed between down-cycling (e.g., using clothes as rags) and putting them in the trash. When asked specifically about discarding jeans and t-shirts, participants responded that t-shirts are less likely (52.2%) to receive a second life but are more often down-cycled (27.8%) or trashed (20.1%). Jeans, on the other hand, are less often down-cycled (14.7%). Interestingly, not only did respondents report a lower share of second life clothes when asked about a specific product category rather than clothes in general, but the Segment 5 high consumers of casual/medium and premium brands indicated no higher share of second life for their unwanted clothes than the other segments (see Appendix A Table 3 for all corresponding descriptive statistics).

4.4. Environmentally Friendly Clothing Consumption Behavior

To assess environmentally friendly clothing consumption behavior, our analysis included measurements of environmental apparel consumption, the monetary value consumers attribute to different clothing materials (with new conventional material as a reference point), and the previous and future intended use of select alternative business models (see Appendix A Table 4 for the full descriptive statistics). Here, the mean environmental apparel consumption is 2.68 (*SD* = 0.80) on a 5-point Likert scale (with a higher value indicating more environmental apparel consumption). Our comparison of consumer segments (Figure 4) reveals that Segments 4 and 5 reported engaging in environmental apparel consumption significantly more often.

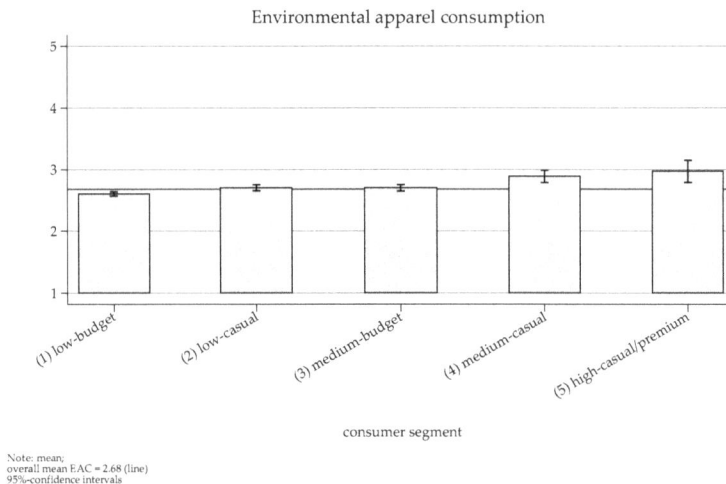

Note: mean;
overall mean EAC = 2.68 (line)
95%-confidence intervals

Figure 4. Environmental apparel consumption by consumer segment.

The value that the average consumer attributes to a pair of jeans and t-shirts made of recycled materials is 64.8% and 62.0%, respectively, of that for these same two items made of new conventional materials. As expected, second-hand clothing is valued even lower, at 36.5% of the value attributed to a pair of jeans made of conventional material. The outcomes are similar for second-hand t-shirts, which are valued at 40.9% of a new conventional t-shirt. The only materials that match the attributed value of new conventional materials are new organic materials, but even these do not exceed the reference value. Hence, if we interpret the attributed value as an indicator for willingness to pay, we could conclude that consumers are on average unwilling to pay more for clothing made of any other material than the conventional materials dominating the market today. A comparison across consumer segments (see Figure 5), however, reveals an interesting difference: Segment 5's valuation (at 11.0%) of organic material (in this case, jeans) over conventional material is higher than that of any other segment. Segment 1, in contrast, attributes a lower value than either Segment 3 or 5 to both jeans and t-shirts made of organic cotton.

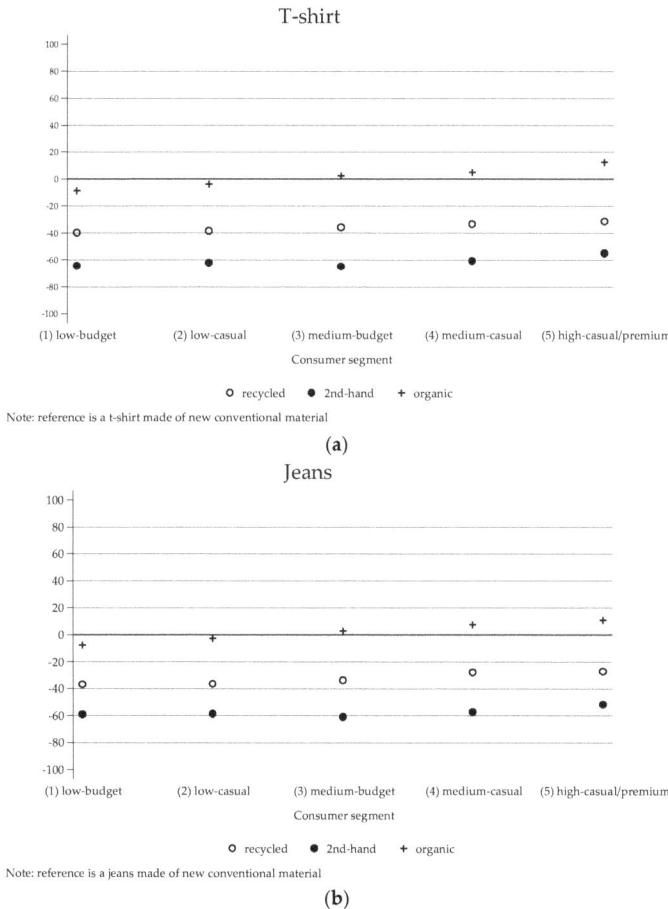

(a)

(b)

Figure 5. Attributed value of material by consumer segment. (a) T-shirts; (b) Jeans.

The most used alternative business models among the consumers surveyed were reselling clothes online (41.1%) and traditional repair services (64.3%), although 10%–20% of the consumers also reported using fashion rentals (17.3%), swap markets (16.5%), incentivized take-back schemes (14.4%), and in-store repair services (11.7%). Only 4.6% and 3.7%, respectively, of the full consumer sample, however, had used the more niche business models of clothing libraries and fashion leasing, with 17.0%

and 10% of Segments 5 and 4, respectively, but under 5% of the other segments indicating previous use of fashion libraries. In fact, Segment 5, followed by Segment 4, accounts for significantly higher use of the alternative business models included in the survey, with the other three segments differing little from each other.

As regards future intended use of alternative business models, the average consumer seems generally unsupportive, indicating only positive intentions for traditional repair services, reselling clothes online, and incentivized take-back schemes. Comparing across segments reveals that Segments 1 to 4 are less likely than Segment 5 to use clothing libraries, fashion rentals, and fashion leasing (see Figure 6), while Segments 4 and 5 have a higher likelihood of using traditional and in-store repair services, perhaps reflecting their prior experience with them. All segments other than Segment 2 show a general positive future intention for online reselling platforms, incentivized take-back schemes, and traditional repair services.

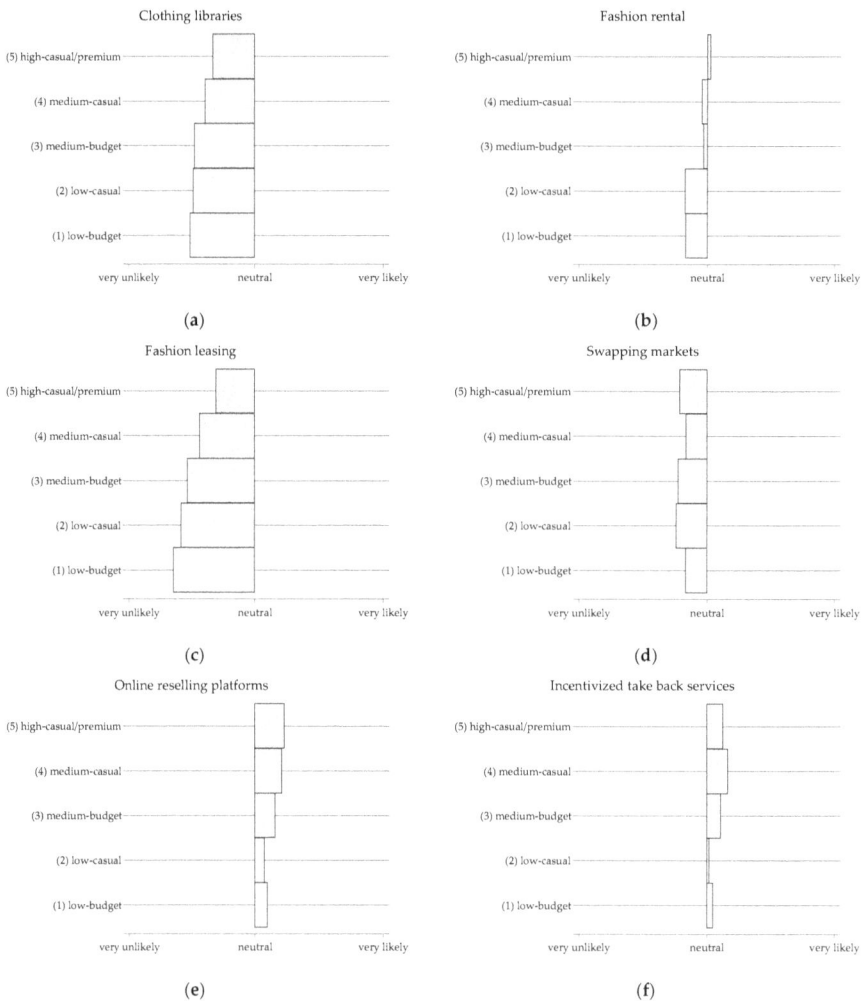

Figure 6. *Cont.*

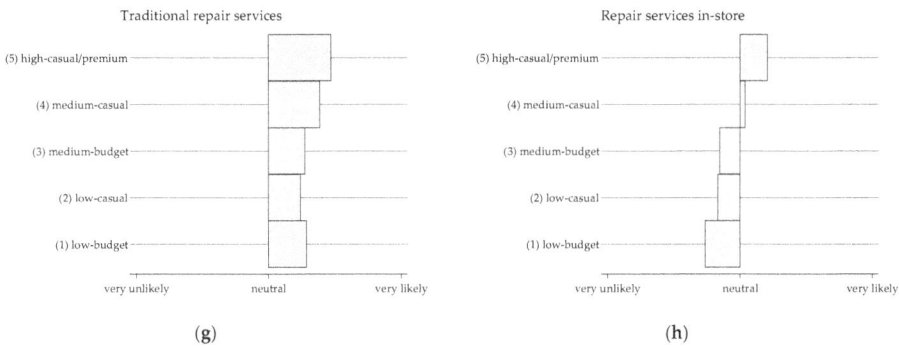

Figure 6. Future use intention of alternative business models by consumer segment. Please add the title for (**a**) clothing libraries, (**b**) fashion rental, (**c**) fashion leasing, (**d**) swapping markets, (**e**) online reselling platforms, (**f**) incentivized take back services, (**g**) traditional repair services, (**h**) repair services in-store.

5. Discussion

Successfully reducing the environmental impact of clothing consumption will require the design and implementation—for all three consumption phases—of behavioral strategies tailored to the characteristics and preferences of different consumer groups. This current paper contributes to the understanding of such strategies by descriptively analyzing different clothing consumer groups based not on traditional segmentation variables such as demographics but on actual purchasing behavior. This approach better encapsulates consumer heterogeneity while more fully identifying clothing consumption patterns. Such identification is highly relevant to developing strategies that foster environmentally friendly clothing consumption because it allows consideration of suitable strategies in relation to the actual purchasing patterns of specific consumer groups. In the following section, therefore, we propose such strategies for the different consumption phases and discuss their applicability to each consumer segment.

5.1. Purchase Phase

For the purchase phase, we propose two main strategies for reducing environmental impact: (1) consuming differently (e.g., purchasing recycled or second-hand products or clothing made of environmentally friendly materials like organic cotton); and (2) consuming less [20]. These strategies are applicable to each of our five consumer groups in the following ways:

Segment 1 (low consumption—budget brands). This largest consumer segment, which possesses the lowest number of t-shirts and jeans bought primarily from budget brands or second-hand outlets, also has the lowest income and is the least open to alternative business models. Although these consumers' relatively low number of clothing purchases may seem environmentally promising and in line with the most environmentally significant purchasing strategy of lowering overall consumption [1], this already low consumption may mean that reduction is not the optimal approach to improving this segment's environmental impact. At the same time, the group's consumption of relatively cheap budget brands, although possibly a reflection of a lack of interest in clothing other than for functional necessity, may be related to their low income. Whichever the case, their budget considerations indicate an unwillingness to pay any additional costs to shift from conventional clothing products to more environmentally friendly alternatives. Hence, although consuming differently could be a more promising avenue for this segment, the question remains of how this strategy would be realized. Not only might budget constraints or lack of interest prevent a shift toward more environmentally friendly and potentially more expensive clothing, but, according to our findings, environmentally friendly materials receive little consumer support. In particular, our respondents' reported willingness to pay for more environmentally friendly materials (e.g., recycled or second-hand) is far lower than their willingness to pay for conventional material. It may thus prove difficult to target this major consumer segment for the promotion of behavioral change. Rather, this segment's environmental impact may be more successfully lowered if the strategies of consuming less and consuming differently are successfully combined. For example, reducing consumption by a few clothing items (e.g., a "1-item less" campaign) could potentially free up monetary resources for investment in more environmentally friendly products. Another possible avenue would be to redirect their preferences toward alternative business models by leveraging their existing use of classic alternative acquisition (e.g., second-hand) to counter their comparably low acceptance of novel but low-cost alternatives (e.g., clothing libraries or swap markets). Strengthening second-hand consumption via image campaigns or new online shops to improve user experiences with such clothing acquisition could foster behaviors that meet the segment's needs but are more environmentally friendly. In general, future interventions targeting these consumers should specifically delineate how they could change their behavior in an environmentally friendly direction without undertaking additional costs.

Segment 2 (low consumption—casual/medium). Although Segment 2 consumption is similar to that of Segment 1 in number of items bought in a three-month period, these consumers enjoy a higher income, spend significantly more, and buy more casual/medium priced brands. This segment can thus be more easily targeted with strategies that foster the purchase of clothing made from more environmentally friendly, albeit more expensive, material.

Segment 3 (medium consumption—budget). This group epitomizes the fast fashion consumer, having a comparatively high consumption rate but a strong preference for budget brands, which in this study, include purchases from supermarkets or other cheap vendors not necessarily seen as fast fashion retailers. Segment 3 is of particular relevance to this research, not only because of its general interest in clothing but also because of its expected high impact on the environment. More specifically, consumers who purchase 8.4 relatively inexpensive items during a three-month period for a total of 33 items per year might be a more promising target group for clothing consumption reduction strategies than the previous two groups. With regard to buying differently, these consumers' unwillingness to pay for alternative materials again implies a reluctance to spend more money on higher quality, more environmentally friendly clothing. Given current marketing tools, however, promoting a consuming less strategy would be even more challenging than compensating one product with another (consuming differently), especially given that the question of how much is enough remains controversial. One behavioral change solution offered by social marketing is the "use of marketing principles and techniques to influence a target audience to voluntarily accept, reject, modify, or abandon a behavior for the benefit of individuals, groups, or society as a whole" ([37], p. 394). Hence, one possible social marketing tool for encouraging consumption would be to adopt a consumer viewpoint rather than making consumers feel guilty [37]. From this perspective, understanding the underlying motivation for Segment 3's consumption patterns would assist in the development of effective behavioral interventions. Alternatively, future interventions might emphasize alternative means of clothes acquisition that have an assumed lower environmental impact (e.g., fashion leasing or rental) without restricting the number of items acquired [48]. At present, however, this segment shows little support for either of these alternatives, which would thus need to be promoted.

Segments 4 (medium consumption—casual/medium) and 5 (high consumption—casual/medium and premium). Although Segments 4 and 5 together comprise the smallest group of consumers, both groups are very interesting in terms of composition and reported behavior. Most notably, both reported the highest clothing purchasing rates, indicating that each spends significantly more on clothing than the other three segments. Nonetheless, Segment 5 differs from Segment 4 in spending distinctly more and buying more premium brands. Interestingly, however, both segments reported purchasing clothing in the most environmentally friendly manner. Given the two groups' behavior patterns and monetary resources, both consuming less and consuming differently could be relevant strategies for these groups. That is, even though the large quantity purchased is the direct opposite of environmental friendliness, both segments exhibit environmental traits such as assigning the highest monetary value to jeans made of recycled and second-hand material and engaging in more consumption of environmental apparel. Even if this latter is due to an increased interest in clothing in general, it could be a promising starting point for introducing the strategies for more environmentally friendly clothing consumption to both segments. Respondents from these groups also reported the highest use of and support for alternative business models like fashion libraries and fashion rental. These tendencies are also promising for pushing Segments 4 and 5 toward more environmentally friendly consumption alternatives without necessarily compromising the quantity purchased. At the same time, raising both segments' awareness about consuming less remains of utmost importance because reducing consumption in these groups would result in a more substantial lowering of environmental impact per consumer than in any other segment. Nonetheless, because promoting behavior change is a balancing act between identifying the meaningful behavior to be changed and the meaningful target group, any strategy needs to take into account that Segments 4 and 5 are very small (6.8% and 2.5%, respectively), which might reduce the penetration of any behavioral intervention.

5.2. Use and Maintenance Phase

In this second phase, the target group (consumer segment, in our case) matters little because rather than identifying notable differences, our analysis highlights mostly similarities. The most noteworthy of these are the time that t-shirts and jeans are kept, the frequency of wearing, and laundry behaviors. Nevertheless, this consumption phase warrants some discussion because of life cycle assessment experts' disagreement over whether it has a significant [33,49] or negligible [1] impact on the environment. Given that a longer product life is generally preferable to a shorter one, retaining jeans and t-shirts for 3–4 years is a more positive outcome than the 2.2 years reported by Gracey and Moon [35]. In fact, all five of our consumer segments indicate the same period, which is particularly surprising given that Segments 1 and 3 purchase primarily budget brands while Segment 5 purchases casual/medium and premium brands. This finding not only contradicts the common environmental literature assumption (e.g., [50]) that premium brand clothing (assumedly of higher quality and durability) is kept longer but also implies that any recommendation to purchase higher quality clothing for environmental reasons will be ineffective if consumers do not simultaneously reduce their overall consumption or use the items for a longer period. In addition, although we are unable to distinguish whether the indicated 3–4 years reflects the active wearing of clothes or includes passive storage, we do know that the 36 to 48 times that both t-shirts and jeans are generally worn over their product lives exceeds the anticipated 22 times for t-shirts but falls drastically short of the anticipated 200 times for jeans [1,33]. Based on a maximum four-year lifetime for jeans and t-shirts, the number of wears, and the number of wears before washing, we estimate a total of 22 washing cycles for a t-shirt and around six washing cycles for a pair of jeans at an average temperature of 40 °C. Whereas washing 1 kg clothes at 40 °C consumes 0.21 kWh of energy, tumble drying it requires 3–4 times as much energy [1], making it the most interesting maintenance practice from an environmental perspective [33,51]. In our study, in line with earlier research [1], around 30% of consumers use a tumble dryer to dry their t-shirts and jeans. (It is worth noting that the use of tumble dryers is much higher in the U.S. (above 80%) compared to the European countries (between ca. 12% in Poland and ca. 20% in Germany and Sweden)) Although the environmental impact of this practice is rather low compared to impacts in the production, purchase, and discard phases [1], for future interventions targeting the use phase, the behavior with the highest potential to reduce impact across all consumer segments is the widespread use of energy gobbling tumble dryers.

5.3. Discard Phase

Lastly, the results related to general clothing disposal practices suggest that consumers widely use environmentally friendly means of discarding their unwanted items, with only 14.1% going into the trash. It should be noted, however, that this finding stands in strong contrast to the 2014 U.S. Environmental Protection Agency statistic of 64.5% of textiles and clothing going into a landfill [34]. Even though this figure is country specific and includes textiles as well as clothing, the difference seems profound. Hence, environmental impact reducing strategies for the disposal phase should focus on the reintroduction of unwanted clothing into the production cycle by facilitating consumer recycling of clothing items to give them a second product life. Achieving this circular flow of materials through in-store take back and other product care services beyond the moment of purchase would benefit the environment by reducing not only waste generation but also the use of virgin materials.

6. Conclusions

Clothing consumption's high environmental impact raises concerns at each phase of a clothing item's life cycle, the severity of which is determined largely by which and how many clothing items consumers purchase and how often, as well as the frequency of item use and the nature of their maintenance and disposal. However, although developing tailored strategies that successfully address consumer decisions across all phases of clothes consumption is a key element in achieving more sustainable clothing consumption, previous research has only fragmentally examined how consumers behave in relation to each phase. This current analysis has thus examined the consumer clothing behavior of large, diverse consumer samples in four Western countries to provide a comprehensive and up-to-date assessment of consumer clothing consumption across four important clothing markets. In doing so, it supplemented the extensive data on self-reported consumer behavior with the environmental concerns generated by each clothing life cycle phase. To address consumer heterogeneity, it divided consumers into five distinct segments based on extent of consumption and price point of product purchased. This segmentation enabled a better understanding of clothing consumption and the development of change interventions for targeting specific behaviors. Basing the segmentation on actual consumption produced five consumer groups offering important insights into both distinctions and similarities in consumer purchasing, use and maintenance, and disposal behavior.

Among the most notable findings are the relatively low clothing consumption-rate by almost half the respondents and their strong preference for budget brand clothing. For the low clothing consumers in Segment 1, shifting behavior toward low cost acquisition alternatives is likely to be a more effective approach than trying to further reduce consumption, whereas both approaches—consuming differently and consuming less—are promising for the high volume and high spending consumers in Segments 4 and 5. Segment 2 consumers, on the other hand, who engage in low consumption but higher spending, could be addressed by strategies that promote consuming differently, whereas strategies to raise awareness of the need to consume less could best serve the high volume, budget brand consumers in Segment 3. The design and implementation of any strategy, however, should take into account that no one message can suit all consumer groups; to be successful, interventions must be adapted to each segments' consumption patterns. The pattern identification and consumer profiling reported here constitutes a first step in this direction, one that provides an important platform for future research aimed at even more comprehensive understanding of clothing consumption. Nonetheless, because simply identifying different behaviors is insufficient to engendering actual behavior change, more research is needed to understand such in-depth aspects as the motivations underlying these actions.

This study is of course not without its limitations, not least the potential for a social desirability or method bias to which all studies of self-reported behavior are subject (see e.g., [52]). A social desirability bias would lead to an over- or underestimation of behavior for all categories, while consumer inability to accurately recall actions in the given time period on a general abstract level would produce different accountings of behavior. The latter is particularly relevant for respondent recall of such past behavior as how many items they purchased in the previous three months, the amount of money spent, and the number of t-shirts and jeans they currently own. In this context, cross-validations of measurements such as surveys and observation experiments or real-time data collection could be a promising way to increase validity and reliability. Another limitation is the cross-sectionality of the study, which may not sufficiently capture the great variation in consumer behavior, especially in such a fast-moving context as the fashion industry. When the study aim is to better understand consumer behavior to enable the design of effective behavioral change interventions, assessing consumption pattern stability and tracing its development is crucial. Finally, although Western countries have some of the largest clothing markets, studying them to the exclusion of highly populated, growing economies such as Brazil, China, and India ignores purchasing, maintenance, and disposal behaviors that may diverge greatly from the Western behavior patterns reported here. Hence, extending the current analysis to developing nations would be an important avenue for future research.

Despite these shortcomings, the present study contributes important and extensive empirical knowledge that can prompt rethinking of previous assumptions about such aspects as clothes purchasing behavior or the relation between age and clothing consumption. Surprisingly, however, we identify no significant age-based differences between our five segments. In fact, the similar age distribution in our medium-budget Segment 3 refutes the commonly accepted notion of the young fast fashion consumer. Although one reason may be that very young consumers (under 18) are not included in the sample, Segment 3's budget purchases are not necessarily made at traditional fast fashion retailers but may take place at nontraditional clothes vendors such as supermarkets. Hence, although the current data provide many interesting insights, they also raise at least as many questions for future investigation. One potential research avenue would be to further explore the segments' demographics or make more detailed comparisons of the different countries. Another important "next step" would be to supplement the findings reported here with psychological insights to provide clearer explanation of the segmental behavior differences based on their psychological underpinnings and to identify which behavioral antecedents could be targeted most effectively in future interventions. Likewise, an assessment of the actual environmental impact of the various consumer segments could support the development of effective behavioral interventions promoting truly environmentally friendly clothing consumption.

Acknowledgments: We gratefully acknowledge the Trash-2Cash project (grant agreement No. 646226) funded by the European Community under Horizon2020 research and innovation program and the Mistra Future Fashion Project Phase II funded by the Swedish Mistra Foundation. This grant does not cover the publication cost for open access. However, the funding source does not hold any competing interest.

Author Contributions: Kristian Steensen Nielsen, Tina Müller and Wencke Gwozdz designed the study and wrote the paper. Wencke Gwozdz carried out the data analyses. All authors provided feedback throughout the research process and proofread the paper.

Conflicts of Interest: The authors declare no conflict of interest.

Appendix A

Table A1. Descriptive statistics for acquisition mode and sociodemographics.

	All		Segment 1 Low-Budget		Segment 2 Low-Casual		Segment 3 Medium-Budget		Segment 4 Medium-Casual		Segment 5 High-Premium	
	Mean	(SD)	Mean	(SD)	Mean	(SD)	Mean	(SD)	Mean	(SD)	Mean	(SD)
Socio-demographics												
Germany (dummy)	0.26	(0.44)	0.20	(0.40)	0.28	(0.45)	0.34	(0.47)	0.33	(0.47)	0.40	(0.49)
Poland (dummy)	0.24	(0.43)	0.35	(0.48)	0.18	(0.38)	0.14	(0.35)	0.13	(0.34)	0.04	(0.20)
Sweden (dummy)	0.25	(0.43)	0.25	(0.43)	0.22	(0.41)	0.31	(0.46)	0.28	(0.45)	0.19	(0.39)
U.S. (dummy)	0.25	(0.43)	0.20	(0.40)	0.33	(0.47)	0.21	(0.41)	0.26	(0.44)	0.37	(0.49)
Age (years)	42.59	(13.54)	42.35	(14.20)	43.55	(13.53)	42.06	(12.78)	42.54	(12.20)	41.05	(11.39)
Male (dummy)	0.44	(0.50)	0.36	(0.48)	0.52	(0.50)	0.45	(0.50)	0.48	(0.50)	0.57	(0.50)
Income (11 categories)	4.69	(3.15)	3.83	(2.82)	4.78	(3.17)	5.28	(3.12)	6.76	(3.01)	8.00	(2.92)

Table A2. Descriptive statistics for the use and maintenance phase.

		All		Segment 1 Low-Budget		Segment 2 Low-Casual		Segment 3 Medium-Budget		Segment 4 Medium-Casual		Segment 5 High-Premium	
		Mean	(SD)	Mean	(SD)	Mean	(SD)	Mean	(SD)	Mean	(SD)	Mean	(SD)
Use													
Items possessing (number)	jeans	6.00	(4.90)	5.08	(4.25)	5.86	(4.40)	6.62	(4.93)	8.51	(6.36)	11.16	(8.29)
	t-shirts	18.56	(12.72)	17.02	(11.85)	18.46	(12.24)	19.75	(13.02)	22.90	(15.38)	24.37	(16.15)
Time keeping [1]	jeans	4.10	(0.95)	4.19	(0.90)	4.18	(0.92)	3.96	(0.98)	3.83	(1.05)	3.52	(1.13)
	t-shirts	3.93	(1.03)	4.05	(0.96)	4.01	(1.03)	3.78	(1.00)	3.47	(1.22)	3.35	(1.18)
Wears on average [2]	jeans	4.30	(1.08)	4.31	(1.14)	4.34	(1.01)	4.28	(1.04)	4.17	(1.04)	4.25	(0.91)
	t-shirts	4.35	(0.91)	4.42	(0.89)	4.36	(0.90)	4.30	(0.91)	4.13	(1.04)	4.24	(0.99)
Wears before washing (number)	jeans	8.24	(9.70)	8.66	(10.16)	8.06	(9.65)	8.14	(9.52)	7.34	(8.11)	6.39	(7.01)
	t-shirts	2.26	(1.87)	2.45	(2.03)	2.20	(1.79)	2.05	(1.69)	1.98	(1.58)	1.92	(1.87)
Maintenance													
Washing temperature (°Celsius)	jeans	38.81	(10.00)	39.57	(9.82)	38.12	(10.61)	38.45	(9.39)	38.11	(9.82)	37.80	(10.97)
	t-shirts	38.06	(9.74)	39.01	(9.63)	37.47	(10.32)	37.45	(8.92)	36.74	(9.47)	36.60	(10.94)
Detergent: none (dummy)	jeans	0.03	(0.18)	0.04	(0.18)	0.03	(0.18)	0.03	(0.17)	0.03	(0.16)	0.04	(0.20)
	t-shirts	0.03	(0.17)	0.03	(0.17)	0.03	(0.17)	0.03	(0.17)	0.04	(0.20)	0.04	(0.20)

Table 2. *Cont.*

		All		Segment 1 Low-Budget		Segment 2 Low-Casual		Segment 3 Medium-Budget		Segment 4 Medium-Casual		Segment 5 High-Premium	
		Mean	(SD)	Mean	(SD)	Mean	(SD)	Mean	(SD)	Mean	(SD)	Mean	(SD)
Detergent: non-eco (dummy)	jeans	0.65	(0.48)	0.73	(0.44)	0.59	(0.49)	0.62	(0.49)	0.56	(0.50)	0.57	(0.50)
	t-shirts	0.65	(0.48)	0.73	(0.45)	0.60	(0.49)	0.62	(0.49)	0.56	(0.50)	0.58	(0.50)
Detergent: eco (dummy)	jeans	0.31	(0.46)	0.23	(0.42)	0.37	(0.48)	0.35	(0.48)	0.42	(0.49)	0.39	(0.49)
	t-shirts	0.31	(0.46)	0.24	(0.43)	0.37	(0.48)	0.35	(0.48)	0.40	(0.49)	0.38	(0.49)
Softener: none (dummy)	jeans	0.49	(0.50)	0.48	(0.50)	0.52	(0.50)	0.51	(0.50)	0.44	(0.50)	0.49	(0.50)
	t-shirts	0.43	(0.50)	0.42	(0.49)	0.46	(0.50)	0.43	(0.50)	0.36	(0.48)	0.45	(0.50)
Softener: non-eco (dummy)	jeans	0.38	(0.49)	0.43	(0.49)	0.33	(0.47)	0.36	(0.48)	0.36	(0.48)	0.33	(0.47)
	t-shirts	0.42	(0.49)	0.47	(0.50)	0.37	(0.48)	0.41	(0.49)	0.39	(0.49)	0.31	(0.46)
Softener: eco (dummy)	jeans	0.13	(0.33)	0.09	(0.29)	0.15	(0.36)	0.13	(0.34)	0.20	(0.40)	0.18	(0.39)
	t-shirts	0.15	(0.36)	0.11	(0.31)	0.17	(0.38)	0.15	(0.36)	0.26	(0.44)	0.24	(0.43)
Dryer use (dummy)	jeans	0.32	(0.47)	0.29	(0.46)	0.36	(0.48)	0.31	(0.46)	0.36	(0.48)	0.38	(0.49)
	t-shirts	0.34	(0.47)	0.31	(0.46)	0.39	(0.49)	0.33	(0.47)	0.34	(0.48)	0.36	(0.48)

[1] Time keeping is measured in 5 categories: 1 "less than 6 months", 2 "less than a year", 3 "1–2 years", 4 "3–4 years", 5 "5 years or more"; [2] Wears on average is measured in five categories: 1 "once a year or less", 2 "less than once every 3 months", 3 "at least once every other month", 4 "at least once a month", and 5 "at least once a week".

Table 3. Descriptive statistics for the discarding phase.

		All		Segment 1 Low-Budget		Segment 2 Low-Casual		Segment 3 Medium-Budget		Segment 4 Medium-Casual		Segment 5 High-Premium	
		Mean	(SD)	Mean	(SD)	Mean	(SD)	Mean	(SD)	Mean	(SD)	Mean	(SD)
Discarding [1]													
Second life (%)	general	70.74	(29.97)	69.03	(31.86)	70.94	(28.98)	73.59	(27.97)	72.42	(27.38)	69.85	(28.07)
	jeans	63.73	(39.52)	60.56	(41.60)	63.58	(38.70)	67.83	(37.58)	68.95	(35.28)	71.79	(32.44)
	t-shirts	52.15	(39.26)	49.72	(39.94)	51.34	(39.17)	55.80	(38.47)	56.34	(37.09)	60.81	(36.76)
Down-cycling (%)	general	15.21	(20.27)	16.24	(22.04)	15.74	(20.21)	12.62	(17.28)	14.30	(17.06)	15.92	(18.41)
	jeans	14.57	(26.35)	15.64	(28.76)	15.46	(26.36)	11.83	(22.81)	13.18	(21.87)	12.98	(19.10)
	t-shirts	27.76	(33.36)	29.89	(35.27)	28.19	(33.03)	24.03	(30.57)	25.25	(30.53)	24.29	(29.46)
Trash (%)	general	14.05	(23.30)	14.73	(24.92)	13.32	(22.02)	13.81	(22.56)	13.28	(20.78)	14.23	(20.27)
	jeans	21.71	(33.97)	23.83	(36.08)	20.97	(32.90)	20.33	(32.65)	17.87	(29.72)	15.23	(26.44)
	t-shirts	20.12	(31.73)	20.44	(32.68)	20.47	(31.53)	20.17	(31.13)	18.41	(30.25)	14.90	(25.58)

[1] Second life, down-cycling and trash together sum up to 100% (within one category).

Sustainability **2017**, *9*, 762

Table 4. Descriptive statistics for environmentally friendly clothing consumption behavior.

		All		Segment 1 Low-Budget		Segment 2 Low-Casual		Segment 3 Medium-Budget		Segment 4 Medium-Casual		Segment 5 High-Premium	
		Mean	(SD)	Mean	(SD)	Mean	(SD)	Mean	(SD)	Mean	(SD)	Mean	(SD)
Environmental apparel consumption [1]													
EAC (mean score)		2.68	(0.80)	2.61	(0.76)	2.70	(0.83)	2.70	(0.76)	2.89	(0.87)	2.98	(0.90)
Value of material [2]													
Recycled	jeans	64.81	(42.47)	63.13	(40.40)	63.58	(43.16)	66.45	(42.81)	72.32	(47.52)	72.71	(49.13)
	t-shirt	62.01	(43.79)	60.21	(41.53)	61.39	(44.12)	64.26	(45.33)	66.67	(47.41)	68.39	(52.63)
Second-hand	jeans	40.85	(37.10)	40.71	(36.50)	41.34	(36.88)	39.09	(35.39)	42.61	(43.35)	47.98	(44.47)
	t-shirt	36.49	(39.12)	35.42	(37.48)	37.97	(40.06)	34.90	(37.26)	39.11	(46.62)	45.26	(47.64)
New organic	jeans	97.51	(43.26)	92.48	(42.42)	97.57	(44.37)	102.90	(42.38)	107.65	(40.01)	111.03	(48.34)
	t-shirt	96.27	(44.18)	91.19	(43.11)	96.02	(45.51)	102.31	(42.88)	105.02	(42.72)	112.39	(49.03)
Alternative business models: past use [3]													
Clothing libraries		0.05	(0.21)	0.03	(0.18)	0.04	(0.20)	0.05	(0.22)	0.10	(0.30)	0.17	(0.38)
Fashion rental		0.17	(0.38)	0.15	(0.36)	0.15	(0.36)	0.20	(0.40)	0.25	(0.43)	0.33	(0.47)
Fashion leasing		0.04	(0.19)	0.02	(0.13)	0.03	(0.18)	0.04	(0.20)	0.09	(0.28)	0.22	(0.42)
Swapping markets		0.16	(0.37)	0.17	(0.37)	0.15	(0.35)	0.16	(0.37)	0.19	(0.40)	0.26	(0.44)
Reselling clothes online		0.41	(0.49)	0.39	(0.49)	0.38	(0.49)	0.45	(0.50)	0.51	(0.50)	0.49	(0.50)
Incentivized take back services		0.14	(0.35)	0.11	(0.31)	0.15	(0.35)	0.17	(0.38)	0.22	(0.41)	0.24	(0.43)
Traditional repair service		0.65	(0.48)	0.66	(0.47)	0.62	(0.49)	0.64	(0.48)	0.69	(0.46)	0.78	(0.42)
In-store repair service		0.12	(0.32)	0.08	(0.28)	0.12	(0.33)	0.12	(0.32)	0.23	(0.42)	0.30	(0.46)
Alternative business models: future use intention [4]													
Clothing libraries		25.74	(29.21)	24.47	(29.08)	25.62	(28.66)	26.11	(28.73)	30.30	(31.07)	33.43	(33.84)
Fashion rental		43.63	(33.90)	41.52	(34.10)	41.38	(33.09)	48.56	(33.36)	47.93	(34.52)	51.30	(35.81)
Fashion leasing		20.85	(26.59)	17.78	(24.65)	20.78	(26.27)	23.20	(27.15)	28.04	(30.35)	34.70	(35.23)
Swapping markets		40.03	(34.41)	41.65	(35.43)	38.00	(33.02)	38.79	(33.45)	41.82	(35.47)	39.40	(35.33)
Reselling clothes online		55.66	(35.73)	54.87	(36.22)	53.59	(35.04)	57.72	(35.08)	60.41	(35.91)	61.40	(37.34)
Incentivized take back services		53.14	(35.29)	52.46	(36.22)	51.01	(34.74)	55.32	(34.12)	58.03	(34.12)	56.20	(35.81)
Traditional repair service		64.28	(33.67)	64.45	(34.47)	62.15	(33.65)	63.83	(33.05)	69.48	(30.89)	73.70	(29.43)
In-store repair service		40.89	(33.53)	36.82	(33.05)	41.66	(33.32)	42.36	(33.08)	51.82	(33.82)	60.10	(32.64)

[1] EAC is a mean score of eight items measured on a five-point scale ranging from 1 "very rarely or never" to 5 "very often or always"; [2] Value of material is measured by the question "If a pair of new conventional jeans is a 100%, how much would you pay for exactly the same pair of … . " "—answer scale is continuous and ranges from 0 to 200; [3] Past use of alternative business models is measured by a dummy 0 "no", 1 "yes"; [4] Future use intention of alternative business models is measured as: 0 "very unlikely", 50 "neutral", and 100 "very likely" on a continuous scale.

References

1. Roos, S.; Sandin, G.; Zamani, B.; Peters, G.; Svanström, M. Will clothing be sustainable? Clarifying sustainable fashion. In *Textiles and Clothing Sustainability*; Muthu, S.S., Ed.; Springer: Singapore, 2017; pp. 1–45.
2. McAfee, A.; Dessain, V.; Sjoeman, A. *Zara: IT for Fast Fashion*; Harvard Business Review: Boston, MA, USA, 2004.
3. Foroohar, R.; Stabe, M. Fabulous fashion: Low-cost companies like Zara and Topshop are emerging as defining and dominant players, not just followers. *Newsweek Int.* **2005**, *17*, 30.
4. Kim, H.; Jung Choo, H.; Yoon, N. The motivational drivers of fast fashion avoidance. *J. Fash. Mark. Manag.* **2013**, *17*, 243–260. [CrossRef]
5. Niinimäki, K.; Hassi, L. Emerging design strategies in sustainable production and consumption of textiles and clothing. *J. Clean. Prod.* **2011**, *19*, 1876–1883. [CrossRef]
6. Choudhury, A.K.R. Environmental impacts of the textile industry and its assessment through life cycle assessment. In *Roadmap to Sustainable Textiles and Clothing, Environmental and Social Aspects of Textiles and Clothing Supply Chain*; Muthu, S.S., Ed.; Springer: Singapore, 2014; pp. 1–39.
7. Boström, M.; Micheletti, M. Introducing the sustainability challenge of textiles and clothing. *J. Consum. Policy* **2016**, *39*, 367–375. [CrossRef]
8. Deloitte-Christiansen, A.M.; Hvidsteen, K.; Haghshenas, B. *Fashioning Sustainability 2013*; Deloitte: Copenhagen, Denmark, 2013.
9. Moore, S.B.; Wentz, M. Eco-labeling for textiles and apparel. In *Sustainable Textiles: Life Cycle and Environmental Impact*; Blackburn, R.S., Ed.; Woodhead Publishing: Cambridge, UK, 2009; pp. 214–230.
10. Textile World. Water and Energy-Saving Solutions. Textile World Special Report. March/April 2008. Available online: http://www.textileworld.com/Issues/2008/March-April/Dyeing_Printing_and_Finishing/Water-And_Energy-Saving_Solutions (accessed on 13 February 2017).
11. Pfister, S.; Koehler, A.; Hellweg, S. Assessing the environmental impacts of freshwater consumption in LCA. *Environ. Sci. Technol.* **2009**, *43*, 4098–4104. [CrossRef] [PubMed]
12. Ecotextiles, O. Why Do We Offer Safe Fabrics? Available online: https://oecotextiles.wordpress.com/ (accessed on 4 January 2017).
13. Greenpeace International. Dirty Laundry 2: Hung out to Dry. 2011. Available online: http://www.greenpeace.org/international/en/publications/reports/Dirty-Laundry-2/ (accessed on 13 February 2017).
14. Peters, G.M.; Granberg, H.; Sweet, S. The role of science and technology in sustainable fashion. In *Routlegde Handbook of Sustainability and Fashion*; Fletcher, K., Tham, M., Eds.; Taylor & Francis: London, UK, 2014; pp. 181–190.
15. Roos, J.M. *Konsumtionsrapporten 2010*; The Consumer Report 2010; Center for Consumer Science, University of Gothenburg: Gothenburg, Sweden, 2010.
16. Roos, S.; Sandin, G.; Zamani, B.; Peters, G. *Environmental Assessment of Swedish Fashion Consumption*; Five Garments–Sustainable Futures; Mistra Future Fashion: Borås, Sweden, 2015.
17. American Apparel and Footwear Association. ApparelStats 2014. Arlington, VA, USA. Available online: www.wewear.org/apparelstats-2014-and-shoestats-2014-reports/ (accessed on 23 March 2017).
18. Connolly, J.; Prothero, A. Sustainable consumption: Consumption, consumers and the commodity discourse. *Consum. Mark. Cult.* **2003**, *6*, 275–291. [CrossRef]
19. Kozar, J.M.; Hiller Connell, K.Y. Socially and environmentally responsible apparel consumption: Knowledge, attitudes, and behaviors. *Soc. Responsib. J.* **2013**, *9*, 315–324. [CrossRef]
20. Roos, S.; Zamani, B.; Sandin, G.; Peters, G.M.; Svanström, M. A life cycle assessment (LCA)-based approach to guiding an industry sector towards sustainability: The case of the Swedish apparel sector. *J. Clean. Prod.* **2016**, *133*, 691–700. [CrossRef]
21. Textile Exchange. Organic Cotton Market Report 2016. Annual Report. 2016. Available online: http://textileexchange.org/wp-content/uploads/2017/02/TE-Organic-Cotton-Market-Report-Oct2016.pdf (accessed on 4 May 2017).
22. Ha-Brookshire, J.E.; Norum, P.S. Willingness to pay for socially responsible products: Case of cotton apparel. *J. Consum. Mark.* **2011**, *28*, 344–353. [CrossRef]
23. Ellis, J.L.; McCracken, V.A.; Skuza, N. Insights into willingness to pay for organic cotton apparel. *J. Fash. Mark. Manag. Int. J.* **2012**, *16*, 290–305. [CrossRef]

24. Mont, O. Institutionalisation of sustainable consumption patterns based on shared use. *Ecol. Econ.* **2004**, *50*, 135–153. [CrossRef]

25. Stamminger, R. Consumer real life behaviour compared to standard in washing and dishwashing. In Proceedings of the WFK 44th International Detergency Conference, Düsseldorf, Germany, 12–14 May 2009; pp. 89–100.

26. Laitala, K.; Boks, C.; Klepp, I.G. Potential for environmental improvements in laundering. *Int. J. Consum. Stud.* **2011**, *35*, 254–264. [CrossRef]

27. Gwozdz, W.; Netter, S.; Bjartmarz, T.; Reisch, L.A. *Survey Results on Fashion Consumption and Sustainability among Young Swedes*; Report Mistra Future Fashion; Mistra Future Fashion: Borås, Sweden, 2013.

28. Van Hoof, G.; Schowanek, D.; Feijtel, T.C. Comparative life-cycle assessment of laundry detergent formulations in the UK. Part I: Environmental fingerprint of five detergent formulations in 2001. *Tenside Surfactants Deterg.* **2003**, *40*, 266–275.

29. Järvi, P.; Paloviita, A. Product-related information for sustainable use of laundry detergents in Finnish Households. *J. Clean. Prod.* **2007**, *15*, 681–689. [CrossRef]

30. Faberi, S. Domestic Washing Machines and Dishwashers. Preparatory studies for Eco-design requirements of EuP. 2007. Available online: https://circabc.europa.eu/sd/a/5eedd0be-bc43-4506-81b2-2a825eb79e01/Lot24_Dish_T4_ENER%20clean_final.pdf (accessed on 6 May 2017).

31. Schmitz, A.; Stamminger, R. Usage behaviour and related energy consumption of European consumers for washing and drying. *Energy Effic.* **2014**, *7*, 937–954. [CrossRef]

32. Siebens, J. *Extended Measures of Well-Being: Living Conditions in the United States: 2011*; United States Census Bureau: Washington DC, USA, 2013; Volume 70, p. 136.

33. Allwood, J.M.; Laursen, S.E.; Rodríquez, C.M.; Bocken, N.M.P. *Well Dressed? The Present and Future Sustainability of Clothing and Textiles in the United Kingdom*; University of Cambridge: Cambridge, UK, 2006.

34. United States Environmental Protection Agency. *Advancing Sustainable Materials Management: 2014 Fact Sheet*; Office of Land and Emergency Management, United States Environmental Protection Agency: Washington, DC, USA, 2016.

35. Gracey, F.; Moon, D. Valuing our Clothes: The Evidence Base. Waste & Resources Action Programme (WRAP). Available online: http://www.wrap.org.uk/sites/files/wrap/10.7.12%20VOC-%20FINAL.pdf (accessed on 13 February 2017).

36. European Commission and the Council. Directive 2008/98/EC on Waste and Repealing Certain Directives. Official Journal of the European Union, 2008. Available online: http://eur-lex.europa.eu/LexUriServ/LexUriServ.do?uri=OJ:L:2008:312:0003:0030:EN:pdf (accessed on 30 March 2017).

37. Farrant, L.; Olsen, S.I.; Wangel, A. Environmental benefits from reusing clothes. *Int. J. Life Cycle Assess.* **2010**, *15*, 726–736. [CrossRef]

38. Morley, N.J.; Bartlett, C.; McGill, I. *Maximising Reuse and Recycling of UK Clothing and Textiles: A Report to the Department for Environment, Food and Rural Affairs*; Oakdene Hollins Ltd.: Aylesbury, UK, 2009.

39. Fisher, K.; James, K.; Maddox, P. *Benefits of Reuse Case Study: Clothing*; WRAP: Banbury, UK, 2011.

40. Koch, K.; Domina, T. Consumer textile recycling as a means of solid waste reduction. *Fam. Consum. Sci. Res. J.* **1999**, *28*, 3–17. [CrossRef]

41. Meade, A.W.; Craig, S.B. Identifying careless responses in survey data. In Proceedings of the 26th Annual Meeting of the Society for Industrial and Organizational Psychology, Chicago, IL, USA, 14–16 April 2011.

42. DeSimone, J.A.; Harms, P.D.; DeSimone, A.J. Best Practice Recommendations for Data Screening. *J. Organ. Behav.* **2015**, *36*, 171–181. [CrossRef]

43. Eurostat. Harmonized Index of Consumer Prices (HCIP). 2016. Available online: http://ec.europa.eu/eurostat/tgm/table.do?tab=table&init=1&plugin=1&language=en&pcode=teicp030 (accessed on 14 February 2017).

44. Hempel, A. *Konsumethik und Premiumsegment. Konzept zur Kundenbindung und Neukundengewinnung im Premiumsegment des Deutschen Modemarktes unter Besonderer Berücksichtigung einer Konsumethik*; Hamburger Schriften zur Marketingforschung; Hampp: Munich, Mering, 2010. (In German)

45. Kim, H.S.; Damhorst, M.L. Environmental concern and apparel consumption. *Cloth. Text. Res. J.* **1998**, *16*, 126–133. [CrossRef]

46. Dagevos, H. Consumers as four-faced creatures. Looking at food consumption from the perspective of contemporary consumers. *Appetite* **2005**, *45*, 32–39. [CrossRef] [PubMed]

47. Wedel, M.; Kamakura, W. *Market Segmentation: Conceptual and Methodological Foundations*, 2nd ed.; Kluwer Academic Publishers: Boston, MA, USA, 2000.

48. Kotler, P.; Roberto, N.; Lee, N. *Social Marketing: Improving the Quality of Life*, 2nd ed.; Sage Publications: Thousand Oaks, CA, USA, 2002.

49. Levi Strauss & Co. The Life Cycle of a Jeans. Understanding the Environmental Impact of a Pair of Levi's® 501® Jeans. 2015. Available online: http://levistrauss.com/wp-content/uploads/2015/03/Full-LCA-Results-Deck-FINAL.pdf (accessed on 13 February 2017).

50. Bhardwaj, V.; Fairhurst, A. Fast fashion: Response to changes in the fashion industry. *Int. Rev. Retail Distrib. Consum. Res.* **2010**, *20*, 165–173. [CrossRef]

51. Weller, I. Sustainable consumption and production patterns in the clothing sector: Is green the new black? In *Sustainability in Fashion and Textiles. Values, Design, Production and Consumption*; Gardetti, M.A., Torres, A.L., Eds.; Greenleaf Publishing: Sheffield, UK, 2013; pp. 184–194.

52. Hiller, A.J. Challenges in researching consumer ethics: A methodological experiment. *Qual. Mark. Res. Int. J.* **2010**, *13*, 236–252. [CrossRef]

![sustainability logo] *sustainability*

MDPI

Article

Fostering Sustainable Travel Behavior: Role of Sustainability Labels and Goal-Directed Behavior Regarding Touristic Services

Elfriede Penz [1,*], Eva Hofmann [2,3] and Barbara Hartl [3,4]

[1]   Department of Marketing, Institute for International Marketing Management, Vienna University of Business and Economics, Vienna 1020, Austria

[2]   Centre for Peace, Trust and Social Relations, Coventry University, Coventry CV1 5FB, UK; eva.hofmann@coventry.ac.uk

[3]   Competence Center for Empirical Research Methods, Vienna University of Business and Economics, Vienna 1020, Austria

[4]   Institute of Organization and Global Management Education, Johannes Kepler University Linz, Linz 4040, Austria; barbara.hartl_1@jku.at

*   Correspondence: elfriede.penz@wu.ac.at; Tel.: +43-1-31336-5102

Academic Editor: Gerrit Antonides
Received: 13 February 2017; Accepted: 13 June 2017; Published: 18 June 2017

Abstract: Individuals around the globe engage in sustainable consumption in their everyday life, e.g., when it comes to individual transportation. Although tourism behavior contributes to global carbon emissions to a considerable extent, consumers' awareness of sustainability in the tourism industry is still underresearched. Placing eco-labels next to tourist offers on websites might direct consumer's perception towards more sustainable offers. By employing eye-tracking techniques and surveys, this research aimed at linking information about sustainable tourist offers, perception of eco-labels and subsequent perception and preferences of tourism services. In Study 1, eight existing hotel offers with sustainability certification (four different labels) were selected and their websites presented to 48 participants (four websites each), whose eye movements were tracked. After looking at each website, they rated the overall appearance of the website. Based on the results, in the second study, participants' (n = 642) awareness of labels, their values and attitudes regarding sustainable behavior were found to influence their preference for certified tour operators. In addition, individuals' ideas of their perfect holidays were captured to allow a better understanding of their motivation. This research proposes implementing appropriate sustainable labeling in the tourism industry to increase awareness about sustainability among travelers and subsequently increase sustainable travel behavior.

Keywords: eco-labels; awareness; perception; trustworthiness and credibility of labels; eye-tracking

---

1. Introduction

According to the World Tourism Organization and the United Nations Environment Programme [1], the tourism industry contributes to 4.6% of global warming and about 5 % of global carbon emissions. The major part of emissions is caused by tourism companies in the transport sector (75%) and the accommodation sector (20%). In addition to the importance of environmental goals in general, there is growing awareness of negative impacts of tourism and the need to behave sustainably. Booking trips and holidays is a typical consumer decision in tourism, yet there are no clear results on whether consumers are willing to change their behavior to help tourism become more sustainable [2–5]. In this respect, sustainable tourism can be described as "tourism that takes full account of its current and future economic, social and environmental impacts, addressing the needs of visitors, the industry, the environment and host communities" ([1], np). At present, there are few regulations of environmental and sustainable practices in the tourism industry and often voluntary approaches guide the industry's pro-environmental, social and economically sustainable performance [6,7].

Consumers vary in their pro-environmental attitudes, which guide their decision-making [8] and determine their booking choice as sustainable or not. Research is scarce exploring whether individuals have associations to the environment or concerns for environmental and social problems when imagining their ideal holiday and subsequently when booking their holiday trip [2–5]. Therefore, understanding individuals' perception of touristic offers and services as part of their decision-making is vital to be able to motivate sustainable tourist behavior. Goals guide decision-making and choices [9,10], which will be examined in this research.

A goal-directed behavior consists of making a deliberate decision for a sustainable option [8]. It is assumed that this deliberate decision leads to a higher preference for a choice, intermediated by awareness and attention, which are significant prerequisites in decision making [11]. The deliberate decision comprises: (i) a pro-environmental attitude (environmental concern) as part of personal goal setting; (ii) the belief that choosing a sustainable tourist option for achieving this goal can make a difference; (iii) knowledge about eco-labels, i.e., that they exist, what they look like, and what they mean; and (iv) trustworthiness of labels and certifications, i.e., they are considered relevant and true.

This is where the current research sets in and aims to investigate the deliberate decision to choose a sustainable tourist option. In particular, we investigate the role of eco-labels at websites in two research questions: We examine prerequisites in decision-making, i.e., whether people are aware of eco-labels when they are presented along information about hotel accommodation on a website and whether the awareness affects the perception of the website (RQ1, impact of awareness on perception). Additionally, we investigate how the search for information is related to the perception of the website (RQ2, impact of search for information on perception).

To test the concept of goal-directed behavior, we analyze how pro-environmental attitudes (environmental concerns), subjective norm, belief to achieve a goal, trustworthiness of labels and certifications and knowledge about eco-labels relates to tourists' preference to choose a certified tour operator, who represents an important intermediary between supply and demand (RQ3, antecedents of preference for certified tour operator).

Finally, we explore whether those who find eco-labels trustworthy and who prefer certified tour operators hold a different image of a perfect holiday and whether environmental and sustainable elements are part of this image (RQ4, image of vacation).

The article is structured according to this conceptualization of goal-directed behavior and decision-making: First, we discuss awareness of eco-labels and perception of offers and develop two hypotheses dealing with the prerequisites for decision-making. Second, we describe the role of tourist operators as important intermediary in the tourism sector and the role of eco-labels and certification. Third, we discuss sustainable travel behavior and develop five hypotheses according to the model of goal-directed behavior. Eventually, we suggest exploring the image of a perfect holiday groups of people with varying trustworthiness in eco-labels and preference for certified tour operators.

1.1. Awareness of Eco-Labels and Perception of Offers

Among the informative tools that raise awareness and promote environmentally friendly practices are certifications, eco-labels and respective awards [2,12]. To identify a product or service as sustainable, consumers depend on a responsible authority to check the status on their behalf and to mark the product accordingly. The most common way of compromising the sustainable status of a product or service is to closely examine the certificate or label. Sustainability labels inform tourists about sustainable holiday and travel choices. However, to do so, tourists have to be aware of the existence of these labels as well as their functions. Moreover, there is only a chance that customers will be willing to change their tourism behavior, if they trust the credibility of these cues [13,14].

Consumers' awareness of respective labels and the impact on travel behavior is a still under-researched topic. Especially when it comes to a change in the behavior of customers, there is so far no evidence that tourists would rather travel with a certified tour operator than one without certification [2–5]. Some studies suggest that customers are not aware of these labels and certifications (e.g., [4]) and other studies found that customers are aware but unwilling to change their behavior (e.g., [15]). Research has further shown that even if tourists consider environmental and sustainability issues, they still need to be aware of sustainability labels and find them to be trustworthy to let them impact their behavior [16].

Although eco-labels have been provided for many years, individuals do not pay particular attention to them when planning their holidays [5]. Some scholars highlight that sustainability certifications may not have the desired impact on potential tourists [2–5]. Due to a general lack of awareness about eco-labels among tourists, many labels were found to be not suitable for reaching potential customers or for influencing their behavior [7]. Although there is growing tourist interest in sustainable holiday experiences [17], many tourists are unaware of the existence of certifications for environmentally responsible holiday offers and therefore do not relate to them when booking their holidays [4]. Even when tourists are considering sustainability issues when booking their holidays, the sustainability of a product still remains only one of many characteristics consumers consider when comparing different offers of tourism products [13]. Consumers, who have a good understanding of what sustainable tourism stands for, tend to interpret eco-labels along those lines compared to tourists with little knowledge about sustainable tourism. This was confirmed in a study on seafood labels [16].

Communication strategies motivate customers to behave sustainably by raising awareness as well as by informing and educating them about activities, offers and consequences of their choices [2]. Environmental awareness has been found to lead to pro-environmental acts [18]. Conceptualized as multidimensional construct, environmental awareness comprises knowledge, values and attitudes towards the environment (e.g., [19]). Knowledge has been argued to be significant for predicting environmental action but it does not always make people act accordingly. Promotion of environmental consciousness, for instance by using eco-labels, seems critical [20]. Activities that build on awareness building fail to establish the link between attitudes, motivation or intention and action [21–24]. Certain tourist segments, for instance eco-tourists [17], seem to be concerned about the environment and know about the (negative) impact of their vacation on the environment, but the majority of tourists do not know about the negative effects and does not choose more sustainable offers over conventional holidays [25].

Eco-labels have the potential to close the psychological gap between the environmental challenges and the actions of individuals by providing valuable information. Consequently, they adapt their behavior towards a more sustainable one, while on vacation [26]. Eco-labels influence consumers' behavior, but they do so in a biased way [27]. It is assumed that eco-labels can empower consumers as they "resolve the information asymmetry between the seller and buyer of a good by providing information to the buyer on how the product was produced" ([16], p. 8197). On the one hand, a high number of eco-labels are suggested to make consumers aware of the issue at their point of choice, as with several eco-labels a high amount of information is presented [8,25]. On the other hand, too much information might confuse consumers [16], make it difficult for consumers to recognize labels and to trust them due to limited transparency of the auditing/certification process and unclear benefit (e.g., [22,28]). The number and variety of awards and certifications are huge and confusing to individuals [5,29], who are simply overwhelmed by an overload of information transmitted by eco-labels [15]. In addition, how an eco-label is presented might influence the perception of the offer. For instance, tourist offers are presented at websites. In this respect, web usability studies show that easy to use and clear websites increase satisfaction with the provider [30–33].

We build on the eye–mind hypothesis [34], suggesting that what individuals are looking at is a reflection of what they are attending to and thus is a measure of awareness. In addition, what individuals are looking at, and how often, can be used as proxy for search activity.

Given the importance of awareness of labels, certifications and awards as antecedent to perception, we develop the following hypotheses:

Hypothesis 1 (H1). *Awareness of eco-labels on a website is related to the perception of the website.*

Hypothesis 2 (H2). *Searching for information regarding eco-labels on a website is related to the perception of the website.*

1.2. Individuals' Preference for Certified Tour Operators

Tour operators are important intermediaries in the tourist sector. About half of the most popular destination choice "beach holidays" was sold through travel retailers including tour operators [35]. Tour operators (including tour guides) were also identified as primarily responsible for providing tourists with information on ethical aspects of tourism [36].

Tour operators have increasingly been using labels to indicate environmental and sustainable offers to improve the image of the organization and to attract further customers [29,37]. Being located in the center of the tourism supply chain, tour operators have the power to influence the behavior of tourism delivery and consumption and are assumed responsible for increasing sustainability in the tourism industry [38]. Tour operators act in a very fragmented industry, consisting of tourist accommodation, transportation (to and from destinations), food services, excursion and activities for tourists [39]. They bundle these products and services and need to make sure that suppliers live up to the criteria of the sustainability award they wish to receive. In this respect, demand from customers has a very strong influence on tour operators [40] and tour operators will only be willing to take efforts to receive certifications, if customers demand sustainable tourism products [14].

Tour operators serve as important information source for tourist choices [41]. In particular, when uncertainty is high, it is considered a professional source that serves high informational needs, for instance if a trip is complex and the quality of the trip should be high. This is the case in both the phase before and after a definite trip decision was made.

Research has studied interrelationships of information, image creation and travel behavior with regard to tourist destination choice. We extend this research by focusing on one specific aspect of tourism, i.e., sustainability communication in the form of a label or certification.

1.3. Sustainable Travel and Goal-Directed Behavior

As outlined above, a goal-directed behavior consists of making a deliberate decision for a sustainable option [8], which is now further developed to the question of how to increase the effectiveness of sustainability communication [22,42].

1.3.1. Pro-Environmental Attitude (Environmental Concern) as Part of Personal Goal Setting

Identification with environmentally conscious consumers and a green personality—a person's "environmentalist" self-perception or identity [43]—are assumed to lead to more sustainable behavior because people who are concerned with the environment feel more attached to a specific behavior, such as organic food consumption [44,45]. While the environmental attitudes of tourists might be strengthened by the information provided by eco-labels, they seem to be not strong enough to overcome behavior. Often, not behaving environmentally friendly is habit-related, convenience or reflects a personal preference [2]. Highly environmentally concerned consumers, who in their daily life are active in environmental protection, do not show the same behavior when on holidays, though. They often engage in vacation behavior with negative environmental consequences and come up with a range of explanations justifying their tourist activities [23]. In addition, despite positive attitudes towards environmentally and socially responsible holidays, individuals are unwilling to pay for more sustainability performance [46,47].

Consequently, we propose:

Hypothesis 3a (H3a). *Environmental concern positively relates to the preference for traveling with a certified tour operator.*

Subjective norms reflect the "perceived social pressure for a person to engage or not to engage in a behaviour" ([48], p. 7). They influence attitudes towards organic purchases, which means that individuals are influenced by the opinions of others towards organic purchases [49]. It is further suggested that subjective norms influence purchase intentions even if people have negative attitudes towards buying sustainably produced food [50]. Similarly, sustainable purchase behavior and subjective norms are positively correlated if the perceived subjective norms correspond with one's personal norms [51]. A recent study on eco-friendly travel choices investigated social comparison feedback and found mixed results on intentions to choose eco-friendly travel options [52]. It is also argued that a change from purchasing conventional to sustainable food products is rather costly, which cannot be compensated by external influence.

Hence, we propose:

Hypothesis 3b (H3b). *Subjective norm to behave sustainably positively relates to the preference for traveling with a certified tour operator.*

1.3.2. Belief to Achieve a Goal

General environmental values can be seen as voluntary commitment, chosen by individuals consciously or unconsciously, and as universal and fundamental values that underlie sustainable development [53]. Reflecting beliefs in certain desirable end states, values serve as antecedents to attitudes and actions [54,55] and general environmental values lead to environmentally sustainable behavior [56]. The values base on the Millennium Declaration of the UN and are freedom, equality, solidarity, tolerance, respect for nature, and shared responsibility [53]. Thus, it is suggested:

Hypothesis 3c (H3c). *General sustainability values positively relates to the preference for traveling with a certified tour operator.*

1.3.3. Trustworthiness of Labels and Certifications

A barrier for consumers not to choose sustainable offers is greenwashing, i.e., referring to "exaggerated benefits or unsupported claims in support of the environment in advertising and other persuasive communications" [57]. They simply mistrust these offers [58] and refrain from purchasing. In addition, individuals do not believe in environmental performance of businesses, limiting the trustworthiness of their offers [3]. Little trustworthiness of eco-labels may be grounded in the belief that during the certification process only a limited selection of criteria is assessed. Individuals are also unable to distinguish between businesses which have failed to meet the certification criteria and those which did not try to receive certifications [3].

Hypothesis 3d (H3d). *Trustworthiness of certifications positively relates to the preference for traveling with a certified tour operator.*

1.3.4. Familiarity with Eco-Labels

Familiarity, defined as the ability to recall an eco-label from the past, helps in developing a knowledge structure. It refers to both information stored in memory and perceived knowledge about a product or service [59]. Recognizing eco-labels plays an important role in explaining purchasing behavior, for instance, of eco-labeled seafood [60]. Based on this, the following hypothesis is developed:

Hypothesis 3e (H3e). *Familiarity with labels positively relates to the preference for traveling with a certified tour operator.*

1.4. Image of Vacation by Consumer Segments

Thus far, predictors of individuals' preference for certified tour operators were described and respective hypotheses developed. However, motivations and intentions of individuals to go on vacation and choose among the variety of offers stem from their image of what a perfect holiday means to them. Thus far, holidays are not associated a lot with sustainability or eco-friendliness, as mentioned above. Even if asked directly, tourists do not rate these criteria highly [61]. In a study on sustainable lifestyles, tourism-based environmental practices were investigated and consumer segments described [34]. Environmental consciousness at home does not translate easily to the context of holidays. Even "committed environmentalists" who show high attachment to nature as part of their holiday experience, would rather buy into compensation schemes than refrain from using air-travel [34]. Young tourists, who value sustainable holiday experiences look for quality in the choice of tour operators and expect support for environmental protection in the local area from them [17]. We assume that those, who find certified tour operators trustworthy and prefer them, might hold a different image of a perfect holiday. Thus, we are interested in exploring the image of their perfect holiday when individuals start their decision whether environmental and sustainable elements are part of this image (RQ4: Image of vacation).

2. Methods and Results

In the following, we investigate the four research questions empirically and present two different studies. While Study 1 comprises a lab experiment using eye-tracking techniques to investigate whether awareness and information search of eco-labels on a website relate to the perception of the website, Study 2 examines related factors of the preference for traveling with a certified tour operator and whether environmental and sustainable elements are part of the image of a perfect holiday using an online questionnaire.

2.1. Study 1

2.1.1. Participants

In total, 48 participants (students at a business school in a major city in Austria) were recruited via an e-mail list from a subject pool (approximately N = 600 bachelor students in the middle of their studies are automatically pool-members) at the Department of Marketing. The mean age was 23.46 years (SD 4.93; range: 19–51 years) and 47.9% were female. Participants were rewarded in the form of course credit for a major marketing course. Their participation is voluntary. Testing took place at a university lab. Each of them viewed four out of eight accommodation offers from hotel websites on a computer screen with eye-tracking glasses on.

2.1.2. Method and Procedure

An experimental study in the lab using eye-tracking technique (SMI Experiment Center™ 3.4, SMI BeGaze™, SensoMotoric Instruments (SMI), Teltow, Germany) was conducted to test whether people are aware of eco-labels when they are presented along other information about hotel accommodation on a website, and how the awareness influences the perception of the website. The procedure involved tracking of eye movements of participants and answering questions. Before starting the data collection, it was necessary to calibrate the equipment for each participant, which took a few minutes.

The websites presented eight hotels with eco-labels on their websites. They were shown to participants as static documents (.pdf) to avoid disturbance through browsing. The material was selected by one psychologist and a research assistant based on desk research and inspection of real offers from hotel websites, which carry the eco-labels as part of their offers. They are also presented at websites on labels and certificates [62,63]. The selection criteria were that labels should represent a cross-section of general and specific logos. In this context "general" implies logos that promote sustainability in different sectors (including tourism), whereas "specific" means logos that only promote sustainability in the tourism and travel industry. Four different labels were eventually chosen based on this comprehensive research. These were two labels focusing on tourism in particular (Travelife, CSR tourism) and two labels focusing on sustainability in general (EMAS, Österreichisches Umweltzeichen). In addition, one label is international (Travelife), two European (EMAS, CSR tourism) and one national (Österreichisches Umweltzeichen) (see Table 1). Hotel and accommodation offers were selected based on the category of the hotel (hotel belonging to hotel chains versus family-run hotel) and what label it carries. In addition, the display of the label on the website was given consideration, ranging from lots of text and small logo on the website (stimulus code: STH, KUR, BSH) to big logo and lots of text (stimulus code: BWP, IIH) and medium size of label and lots of pictures (stimulus code: BH, BSPH, AS). Text-based websites had only small labels displayed while image-based websites display labels much bigger. The combination of labels (four labels) and hotel websites (two per label) resulted in a total of eight websites, which were randomly assigned to participants during data collection. Each participant rated four out of the eight websites.

Table 1. Background information about and selection criteria for eco-labels (Study 1).

Selection Criterion	Label	Awarded by	Hotel Type: Stimulus (No of Subjects)
Specific area: Tourism (CSR)	CSR Tourism	non-profit organization TourCert (Stuttgart, Germany)	Hotel chain: BWP (N = 26) Hotel chain: IIH (N = 19)
Specific area: Tourism (Sustainability)	Travelife	Travelife Ltd. (London, UK)	Hotel chain: KUR (N = 26) Family-run: AS (N = 24)
General area	EMAS	European Eco-Management and Audit Scheme (EMAS) logo is the eco-label of the European Union	Hotel chain: BSPH (N = 25) Family-run: BSH (N = 20)
General area	Österreichisches Umweltzeichen	Austrian Federal Ministry of Agriculture, Forestry, Environment and Water Management (initiative by the Austrian government)	Hotel chain: BH (N = 26) Family-run: STH (N = 20)

The participants were asked to look at the website offer for as long as they felt was necessary to understand it. During this time frame, their eye movements were tracked and recorded. After showing the website, participants rated the overall appearance of the website ("How did you perceive the design of the website?") on two items on their perception: clarity (1 = clear, 5 = unclear) and appeal (1 = appealing, 5 = unappealing). Additional items not relevant for the current study regarding the evaluation of the offer of the hotel on several aspects (destination, offer, environment, activities, images, appealing description), ranging from 1 = very attractive to 5 = very unattractive were asked. To test our hypotheses, we will only use the overall perception of the website as clear and appealing (Cronbach's $\alpha = 0.96$).

Two types of eye movements are usually modeled to gain insight into the overt localization of visual attention: fixations and saccades (glances). While fixations are eye movements that stabilize the retina over an object (with a minimum time of eye stability of 50 ms in our study), saccades are used in repositioning the fovea to a new location in the visual environment, such as a website [64]. Fixations correspond to the desire to maintain one's gaze on an object and therefore are a physiological measure of awareness. Saccades (glances), which are voluntary, are considered manifestations of the desire to change the focus of attention. Eye movement analysis considers a third movement, i.e., smooth pursuits, which occur when tracking moving objects. For our study, we will focus on fixations and saccades as physiological measures of attention. What individuals are looking at is a reflection of what they are attending to and thus measures awareness [63]. In more detail, we produce the following eye tracking data [65]: fixation count (i.e., number of fixations on stimulus) and average fixation duration (i.e., how long on average respondents fixated the stimulus). The more fixations and the longer the duration, the more interesting, important or noticeable is the stimulus. In addition, first fixation, which measures how much time respondents spent on the stimulus (first fixation duration; the longer, the more difficult to understanding or more engaging) is used.

As a measure of what individuals are looking at, we use glances count, i.e., the number of gazes on the stimulus. The higher the number of glances, the more searching takes place [65].

Finally, we split the entire website into several Areas of Interests (AOI), i.e., sub-regions of the page, to be able to extract data about fixations and glances exactly for the shown labels.

Thus, the study was designed as follows: Eight websites contains different labels in different sizes with different kinds of hotels whereby each participant randomly received four of these websites for evaluation. The independent variables are the measured eye movements (IV: Eye movements) which were registered with the different websites and the dependent variable is the reported perception of the website as clear and appealing (DV: Perception, mean of items clarity and appeal).

2.1.3. Results

The Austrian Eco-label ("Österreichisches Umweltzeichen") was by far the most familiar of the four labels. Overall, 33 participants were familiar with the label, while the label "Travelife" was the least familiar label, with only six participants being familiar with the label. The survey showed that 14 respondents were familiar with the label issued by the European Eco-Management and Audit Scheme ("EMAS"); 11 participants were familiar with the label "CSR tourism". Table 2 shows some descriptive information about the stimuli.

Table 2. Descriptive information about stimulus websites (aggregate data, Study 1).

Stimulus	Label	Sequence of Fixation	AOI Coverage [%] *	First Fixation Duration [ms]	Glances Count	Fixation Count	Average Fixation [ms]
BWP [1]	CSR Tourism	7	1.30	256.42	0.92	2.12	229.49
IIH [1]	CSR Tourism	8	1.10	197.50	0.87	1.30	178.04
BSH [2]	EMAS	8	0.20	59.00	0.25	0.25	52.33
BSPH [1]	EMAS	7	0.80	169.50	1.36	1.56	195.10
AS [2]	Travelife	7	0.70	250.40	1.50	1.92	266.10
KUR [1]	Travelife	9	0.20	86.87	0.48	0.56	82.15
BH [1]	Österreichisches Umweltzeichen	6	3.40	164.79	2.31	7.62	185.35
STH [2]	Österreichisches Umweltzeichen	7	0.20	n/a	0.10	0.10	16.20

Notes: * AOI = Area of Interest; coverage (%) relates the selected AOI to all other AOIs (website): The higher the number, the bigger the label on the website. n/a: Due to a low number of fixations (only two), the duration was not captured. [1] = hotel chain; [2] = family-run hotel.

To test whether eye movements are related to perception (H1 and H2), a repeated measure regression is conducted using STATA, controlling for age, gender and education. The analysis ($F_{(8, 46)} = 2.47$, $p = 0.026$, $R^2 = 0.08$) reveals a significant effect for fixation count, $\beta = -0.18$, $t(183) = -2.24$, $p = 0.030$ and first fixation durations, $\beta = -0.30$, $t(183) = -2.06$, $p = 0.045$, but no significant effect of glances count ($p = 0.164$) or average fixations ($p = 0.146$). The effect of first fixation durations and fixation count is based on the size of the label. Two t-tests comparing first fixation durations and fixation count for high and low coverage of the label reveal that first fixation durations is longer for large labels ($M_{low} = 119.88$, SD = 177.93; $M_{high} = 206.51$, SD = 258.27; $t(183) = -2.70$, $p = 0.008$) and that fixation count is more often with larger labels ($M_{low} = 0.92$, SD = 1.42; $M_{high} = 3.94$, SD = 5.79; $t(183) = -5.33$, $p < 0.001$).

Overall, the awareness of eco-labels on a website influences the perception of the website; however, when the size of the label is taken into account, first fixation durations and fixation count durations and fixation depend on it, supporting partly H1. The search for information regarding eco-labels does not seem to influence the perception, rejecting H2.

While Study 1 showed that awareness of eco-labels in general has a positive effect on the perception of websites, it is not clear what consumers consider when deciding for a sustainable tour operator and whether they consider sustainability for their perfect holiday. Therefore, we conducted Study 2.

2.2. Study 2

2.2.1. Participants

A convenience sample of 642 participants (62.1% female, $M_{age} = 26.90$, SD = 4.93, mainly students) completed an online questionnaire. Participants stated that they mainly use tour operators for gathering information online (mean = 3.58, SD = 1.14; 1 = seldom, 5 = always) or directly booking online (mean = 3.28, SD = 1.46; 1 = seldom, 5 = always). On average, they state to travel 3.76 times per year; in more detail, they book city trips (mean = 3.21, SD = 3.83; 1 = seldom, 5 = always) and beach holidays (mean = 2.61, SD = 1.37; 1 = seldom, 5 = always). They travel with friends (mean = 3.08, SD = 1.43; 1 = seldom, 5 = always) or with their partner (mean = 3.07, SD = 1.74; 1 = seldom, 5 = always).

2.2.2. Method and Procedure

An online questionnaire was developed consisting of two parts to answer what are predictors of individuals' preferences for traveling with a certified tour operator and what image of the perfect holiday groups of individuals hold and what environmental and sustainable elements part of this image are. The first part of the questionnaire started with an open question to capture individuals' image of vacation ("a perfect holiday means to me . . . "). Participants had to note a minimum of three associations, but could not report more than five. All reported associations were used in the analysis.

In the second part of the survey, participants were asked 12 questions on their general sustainability values, which they had to answer by rating their agreement or disagreement on a 5-point Likert scale. In order to guarantee reliability and validity a shortened version [66] of the Sustainability Values scale [53] has been applied. These questions were used to find out if participants show general concern for sustainability issues (Cronbach's α = 0.73). In order to find out about their level of familiarity with labels, participants were shown the most common sustainability certifications for tourism providers in Austria (nine labels) and were asked about their level of familiarity and their experience with these certifications (Cronbach's α = 0.98). This list included the labels used in Study 1 (EMAS, CSR tourism, Travelife, Österreichisches Umweltzeichen). Next, evaluations of participants on the trustworthiness of sustainability certifications for tour operators were measured [67]. Participants were asked to state the extent to which they agree or disagree with eight statements regarding trustworthiness of certifications on a 5-point Likert scale (Cronbach's α = 0.80). The preference to choose a certified tour operator was measured using a single-item ("I would travel with a tour operator if he'd been awarded a sustainability certificate") on a 5-point Likert scale (mean = 3.02, SD = 1.11; 1 = disagree, 5 = agree).

Finally, questions on general environmental concern (Cronbach's α = 0.74, eight items) and subjective norm (Cronbach's α = 0.83, five items) of the participants as well as demographic questions regarding age, gender, education, living situation, nationality and income of the participants followed. The questionnaire included further questions (booking and traveling behavior, eight items; importance ranking of eight factors in the booking decision [68]).

2.2.3. Results

To test the concept of goal-directed behavior and whether pro-environmental attitude (environmental concern (H3a) and subjective norm (H3b)), belief to achieve a goal (general sustainability values (H3c)), trust of labels and certifications (trustworthiness of certifications (H3d)), and knowledge about eco-labels (familiarity with eco-labels (H3e)) are related to individuals' preferences for traveling with a certified tour operator, a step-wise regression (method: enter) was run using SPSS (Correlation matrix see Table 3).

Table 3. Correlation matrix (Study 2).

	(1)	(2)	(3)	(4)	(5)
(1) Sustainability Values					
(2) Environmental Concern	−0.315 **				
(3) Subjective Norm	−0.257 **	0.487 **			
(4) Familiarity with Labels	−0.088 *	−0.034	−0.021		
(5) Trustworthiness of Labels	−0.163 **	0.371 **	0.454 **	0.014	
(6) Preference Certified Tour Operator	−0.260 **	0.355 **	0.454 **	0.012	0.671 **

Note: * $p < 0.05$; ** $p < 0.001$.

Step 1 (model 1) included subjective norm, general sustainability values and environmental concern $F(3,638) = 67.78$, $p < 0.001$, $R^2 = 0.24$), the second step (model 2) added familiarity with labels and trustworthiness of labels ($F(5,636) = 122.13$, $p < 0.001$, $R^2 = 49$). The analysis reveals a significant relation with general sustainability values ($\beta = 0.12$, $t(641) = 3.88$, $p < 0.001$), subjective norm ($\beta = 0.15$, $t(641) = 4.25$, $p < 0.001$) and trustworthiness of certifications ($\beta = 0.57$, $t(641) = 17.58$, $p < 0.001$).

The relevance of sustainability in the booking decision will be explored by considering the freely associated open answers to the image of the perfect holiday. To answer what image of the perfect holiday individuals hold and whether environmental and sustainable elements are part of this image, a correspondence analysis was conducted on the frequency of associations towards the "perfect holiday" (see Figure 1). The correspondence analysis (Anacor, normalization "canonical") is an exploratory method for the graphical display of categorical data, which allows the simultaneous treatment of variables. The closer one association is to a group or another association the more often they are stated together with this group or association [69].

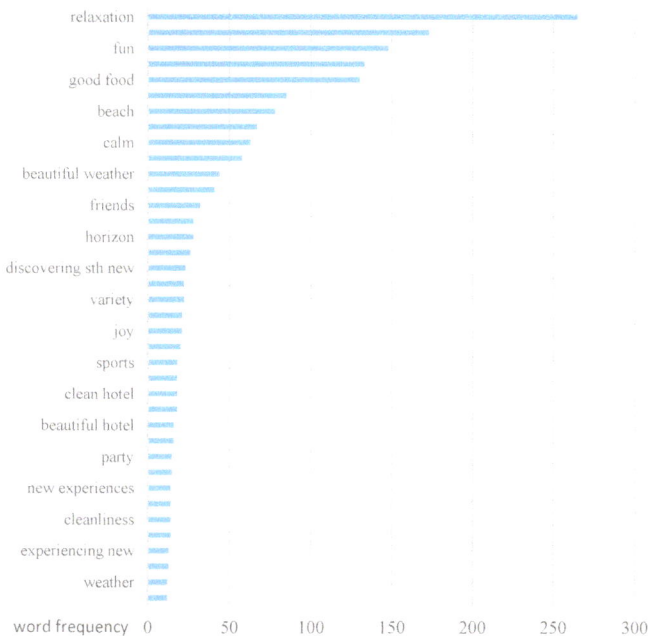

Figure 1. Frequencies of free associations (Study 2); associations f > 10 are displayed.

The analysis starts with a table of frequencies, where in the current analysis the rows represent the different free associations to a perfect holiday and the four columns represent the groups high and low trustworthiness of labels (trust-high and trust-low) and high and low preferences for certified tour operators (pref-high and pref-low). For these two grouping variables, we split the sample (median) into two groups (high/low) per variable, resulting in four groups. Two dimensions were extracted, which contribute 82.4% of variance to the overall solution. The overall spatial variation (total inertia) was 0.13, indicating that the correlation between row points (associations categories) and column points (groups of individuals) is fairly low. For interpretation purposes, the row and column points, which contributed significantly to the two dimensions, were taken into consideration [70]. In the following, the two dimensions are described (see Figure 2).

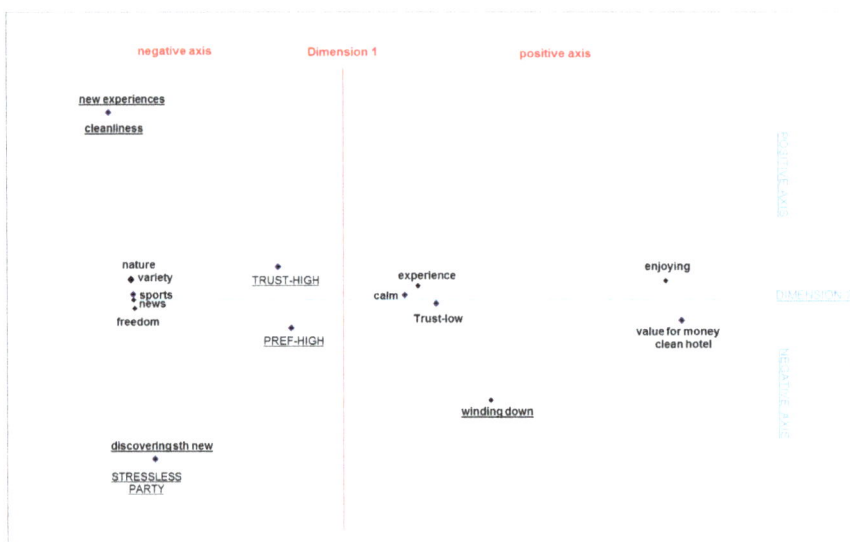

Figure 2. Correspondence analysis (Study 2). Note: Associations and groups contributing to **dimension 1** are presented in bold letters; those contributing to DIMENSION 2 in uppercase; and associations and groups contributing to **both dimensions** appear bold and underlined.

Only associations mentioned more than ten times by respondents are included in the analysis. Associations and variables that significantly explain the dimensions are displayed.

Dimension 1 distinguishes between "value-added chill out" (positive axis: expressed by the associations calm, experience, enjoying, value for money, clean hotel and winding down) and "excitement and discovery" (negative axis: expressed by the associations nature, sports, freedom, news, variety, new experiences, cleanliness, and learn something new). The positive axis also includes people with low trustworthiness towards certifications. Nature is the only association that refers to the environment; it can be found in the "excitement and discovery" part of dimension 1 and does not seem to be close to any group.

Dimension 2 separates the themes "finding purity" (positive axis: expressed by associations new experiences and cleanliness) and "carefree" (negative axis: expressed by the associations party, stressless, winding down, and learn something new). The dimension further distinguishes between people who believe in the trustworthiness of certifications (positive axis) and who have high preferences for traveling with certified tour operators (negative axis). It seems that people interested in enjoyment and value for money are rather skeptical about certifications. Those who find certifications trustworthy put more emphasis on variety in their holiday. Eventually, people who imagine their perfect holiday to be "carefree" show preference for traveling with certified tour operators.

3. Discussion

This research set out to understand individuals' perception of touristic offers and services in order to motivate them to choose sustainable alternatives when going on vacations. Eco-labels provide valuable information to consumers—they empower them—if seen and processed; thus, they need to be made visible, accessible and salient. However, the interpretation of information differs, depending on individuals' understanding of the cue (e.g., [11]). In particular, we investigated whether and how cues can raise awareness, how preferences for traveling with certified tour operators are shaped and whether those, who trust and prefer certified tour operators hold a different image of a perfect holiday.

Using eye-tracking and an online questionnaire, the current research shows that the awareness of eco-labels influences the perception of the website using the label (Study 1) and influences sustainable travel behavior, together with values and attitudes regarding sustainable behavior (Study 2). The current research proposes implementing appropriate sustainable labeling in the tourism industry to increase positive perception of websites including such labels among travelers and subsequently increase sustainable travel behavior. It might help in identifying opportunities for tour operators to improve the offers of sustainable tours and initiate more sustainability.

In particular, regarding the question concerning the relation between the awareness of and search for eco-labels and the perception of a website of hotels (RQ1 and RQ2), this means that when individuals browse an offer, their searching for relevant information does not influence their perception, but once some evidence for certification (in our case sustainability certification) is processed, the overall perception is positive. It does not matter in what sequential order the information is perceived (eco-labels are looked rather late) and it seems that bigger displays are better recognized. As regards the question of possible influences on tourists' preference to choose a certified tour operator (RQ3), the current study shows that trustworthiness of certifications influence the decision to choose operators with certifications. In addition, the social environment and sustainability values have an impact. Environmental concern, mentioned in past research with an unclear role, was not influential in our research. While we found support that awareness of labels impact the perception of a website in a positive way, we could not find an influence of individuals' familiarity with labels on their actual preference for choosing certified tour operators. To conclude, people prefer to travel with certified tour operators the more they think that certifications for tour operators are trustworthy, the more they feel dependent on how others think one should travel and the more they agree with general sustainability values.

However, the awareness and the familiarity with eco-labels in the tourist sector is generally low. Consumers' unawareness of eco-labels may partially result from their confusion due to the current proliferation of labels and certifications. Their confusion may further lead consumers to ignore green messages [71]. On the other hand, consumers may be unaware of eco-labels in the tourist sector, as the majority of consumers do not think about sustainable issue when planning their holiday [2–5].

To explore further whether those, who trust and prefer certified tour operators, hold a different image of a perfect holiday and whether environmental and sustainable elements are part of the image (RQ4, image of vacation), our research explored the general meaning and understanding of the concept "holiday" for individuals. Generally, the concept of traveling and holiday is (still) not linked to sustainability. A perfect holiday is rather associated with relaxation, recreation and fun. In addition, price for value and quality/comfort are relevant decision criteria while impact on environment and social responsibility are the least important criteria when booking. This is in line with research showing that a holiday is perceived as "different" to everyday life [34]. Many consumers do not consider environmental issues when planning their holidays [72]. Unlike other behaviors, such as switching off lights or purchasing organic foods, it seems that sustainable travel behavior cannot be easily embedded into daily life practices [34]. This indicates that the promotion of sustainable behavior is still a challenge in the context of tourism.

In the current study, we identified associations group under the term "nature" as closest to the concept of environment, next to a "carefree" holiday and could link it to individuals who would travel with certified tour operators. Another group with high sustainable values views holidays as offering amenities and have a compound view of holidays. Those people who associate their perfect holiday with "value for money" would rather not prefer certified tour operators and do not find certifications trustworthy.

There are certainly economic implications of tourist preferences; sustainable consumption is seen as a business opportunity. However, tourists need to be convinced and willing to make efforts to improve their behavior [47]. Our research points to the role of businesses to raise awareness of eco-labels [16]. It seems that consumers' demand for sustainable options and voluntary certification of some tour operators, etc. are not strong enough to generate respective and many offers. Governmental and non-governmental pressure and encouragement could force businesses to adapt certification schemes. This is important also because government programs are more efficient than private ones [73].

As regards practical implications, communication strategies should be applied to increase the awareness and credibility of eco-labels [13,27] in the tourism industry. Low credibility of eco-labels can be encountered using recognized and official certifications and making the awarding and auditing process clear and transparent [12,22,57]. It seems that few labels that communicate clearly their purpose (e.g., CSR) are to be preferred over a variety of less clear labels or schemes (EMAS) to avoid consumer confusion. Simple seal-of-approval logos and labels have been found to affect consumer behavior more than complex information-disclosure labels [73]. The design of logos might be vital as well, following our study results, they should be big and well-known (Study 1 and Study 2). However, big logos are looked at promptly (first fixation durations). Thus, the logo size on a website should be carefully chosen depending on the purpose of communication.

In general, labels need to be salient and accessible for consumers to allow individuals processing and understanding the information that it expresses [22]. This means that labels need to be made visible by e.g., placing them next to an accommodation offer on a website. For instance, analyzing Internet advertising in the tourism industry, it was found that increased exposure to information increases attention and appropriate content that fits individuals' preferences increases involvement with the offer. Both increase the effectiveness of the information. Moreover, using imagery that stands out from other visual information is easier to process, and should be used in combination with text [74,75].

Besides its merits the two studies hold also some limitations. Study 1 presents an experiment where different websites are randomly allocated to different participants. The websites vary over several aspects: chain versus family hotel, kind of label, and size of label. In a standard experiment, these variations would have been too many, but in the current case not the websites with the labels are the independent variables but the registered eye movements that they trigger. In the current study these variations assure that a great variety of different websites with labels stimulate several different eye movements that are related to the perceptions of the websites. One problem, which is usually the case with eye-tracking methodology in social research, is the small sample size [76]. Due to the small sample size, additional control variables could not be included in the analysis. Further research should particularly pay attention to the role of familiarity as confounding variable, as familiarity with logos is an important determinant of attention to labels [77]. In their review, Wedel and Pieters [78] discuss familiarity as a top-down influencing factor of eye-movement patterns. In the current study, familiar eco-labels may have attracted less attention than new, unfamiliar labels. Consumers who are familiar with a label may look at it for a short time, because they have previously viewed the label extensively and think that a further examination is unnecessary (cf. research on nutrition label use; [79]).

Study 2 helps us in identifying relations in goal-directed behavior but further research needs to identify causal instead of relational relationships using appropriate methodology and instead of using a single-item for preferences use a multiple item scale to increase validity. Answering RQ4, Study 2 presents a correspondence analysis, where free associations are categorized according to two different variables (trustworthiness of certifications, preference for traveling with a certified tour operator). For grouping these two variables, a median split was undertaken resulting in four different groups of low and high characteristics. These median splits result in artificial groups, which not exactly reflect the original values of the variables. Nevertheless, for the current analysis, a reduction of complexity is needed. As the correspondence analysis shows, even with this reduction of complexity, we find differences between different groups.

Future research therefore could build on our findings that awareness of eco-labels impact perception positively. To delve deeper into the dynamics of designing eco-labels and online travel websites, systemic eye-tracking studies that test the size, position and meaning of eco-labels for a specific tourist offer could be conducted. In addition, the impact of communication efforts by different senders (e.g., governmental, non-governmental, and private organization) would show which authority is most effective in promoting eco-labels. Eventually, to make the perfect holiday a sustainable holiday, a behavioral spillover [55] from sustainable behaviors of individuals' everyday practices, for instance using public transportation instead of a car, to sustainable travel behavior could be investigated. Research so far looked at different contexts (household and hospitality/hotel) and found that the vacation context is hedonic and therefore spillover is less likely [80,81].

Summing up the current research shows that cues such as eco-labels are essential for eco-tourist to decide for sustainable tourism options. Especially trustworthiness of the labels is of importance when selecting a sustainable tour operator. However, tourism industry needs to raise awareness of the importance of sustainable tourism offers, as a perfect holiday is not linked to sustainability yet.

Acknowledgments: We thank Katrin Eder and Saba Sonnleitner for their support in the data collection and Stefan Wiesel-Severin for his support in collecting and analyzing the eye-tracking data. Partly financed by the Austrian Science Fund (Project number: P 29693-G29). The Vienna University of Economics and Business contributed to the funding of data collection (Study 1) and covered the cost to publish in open access.

Author Contributions: Elfriede Penz designed the studies and collected the data; and Elfriede Penz, Eva Hofmann and Barbara Hartl analyzed the data and wrote the paper.

Conflicts of Interest: The authors declare no conflict of interest.

References

1. UNEP; UNWTO. *Making Tourism More Sustainable—A Guide for Policy Makers*; World Tourism Organization UNWTO: Madrid, Spain, 2005; pp. 11–12.
2. Budeanu, A. Sustainable tourist behaviour—A discussion of opportunities for change. *Int. J. Consum. Stud.* **2007**, *31*, 499–508. [CrossRef]
3. Erskine, C.C.; Collins, L. Eco-labelling: Success or failure? *Environmentalist* **1997**, *17*, 125–133. [CrossRef]
4. Fairweather, J.R.; Maslin, C.; Simmons, D.G. Environmental values and response to ecolabels among international visitors to New Zealand. *J. Sustain. Tour.* **2005**, *13*, 82–98. [CrossRef]
5. Reiser, A.; Simmons, D.G. A quasi-experimental method for testing the effectiveness of ecolabel promotion. *J. Sustain. Tour.* **2005**, *13*, 590–616. [CrossRef]
6. Ding, P.; Pigram, J.J. Environmental audits: An emerging concept in sustainable tourism development. *J. Tour. Stud.* **1995**, *6*, 2–10.
7. Font, X.; Tribe, J. Promoting green tourism: The future of environmental awards. *Int. J. Tour. Res.* **2001**, *3*, 9–21. [CrossRef]
8. Thøgersen, J. Psychological determinants of paying attention to eco- labels in purchase decisions: Model development and multinational validation. *J. Consum. Policy* **2000**, *23*, 285–313. [CrossRef]
9. Bagozzi, R.P.; Dholakia, U. Goal setting and goal striving in consumer behavior. *J. Mark.* **1999**, *63*, 19–32. [CrossRef]
10. Gollwitzer, P.M. Planning and coordinating action. In *The Psychology of Action: Linking Cognition and Motivation to Behavior*; Gollwitzer, P.M., Bargh, J.A., Eds.; Guilford Press: New York, NY, USA, 1996; pp. 283–312.

11. Hoyer, W.D.; MacInnis, D.J.; Pieters, R. *Consumer Behavior*, 6th ed.; South-Western Cengage Learning: Mason, OH, USA, 2013; pp. XIX, 497, [442] S.

12. Minoli, D.M.; Goode, M.M.H.; Smith, M.T. Are eco labels profitably employed in sustainable tourism? A case study on Audubon certified golf resorts. *Tour. Manag. Perspect.* **2015**, *16*, 207–216. [CrossRef]

13. Buckley, R.C. Tourism ecolabels. *Ann. Tour. Res.* **2002**, *29*, 183–208. [CrossRef]

14. Tepelus, C.M. Aiming for sustainability in the tour operating business. *J. Clean. Prod.* **2005**, *13*, 99–107. [CrossRef]

15. McKercher, B.; Prideaux, B. Are tourism impacts low on personal environmental agendas? *J. Sustain. Tour.* **2011**, *19*, 325–345. [CrossRef]

16. Gutierrez, A.; Thornton, T. Can consumers understand sustainability through seafood eco-labels? A U.S. and UK case study. *Sustainability* **2014**, *6*, 8195–8217. [CrossRef]

17. Buffa, F. Young tourists and sustainability. Profiles, attitudes, and implications for destination strategies. *Sustainability* **2015**, *7*, 14042–14062. [CrossRef]

18. Kristensen, K.; Grunert, S.C. The green consumer: Some danish evidence. *Xingxiao Pinglun* **1994**, *8*, 138–145.

19. Kollmuss, A.; Agyeman, J. Mind the gap: Why do people act environmentally and what are the barriers to pro-environmental behavior? *Environ. Educ. Res.* **2002**, *8*, 239–260. [CrossRef]

20. Roy, D.; Verplanken, B.; Griffin, C. Making sense of sustainability: Exploring the subjective meaning of sustainable consumption. *Appl. Environ. Educ. Commun.* **2015**, *14*, 187–195. [CrossRef]

21. De Koning, J.I.J.C.; Ta, T.H.; Crul, M.R.M.; Wever, R.; Brezet, J.C. Getgreen Vietnam: Towards more sustainable behaviour among the urban middle class. *J. Clean. Prod.* **2016**, *134*, 178–190. [CrossRef]

22. Gössling, S.; Buckley, R. Carbon labels in tourism: Persuasive communication? *J. Clean. Prod.* **2016**, *111*, 358–369. [CrossRef]

23. Juvan, E.; Dolnicar, S. The attitude–behaviour gap in sustainable tourism. *Ann. Tour. Res.* **2014**, *48*, 76–95. [CrossRef]

24. Reje, A.; Dreger, E.; Vanyushyn, V.; Nylén, U. *Marketing Sustainability in Charter Tourism: The Influence of Brands, Eco-Labels and Their Combination on the Swedish Charter Tourist's Decision Making*; Umeå University: Umeå, Sweden, 2014.

25. Russillo, A.; Honey, M.; Rome, A.; Bien, A. Practical Steps for Marketing Tourism Certification. Available online: http://www.ecotourism.org/sites/ecotourism.org/files/document/Certification/Ecotourism%20Handbook%20III%20-%20Practical%20steps%20for%20Marketing%20Tourism%20Certification.pdf (accessed on 23 October 2016).

26. Anderson, L.; Mastrangelo, C.; Chase, L.; Kestenbaum, D.; Kolodinsky, J. Eco-labeling motorcoach operators in the North American travel tour industry: Analyzing the role of tour operators. *J. Sustain. Tour.* **2013**, *21*, 750–764. [CrossRef]

27. Björk, P. Applying Swedish eco-labelling to finnish tourism operation: Which associations does it elicit amongst customers. *Scand. J. Hosp. Tour.* **2004**, *4*, 25–41. [CrossRef]

28. Tepelus, C.M.; Córdoba, R.C. Recognition schemes in tourism—From 'eco' to sustainability'? *J. Clean. Prod.* **2005**, *13*, 135–140. [CrossRef]

29. Font, X. Regulating the green message: The players in ecolabelling. In *Tourism ecolabelling. Certification and promotion of sustainable management*; Front, X., Buckley, R.C., Eds.; CABI Publishing: Oxfordshire, UK, 2001.

30. Dov, T. Review: A cognitive-affective model of organizational communication for designing it. *MIS Q.* **2001**, *25*, 251–312.

31. Flavián, C.; Guinalíu, M.; Gurrea, R. The role played by perceived usability, satisfaction and consumer trust on website loyalty. *Inform. Manag.* **2006**, *43*, 1–14. [CrossRef]

32. Penz, E.; Kirchler, E. Affective states, purchase intention and perceived risk in online shopping. In *Impact of E-Commerce on Consumers and Small Firms*; Zappalà, S., Gray, C., Eds.; Ashgate: Aldershot, UK, 2006; pp. 191–205.

33. Sinkovics, R.R.; Penz, E. Empowerment of sme websites—Development of a web-empowerment scale and preliminary evidence. *J. Int. Entrep.* **2006**, *3*, 303–315. [CrossRef]

34. Barr, S.; Shaw, G.; Coles, T.; Prillwitz, J. 'A holiday is a holiday': Practicing sustainability, home and away. *J. Transp. Geogr.* **2010**, *18*, 474–481. [CrossRef]

35. Bremner, C. *Travel 2016 Key Insights*; Passport Euromonitor: London, UK, September 2016.

36. Goodwin, H.; Francis, J. Ethical and responsible tourism: Consumer trends in the UK. *J. Vacat. Mark.* **2003**, *9*, 271–284. [CrossRef]

37. Miller, G. Corporate responsibility in the UK tourism industry. *Tour. Manag.* **2001**, *22*, 589–598. [CrossRef]

38. Budeanu, A. Impacts and responsibilities for sustainable tourism: A tour operator's perspective. *J. Clean. Prod.* **2005**, *13*, 89–97. [CrossRef]

39. Schwartz, K.; Tapper, R.; Font, X. A sustainable supply chain management framework for tour operators. *J. Sustain. Tour.* **2008**, *16*, 298–314. [CrossRef]

40. Carey, S.; Gountas, Y.; Gilbert, D. Tour operators and destination sustainability. *Tour. Manag.* **1997**, *18*, 425–431. [CrossRef]

41. Bieger, T.; Laesser, C. Information sources for travel decisions: Toward a source process model. *J. Travel Res.* **2004**, *42*, 357–371. [CrossRef]

42. UNEP. Tourism. Investing in Energy and Resource Efficiency. Available online: http://www.unep. org/resourceefficiency/Portals/24147/scp/business/tourism/greeneconomy_tourism.pdf (accessed on 28 October 2016).

43. Thøgersen, J.; Noblet, C. Does green consumerism increase the acceptance of wind power? *Energy Policy* **2012**, *51*, 854–862. [CrossRef]

44. Bartels, J.; Hoogendam, K. The role of social identity and attitudes toward sustainability brands in buying behaviors for organic products. *J. Brand Manag.* **2011**, *18*, 697–708. [CrossRef]

45. Thomas, C.; Sharp, V. Understanding the normalisation of recycling behaviour and its implications for other pro-environmental behaviours: A review of social norms and recycling. *Resour. Conserv. Recycl.* **2013**, *79*, 11–20. [CrossRef]

46. Manaktola, K.; Jauhari, V. Exploring consumer attitude and behaviour towards green practices in the lodging industry in India. *Int. J. Contemp. Hosp. Manag.* **2007**, *19*, 364–377. [CrossRef]

47. Pulido-Fernández, J.; López-Sánchez, Y. Are tourists really willing to pay more for sustainable destinations? *Sustainability* **2016**, *8*, 1240. [CrossRef]

48. Aertsens, J.; Verbeke, W.; Mondelaers, K.; Van Huylenbroeck, G. Personal determinants of organic food consumption. *Rev. Br. Food J.* **2009**, *111*, 1140–1167. [CrossRef]

49. Tarkiainen, A.; Sundqvist, S. Product involvement in organic food consumption: Does ideology meet practice? *Psychol. Mark.* **2009**, *26*, 844–863. [CrossRef]

50. Vermeir, I.; Verbeke, W. Sustainable food consumption: Exploring the consumer "attitude–behavioral intention" gap. *J. Agric. Environ. Ethics* **2006**, *19*, 169–194. [CrossRef]

51. Biel, A.; Thøgersen, J. Activation of social norms in social dilemmas: A review of the evidence and reflections on the implications for environmental behaviour. *J. Econ. Psychol.* **2007**, *28*, 93–112. [CrossRef]

52. Doran, R.; Hanss, D.; Øgaard, T. Can social comparison feedback affect indicators of eco-friendly travel choices? Insights from two online experiments. *Sustainability* **2017**, *9*, 196. [CrossRef]

53. Shepherd, D.A.; Kuskova, V.; Patzelt, H. Measuring the values that underlie sustainable development: The development of a valid scale. *J. Econ. Psychol.* **2009**, *30*, 246–256. [CrossRef]

54. Spash, C.L. The brave new world of carbon trading. *New Political Econ.* **2010**, *15*, 169–195. [CrossRef]

55. Thøgersen, J.; Ölander, F. Spillover of environment-friendly consumer behaviour. *J. Environ. Psychol.* **2003**, *23*, 225–236. [CrossRef]

56. Thøgersen, J. Spillover processes in the development of a sustainable consumption pattern. *J. Econ. Psychol.* **1999**, *20*, 53–81. [CrossRef]

57. Sheehan, K.B. The many shades of greenwashing. In *Communicating Sustainability for the Green Economy*; Kahle, L.R., Gurel-Atay, E., Eds.; Society for Consumer Psychology: New York, NY, USA, 2014; pp. 43–55.

58. Lebe, S.S.; Vrečko, I. Eco-labels and schemes: A requisitely holistic proof of tourism's social responsibility? *Syst. Res. Behav. Sci.* **2015**, *32*, 247–255. [CrossRef]

59. Taufique, K.; Siwar, C.; Talib, B.; Sarah, F.; Chamhuri, N. Synthesis of constructs for modeling consumers' understanding and perception of eco-labels. *Sustainability* **2014**, *6*, 2176–2200. [CrossRef]

60. Jonell, M.; Crona, B.; Brown, K.; Rönnbäck, P.; Troell, M. Eco-labeled seafood: Determinants for (blue) green consumption. *Sustainability* **2016**, *8*, 884. [CrossRef]

61. Wehrli, R.; Egli, H.; Lutzenberger, M.; Pfister, D.; Schwarz, J.; Stettler, J. *Is There Demand for Sustainable Tourism?—Study for the World Tourism Forum Lucerne 2011*; Citeseer: Lucerne, Switzerland, 2011.

62. Arbeitskreis Tourismus & Entwicklung (akte). Orientierungshilfe im Touristischen Labeldschungel. Available online: http://www.fairunterwegs.org/vor-der-reise/labelfuehrer/ (accessed on 15 January 2017).

63. ECOTRANS. Destinet Services: Sustainable Tourism Certification Worldwide. Available online: http://destinet.eu/who-who/market-solutions/certificates/fol442810 (accessed on 15 January 2017).

64. Duchowski, A.T. *Eye Tracking Methodology: Theory and Practice*, 2nd ed.; Springer: London, UK, 2007.

65. Ehmke, C.; Wilson, S. Identifying Web Usability Problems from Eye-Tracking Data. In *Proceedings of the 21st British HCI Group Annual Conference on People and Computers: HCI... but not as we know it, Lancaster, UK, 3–7 September 2007*; British Computer Society: Lancaster, UK, 2007; Volume 1, pp. 119–128.

66. Sirakaya-Turk, E.; Baloglu, S.; Mercado, H.U. The efficacy of sustainability values in predicting travelers' choices for sustainable hospitality businesses. *Cornell Hosp. Q.* **2014**, *55*, 115–126. [CrossRef]

67. Thøgersen, J.; Haugaard, P.; Olesen, A. Consumer responses to ecolabels. *Eur. J. Mark.* **2010**, *44*, 1787–1810. [CrossRef]

68. Hudson, S.; Ritchie, B. Understanding the domestic market using cluster analysis: A case study of the marketing efforts of travel Alberta. *J. Vacat. Mark.* **2002**, *8*, 263–276. [CrossRef]

69. Greenacre, M. *Correspondence Analysis in Practice*; Chapman & Hall/CRC: London, UK, 2007.

70. Matiaske, W.; Dobrov, I.; Bronner, R. Anwendung der Korrespondenzanalyse in der Imageforschung. *Mark. ZFP* **1994**, *1*, 42–54.

71. Font, X. Environmental certification in tourism and hospitality: Progress, process and prospects. *Tour. Manag.* **2002**, *23*, 197–205. [CrossRef]

72. Hares, A.; Dickinson, J.; Wilkes, K. Climate change and the air travel decisions of UK tourists. *J. Transp. Geogr.* **2010**, *18*, 466–473. [CrossRef]

73. Banerjee, A.; Solomon, B.D. Eco-labeling for energy efficiency and sustainability: A meta-evaluation of US programs. *Energy Policy* **2003**, *31*, 109–123. [CrossRef]

74. Mosteller, J. The influence of visual information on environmentally significant behavior. In *Communicating Sustainability for the Green Economy*; Kahle, L.R., Gurel-Atay, E., Eds.; M.E. Sharpe: New York, NY, USA, 2014.

75. Wu, S.-I.; Wei, P.-L.; Chen, J.-H. Influential factors and relational structure of internet banner advertising in the tourism industry. *Tour. Manag.* **2008**, *29*, 221–236. [CrossRef]

76. Gegenfurtner, A.; Lehtinen, E.; Säljö, R. Expertise differences in the comprehension of visualizations: A meta-analysis of eye-tracking research in professional domains. *Educ. Psychol. Rev.* **2011**, *23*, 523–552. [CrossRef]

77. Bialkova, S.; van Trijp, H. What determines consumer attention to nutrition labels? *Food Qual. Preference* **2010**, *21*, 1042–1051. [CrossRef]

78. Wedel, M.; Pieters, R. A review of eye-tracking research in marketing. In *Review of Marketing Research*; Emerald Group Publishing Limited: Bingley, UK, 2008; pp. 123–147.

79. Graham, D.J.; Orquin, J.L.; Visschers, V.H.M. Eye tracking and nutrition label use: A review of the literature and recommendations for label enhancement. *Food Policy* **2012**, *37*, 378–382. [CrossRef]

80. Dolnicar, S.; Cvelbar, L.K.; Grün, B. Do pro-environmental appeals trigger pro-environmental behavior in hotel guests? *J. Travel Res.* **2016**, 1–10. [CrossRef]

81. Miao, L.; Wei, W. Consumers' pro-environmental behavior and the underlying motivations: A comparison between household and hotel settings. *Int. J. Hosp. Manag.* **2013**, *32*, 102–112. [CrossRef]

![sustainability logo] *sustainability*

MDPI

Article

Can Social Comparison Feedback Affect Indicators of Eco-Friendly Travel Choices? Insights from Two Online Experiments

Rouven Doran [1,*], Daniel Hanss [2] and Torvald Øgaard [3]

1   Department of Psychosocial Science, University of Bergen, 5015 Bergen, Norway
2   Department of Social and Cultural Sciences and Social Work,
    Hochschule Darmstadt—University of Applied Sciences, 64295 Darmstadt, Germany;
    daniel.hanss@h-da.de
3   Norwegian School of Hotel Management, University of Stavanger, 4036 Stavanger, Norway;
    torvald.ogaard@uis.no
*   Correspondence: rouven.doran@uib.no; Tel.: +47-55-582-336

Academic Editor: Gerrit Antonides
Received: 10 November 2016; Accepted: 19 January 2017; Published: 29 January 2017

Abstract: Two online experiments explored the effects of social comparison feedback on indicators of eco-friendly travel choices. It was tested whether the chosen indicators are sensitive to the information conveyed, and if this varies as a function of in-group identification. Study 1 (N = 134) focused on unfavourable feedback (i.e., being told that one has a larger ecological footprint than the average member of a reference group). People who received unfavourable feedback reported stronger intentions to choose eco-friendly travel options than those who received nondiscrepant feedback, when in-group identification was high (not moderate or low). Perceived self- and collective efficacy were not associated with the feedback. Study 2 (N = 323) extended the focus on favourable feedback (i.e., being told that one has a smaller ecological footprint than the average member of a reference group). Neither unfavourable nor favourable feedback was associated with behavioural intentions, self- or collective efficacy. This means that Study 2 failed to replicate the finding of Study 1 that behavioural intentions were associated with unfavourable feedback, given that in-group identification is high. The findings are discussed in light of the existing literature. Suggestions are made for future studies investigating social comparison feedback as a means to motivate people to make eco-friendly travel choices.

Keywords: sustainable tourism; travel choices; ecological footprint; feedback strategies; social comparison

1. Introduction

The choices which people make, both before and during their vacation, can play an important part in creating a more sustainable tourism sector [1,2]. For example, choosing accommodation and transportation with low carbon dioxide (CO_2) emissions, can place pressure on the tourism industry to supply products and services that help to satisfy these demands [1]. This calls for research on what motivates people to consider environmental issues when they choose between different vacation options.

There has been some discussion on whether online calculators, designed to give feedback on the environmental impact of certain lifestyles, can assist people in choosing vacation options considered to reduce negative impacts in this regard [3,4]. Feedback can instigate behavioural change because recipients are made aware of the consequences (positive or negative) associated with the targeted behaviour [5]. Whilst many studies attest to the effectiveness of feedback in promoting conservation behaviour, there is also evidence that effects vary as a function of how and to whom feedback is presented [6].

This paper focuses on social comparison feedback, which is when people receive feedback about their own ecological footprint relative to the ecological footprint of the average member of a reference group (cf. [7]). The aims were to investigate (i) whether the information conveyed through such feedback affects indicators of eco-friendly travel choices, along with (ii) whether these effects vary as a function of in-group identification.

1.1. Social Comparison Feedback and Pro-Environmental Behaviour

Social comparison feedback has been proven effective for instigating behavioural change with environmental significance, most notably that associated with energy saving (e.g., [8,9]; for contrasting evidence, see e.g., [10]). For example, Brook [11] found that informing people that they have a larger than average ecological footprint can affect subsequent behaviour. Whilst people who based their self-esteem on environmentalism showed increases in pro-environmental behaviour, decreases were observed among those who did not base their self-esteem on environmentalism. Another study that used the ecological footprint for investigating responses to social comparison feedback comes from Toner et al. [12]. They measured the strongest pro-environmental intentions in response to individual feedback that was worse than that of the average member of an important peer group. People who received this information (presented as results from a bogus carbon footprint calculator) expressed stronger intentions than those who were informed that they were doing either similar to, or better than, their peers.

Aitken et al. [13] tested whether comparative feedback (own household vs. average household) can stimulate changes in residential water consumption. Those who learned that the average household was using less than them showed decreases in water usage after receiving such feedback, whereas households using far below-average responded with increases in water usage if no additional information was provided. Schultz et al. [14] made similar observations when they provided residents with feedback about the average energy consumption in the neighbourhood. This led to decreases in energy usage for above-average consumption households, and, unless accompanied by information indicating social approval of energy saving, increases in energy usage for below-average consumption households. This finding implies that feedback indicating below-average consumption may not only be ineffective in promoting desired behavioural change, but in fact, may sometimes result in "unintended and undesirable boomerang effects" [14] (p. 430). Henceforth, the term unfavourable indicates feedback that one's own footprint is larger, and the term favourable describes feedback that one's own footprint is smaller, when compared to the ecological footprint of an average reference group member. Based on the above studies, the following hypotheses (H1a and H1b) were formulated:

H1a. *Unfavourable (vs. nondiscrepant) social comparison feedback strengthens intentions to choose eco-friendly travel options.*

H1b. *Favourable (vs. nondiscrepant) social comparison feedback weakens intentions to choose eco-friendly travel options.*

1.2. Social Comparison Feedback and Perceived Efficacy

People's beliefs that they can affect desired changes through their own actions play a pivotal role in human functioning [15]. Research shows that these beliefs are also important for explaining variability in consumption motivated by sustainability concerns. For instance, consumers who believe that they can personally promote sustainability goals through their purchases also seem more likely to buy sustainable instead of conventional product alternatives, than consumers who question their abilities in this regard (e.g., [16–18]).

Different lines of research have used different terms to refer to these types of personal beliefs [17]. The present paper builds on the literature that construes issues of environmental sustainability as social dilemmas (e.g., [19]), and uses the term self-efficacy to refer to an individual's perceived ability to personally contribute to collectively-beneficial outcomes (here: improvements in sustainable development; see also [20]). Specifically, this paper focuses on whether a person feels confident that his/her choices as a tourist provide a significant contribution to protecting the environment (cf. [16]).

If a desired outcome can only be accomplished by collective efforts, perceptions of efficacy are derived from one's own as well as others' performances [15,21]. This makes collective efficacy an important determinant for individual responses to large-scale societal challenges, such as climate change [22]. Collective efficacy is less about whether each individual action provides a significant additive for the pursuit of a set goal. Instead, it captures beliefs about the group's joint ability for achieving a desired outcome [23]. Previous research has demonstrated that perceptions about the effectiveness of collective action are indeed characteristic of those willing to make personal efforts to tackle environmental problems [22,24], with some studies suggesting that collective efficacy could be more important than self-efficacy in this context [16,25].

Bandura [23] noted that comparing one's own performances with those of others (as a form of vicarious experience) constitutes an important source for perceptions of efficacy, especially when perceived similarity with the referent is high. Research indeed suggests that exposure to social comparison information can alter perceived self-efficacy and individual performances [26,27]. Information of this kind has been further identified as a contributing factor to group performances via its association with perceived collective efficacy [28].

Pro-environmental behaviour often requires individuals to set personal interests aside, knowing that this behaviour only matters when echoed by a sufficient number of others (cf. [29]). We suggest that people may rely on social comparison information as a source for estimating perceived efficacy, particularly when individual and group feedback are combined (see above). Unfavourable feedback is expected to have strengthening effects as other people may appear extra willing to make an effort to protect the environment, and favourable feedback is expected to have weakening effects as other people are seemingly less engaged than oneself. The underlying assumption is that the former decreases, while the latter increases, the perceived likelihood that personal efforts (e.g., choosing eco-friendly travel options in spite of being costlier) are rendered insignificant considering the behaviour shown by others. Hence, the following hypotheses (H2a and H2b) are presented:

H2a: *Unfavourable (vs. nondiscrepant) social comparison feedback strengthens perceived self- and collective efficacy.*

H2b: *Favourable (vs. nondiscrepant) social comparison feedback weakens perceived self- and collective efficacy.*

1.3. Social Comparison Feedback and In-Group Identification

The degree to which a person defines or views himself/herself as being a member of a given group has been described as in-group identification [30,31]. Research in this domain shows that people tend to ascribe similar characteristics to themselves as to their fellow group members (e.g., [32]) and evaluate in-group membership more positively than out-group membership (e.g., [33]). Moreover, making group membership salient promotes behaviours that focus on collective rather than personal welfare [34]. It has been further demonstrated that strong in-group identification increases the likelihood of behavioural adherence to norms that are dominant within that group, including those concerned with environmental issues (e.g., [35–37]).

Rabinovich and Morton [38] informed participants about their own carbon footprint (i.e., individual feedback) relative to that of an average citizen of the same nation (i.e., group feedback). They found that individual responses to discrepant feedback varied at different levels of identification with the reference group. For instance, negative group feedback combined with positive individual feedback only strengthened perceptions about the need for societal change when group identification was strong. Graffeo et al. [39] tested whether comparative feedback can motivate energy conservation among students residing on campus. In addition, the reference frame in which the feedback was provided was varied systematically (in-group vs. out-group, identified vs. unidentified). Feedback led to an increase in the intention to save energy compared to a non-feedback condition. Most effective in this regard was feedback involving a comparison with others from the same neighborhood without providing further details (i.e., in-group and unidentified). It was more effective than any other feedback, including the comparison with a statistically average household. Therefore, the following hypothesis (H3) is presented:

H3: *Effects of social comparison feedback vary as a function of in-group identification.*

2. Study 1

A 1 (individual feedback: highly negative) × 2 (group feedback: highly negative vs. moderately negative) between-subjects design was employed. The aim was to study the effect of unfavourable social comparison feedback; information indicating that one's own ecological footprint is larger than that of an average reference group member.

2.1. Materials and Methods

2.1.1. Participants

The participants (M_{age} = 21.84, SD_{age} = 3.49, 17–40 years, one person provided no age) were 134 students (91 female) from the same university who took part in return for a shopping voucher worth 100 NOK. Recruitment was conducted during lectures as well as through advertising the study on campus. Participants were told that the aim was to better understand how people in Norway think and feel about environmental issues, such as their personal ecological footprint. It can be assumed that they were naïve about the actual purpose of the study. Those consenting to participate signed up with an e-mail address on a recruiting webpage or on a paper-and-pencil sheet.

2.1.2. Procedures

Participants received a standardized invitation e-mail that included a personalized link directing them to a webpage (one reminder). The webpage (page 1) included a brief description about the study's aims (e.g., to understand public opinions of environmental issues), practical issues (e.g., duration, possibility to quit at any time), and contact information. After providing information about their gender, age, and identification with other students at their university (page 2), participants were informed (page 3) that they would be presented with a list of different types of behaviour that can directly or indirectly impact the environment, that a calculator would estimate their personal ecological footprint based on their answers, and that they would get information about the ecological footprint of an average student at their university. These instructions concluded with a formal description of what the term ecological footprint stands for, as defined by the World Wide Fund for Nature [40].

Participants were told to choose the answer that best described their lifestyle (page 4). Questions about the respective behaviours were clustered under the following categories: food products (4 items: e.g., How often do you eat meat?), consumption (2 items: e.g., How often do you buy new clothes, shoes, and/or sport goods), energy and recycling (5 items: e.g., How much of the paper you use do you recycle?), as well as mobility and transportation (5 items: e.g., How often do you cycle or walk from one place to another (more than 2km distance)?). The covered behaviours were similar to those typically included in online footprint calculators (for an example, see [41]). After pressing a button labelled calculate, a dynamic graphic appeared, counting down from 15 s in order to simulate the calculation process (page 5). This was followed by the provision of bogus feedback, in which a participant's own ecological footprint was compared to that of an average student at their university (page 6).

Feedback information stated how many earths would be needed if everybody were to maintain a lifestyle similar to the one of the participant (i.e., individual feedback), and how many earths would be needed if everybody were to maintain a lifestyle similar to that of an average student at their university (i.e., group feedback). This information was also illustrated graphically (cf. [12]). Participants were randomly allocated nondiscrepant/highly negative (coded = 0) or discrepant/unfavourable (coded = 1) feedback: $t(131)_{age} = -0.96$, $p = 0.340$; $\chi^2(1)_{gender} < 0.01$, $p = 0.958$; $t(132)_{identification} = 0.40$, $p = 0.968$. A detailed description of these conditions can be found in Table 1 and Appendix A. Similar to Toner et al. [12], we chose moderately negative rather than neutral feedback as a reference point for a relatively low environmental impact. This has been recommended as people are likely to think that their current behaviours have some sort of negative impact on the environment [11,12].

Table 1. Summary for the different feedback conditions.

The following pages (page 7–9) included items for measuring the dependent variables and for running the manipulation checks. All participants were debriefed (page 10), before being provided with information about how to receive a shopping voucher as compensation (page 11).

Study	Feedback Description	Individual Feedback	Group Feedback
Study 1			
Condition 1	nondiscrepant/high. negative	high. negative	high. negative
Condition 2	discrepant/unfavourable	high. negative	mod. negative
Study 2			
Condition 1	nondiscrepant/high. negative	high. negative	high. negative
Condition 2	discrepant/unfavourable	high. negative	mod. negative
Condition 3	discrepant/favourable	mod. negative	high. negative
Condition 4	nondiscrepant/mod. negative	mod. negative	mod. negative

Note: mod. negative = moderately negative; high. negative = highly negative.

2.1.3. Measures

In-group identification was assessed with the Inclusion of Ingroup in the Self measure from Tropp and Wright [32]. This single-item measure asks people to choose among seven pairs of circles (one reflects the self and one reflects the in-group) with varying degrees of overlap. Participants in this particular study were asked to think about students at their university as a group, and then to indicate the degree to which they identified with members of that group. Responses were coded from 1 (no overlap) to 7 (high degree of overlap), with higher numbers indicating higher levels of in-group identification (cf. [32]).

Participants received information that suggested a link between tourism and the environment. Specifically, it was stated that contemporary tourism activities are a significant factor considering negative impacts on the environment, mentioning the contribution to global climate change via CO_2 emissions as an example (see [2]). Participants were then asked to indicate the likelihood that they would perform a set of behaviours when it comes to their next travel (1 = Very unlikely, 10 = Very likely). It was explicitly stated that these were possible measures to reduce negative environmental impacts stemming from tourism activities. Each behaviour has been identified in the literature as an area for implementing behavioural change to reduce CO_2 emissions from tourism [1]. Higher scores on the respective items indicated stronger behavioural intentions (6 items, $\alpha = 0.88$).

Perceived efficacy was operationalized similar to past studies on consumption preferences at home (e.g., [17]) and in tourism (e.g., [16]). Items asked participants to indicate their level of agreement with statements about the effectiveness of their own (i.e., self-efficacy; 3 items, $\alpha = 0.87$) and tourists' (i.e., collective efficacy; 3 items, $\alpha = 0.93$) actions (1 = Strongly agree, 10 = Strongly disagree). Responses were recoded so that higher scores indicated stronger perceived efficacy. Means and standard deviations are reported in Table 2. For a complete list of items, see Appendix B.

Two items asked participants to indicate, considering the feedback that they had just received, how many earths would be needed to sustain a lifestyle like their own, or to sustain the lifestyle of an average student at their university (nine answer options ranging from 1–2 ... , 9–10). Responses to each item were coded from 1 (1–2 earths) to 9 (9–10 earths). Another item asked participants to judge whether the information presented to them, concerning individual and group feedback, was trustworthy (1 = Very untrustworthy, 10 = Very trustworthy).

Table 2. Means and standard deviations for the moderator and the dependent variables.

Study	Condition 1		Condition 2		Condition 3		Condition 4	
	n	*M (SD)*	*n*	*M (SD)*	*n*	*M (SD)*	*n*	*M (SD)*
Study 1								
In-group identification	69	3.58 (1.56)	65	3.57 (1.45)				
Behavioural intentions	68	3.91 (1.72)	62	4.54 (2.18)				
Self-efficacy	67	6.85 (2.25)	59	7.20 (2.17)				
Collective efficacy	67	7.37 (2.45)	59	7.24 (2.35)				
	n	*M (SD)*	*n*	*M (SD)*	*n*	*M (SD)*	*n*	*M (SD)*
Study 2								
In-group identification	76	4.01 (1.52)	82	3.94 (1.53)	87	4.33 (1.53)	78	4.12 (1.50)
Behavioural intentions	73	4.57 (2.03)	77	4.89 (2.12)	84	4.12 (2.07)	75	4.33 (1.96)
Self-efficacy	72	6.99 (2.05)	76	6.76 (2.18)	83	6.49 (2.23)	75	6.41 (2.21)
Collective efficacy	72	7.74 (1.75)	76	7.22 (2.22)	83	7.41 (2.43)	75	7.32 (2.14)

Note: Condition 1 = highly negative individual feedback and highly negative group feedback; Condition 2 = highly negative individual feedback and moderately negative group feedback; Condition 3 = moderately negative individual feedback and highly negative group feedback; Condition 4 = moderately negative individual feedback and moderately negative group feedback.

2.1.4. Statistics

Cronbach's alpha was calculated to explore the internal consistency of the item measures (see above). Independent *t*-tests explored perceptions regarding the information conveyed in the different feedback conditions. Descriptive statistics were inspected to explore whether the information was perceived as trustworthy. This was completed in IBM SPSS Statistics (v.23). Hypotheses were tested in a model of simple moderation (Model 1; [42]) with feedback condition as a categorical independent variable, and in-group identification as a continuous moderator variable. Significant interactions were explored by simple slope analyses of low ($M - 1\ SD$), moderate (M), and high ($M + 1\ SD$) values for the moderator variable [43]. There were some participants with missing values for the dependent variables; these cases were removed from the analyses: $n = 4$ for behavioural intentions; $n = 8$ for self-efficacy; $n = 8$ for collective efficacy. These analyses were computed using v.2.15 of the PROCESS macro for SPSS [42].

2.2. Results

2.2.1. Manipulation Checks

For perceptions about individual feedback, there was no significant difference between participants in the nondiscrepant/highly negative or discrepant/unfavourable condition, $t(69.89) = 1.15$, $p = 0.254$. For perceptions about group feedback, participants who received nondiscrepant/highly negative feedback reported significantly higher ratings than those who received discrepant/unfavourable feedback, $t(116.99) = 15.00$, $p < 0.001$. Trustworthiness ratings were close to the midpoint of the scale in both conditions: nondiscrepant/highly negative feedback, $M = 6.54$, $SD = 2.24$; discrepant/unfavourable feedback, $M = 5.22$, $SD = 2.32$. In sum, participants recalled the presented information and trustworthiness ratings were acceptable.

Table 3. Linear model of predictors of the dependent variables in Study 1 and Study 2.

Study	Behavioural Intentions			Self−Efficacy			Collective Efficacy		
	B	SE B	t	B	SE B	t	B	SE B	t
Study 1									
Constant	4.22 [3.88, 4.56]	0.17	24.65 ***	7.01 [6.61, 7.41]	0.20	34.71 ***	7.31 [6.88, 7.74]	0.22	33.42 ***
In−group identification (II)	0.04 [−0.21, 0.28]	0.12	0.30	<0.01 [−0.26, 0.26]	0.13	0.01	0.12 [−0.14, 0.38]	0.13	0.89
Condition 1 vs. Condition 2 (C1 vs. C2)	0.64 [−0.05, 1.32]	0.35	1.84	0.36 [−0.44, 1.16]	0.40	0.89	−0.13 [−1.00, 0.74]	0.44	−0.30
C1 vs. C2 × II	0.64 [0.14, 1.13]	0.25	2.52 *	<0.01 [−0.53, 0.53]	0.27	<0.01	−0.09 [−0.62, 0.43]	0.26	−0.35
	$R^2 = 0.08$			$R^2 = 0.01$			$R^2 = 0.01$		
	$F(3, 126) = 2.79 *$			$F(3, 122) = 0.26$			$F(3, 122) = 0.41$		
	B	SE B	t	B	SE B	t	B	SE B	t
Study 2									
Constant	4.57 [4.10, 5.05]	0.24	19.05 ***	6.99 [6.51, 7.48]	0.25	28.40 ***	7.74 [7.33, 8.15]	0.21	36.89 ***
In−group identification (II)	0.13 [−0.25, 0.51]	0.19	0.68	0.04 [−0.30, 0.38]	0.17	0.22	−0.06 [−0.33, 0.22]	0.14	−0.41
Condition 1 vs. Condition 2 (C1 vs. C2)	0.33 [−0.34, 1.01]	0.34	0.98	−0.22 [−0.91, 0.47]	0.35	−0.62	−0.52 [−1.18, 0.14]	0.33	−1.56
Condition 1 vs. Condition 3 (C1 vs. C3)	−0.47 [−1.12, 0.19]	0.33	−1.41	−0.53 [−1.21, 0.16]	0.35	−1.51	−0.34 [−1.01, 0.32]	0.34	−1.01
Condition 1 vs. Condition 4 (C1 vs. C4)	−0.25 [−0.90, 0.40]	0.33	−0.75	−0.57 [−1.27, 0.13]	0.36	−1.59	−0.43 [−1.07, 0.22]	0.33	−1.31
C1 vs. C2 × II	0.03 [−0.49, 0.54]	0.26	0.10	0.08 [−0.38, 0.55]	0.24	0.36	0.03 [−0.40, 0.45]	0.22	0.12
C1 vs. C3 × II	−0.07 [−0.53, 0.40]	0.24	−0.29	0.08 [−0.38, 0.53]	0.23	0.33	0.11 [−0.33, 0.55]	0.22	0.49
C1 vs. C4 × II	−0.21 [−0.65, 0.24]	0.23	−0.92	0.09 [−0.36, 0.54]	0.23	0.38	<0.01 [−0.44, 0.45]	0.23	0.01
	$R^2 = 0.03$			$R^2 = 0.02$			$R^2 = 0.01$		
	$F(7, 301) = 1.26$			$F(7, 298) = 0.79$			$F(7, 298) = 0.47$		

Note: Condition 1 = highly negative individual feedback and highly negative group feedback; Condition 2 = highly negative individual feedback and moderately negative group feedback; Condition 3 = moderately negative individual feedback and highly negative group feedback; Condition 4 = moderately negative individual feedback and moderately negative group feedback. Shown are unstandardized coefficients and 95% confidence intervals based on mean−centred products and heteroscedasticity−consistent SEs (cf. [44]). For behavioural intentions in Study 1: $R^2_{change} = 0.06$, $F(1, 126) = 6.37$, $p = 0.013$. *** $p < 0.001$. * $p < 0.05$.

2.2.2. Dependent Variables

Table 3 shows that feedback condition and in-group identification were not significantly associated with intentions to choose eco-friendly travel options. However, the interaction term of the two variables was significant. Simple slope analyses revealed that participants who received discrepant/unfavourable feedback reported stronger behavioural intentions than those who received nondiscrepant/highly negative feedback when in-group identification was high, $B = 1.57$, 95% CI (0.44, 2.71), $t = 2.74$, $p = 0.007$, but not when it was moderate, $B = 0.64$, 95% CI (-0.05, 1.32), $t = 1.84$, $p = 0.069$, or low, $B = -0.30$, 95% CI (-1.15, 0.56), $t = -0.69$, $p = 0.491$.

Feedback condition and in-group identification showed no significant association with self-efficacy; neither was there a significant interaction. Results for collective efficacy were similar. There was no significant association with feedback condition or in-group identification, and no significant interaction. A detailed report of these results can be found in Table 3.

2.3. Discussion

Previous research suggests that individual responses to social comparison feedback can vary in relation to the degree to which recipients identify with the reference group (see e.g., [38]). Indeed, feedback indicating that one is doing worse than an average reference group member was effective in bringing about stronger behavioural intentions when it was met with high in-group identification, but not when it was met with moderate or low in-group identification. These findings suggest that unfavourable social comparison feedback can strengthen intentions to choose eco-friendly travel options, but that this effect depends on the level of identification with the reference group.

Social comparison information has been identified as an antecedent for perceived efficacy at an individual and group level (see e.g., [27,28]). Yet, our hypothesis that unfavourable social comparison feedback would strengthen perceived self- and collective efficacy was not supported by the data. Furthermore, other than for behavioural intentions, similar patterns emerged for all participants irrespective of the degree to which they identified with the reference group.

3. Study 2

It remains unclear from the reported results how participants would respond to favourable social comparison feedback; information indicating that one's own ecological footprint is smaller than that of an average reference group member. A 2 (individual feedback: highly negative vs. moderately negative) × 2 (group feedback: highly negative vs. moderately negative) between-subjects design addressed this.

3.1. Materials and Methods

3.1.1. Participants

Recruitment was similar to Study 1. Participants were promised a shopping voucher (50 NOK) and a chance of winning an extra shopping voucher (500 NOK). This led to a sample of 323 students (224 female) from the same university ($M_{age} = 21.99$, $SD_{age} = 3.57$, 18–48 years, one person provided no age).

3.1.2. Procedures

Study invitations were sent out via e-mail (two reminders). Procedures were similar to Study 1, except for the use of additional questions as a base for calculating the ecological footprint. This was meant to increase the trustworthiness of the provided information as well as the salience of tourism as a contributor to environmental problems. Additional questions (5 items: e.g., How often do you choose to pay extra in order to compensate for carbon emissions generated from your air travel?) addressed domains considered important for lowering CO_2 emissions from tourism (see [1]).

Participants were randomly assigned nondiscrepant/highly negative (coded = 0), discrepant/ unfavourable (coded = 1), discrepant/favourable (coded = 2), or nondiscrepant/ moderately negative (coded = 3) feedback: $F(3, 318)_{age} = 1.26$, $p = 0.290$; $\chi^2(3)_{gender} = 0.68$, $p = 0.878$; $F(3, 319)_{identification} = 1.07$, $p = 0.361$. A description for each condition is provided in Appendix A.

3.1.3. Measures

In-group identification, dependent variables, and manipulation checks were similar to those of Study 1, with the exception of the use of different scale labels for items addressing self- and collective efficacy (1 = Strongly disagree, 10 = Strongly agree). Internal consistencies were $\alpha = 0.88$ (behavioural intentions), $\alpha = 0.83$ (self-efficacy), and $\alpha = 0.90$ (collective efficacy). For a summary of the means and standard deviations, see Table 2.

3.1.4. Statistics

Statistical analyses were similar to those in Study 1. Following recommendations in the literature (cf. [44]), feedback condition was dummy coded prior to the analysis with nondiscrepant/highly negative feedback as the reference category. Participants with missing values for the dependent variables were excluded from further analyses: $n = 14$ for behavioural intentions; $n = 17$ for self-efficacy; $n = 17$ for collective efficacy.

3.2. Results

3.2.1. Manipulation Checks

For perceptions of individual feedback, participants who received highly negative information about their own footprint reported significantly higher ratings than those who received moderately negative information, $t(304) = 27.92$, $p < 0.001$. For perceptions of group feedback, participants given highly negative information about the average footprint reported significantly higher ratings than those given moderately negative information, $t(304) = 19.17$, $p < 0.001$. Trustworthiness ratings across conditions were comparable to Study 1: nondiscrepant/highly negative, $M = 6.68$, $SD = 2.27$; discrepant/unfavourable, $M = 5.41$, $SD = 2.13$; discrepant/favourable, $M = 7.20$, $SD = 1.99$; nondiscrepant/moderately negative, $M = 6.76$, $SD = 2.06$. In sum, participants recalled the information communicated to them and levels of trustworthiness were acceptable.

3.2.2. Dependent Variables

Feedback condition and in-group identification did not show a significant association with intentions to choose eco-friendly travel options; neither were any of their interaction terms significant (see Table 3). Results for the other variables were similar as self- and collective efficacy were not significantly affected by the feedback condition (see Table 3). In each case, there was no significant association with in-group identification, and the analysis did not reveal significant interactions for the variables.

3.3. Discussion

A central aim of Study 2 was to replicate our prior finding on the effect of unfavourable social comparison feedback. In contrast to Study 1, however, intentions to choose eco-friendly travel options were not strengthened in response to unfavourable social comparison feedback, with similar effects at varying levels of in-group identification. The same was reported in connection with self- and collective efficacy.

Some research (e.g., [14]) shows that feedback on environmental performances can make one's own consumption level increase, in cases when it indicates that one is already better off than the group average. Our hypothesis that favourable social comparison feedback would weaken intentions to choose eco-friendly travel options was not supported by the data; neither were there any differences due to in-group identification. Similar results were reported with self- and collective efficacy as dependent variables.

4. General Discussion

The present paper started by examining the literature on feedback to accomplish behavioural change for environmental causes. This literature shows that there are situations in which the provision of feedback is an effective means to motivate conservation behaviour [5,7]. Study 1 suggested that unfavourable social comparison feedback can affect intentions to choose eco-friendly travel options under certain conditions, namely when in-group identification is high. In that case, self-reported behavioural intentions were highest when participants received information indicating that their own ecological footprint is larger than (vs. similar to) that of an average reference group member. It is consistent with studies where group norms promoted pro-environmental attitudes and behaviours when referencing in-group behaviour, but not when referencing out-group behaviour [36,37].

Study 2 failed to replicate the effect of unfavourable social comparison feedback on intentions to choose eco-friendly travel options. This finding adds to an existing body of research where feedback employing social comparison failed to promote conservation efforts (e.g., [10]; see also [6]). One reason for why norm-based interventions may be ineffective is a lack of credibility of the conveyed information [45]. Consequently, we checked whether the feedback information was judged equally trustworthy across the two studies in order to explore if this could have accounted for the null findings in Study 2. The fact that adding further items to the questionnaire led to a marginal increase in the trustworthiness rating, however, suggests that a lack of credibility alone does not offer a sufficient explanation for the different results.

Another plausible explanation concerns possible differences in sample characteristics. Norm-based interventions have greater potential for promoting behavioural change when there is attitudinal support for the targeted behaviour [45]. We cannot rule out that participants in Study 2 were less concerned about environmental issues than participants in Study 1, and that this may have affected their responses. This may also explain the null findings reported for the hypothesized effect of favourable social comparison feedback on intentions to choose eco-friendly travel options. Considering factors suspected to affect the receptiveness for normative messages, such as environmental attitudes, could allow an exploration into the importance of individual differences in this regard (for similar views, see [38,46]).

We gave an account of, and the reasons for, considering perceived efficacy in relation to social comparison feedback. It extends previous works suggesting that changes in perceived efficacy are a possible mechanism underlying feedback effects in the environmental domain [5,47]. We drew upon the more general notion that comparing one's own performance with that of others constitutes an important source for estimating these perceptions [23]. There was a match between the results from the two studies in that a participant's sense of self- and collective efficacy was not associated with the assigned feedback condition.

This is one of the first attempts to examine perceived efficacy in connection with feedback combining individual (e.g., ecological footprint of oneself) and group (e.g., ecological footprint of others) environmental performances. Yet, our results are compatible with another study that focused on group feedback as a strategy for encouraging energy conservation in organizational settings [47]. This study found group-level feedback to be effective in motivating conservation efforts among employees, despite there being no association between feedback exposure and the perception of whether changing group behaviour can increase energy savings. Without rejecting the idea that perceived efficacy may help to explain feedback effects in some contexts, there is room to consider alternative explanations. Other mechanisms that could account (at least partly) for the effects of norm-based interventions are that they induce negative emotions such as guilt or shame, particularly in public settings [45], or that they stimulate information-seeking behaviour [48].

5. Limitations

There are some limitations in the present investigation. First, participants were recruited from the local student population. This allowed us to rely on existing social structures for making social comparison more meaningful, as proposed by Kurz et al. [10]. It limits the generalizability of our findings as participants were not representative of the general public. Additional research with samples other than students is therefore recommended. Secondly, effects of social comparison feedback were tested on behavioural intentions and perceived efficacy; actual behaviour was not investigated. Including measures of actual behaviour would heighten the practical implications of research employing designs similar to the present investigation. This concurs with recent calls in the tourism literature for using objective instead of subjective behavioural measures, as these avoid problems such as social desirability bias [49]. Third, social comparison feedback may evoke stronger individual responses when the referents are identifiable rather than anonymous (see [10]; but see also [39]). The participant instructions explicitly stated that all information would be treated confidentially and would only be used for research purposes. This, in combination with the fact that participants allegedly received the feedback in private, could have affected their responses. Finally, a larger number of participants for each condition, and thus an increased statistical power, would have given extra credence to the findings.

6. Conclusions

This paper reported mixed results regarding the effects of social comparison feedback on indicators of eco-friendly travel choices. More research is needed to elucidate whether exposure to feedback involving social comparison information causally contributes to eco-friendly travel choices, and what factors may moderate this relationship. One promising avenue in this regard is to look at the characteristics of the reference group [7]. The two studies presented in this paper employed information about the ecological footprint of an average student at the same university, without providing any further indication of similarity with the recipient. Increasing perceived similarity, and probably the behavioural relevance of the feedback, might be accomplished by providing socio-demographics (like age or gender) that match the characteristics of the recipient. The underlying thinking is that social comparisons are more relevant for self-evaluative processes when perceived similarity with the referent is high [23,50]. If future studies do not demonstrate stronger effects on indicators of eco-friendly travel choices, and eventually actual behaviour, the provision of social comparison feedback may not be an efficient route to stimulate changes in the way in which people plan their vacation.

Acknowledgments: This research was part of the doctoral thesis of the first author. We express our gratitude to the Meltzer foundation who contributed to the funding of the studies, Matiss Macs for designing the webpages employed for the purpose of data collection, and Svein Larsen for discussing the findings. The research was registered at the Norwegian Social Science Data Services (NSD).

Author Contributions: Rouven Doran and Daniel Hanss designed the studies and collected the data; Rouven Doran analysed the data and wrote the first draft of the manuscript. Torvald Øgaard commented on the data analyses. All authors read and approved the final draft of the manuscript.

Conflicts of Interest: The authors declare no conflict of interest. The founding sponsors had no role in the design of the studies; in the collection, analyses, or interpretation of the data; in the writing of the manuscript, and in the decision to publish the results.

Appendix A.

Appendix A.1. Condition 1: Nondiscrepant/Highly Negative (Translated from Norwegian)

Based on your answers to the questionnaire, if everyone living on earth had lived like you do now, we would have needed 4.46 earths to sustain this lifestyle (see picture 1). This means that you use 4.46 times as many resources as the earth actually can endure per individual.

Based on answers in earlier investigations among [university name] students, if everyone living on earth had lived like an average [university name] student is doing now, we would have needed 4–5 earths to sustain this lifestyle (see picture 2). This means that an average student at [university name] uses about as much resources as you.

Appendix A.2. Condition 2: Discrepant/Unfavourable (Translated from Norwegian)

Based on your answers to the questionnaire, if everyone living on earth had lived like you do now, we would have needed 4.46 earths to sustain this lifestyle (see picture 1). This means that you use 4.46 times as many resources as the earth actually can endure per individual.

Based on answers in earlier investigations among [university name] students, if everyone living on earth had lived like an average [university name] student is doing now, we would have needed 2–3 earths to sustain this lifestyle (see picture 2). This means that an average student at [university name] uses fewer resources than you.

Appendix A.3. Condition 3: Discrepant/Favourable (Translated from Norwegian)

Based on your answers to the questionnaire, if everyone living on earth had lived like you do now, we would have needed 2.46 earths to sustain this lifestyle (see picture 1). This means that you use 2.46 times as many resources as the earth actually can endure per individual.

Based on answers in earlier investigations among [university name] students, if everyone living on earth had lived like an average [university name] student is doing now, we would have needed 4–5 earths to sustain this lifestyle (see picture 2). This means that an average student at [university name] uses more resources than you.

Appendix A.4. Condition 4: Nondiscrepant/Moderately Negative (Translated from Norwegian)

Based on your answers to the questionnaire, if everyone living on earth had lived like you do now, we would have needed 2.46 earths to sustain this lifestyle (see picture 1). This means that you use 2.46 times as many resources as the earth actually can endure per individual.

Based on answers in earlier investigations among [university name] students, if everyone living on earth had lived like an average [university name] student is doing now, we would have needed 2–3 earths to sustain this lifestyle (see picture 2). This means that an average student at [university name] uses about as much resources as you.

Appendix B.

Appendix B.1. Behavioural Intentions Items (Translated from Norwegian)

I am going to . . .

. . . avoid transportation means that produce a lot of carbon dioxide (e.g., plane), even if the alternatives take longer time.

. . . use extra time in the planning stage of my travel to find out how to best take the environment into account.

. . . choose nearby holiday places (e.g., in Nordic countries) if this helps to stop environmental problems stemming from tourism activities.

. . . avoid transportation means that produce a lot of carbon dioxide (e.g., plane) even if the alternatives are more expensive.

. . . choose accommodation places that are certified as environmentally friendly (e.g., low energy use), even if conventional offers are cheaper.

. . . pay extra money to reduce negative impacts on the environment that can be linked to my travel (e.g., voluntary participation in "carbon offsetting"-programs).

Appendix B.2. Self-Efficacy Items (Translated from Norwegian)

By avoiding transportation means that produce a lot of carbon dioxide (e.g., plane), I can contribute to stop environmental problems stemming from tourism activities.

By choosing accommodation places that are certified as environmentally friendly (e.g., low energy use), I can help to protect the environment.

By choosing nearby holiday places (e.g., Nordic countries), I can contribute to reduce negative impacts on the environment.

Appendix B.3. Collective Efficacy Items (Translated from Norwegian)

By choosing transportation means with low negative impact on the environment, we as tourists can contribute to stop environmental problems.

By asking for environmentally friendly travel alternatives (e.g., low carbon dioxide emissions), we as tourists can make a difference when it comes to environmental preservation.

We as tourists can actively contribute to protect the environment by choosing nearby holiday places.

References

1. Simpson, M.C.; Gössling, S.; Scott, D.; Hall, C.M.; Gladin, E. *Climate Change Adaptation and Mitigation in the Tourism Sector: Frameworks, Tools and Practices*; UNEP, University of Oxford, UNWTO,WMO: Paris, France, 2008.
2. United Nations World Tourism Organization. *From Davos to Copenhagen and Beyond: Advancing Tourism's Response to Climate Change*; UNWTO background paper; UNWTO: Madrid, Spain, 2009.
3. Filimonau, V. Carbon calculators as a tool for carbon impact appraisal of holiday travel: A critical review. *Worldw. Hosp. Tour. Themes* **2012**, *4*, 302–331. [CrossRef]
4. Juvan, E.; Dolnicar, S. Can tourists easily choose a low carbon footprint vacation? *J. Sustain. Tour.* **2014**, *22*, 175–194. [CrossRef]
5. Abrahamse, W.; Steg, L.; Vlek, C.; Rothengatter, T. A review of intervention studies aimed at household energy conservation. *J. Environ. Psychol.* **2005**, *25*, 273–291. [CrossRef]
6. Karlin, B.; Zinger, J.F.; Ford, R. The effects of feedback on energy conservation: A meta-analysis. *Psychol. Bull.* **2015**, *141*, 1205–1227. [CrossRef] [PubMed]
7. Abrahamse, W.; Steg, L. Social influence approaches to encourage resource conservation: A meta-analysis. *Glob. Environ. Chang.* **2013**, *23*, 1773–1785. [CrossRef]
8. Siero, F.W.; Bakker, A.B.; Dekker, G.B.; van Den Burg, M.T.C. Changing organizational energy consumption behaviour through comparative feedback. *J. Environ. Psychol.* **1996**, *16*, 235–246. [CrossRef]
9. Dixon, G.N.; Deline, M.B.; McComas, K.; Chambliss, L.; Hoffmann, M. Using comparative feedback to influence workplace energy conservation: A case study of a university campaign. *Environ. Behav.* **2015**, *47*, 667–693. [CrossRef]
10. Kurz, T.; Donaghue, N.; Walker, I. Utilizing a social-ecological framework to promote water and energy conservation: A field experiment. *J. Appl. Soc. Psychol.* **2005**, *35*, 1281–1300. [CrossRef]
11. Brook, A. Ecological footprint feedback: Motivating or discouraging? *Soc. Influ.* **2011**, *6*, 113–128. [CrossRef]
12. Toner, K.; Gan, M.; Leary, M.R. The impact of individual and group feedback on environmental intentions and self-beliefs. *Environ. Behav.* **2014**, *46*, 24–45. [CrossRef]
13. Aitken, C.K.; McMahon, T.A.; Wearing, A.J.; Finlayson, B.L. Residential water use: Predicting and reducing consumption. *J. Appl. Soc. Psychol.* **1994**, *24*, 136–158. [CrossRef]
14. Schultz, P.W.; Nolan, J.M.; Cialdini, R.B.; Goldstein, N.J.; Griskevicius, V. The constructive, destructive, and reconstructive power of social norms. *Psychol. Sci.* **2007**, *18*, 429–434. [CrossRef] [PubMed]
15. Bandura, A. Toward a psychology of human agency. *Perspect. Psychol. Sci.* **2006**, *1*, 164–180. [CrossRef] [PubMed]
16. Doran, R.; Hanss, D.; Larsen, S. Intentions to make sustainable tourism choices: Do value orientations, time perspective, and efficacy beliefs explain individual differences? *Scand. J. Hosp. Tour.* **2016**. [CrossRef]

17. Hanss, D.; Böhm, G.; Doran, R.; Homburg, A. Sustainable consumption of groceries: The importance of believing that one can contribute to sustainable development. *Sustain. Dev.* **2016**, *24*, 357–370. [CrossRef]
18. Hanss, D.; Böhm, G. Can I make a difference? The role of general and domain-specific self-efficacy in sustainable consumption decisions. *Umweltpsychologie* **2010**, *14*, 46–74.
19. Gupta, S.; Ogden, D.T. To buy or not to buy? A social dilemma perspective on green buying. *J. Consum. Mark.* **2009**, *26*, 376–391. [CrossRef]
20. Kerr, N.L. "Does my contribution really matter?": Efficacy in social dilemmas. *Eur. Rev. Soc. Psychol.* **1996**, *7*, 209–240. [CrossRef]
21. Bandura, A. Exercise of human agency through collective efficacy. *Curr. Dir. Psychol. Sci.* **2000**, *9*, 75–78. [CrossRef]
22. Rees, J.H.; Bamberg, S. Climate protection needs societal change: Determinants of intention to participate in collective climate action. *Eur. J. Soc. Psychol.* **2014**, *44*, 466–473. [CrossRef]
23. Bandura, A. *Self-Efficacy: The Exercise of Control*; W.H. Freeman and Company: New York, NY, USA, 1997.
24. Homburg, A.; Stolberg, A. Explaining pro-environmental behavior with a cognitive theory of stress. *J. Environ. Psychol.* **2006**, *26*, 1–14. [CrossRef]
25. Chen, M.-F. Self-efficacy or collective efficacy within the cognitive theory of stress model: Which more effectively explains people's self-reported proenvironmental behavior? *J. Environ. Psychol.* **2015**, *42*, 66–75. [CrossRef]
26. Miyake, M.; Matsuda, F. Effects of generalized self-efficacy and negative social comparison feedback on specific self-efficacy and performance. *Psychol. Rep.* **2002**, *90*, 301–308. [CrossRef] [PubMed]
27. Steyn, R.; Mynhardt, J. Factors that influence the forming of self-evaluation and self-efficacy perceptions. *S. Afr. J. Psychol.* **2008**, *38*, 563–573. [CrossRef]
28. Prussia, G.E.; Kinicki, A.J. A motivational investigation of group effectiveness using social-cognitive theory. *J. Appl. Psychol.* **1996**, *81*, 187–198. [CrossRef]
29. Koletsou, A.; Mancy, R. Which efficacy constructs for large-scale social dilemma problems? Individual and collective forms of efficacy and outcome expectancies in the context of climate change mitigation. *Risk Manag.* **2011**, *13*, 184–208. [CrossRef]
30. Tajfel, H.; Turner, J. An integrative theory of intergroup conflict. In *The Social Psychology of Intergroup Relations*; Austin, W.G., Worchel, S., Eds.; Brooks/Cole: Monterey, CA, USA, 1979; pp. 33–47.
31. Tajfel, H.; Turner, J.C. The social identity theory of intergroup behavior. In *Psychology of Intergroup Relations*; Nelson-Hall: Chicago, IL, USA, 1986; pp. 7–24.
32. Tropp, L.R.; Wright, S.C. Ingroup identification as the inclusion of ingroup in the self. *Personal. Soc. Psychol. Bull.* **2001**, *27*, 585–600. [CrossRef]
33. Perreault, S.; Bourhis, R.Y. Ethnocentrism, social identification, and discrimination. *Personal. Soc. Psychol. Bull.* **1999**, *25*, 92–103. [CrossRef]
34. De Cremer, D.; van Vugt, M. Social identification effects in social dilemmas: A transformation of motives. *Eur. J. Soc. Psychol.* **1999**, *29*, 871–893. [CrossRef]
35. Bamberg, S.; Rees, J.; Seebauer, S. Collective climate action: Determinants of participation intention in community-based pro-environmental initiatives. *J. Environ. Psychol.* **2015**, *43*, 155–165. [CrossRef]
36. White, K.M.; Smith, J.R.; Terry, D.J.; Greenslade, J.H.; McKimmie, B.M. Social influence in the theory of planned behaviour: The role of descriptive, injunctive, and in-group norms. *Br. J. Soc. Psychol.* **2009**, *48*, 135–158. [CrossRef] [PubMed]
37. Smith, J.R.; Louis, W.R. Do as we say and as we do: The interplay of descriptive and injunctive group norms in the attitude-behaviour relationship. *Br. J. Soc. Psychol.* **2008**, *47*, 647–666. [CrossRef] [PubMed]
38. Rabinovich, A.; Morton, T.A. Sizing fish and ponds: The joint effects of individual- and group-based feedback. *J. Exp. Soc. Psychol.* **2012**, *48*, 244–249. [CrossRef]
39. Graffeo, M.; Ritov, I.; Bonini, N.; Hadjichristidis, C. To make people save energy tell them what others do but also who they are: A preliminary study. *Front. Psychol.* **2015**, *6*. [CrossRef] [PubMed]
40. World Wide Fund for Nature Økologisk Fotavtrykk (Ecological Footprint). Avaliable online: http://www.wwf.no/dette_jobber_med/norsk_natur/naturmangfold/okologisk_fotavtrykk/ (accessed on 5 October 2015).
41. World Wide Fund for Nature Footprint Calculator. Avaliable online: http://footprint.wwf.org.uk/ (accessed on 23 May 2016).

42. Hayes, A.F. *Introduction to Mediation, Moderation, and Conditional Process Analysis: A Regression-Based Approach*; The Guilford Press: New York, NY, USA, 2013.
43. Aiken, L.S.; West, S.G. *Multiple Regression: Testing and Interpreting Interactions*; SAGE Publications: Newbury Park, CA, USA, 1991.
44. Field, A. *Discovering Statistics Using IBM SPSS Statistics*, 4th ed.; SAGE Publications: London, UK, 2013.
45. Miller, D.T.; Prentice, D.A. Changing norms to change behavior. *Annu. Rev. Psychol.* **2016**, *67*, 339–361. [CrossRef] [PubMed]
46. Brandon, G.; Lewis, A. Reducing household energy consumption: A qualitative and quantitative field study. *J. Environ. Psychol.* **1999**, *19*, 75–85. [CrossRef]
47. Carrico, A.R.; Riemer, M. Motivating energy conservation in the workplace: An evaluation of the use of group-level feedback and peer education. *J. Environ. Psychol.* **2011**, *31*, 1–13. [CrossRef]
48. Harries, T.; Rettie, R.; Studley, M.; Burchell, K.; Chambers, S. Is social norms marketing effective? A case study in domestic electricity consumption. *Eur. J. Mark.* **2013**, *47*, 1458–1475. [CrossRef]
49. Dolnicar, S.; Cvelbar, L.K.; Grün, B. Do pro-environmental appeals trigger pro-environmental behavior in hotel guests? *J. Travel Res.* **2016**. [CrossRef]
50. Festinger, L. A theory of social comparison processes. *Hum. Relat.* **1954**, *7*, 117–140. [CrossRef]

sustainability

MDPI

Article

Collaborative Consumption: A Proposed Scale for Measuring the Construct Applied to a Carsharing Setting

Helena Dall Pizzol [1], Stefânia Ordovás de Almeida [2] and Mauren do Couto Soares [3,*]

[1] Management and Marketing Department, School of Advertising and Marketing—ESPM-Sul, RS 90640-040 Porto Alegre, Brazil; hpizzol@espm.br
[2] Business School, Pontifical Catholic University of Rio Grande do Sul—PUCRS, RS 90619-900 Porto Alegre, Brazil; stefania.almeida@pucrs.br
[3] Department of Statistics and Quantitative Methods, School of Advertising and Marketing—ESPM-Sul, RS 90640-040 Porto Alegre, Brazil
* Correspondence: mauren_soares@hotmail.com; Tel.: +55-51-3320-3524

Academic Editor: Gerrit Antonides
Received: 26 January 2017; Accepted: 26 April 2017; Published: 28 April 2017

Abstract: In recent years, there has been a significant shift towards greater collaboration in various spheres of society, in which the creation of value from shared resources while balancing self-interest and community well-being is emphasized. Consumption has ceased to be characterized exclusively by the purchase and possession of goods; instead new collaborative initiatives represented by exchanges, loans, renting, and other forms of sharing that allow consumers access to a good or service only in the time they are necessary have appeared. However, few studies have attempted to measure the reasons that lead consumers to practice collaborative consumption. Therefore, the main objective of this article is to propose a scale that measures the motivators, facilitators, and constraints for this mode of consumption. For this, a study was conducted among carsharing users in Brazil, which aimed to purify and validate the proposed scale. The results indicate that collaborative consumption applied to a carsharing setting is composed of six dimensions and confirm the validity and reliability of the studied construct. The discussion highlights the study findings and offers suggestions for further research into this topic.

Keywords: consumer behavior; collaborative consumption; carsharing

1. Introduction

Changes in society and its members influence new forms of consumption of goods and services. Various cultural and structural factors such as increased purchasing power, an aging population, and the increasing value attributed to quality of life are seen to be among the elements responsible for the entry of new consumers and new consumption practices. Added to this are motivations related to the appreciation of environmental and social issues of greatest impact on people's daily lives, such as traffic congestion, problems caused by global warming, population growth, and a greater awareness of the importance of sustainability, which often lead individuals to seek radical solutions to their problems [1–3].

There is an ongoing theoretical and managerial debate on collaborative consumption, taking place mainly in Europe and North America, regarding consumption practices related to what is described as sharing [4–6], commercial sharing systems [7], and access-based consumption [8]. According to Leismann et al. [9], services that promote the use rather than the possession of a good need to be expanded, while product sharing, as well as the new collaborative models, have great potential to alter consumption patterns and lifestyles. Among the wide range of solutions that combine products and services capable of satisfying consumer needs are commercial systems for shared use (in the short or long term), as well as services that lead to the recovery and reuse of components and goods, such as exchange and donation. These assertions corroborate the basic assumption underlying collaborative consumption that is based on collaboration between individuals and enabled primarily by virtual platforms.

At the core of this transformation, understanding the influences and determinants of consumer behavior is a key issue, and thus a new research field within the scope of consumer behavior studies has emerged. From the academic point of view, some studies show that tangible benefits such as access, mobility, reward, and cost reduction can be obtained through the new consumption model based on the sharing of goods and services in the most varied segments such as transportation, food, financial services, and lodging, among others.

From a business perspective, managerial studies have also contributed to developing an understanding of the topic. A great number of such initiatives are being developed around the world and companies such as Netflix, Zipcar, and Airbnb are recognized examples of initiatives in several markets [10]. Concerning the collaborative consumption platform used in this study, carsharing, the worldwide market today encompasses nearly 5.8 million customers. In the Asia-Pacific region, the largest market, there are 2.3 million users and 33,000 vehicles. The largest service per capita, however, is in Europe, with 2.1 million users and 31,000 vehicles. On the other hand, North America accounts for 1.5 million users sharing 22,000 vehicles [11]. By 2021, according to the Boston Consulting Group [11] (p. 2) '35 million users will book 1.5 billion minutes of driving time each month and generate annual revenues of €4.7 billion'.

This view is consistent with the findings reported by Kang et al. [12] (p. 10); 'that carsharing demand is high in an area where a higher proportion of building floor area is used for business, and which has a higher proportion of young residents in their 20s and 30s'. That is why this result can be used to forecast carsharing demand, especially in Asian cities with urban conditions similar to Seoul, where the study occurred. Another example, implemented in Barcelona, Paris, Berlin, and Rotterdam, is electric vehicle sharing (EVS), an alternative providing a cleaner transport mode [13].

Compared to other markets, Brazilian initiatives are still timid, yet new collaborative consumer businesses have emerged. The growing trend could seem contradictory, since it competes with national economic growth that took place in Brazil until early 2014, driven by policies designed to stimulate consumption, with increased credit and a consequent growth in the retail sector. However, the two models seemed to coexist within contemporary society in which we have an economy where ownership rivals convenience of access and encourages changes in consumption behavior. Among the existing Brazilian options, consumers can find services such as carsharing, monthly toy rotation, community bicycles, sites offering free loans, and the renting of objects that are enabled through platforms or online consumer systems [14].

Although all the existing academic and managerial research has been fundamental to the production of knowledge regarding the sharing of goods and its motivations and constraints, there is a notable absence of studies that provide a complete and valid scale for evaluating the dimensions that make up collaborative consumption. Möhlmann [15] proposed a framework based on the determinants of satisfaction with a sharing option and the likelihood of choosing a sharing option, but the author's focus was on motivators and their relation to outcomes and was largely based on trends and technology, while failing to mention the constraints. Therefore, it is of fundamental importance to better understand the variables present in this new consumer behavior.

Accordingly, the main objective of this article is to propose and test a scale for measuring the construct of collaborative consumption applied in a carsharing setting. To do so, firstly, research of an exploratory nature was undertaken to better understand the dimensions that make up collaborative consumption and to generate items for the construction of a measurement scale. Subsequently, a descriptive analysis was carried out to purify and validate the measurement items by applying the scale to a sample of carsharing users in Brazil.

2. Literature Review

2.1. Collaborative Consumption Definitions

The determinants of collaboration between individuals and the predisposition to sharing can be evaluated according to the theoretical assumptions of collective action. Olson [16] argues that individuals must undergo external pressure to act cooperatively in building and managing common assets and to secure their own long-term interest. In Ostrom's [17] view, collaborative behaviors require a certain level of cooperation and identification among the participants. Therefore, for collective action to occur the individuals need to be more likely to collaborate and there must be mutual trust between them.

To define the concept of collaborative consumption, according to Belk [4], it is necessary to consider the acquisition and distribution of resources during activities among individuals. From this premise, collaborative consumption occurs in coordinated events between consumers for the acquisition and distribution of a resource based on a value or other form of reward, such as barter, trade, and exchanges involving non-monetary compensation.

Belk [6] emphasizes that this definition of collaboration excludes gift giving, which is characterized by the permanent transfer of ownership, while the terrain occupied by collaborative consumption is a compromise between sharing and market transactions, bringing together properties inherent to both. Add to this the premise that the sharing of goods (tangible and intangible) 'is an interpersonal process that is sanctioned and prescribed by culture', and, although it has not been well differentiated in the literature, sharing can be seen as a third form of distribution distinct from the exchange of goods and donation [4] (p. 130).

Along the same lines, Bardhi and Eckhardt [8] describe the domain and motivation of collaborative consumption as temporary access to goods and consumption experiences, rather than purchase and possession; that is, a market-mediated access. According to Botsman and Rogers [1], the strengthening of a new form of consumption accompanies the emergence of a socioeconomic era in which hyper consumption has begun to show signs of waning and is no longer at the center of human motivation. In its place, a greater concern with the exhaustion of natural resources encourages the better use of products. The idea of reusing products during the useful life of the good in the form of loans, rent, exchange, or resale is translated into the awareness that one must extract the maximum from what is consumed. This assumption is aligned with the belief in the common good, that is, to the understanding that the performance of some action, taking into account the general good of the community or an individual, is one of the essential principles of shared consumption [1].

Collaborative consumption, in the conception of Botsman and Rogers [1], is based on the technologies and behavior related to online social networks. Such interactions would seem to suggest the concept that collaboration does not have to occur to the detriment of individualism; rather, it enables a system in which people share resources without losing personal liberties and without sacrificing their lifestyle.

2.2. Collaborative Consumption Systems

Participation in collaborative consumption occurs in different forms and varies in terms of scale, maturity, and purpose. Botsman and Rogers [1] identify three distinct systems of collaboration, described below.

Product service systems are defined as a form of consumption in which one pays for the use of a product without the need to acquire it. The key benefit of this system is the absence of any obligation to definitively purchase the product on the part of the user, and, in the case of increased need to use the product or service, access for consumption can also be increased. For Lamberton and Rose [7], the presence of rivalry, exclusivity, and the availability of the shared products are essential characteristics to be added to this model.

Redistribution markets are characterized by relationships of exchange and donation such as the donation of furniture, the exchange or loan of books, and the exchange or donation of clothes. In this case, donation and exchange are related to the transfer of ownership. This system encourages the use and redistribution of old or unused items and contributes significantly to waste reduction.

Finally, collaborative lifestyles consist of the interaction of people with similar interests and the desire to share less tangible assets such as knowledge, resources, space, skills, and time, such as sharing time to learn a language. In addition, because it concerns sharing based on social interaction, a high degree of trust among the participants of the system is required.

2.3. Motivators, Facilitators and Constraints of Collaborative Consumption

Research shows that consumer participation in collaborative systems is generally associated with sustainable behavior that reverts to positive social and environmental outcomes [3], assuming that the use efficiency associated with reducing waste and absorbing surplus created by excess production and consumption are also motivating factors for collaboration, as they provide significant environmental benefits.

Rational and economic attributes such as the maximization of the use of the goods and cost savings are also pointed out as advantages associated with the collaborative consumption [4,7]. Along the same lines, Sacks [18] claims that individuals tend to engage in collaborative consumer systems because they allow access at lower costs.

Another important aspect that is considered a facilitator of collaborative practices is the trust placed in social relations as well as in organizational and institutional relationships [1,16]. To establish trust, there are some essential conditions, among which facing risks, a perception of loss, interdependence between the interests of the parties involved, the choices and alternatives available, and uncertainty about the expectations of other parties stand out. Lamberton and Rose [7] add that trust between individuals with similar behaviors can generate a high level of sharing with other similar individuals regardless of the pattern and intensity of use of the good or service being shared. In this context, it can be inferred that the social relations established among the individuals participating in the collaborative consumption can be facilitated by the presence of bonds of trust. Hence, trust will be seen as a facilitator for collaborative consumption practices in this study.

The studies by Hamari et al. [19] found that the extrinsic motives that lead users to use collaborative consumer platforms are focused on practical needs related to benefits in terms of economy, time, and recognition or reputation, which have a significant effect on people and their readiness to participate in sharing initiatives. On the other hand, the intrinsic motives are social and environmental in nature, being associated with ecological sustainability and pleasure, such as meeting or helping people and contributing to a sustainable and healthy environment, and have a greater impact on people's attitudes towards shared consumption.

Included in this discussion are findings from the study by Lamberton and Rose [7], wherein the results showed that the perceived risk of scarcity has a determinant effect on the probability of sharing, i.e., the consumer not only considers their own participation in these systems but also the participation and the demand from the partners in the sharing system. Sharing can also be considered a form of resistance to consumption, translated into actions based on anti-consumption attitudes. In this case, goods, when shared, become co-owned and consequently there is a natural reduction in the expectation of individual purchases by consumers [4,20].

Feelings of possessiveness and attachment made explicit by the importance given to what is possessed are mentioned by Belk [5] as possible impediments to sharing. Possessiveness affects the intention and willingness to share because of people's strong emotional connection and the feeling of domain over and attachment to their possessions. Similarly, Mont [21] postulates that current consumption patterns can be considered barriers to sharing since a large number of individuals are predisposed to the instinctive accumulation of what money can buy.

Ornellas [22] also noted some implications considered unfavorable to the practice of sharing in Brazil, such as insecurity *vis-à-vis* the availability of goods when the need for use arises. Attachment to things is also seen as a constraint because it involves not using one's own good, considered by many consumers as a symbol of social status.

From the business perspective, managerial studies have also contributed to the understanding of the topic. The adherence of consumers to a shared transportation option includes motivators such as reducing the periodic expenses associated with owning a vehicle (taxes, maintenance, and fuel), concern for the environment, and issues related to the convenience of use that the service offers [23].

Table 1 presents a summary of the motivators, facilitators (trust) and constraints to the practice of collaborative consumption, based on the bibliographic review.

Table 1. Synthesis of the motivators, facilitators, and constraints of collaborative consumption.

Motivators/Facilitators	Conceptual Definitions	References
Socio-environmental consciousness	Sustainable behavior that reverts to positive social and environmental outcomes. The efficiency of use associated with the reduction of waste and the absorption of surplus goods.	[1,3,24]
Cost savings	The ability to reduce spending on product acquisition or access to lower costs.	[1,7,25,26]
Trust	Trust placed in both social and organizational relationships, regardless of the standard or intensity of use of the good.	[7,16]
Convenience	The ability to provide comfort or well-being to the individual and facilitate their routine.	[7,22,26]
Resistance to consumption	Reduction in the expectation of purchases when the goods are shared (joint ownership).	[4,20]
Constraints	**Conceptual Definitions**	**References**
Risk	The expectation of problems and consideration of uncertainties in the search for lower risk in the decision-making process.	[7]
Possessiveness and attachment	A strong emotional bonding of people and sense of domain over and attachment to their possessions.	[4,5,21,22]
Privacy	Care taken with the shared good, manifestations of concern with the maintenance of the good state of belongings and with the collective living environment.	[5]

3. Carsharing as a Collaborative Consumer Platform

Carsharing, which is recognized as a form of goods supply service, is intended for consumers seeking to meet the need for individual mobility but who do not necessarily need to own the car, thus reducing journeys with the private vehicle and leading the consumer to adopt more sustainable behavior [2]. Carsharing is the sharing platform used in the present study.

The carsharing market is rapidly expanding and, according to a research report by Navigant Research [27], the projected worldwide revenue from carsharing services will be about $6.2 billion by 2020. Studies by Millard-Ball et al. [28] indicate that shared use of private cars plays an important role in reducing congestion and pollution rates because many individuals reduce or cancel car purchases or sales after becoming members of carsharing programs. This implies a reduction in the number of vehicles on the road and demonstrates an environmentally friendly strategy for organizations.

Notably, for some cultures, the possession of a private car has long been associated with a form of status and freedom. However, Efthymiou et al. [29] showed that this perception is beginning to change, particularly among younger people, driven by the emergence of a new ethos of collaborative consumption, in which access to the good or service, rather than its ownership, is seen as being primordial among a generation that seeks the ease and convenience of using a product and is willing to give up a little flexibility in exchange for participation in a collaborative consumption system.

In Brazil, carsharing is rapidly growing. There are now more than six carsharing companies operating in Brazilian cities [30], including Zazcar, the first one to launch the service in 2009 in São Paulo [31]. Currently, Zazcar has about 7.5 thousand registered users, with a fleet of vehicles distributed across 50 points within the city of São Paulo [32].

In essence, carsharing appears to be a catalyst for a wide variety of commercial systems that can provide the consumer the benefits of service access and regular use of goods, especially in large urban conglomerates, given the intensity of use, occupancy of physical space, and the costs of acquisition and maintenance of the good by the owner.

4. Methodology

The research was carried out in two main stages, the first being exploratory in nature and the second descriptive. The process of developing the proposed scale will be presented considering both stages. Finally, the process of validating the scale is presented. All procedures were performed in accordance with the recommendations of Churchill [33] and DeVellis [34].

4.1. Developing the Scale—The Exploratory Stage

The exploratory stage consisted of specifying the construct domain and generating items for the scale by reviewing the measurement items identified in the literature and supported by in-depth interviews. A bibliographic investigation was conducted to interpret information relevant to the purpose of the research, based on academic studies of diverse empirical natures on collaborative consumption. Journals from the area of marketing and psychology were consulted to find articles related to collaborative consumption, its motivators, facilitators, and constraints. The knowledge acquired on the research topic served as the basis for the elaboration of the script for the in-depth interviews and permitted the visualization of items to be used on the scale.

Nine in-depth interviews were conducted with users, experts, and managers of carsharing companies in Brazil and abroad who reported their experiences of sharing goods. The sample members were selected based on their experience and habits of use. The contents of the interviews were categorized, and a strong convergence was found between the collaborative consumption motivators, facilitators, and constraints present in the literature and those mentioned by the interviewees. Accordingly, when elaborating the scale, the measurement items were mainly adapted from the studies by Hamari et al. [19], Shaefers [26], Lamberton and Rose [7], and Ornellas [22], with the support of the in-depth interviews. Afterwards, we proceeded with the process of confirming the theoretical structure of the scale through conversations with three experts from the marketing area and two experts on the topic of collaborative consumption in Brazil. The items with no Portuguese language version were translated considering the distinction between the original studies and the proposed study.

Following DeVellis' [34] guidelines, two marketing academics and a market expert later evaluated the comprehensiveness of each of the translated items and suggested adjustments to the scale items. Thus, the first version of the scale included 30 items that could compose the collaborative consumption construct, divided into seven broad dimensions: cost savings; convenience; socio-environmental consciousness; belief in the common good; social identity, defined as motivators; trust, defined as a facilitator; and risks, defined as a constraint. Table 2 shows the first version of the scale to measure the collaborative consumption construct.

Table 2. Proposed scale for the measurement of collaborative consumption.

Dimension	Code	Item	Adapted from
Cost savings	CC1	I use the carsharing service because, by doing so, I can cut my costs.	[18,22]
	CC2	Participating in carsharing benefits me financially.	[19]
	CC3	I use carsharing because it is cheaper than other means of transportation.	[26]
	CC4	I use carsharing because I only pay for the usage time.	*
Convenience	CC5	I appreciate using the shared car and not having to worry about parking spaces or parking.	[7,22,26]
	CC6	I appreciate not having to worry about collective transportation schedules (bus, subway, train, ferry, catamaran) for my trips.	*
	CC7	I appreciate not having to worry about filling the tank in the car.	*
	CC8	Carsharing means there is always a vehicle available for use when I need one.	[7]
	CC9	I prefer the freedom of using my car at any time to using a shared car. **	[22]
	CC10	The possibility of using different models of vehicles, according to my need, is an attraction of carsharing.	[7,22]
	CC11	Using the shared car saves me time.	[19]
	CC12	I appreciate the convenience of using the shared car for my trips.	[29]
Socio-environmental consciousness	CC13	Using a shared car is a sustainable mode of consumption.	[19]
	CC14	Using a shared car reduces the consumption of natural resources.	[7]
	CC15	Using carsharing services means thinking about the environment.	[19]
Belief in the common good	CC16	Leaving a car idle and unused for most of the day seems inappropriate to me.	[7]
	CC17	Using carsharing services means thinking about others and the community.	*
	CC18	I feel good when I share resources and avoid overconsumption.	[20]
Social identity	CC19	Using carsharing allows me to be part of a group of people with similar interests.	[7]
	CC20	Using carsharing improves my image *vis-à-vis* the community and society.	[19]
	CC30	I feel accepted by the community and society when I use carsharing.	[35]
Trust	CC21	I trust the carsharing operating model.	[7]
	CC22	I trust the carsharing services I use.	[7]
	CC23	I trust the members who participate in the carsharing program.	[7]
	CC24	The carsharing service is safe.	[26]
Risks	CC25	I'm afraid of not being able to use the shared car when I need to use it. **	[7]
	CC26	I'm afraid of not being able to familiarize myself with the controls of different cars every time I use them. **	[7]
	CC27	I fear the car will not be suitable for use (maintenance, cleaning) when I need to use it. **	*
	CC28	Having to book the car every time I need to use it is inconvenient. **	[7]
	CC29	Having to find the car pick-up point is inconvenient. **	[7]

* Proposed item for the study; ** Reverse item.

4.2. Developing and Validating the Scale—The Descriptive Stage

The descriptive stage of the process of developing the collaborative consumption scale began with a pre-test of the data collection instrument conducted among six people from the same study population, with the aim of minimizing bias in the responses and identifying variables in which there were problems related to comprehension. Following that analysis, the recommended items were modified in order to increase the comprehensibility and clarity of the instrument.

To test, purify, and validate the scale, the survey was applied to a population composed of active users of the carsharing service. The participants were selected from the customer database, which was provided by the main carsharing company in Brazil, Zazcar [36]. The consumers researched were residents of the biggest Brazilian city, São Paulo. In this sense, Kang et al. [12] emphasizes the importance of studies based on real carsharing usage data.

Data collection was carried out in late December 2014, considering a cross-sectional sample. A questionnaire containing the developed collaborative consumption scale and other questions designed to characterize the respondent's demographics and usage profile. The data were collected by sending emails containing the survey link to the company's customer base. The online application format was chosen based on the sample profile and the convenience of sending it to different individuals [36]. Approximately 1800 active users (60% of the total company base at the time) received the link with the survey, and at the end of the collection period a sample of 124 completed questionnaires was registered, representing a return rate of 6.9% of the base used.

The procedures used to test and purify the scale were based on the recommendations of DeVellis [34], in which exploratory factor analysis (EFA), the communalities of the items, the measure of reliability through Cronbach's alpha, and the consequent item-to-item and item-total correlations were used. The analysis was made with the aid of SPSS (IBM, New York, NY, USA). In addition, following the orientations of Hair et al. [37], the univariate outliers were examined using the Z coefficient test, and the presence of multivariate outliers was also analyzed by measuring the Mahalanobis distance (D^2) [38,39]. Minor problems of normality were eliminated following the criteria suggested by Kline [39].

All the items in the scale were measured using Likert-type scales with seven points and subtitled at the extremes. The collaborative consumption scale was validated based on its content validity and construct validity. Validation of the construct was achieved through confirmatory factor analysis (CFA), using AMOS software.

5. Results

Regarding the sample profile, the majority of the respondents were men (76%), 25 years and over, and with a college degree (85%). Almost 80% of the sample does not own a car. Concerning carsharing usage, 70% stated they use the car for leisure and 50% use it for shopping (in a multiple-choice question).

5.1. Scale Development and Purification

To achieve the broader goal of this study, we started eliminating redundant items or those with low factor loadings, thus improving the scale's properties. We used principal component analysis with an orthogonal rotation to examine and interpret the factors [34]. The cut-off criterion for factor retention was an eigenvalue equal to or larger than 1 [36]. The Kaiser-Meyer-Olkin (KMO) test was used to indicate the adequacy of the data to the factor analysis. The sample is adequate if the value of KMO is greater than 0.6. Bartlett's test of sphericity was also checked, and the null hypothesis of no correlations between the variables was rejected for all the analyses.

Acceptable values for each of the other tests are explained in the literature. According to Hair et al. [37], items with communalities lower than 0.5 should be removed. To examine the scale's reliability, we calculated the Cronbach's alpha (minimum recommended of 0.6) and the item-total correlations, for which values above 0.5 were expected [34,36]. We also assessed the item-to-item correlations, for which the maximum score of 0.8 for a correlation between two variables was considered [39].

In addition, regarding the exploratory factor analysis (EFA), Hair et al. [37] suggest only interpreting factor loadings with an absolute value greater than 0.4, the guideline that was followed in this study. To perform the reliability and correlation tests, some items were regrouped according to their conceptual coherence and their factor loadings.

To make the final rotated solution satisfactory, factor analysis was processed ten times. The results obtained before the adoption of the final scale, in general, presented inadequate structures, with the presence of cross-loading items and items with low communalities, as well as the existence of theoretical mismatch of some items in their original dimensions. Table 3 summarizes the EFA process and specifically indicates the items that were eliminated (and why) during the development of the collaborative consumption scale.

Table 3. Summary of the exploratory factor analysis (EFA) process.

Factor Analysis	Eliminated Item	Reason for Elimination
1	CC16	Low communality
2	CC23	Cross-loaded on more than one factor
3	CC4	Magnitude of the factor loading
4 and 5	CC7; CC8	Low communalities and unacceptable item-total correlations
6	CC26	Magnitude of the factor loading, alpha level, and unacceptable item-total correlation
7	CC5	Magnitude of the factor loading, alpha level, and unacceptable item-total correlation
8	CC9	Cross-loaded on more than one factor, alpha level, and unacceptable item-total correlation
9	CC3	Alpha level, unacceptable item-total correlation, and lack of theoretical adherence between the item and the loaded factor

Thus, the final structure for validation was composed of six factors (Table 4). Items originally associated with two distinct dimensions, socio-environmental consciousness and belief in the common good, were clustered around a single factor, Factor 1. A strong conceptual relationship is assumed to exist between the two dimensions since motivation and greater awareness of social and environmental issues lead to an increasing number of people seeking alternative solutions to their individual problems as well as collective issues. Hence, the items were included in a single dimension referred to as socio-environmental consciousness. The reliability measures were acceptable, with alpha statistics higher than 0.6. The KMO test of sampling adequacy was 0.749, and Bartlett's test of sphericity was found to be significant. The total variance explained was 70.216; the percentages for each factor are presented in Table 4. The results of this final orthogonal rotation were also confirmed in an oblique rotation, which sustained its robustness.

Table 4. Exploratory factor analysis: final structure.

Code	Item	Factor Loading	Com. [1]
Factor 1—Socio-environmental consciousness Cronbach alpha 0.882 Percentage of Variance Explained 15.859			
CC15	Using carsharing services means thinking about the environment.	0.898	0.884
CC14	Using a shared car reduces the consumption of natural resources.	0.887	0.847
CC13	Using a shared car is a sustainable mode of consumption.	0.745	0.718
CC17	Using carsharing services means thinking about others and the community.	0.684	0.690
CC18	I feel good when I share resources and avoid overconsumption.	0.557	0.560
Factor 2—Social identity Cronbach alpha 0.868 Percentage of Variance Explained 12.424			
CC20	Using carsharing improves my image *vis-à-vis* the community and society.	0.818	0.805
CC30	I feel accepted by the community and society when I use carsharing.	0.807	0.765
CC19	Using carsharing allows me to be part of a group of people with similar interests.	0.786	0.751
Factor 3—Trust Cronbach alpha 0.862 Percentage of Variance Explained 12.289			
CC22	I trust the carsharing services I use.	0.882	0.818
CC24	The carsharing service is safe.	0.835	0.732
CC21	I trust the carsharing operating model.	0.803	0.745
Factor 4—Risks Cronbach alpha 0.687 Percentage of Variance Explained 10.365			
CC29	Having to find the car pick-up point is inconvenient.	0.773	0.645
CC28	Having to book the car every time I need to use it is inconvenient.	0.696	0.583
CC25	I'm afraid of not being able to use the shared car when I need to use it.	0.682	0.527
CC27	I fear the car will not be suitable for use (maintenance, cleaning) when I need to use it.	0.680	0.464

Table 4. *Cont.*

Code	Item	Factor Loading	Com. [1]
Factor 5—Convenience Cronbach alpha 0.686 Percentage of Variance Explained 9.900			
CC11	Using the shared car saves me time.	0.765	0.714
CC10	The possibility of using different models of vehicles, according to my need, is an attraction of carsharing.	0.754	0.654
CC12	I appreciate the convenience of using the shared car for my trips.	0.634	0.600
CC6	I appreciate not having to worry about collective transportation schedules (bus, subway, train, ferry, catamaran) for my trips.	0.525	0.546
Factor 6—Cost savings Cronbach alpha 0.856 Percentage of Variance Explained 9.379			
CC1	I use the carsharing service because, by doing so, I can cut my costs.	0.902	0.854
CC2	Participating in carsharing benefits me financially.	0.905	0.842

[1] Communalities.

5.2. Scale Validation

Being a procedure that does not involve statistical tests but instead depends on the subjective assessment of the researcher [40], content validity was established through a literature review combined with discussions with experts on the topic and thus met the methodological rigor used in the development and refinement of the scale.

To verify the construct validity and confirm the six-factor solution of the scale, we performed confirmatory factor analysis (CFA). This procedure can be considered preliminary, as the same data set was used for purification and validation. In this way, we estimated six measurement models; one for each dimension of the collaborative consumption scale. This method is widely used in marketing research to determine construct validity [41,42]. In particular, we assessed the unidimensionality, reliability, convergent validity, and discriminant validity, as well as the fit statistics described in the literature [39].

Table 5 shows the following fit indexes for the constructs of socio-environmental consciousness, social identity, trust, risks, and convenience; the chi-square index divided by degrees of freedom (χ^2/df), goodness-of-fit index (GFI), adjusted goodness-of-fit index (AGFI), Tucker-Lewis index (TLI), comparative fit index (CFI), and root mean square error of approximation (RMSEA).

Table 5. Fit statistics for the constructs.

Fit Statistics	Socio-Environmental Consciousness	Social Identity	Trust	Risks	Convenience
χ^2/df	1.490	3.774	2.118	1.042	1.155
GFI	0.995	0.980	0.989	0.996	0.991
AGFI	0.928	0.879	0.931	0.958	0.953
TLI	0.986	0.959	0.981	0.997	0.989
CFI	0.999	0.986	0.994	1.000	0.996
RMSEA	0.063	0.150	0.095	0.018	0.035

Most of the fit indexes are acceptable. For example, most of the values of GFI, AGFI, TLI, and CFI were above the commonly recommended 0.9 limit [39,43]. Moreover, the RMSEA was less than the 0.08 cut-off value for the constructs of socio-environmental consciousness, risks, and convenience. For the trust and social identity dimensions, the RMSEA, and the AGFI for the latter, were outside the suggested range. Ullman [44] believes that the AGFI is equivalent to the GFI but is adjusted, considering the number of parameters in the adjusted model. The RMSEA index, on the other hand, shares the same theoretical nature as the CFI, according to Raykov and Marcoulides [45]. Thus, due to the high CFI values obtained, the analyzed dimensions were considered validated. It should be noted that the existence of only two or three items in certain dimensions may explain the occurrence of improper statistics; hence the number of items should be reviewed in future studies.

Construct validation of the cost savings dimension was unfeasible due to the low conceptual explanatory capacity intrinsic to models with only two items [42]. However, considering its theoretical relevance to the studied phenomenon, related to its content validity, and its good performance in the exploratory phase of the study, it was decided to retain this construct in the scale so that its construct validation might be confirmed in future research.

Unidimensionality was achieved by examining the standardized residuals, which could indicate items with an unacceptable fit to the model [42,43]. According to the literature, for a dimension to be considered unidimensional, all its standardized residuals should be less than 2.58. The highest value found in this study was 0.692 in the convenience dimension. From this information, we can conclude that we found evidence of unidimensionality for our measurements.

The reliability tests used were intended to overcome the limitations associated with the Cronbach's alpha coefficients [42]. Thus, the composite reliability and variance extracted from all constructs values were calculated. Composite reliabilities were high, surpassing the recommended threshold level of 0.7. Whereas the variance extracted for the dimensions of socio-environmental consciousness, social identity, trust, and convenience exceeded the required 0.5, the variance extracted for risks fell slightly below the minimum level. This result suggests that there are opportunities for further item refinement in this construct. Given the exploratory nature of this study, the risks dimension can also be considered reliable. Table 6 presents the composite reliabilities and variance extracted for the dimensions, as well as their respective standardized factor loadings and t-values.

Table 6. Reliability and convergent validity.

Dimensions	Reliability		Convergent Validity	
	Composite Reliability	Variance Extracted	Standardized Loading [1]	T-Value [2]
Socio-environmental consciousness	0.920	0.700	0.597	6.123
Social identity	0.930	0.810	0.684	8.835
Trust	0.920	0.790	0.749	8.939
Risks	0.720	0.400	0.434	3.157
Convenience	0.790	0.500	0.490	3.853

[1,2] Lowest value on each factor.

Byrne [38] (p. 288) described convergent validity as 'the extent to which independent measures of the same trait are correlated'. Specifically, convergent validity is reflected in the magnitude of the standardized factor loadings and t-values for all constructs involved in the scale [41,42]. As shown in Table 6, two dimensions, risks and convenience, displayed items with factor loadings below the limit of 0.5. Again, this may occur in newly developed scales. T-values, however, were found to exceed the minimum level of 2.0, proposed by Bagozzi et al. [41]. Hence, the results support the convergent validity.

Finally, we examined the discriminant validity. According to Kline [39] (p. 72), 'a set of variables presumed to measure different constructs shows discriminant validity if their intercorrelations are not too high'. In testing for evidence of discriminant validity among the dimensions for the scale of collaborative consumption, we contrasted the squared correlation of each dimension pair with the variance extracted from each dimension, following the procedure described by Fornell and Larcker [46]. Discriminant validity is exhibited only if each variance extracted is larger than all correlations. In each case, the variance extracted (square root, the value in bold) exceeded the correlation, supporting discriminant validity (Table 7).

Table 7. Discriminant validity [1].

	SEC [2]	Trust	SI	CNV	Risks
SEC	0.84				
Trust	0.307	0.89			
SI	0.556	0.171	0.90		
CNV	0.291	0.357	0.375	0.71	
Risks	0.002	0.192	−0.135	−0.011	0.63

[1] For the correlations we calculated the mean of variable indicators. [2] SEC: Socio-environmental consciousness; SI: Social identity; CNV: Convenience.

In summary, the results of the CFA support the scale's unidimensionality, reliability, convergent validity, and discriminant validity. Taken together, these tests confirm the validation process of the proposed scale for measuring the construct of collaborative consumption.

6. Discussion and Conclusions

Concerning the theoretical implications of this research, it is understood that the scale development and test fills a gap identified in the literature, providing greater theoretical understanding regarding the dimensions that compose the collaborative consumption construct. In this sense, this study provides an important contribution to the understanding of consumer behavior by identifying and offering insights into the composition of collaborative consumption applied to a carsharing setting.

The first strength of the research refers to the relevance of the purification process since only empirical evidence could prove that a few items were not part of the construct of collaborative consumption. Nevertheless, further item refinement might be needed, especially for the dimensions formed by two or three indicators like social identity, trust, and cost savings. Future studies might enhance the conceptual richness of the proposed dimensions and consequently offer a better representation of the construct.

It is important to note that through the scale's development and purification process, poorly loading items, and cross-loading items were removed from the factor analysis to achieve a better solution. Prior to EFA, the wording of the scale was adapted to improve the understandability of the items in each dimension. Therefore, the EFA results were submitted to content analysis to ensure that statistical results meet content criteria [40].

Another contribution relates to the verification and confirmation of the measures that compose the collaborative consumption construct through the CFA analysis. In this case, the findings indicate good results for the scale's unidimensionality, reliability, and convergent and discriminant validity. The fit statistics for the analyzed dimensions also show a reasonable level of model fit for a new scale, which supports the construct validity. This study was performed with a sample of real users, indicating the high external validity of the results.

Notwithstanding its potential contributions, the research has several limitations. The findings of the refinement process revealed reliable measures but with some unadjusted items and dimensions, which, therefore, deserve further evaluation. The cost savings dimension was not statistically validated due to the small number of items, but its relevance and adherence to the construct of collaborative consumption was proven in the exploratory stage. In this sense, this limitation should be overcome in future studies that must provide new measurement items for the cost savings dimension.

In addition, one must consider the limitations relative to the use of the same data set for purification and validation procedures, which proved necessary in this case due to the relatively small sample size that was impractical to split. For this reason, it is recommended that CFA is repeated in a fresh sample in the future with the new aforementioned measurement items. The profile and size of the population used in this study in Brazil, as well as the limited availability of the database, make it difficult both to replicate the study and also to compare the respondent profile with that of the non-respondents. Moreover, performing a survey among users and non-users of the carsharing services would be an interesting avenue for further research.

Another limitation refers to the application of the survey related to carsharing users in one Brazilian metropolis. In this sense, to ensure a highly generalizable scale, future studies could investigate the applicability of the dimensions of collaborative consumption in different national and cultural contexts.

Kang et al. [12] argue that, particularly in American cities, carsharing is expected to be associated with high-density areas, where privately owned vehicles should be less present. In addition, carsharing is also offered jointly with other public transportation solutions such as trains and subways in such areas. When we compare São Paulo, where this study took place, to another metropolis abroad, it has a poor public transportation system, with only five subway lines and insufficient buses to meet the needs of the population. Many people who can afford a car buy one in order to better provide for their transportation needs, but parking is expensive in central areas, which can be a constraint for carsharing systems as well. In this sense, while this study sheds new light on the little studied areas of collaborative consumption and the carsharing market, it also confirms the need for replication in other locations.

The fact that it is context specific may also be a weakness of this study, although it provides important avenues for future research in order to provide generalizability for the proposed scale. While largely based on collaborative consumption theory, in order to be feasible to be applied in the carsharing setting as an example of collaborative consumption, the proposed scale suffered from the need for item specificity in some of the theoretical dimensions studied. Scale items such as 'I fear the car will not be suitable for use (maintenance, cleaning) when I need to use it' from the risks dimension and 'I appreciate the convenience of using the shared car for my trips' and 'I appreciate not having to worry about collective transportation schedules (bus, subway, train, ferry, catamaran) for my trips' from the convenience dimension should suffer major changes when applying the proposed scale to other kinds of collaborative consumption settings. Thus, adapting and applying the proposed scale in other collaborative consumption platforms and contexts, such as accommodation, tourism, clothing, and others, would offer the opportunity to validate the scale in a broader spectrum of collaborative consumption needs.

The examination of a model that includes antecedents and consequences of the construct is also recommended to provide a more comprehensive picture of consumer behavior and to generate a better understanding of how the dimensions of the collaborative consumption concept are affected and affect other constructs. In a study performed in Germany by Möhlmann [15], trust appeared as an antecedent for satisfaction in a carsharing system, and community belonging/identity was a relevant predictor for choosing the sharing option again. Future studies with this proposed scale can test a theoretical model and verify the role of trust as a facilitator for collaborative consumption.

The alternative pattern of consumption, motivated by emotional, rational, or utilitarian issues, demonstrates that obtaining the acceptance, adoption, and diffusion of collaborative forms of businesses among consumers constitutes a great managerial challenge. According to the results, convenience of use, sense of belonging to a community, greater social and sustainable awareness, trust in strangers, and preference for accessibility rather than ownership are the main drivers of collaborative consumption. More rational and utilitarian aspects, such as cost savings, are equally important variables that need to be explored by companies when creating, communicating, and disseminating new collaborative practices. We must also mention that the proposed scale is built for people already engaged in collaborative consumption, otherwise he/she could not feel social identity, perceive risks and costs, and so on. With the scale dimensions and a profile identification, a manager can certainly identify the kind of person most involved in collaborative consumption among those already engaged in this sort of platform.

Using this scale in different platforms of collaborative consumption (with minor adjustments for each platform) one can measure the strength of the motivators and the impact of the constraints consumers feel when engaging in such collaborative platforms, as well as the facilitating role of trust in this mode of consumption. If the motivators are high, continued use of the collaborative consumption platform analyzed would be a logical future intention. On the other hand, if constraints are higher, the probability of abandoning collaborative consumption must be considered. Based on these answers, obtained through research scores from the collaborative consumption scale, companies can better provide offers to their consumers, increasing the practice of collaborative consumption while reducing the perception of risk and supporting motivations. Hence, we suggest that future studies test the predictive validity of the proposed scale by applying it in different samples and collaborative consumption contexts. Taking all this into account, the proposed scale can be considered to have only been preliminarily validated; hence future studies are encouraged to replicate it and improve upon it.

The results of this paper also offer important insights that can be considered by managers seeking to adapt their business activities to build a sense of community belonging and trust, strategically competitive advantages in a market in which the acquisition and retention of customers have high relevance. Finally, a more accurate understanding of the nature and impact of shared activities and the potential growth of the carsharing market offers collaborative consumption opportunities like the development of new business propositions with less environmental impact and more meaningful experiences for users. Governments could also use these insights to promote collaborative consumption, especially in big cities. Identifying personal characteristics that relate to shared consumption, therefore, is critical for companies that want to win new consumers, even if this involves initially appealing to a limited number of individuals who share beliefs and motivations that are distinct from those held by the majority.

This study also offers managers a better understanding of user profiles, congruent with prior research. In this study, as in previous ones, males reported using carsharing more often than females (see Kang et al. for a revision) [12]. Usage for leisure purposes and daily activities such as shopping also showed congruence with earlier studies [13]. In sum, consumer behavior relative to collaborative consumption is a research focus with potential impacts for scholars, managers, and governments.

Acknowledgments: This study had no third-party research funds, but we acknowledge Zazcar for providing consumer contacts for data collection.

Author Contributions: Helena Dall Pizzol and Stefânia Ordovás de Almeida conceived and designed the scale; Helena Dall Pizzol collected data; Helena Dall Pizzol and Mauren do Couto Soares analyzed the data; and all authors wrote and revised the paper.

Conflicts of Interest: The authors declare no conflict of interest.

References

1. Botsman, R.; Rogers, R. *O Que É Meu É Seu: Como o Consumo Colaborativo Vai Mudar o Mundo*; Bookman: Porto Alegre, Brazil, 2011.
2. Frost, S. Sustainable and Innovative Personal Transport Solutions: Strategic Analysis of Car Sharing Market in Europe. 2010. Available online: http://www.frost.com/prod/servlet/svcg.pag/AT00 (accessed on 17 May 2013).
3. Prothero, A.; Dobscha, S.; Freund, J.; Kilbourne, W.E.; Luchs, M.G.; Ozanne, L.K.; Thøgersen, J. Sustainable consumption: Opportunities for consumer research and public policy. *J. Public Policy Mark.* **2011**, *30*, 31–38. [CrossRef]
4. Belk, R. Why Not Share Rather Than Own? *Ann. Am. Acad. Political Soc. Sci.* **2007**, *611*, 126–140. [CrossRef]
5. Belk, R. Sharing. *J. Consum. Res.* **2010**, *36*, 715–734. [CrossRef]
6. Belk, R. You are what you can access: Sharing and collaborative consumption online. *J. Bus. Res.* **2014**, *67*, 1595–1600. [CrossRef]
7. Lamberton, C.; Rose, R. When is ours better than mine? A framework for understanding and altering participation in commercial sharing systems. *J. Mark.* **2012**, *76*, 109–125. [CrossRef]
8. Bardhi, F.; Eckhardt, G. Access based consumption: The case of car sharing. *J. Consum. Res.* **2012**, *39*, 881–898. [CrossRef]
9. Leismann, K.; Schmitt, M.; Rohn, H.; Baedeker, C. Collaborative Consumption: Towards a Resource-Saving Consumption Culture. *Resources* **2013**, *2*, 184–203. [CrossRef]
10. Owyang, J.; Tran, C.; Silva, C. The Collaborative Economy: Products, Services, and Market Relationships Have Changed, as Sharing Startups Impact Business Models. Available online: http://www.altimetergroup.com/research/reports/collaborative-economy (accessed on 16 June 2013).

11. Bert, J.; Collie, B.; Gerrits, M.; Xu, G. *What's Ahead for Car Sharing? The New Mobility and Its Impact on Vehicle Sales*; The Boston Consulting Group: Boston, MA, USA, 2016; pp. 1–17. Available online: http://www.bcg.de/documents/file206078.pdf (accessed on 18 December 2016).

12. Kang, J.; Hwang, K.; Park, S. Finding Factors that Influence Carsharing Usage: Case Study in Seoul. *Sustainability* **2016**, *8*, 709. [CrossRef]

13. Wang, N.; Yan, R. Research on Consumers' Use Willingness and Opinions of Electric Vehicle Sharing: An Empirical Study in Shanghai. *Sustainability* **2016**, *8*, 7. [CrossRef]

14. Moura, M. *Para Tirar Vocês do Trânsito Com Ideias Simples de Compartilhamento de Bens e Dados, a Sociedade Começa a Desatar os Nós Das Ruas*; Época: São Paulo, Brazil, 2013; Available online: epoca.globo.com/vida/noticia/2013/11/como-empresas-e-escolas-podem-ajudar-bdesafogar-o-trafegob.html (accessed on 28 October 2013).

15. Möhlmann, M. Collaborative Consumption: Determinants of satisfaction and the likelihood of using a sharing economy option again. *J. Consum. Behav.* **2015**, *14*, 193–207. [CrossRef]

16. Olson, M. *The Logic of Collective Action: Public Goods and the Theory of Groups*; Harvard University Press: Cambridge, MA, USA, 1965.

17. Ostrom, E. Collective Action and the Evolution of Social Norms. *J. Econ. Perspect.* **2000**, *14*, 137–158. [CrossRef]

18. Sacks, D. The Sharing Economy. Fast Company. Available online: http://www.fastcompany.com/magazine/155/the-sharing-economy.htm (accessed on 30 May 2013).

19. Hamari, J.; Sjöklint, M.; Ukkonen, A. The Sharing Economy: Why People Participate in Collaborative Consumption. *SSRN* **2013**, *67*, 2047–2059. [CrossRef]

20. Ozanne, L.K.; Ballantine, P.W. Sharing as a form of anti-consumption? An examination of toy library users. *J. Consum. Behav.* **2010**, *9*, 485–498. [CrossRef]

21. Mont, O. Institutionalization of sustainable consumption patterns based on shared use. *Ecol. Econ.* **2004**, *50*, 135–153. [CrossRef]

22. Ornellas, R.S. *O Consumo Colaborativo de Transporte Individual Car Sharing e o Processo Decisório do Consumidor na Cidade de SP*. Master's Thesis, Universidade de São Paulo, São Paulo, Brazil, 2012.

23. Reuters Brazil. Zazcar Aproveita geração da Internet e Caos no Trânsito para Crescer. Available online: http://br.reuters.com/article/internetNews/idBRSPE92H00920130318?sp=true (accessed on 11 January 2014).

24. Seyfang, G. Shopping for sustainability: Can sustainable consumption promote ecological citizenship? *Environ. Politics* **2005**, *14*, 290–306. [CrossRef]

25. Kozinets, R.V.; Hemetsberger, A.; Schau, H.J. The Wisdom of Consumer Crowds: Collective Innovation in the Age of Networked Marketing. *J. Macromark.* **2008**, *28*, 339–354. [CrossRef]

26. Schaefers, T. Exploring carsharing usage motives: A hierarchical means-end chain analysis. *Trans. Res. Part A* **2013**, *47*, 69–77. [CrossRef]

27. Navigant. Car-sharing Membership and Vehicle Fleets, Personal Vehicle Reduction, and Revenue from Car-sharing Services: Global Market Analysis and Forecasts. Available online: http://www.navigantresearch.com/wp-assets/uploads/2013/08/CSHP-13-Executive-Summary.pdf (accessed on 27 August 2013).

28. Millard-Ball, A.; Murray, G.; ter Schure, J. Car-Sharing as a Parking Management Strategy. In Proceedings of the 85th Annual Meeting of the Transportation Research Board, Washington, DC, USA, 1–2 November 2006.

29. Efthymiou, D.; Antoniou, C.; Waddell, P. Factors affecting the adoption of vehicle sharing systems by young drivers. *Transp. Policy* **2013**, *29*, 64–73. [CrossRef]

30. Carrigan, A. Four Facts about Carsharing in Emerging Markets that Might Surprise You. TheCityFix. Available online: http://thecityfix.com/blog/four-facts-carsharing-report-emerging-markets-surprise-you-aileen-carrigan/ (accessed on 18 December 2016).

31. Poggetto, P.D. Serviço de Compartilhamento de Carro Começa a ter Espaço No Brazil. Auto Esporte. Available online: http://g1.globo.com/carros/noticia/2013/04/servico-de-compartilhamento-de-carro-comeca-ter-espaco-no-brzsil.html (accessed on 18 December 2016).

32. Olivette, C. Compartilhamento de Veículos altera a Mobilidade Urbana. Estadão—Portal do Estado de São Paulo. Available online: http://economia.estadao.com.br/blogs/sua-oportunidade/compartilhamento-de-veiculos-altera-a-mobilidade-urbana/ (accessed on 18 December 2016).

33. Churchill, G.A., Jr. *Marketing Research: Methodological Foundations*; The Dryden Press: Orlando, FL, USA, 1979.

34. DeVellis, R.F. *Scale Development: Theory and Applications*; Sage Publications: Thousand Oaks, CA, USA, 2003.

35. Malone, G.P.; Pillow, D.R.; Osman, A. The general belongingness scale (GBS): Assessing achieved belongingness. *Personal. Individ. Differ.* **2012**, *52*, 311–316. [CrossRef]
36. Zazcar. Available online: http//www.zazcar.com.br (accessed on 20 February 2014).
37. Hair, J.F., Jr.; Babin, B.; Money, A.H.; Samouel, P. *Fundamentos de Métodos de Pesquisa em Administração*; Bookman: Porto Alegre, Brazil, 2007.
38. Byrne, B.M. *Structural Equation Modeling with AMOS: Basic Concepts, Applications, and Programming*, 2nd ed.; Routledge Taylor & Francis Group: New York, NY, USA, 2010.
39. Kline, R.B. *Principles and Practice of Structural Equation Modeling*, 3rd ed.; The Guilford Press: New York, NY, USA, 2011.
40. Rossiter, J. The C-OAR-SE Procedure for Scale Development in Marketing. *Int. J. Res. Mark.* **2002**, *19*, 305–335. [CrossRef]
41. Bagozzi, R.P.; Yi, Y.; Phillips, L.W. Assessing Construct Validity in Organizational Research. *Adm. Sci. Q.* **1991**, *36*, 421–458. [CrossRef]
42. Garver, M.S.; Mentzer, J.T. Logistics Research Methods: Employing Structural Equation Modeling to Test for Construct Validity. *J. Bus. Logist.* **1999**, *20*, 33–57.
43. Hair, J.F., Jr.; Anderson, R.E.; Tatham, R.L.; Black, W.C. *Análise Multivariada de Dados*, 6th ed.; Bookman: Porto Alegre, Brazil, 2009.
44. Ullman, J.M. Structural Equation Modeling. In *Using Multivariate Statistics*; Tabachnick, B., Fidell, L., Eds.; Allyn & Bacon: Boston, MA, USA, 2000.
45. Raykov, T.; Marcoulides, G.A. *A First Course in Structural Equation Modeling*; Lawrence Erlbaum Associates: Mahwah, NJ, USA, 2000.
46. Fornell, C.; Larcker, D.F. Evaluating Structural Equation Models with Unobservable Variables and Measurement Error. *J. Mark. Res.* **1981**, *18*, 39–50. [CrossRef]

![sustainability logo] *sustainability*

MDPI

Article

Consumers' Willingness to Pay a Premium for Eco-Labeled LED TVs in Korea: A Contingent Valuation Study

Seo-Hyeon Min, Seul-Ye Lim and Seung-Hoon Yoo *

Department of Energy Policy, Graduate School of Energy & Environment, Seoul National University of Science & Technology, 232 Gongreung-Ro, Nowon-Gu, Seoul 01811, Korea; shmin@seoultech.ac.kr (S.-H.M.); sylim@seoultech.ac.kr (S.-Y.L.)
* Correspondence: shyoo@seoultech.ac.kr; Tel.: +82-2-970-6802

Academic Editor: Gerrit Antonides
Received: 31 January 2017; Accepted: 4 May 2017; Published: 13 May 2017

Abstract: Although the production costs and prices of eco-labeled products are higher than those of conventional ones, the use of greener products can lead to better environmental outcomes. Thus, the consumers' preferences for eco-labeled products should be investigated to understand the potential of markets with green products. This study attempts to examine the consumers' preference or willingness to pay (WTP) a premium for eco-labeled products using a specific case study of a 43-inch LED TV, which is a common home appliance in Korea. For this purpose, a contingent valuation survey of 1000 Korean consumers was conducted in June 2016. We used a one-and-one-half-bounded dichotomous choice question to derive the additional WTP responses and a spike model to analyze zero additional WTP responses. The mean additional WTP a premium for the eco-labeled 43-inch LED TV is estimated to be KRW 29,007 (USD 24.8), which is statistically meaningful at the 1% level. This value amounts to 3.9% of the price of a conventional 43-inch LED TV (KRW 750,000 or USD 640.5) and can be interpreted as the external benefit of an eco-labeled LED TV. We can conclude that Korean consumers are ready to pay a significant premium for eco-labeled LED TVs. Moreover, we examined the consumer's characteristics that affect the probability that the person will be willing to pay a premium for an eco-labeled LED TV and found that it would be effective to set high-income, older, highly-educated, and female consumers with children as marketing targets.

Keywords: eco-labeled LED TV; consumer preference; willingness to pay; premium; contingent valuation

1. Introduction

Various pollutants, such as air pollutants, waste water, and waste, are emitted into the environment in the course of manufacturing electronic products [1,2]. These emitted pollutants exert negative effects on human health, as well as the environment [3]. The Korean government has introduced a scheme for environmentally-friendly products that are created using less water and electricity and emitting fewer pollutants. In other words, the Korean government grants eco-label certification to eco-friendly products that may cause less environmental pollution or save resources compared with other products intended for the same use. The certification is based on the Support for Environmental Technology and Environmental Industry Act. The attached eco-label indicates that the product is manufactured using an eco-friendly process and production method (PPM) [4,5].

Some consumers prefer an eco-labeled product to a conventional one without an eco-label. In this case, an eco-label can help consumers participate voluntarily in increasing the use of eco-friendly PPMs. Consumers' desires to purchase eco-labeled products leads firms to develop and manufacture environmentally-friendly products. However, the production costs of eco-labeled products are higher than those of conventional ones because the PPMs for eco-labeled products require careful management from the raw materials and subsidiary materials to the packaging [6–9].

For example, the eco-label in Korea demands that the chemical contents of the product must follow the EU's Directive 2006/66/EC. The housing of a product's materials must not contain halogen synthetic resins, such as polyvinyl chloride. Thus, the prices of eco-labeled products are usually higher than those of conventional ones with no eco-label, although there are no differences for consumers' usage between eco-labeled products and conventional ones. In this regard, the consumers' preference for eco-labeled products over conventional products with no eco-label should be investigated. Moreover, market planners and product developers frequently need to assess the market potential of an eco-labeled products that is not yet available for actual test marketing. The contingent valuation (CV) technique for assigning a social value to non-market environmental resources can be ideally suited to estimating the premium for an eco-labeled product over a non-eco-labeled product.

Both the government and chief executive officers of LED TV industry in Korea are currently addressing the likely effectiveness of a provision of an eco-labeled LED TV. If provided, additional costs will be incurred, with the expectation that inhabitants in Korea will reap the ensuing benefits. Employing financial viability as the sole criterion, whether to provide an eco-labeled LED TV or not can be evaluated in a conventional financial feasibility analysis context. In other words, implications of whether to provide the product could, in principle, be deduced from an examination of costs and revenues associated with the product. Moreover, an important first step in fostering a productive debate over how to provide the product is a better understanding of its costs and revenues.

In order to make an informed decision, some information on the expected revenues would be useful. This study addresses a component of the revenues that such an analysis would consider: the additional willingness to pay (WTP) for the eco-labeled product over a non-eco-labeled product. This paper tries to contribute to the current literature. Therefore, the objective of this study is to examine the consumers' WTP a premium for eco-labeled LED TVs. This objective is carried out using a survey approach called the CV method.

CV is a standardized and widely-used survey method for estimating WTP, it involves constructing a hypothetical market or referendum scenario in a survey. The proposed increase (if respondents pay) or decrease (if respondents do not pay) in the quantity or quality of the goods is communicated to respondents in words and with visual aids. Next, respondents are informed of how they will pay for the proposed quantity or quality. Then the provision rule is made clear: if you agree to pay, you get the proposed quantity or quality; if you do not pay, you remain at the current quantity or quality level. Respondents use the hypothetical market to state their WTP or vote for or against a product.

The CV method is based on the premise that the maximum amount of money an individual is willing to pay for a product is an indicator of the value to him/her of that service. In considering their maximum additional WTP for an eco-labeled LED TV over a non-eco-labeled LED TV, individuals should take into account all factors that are important to them in the provision of the product. In this respect, the message of this paper, which uses the CV technique to look into the consumers' WTP a premium for eco-labeled LED TVs, can be quite useful. Moreover, the validity and accuracy of the CV method results is tied, in part, to the accuracy and unbiasedness of the information contained in the survey and the survey implementation [10,11].

Most of the previous studies that examined consumers' additional WTP a premium for eco-friendly products employed stated preference techniques, such as CV and a choice experiment (CE). For example, Milovantseva [3] used a CV method to analyze American households' WTP a premium for green consumption of information and communication technologies and found that the premium was USD 29.6 per household. Mostafa [12] examined Egyptian consumers' WTP for carbon-labeled products using a CV approach and discovered that the additional WTP ranged from EGP 75 (or USD 10.5) to EGP 90 (or USD 12.6) per product.

On the other hand, Sammer and Wüstenhagen [8] examined the influence of eco-labeling on consumer behavior regarding washing machines using CE and detected that consumers' WTP a premium for an eco-labeled product was more than CHF 1220 (EUR 800). Using CE, Ward et al. [13] investigated how the ENERGY STAR label affects consumers' preferences for refrigerators. The additional WTP for an ENERGY STAR-labeled refrigerator ranged from USD 249.8 to USD 349.3 per product. Lanzini et al. [14] elicited drivers' WTP a premium for biofuels using CE. The premium was estimated to be a surcharge of EUR 0.01 to 0.14 per liter of biofuel.

Gaspar and Antunes [15] analyzed the consumer profiles and choice determinants for appliance purchases. The cost positively correlated with consideration of energy efficiency class in consumer choices. Furthermore, the consumer profiles were identified based on gender, age, and whether or not the purchaser was accompanied when decisions were made. Murray and Mills [16] examined the correlation with consumers' awareness of the Energy Star label and factors associated with the choice of Energy Star labeled appliances. This study found household characteristics have a much stronger association with consumers' awareness of labels than with the choice of Energy Star appliances. Moreover, if eliminating the socio-economic variables' gap in Energy Star appliance adoption, it decreases an electricity cost in house USD 164 million per year and reduces carbon emissions by about 1.1 million metric tons per year. Taufiquea et al. [17] discovered that both general environmental knowledge and knowledge of eco-labels positively influence consumers' attitudes towards environment in driving ecologically conscious consumer behavior. Park [18] investigated a price premium for Korea's Energy Efficiency Grade Label and suggested the need of careful design of labeling programs because energy-efficient products already had higher prices before the introduction of the energy efficiency label.

Of the above-mentioned nine case studies, CV or CE methods are used in accordance with the author's preference and research topic. The CV method is one of the most popular methods used by environmental and resource economists to value environmental and non-market goods [19–21]. In the literature, the authors found various pieces of empirical evidence that people are willing to pay a premium for eco-friendly products. If people accept an additional surcharge for a 43-inch eco-labeled LED TV, they could be interpreted as having a positive preference for a 43-inch eco-labeled LED TV.

Therefore, this study attempts to investigate the public preference, or WTP a premium, for eco-labeled products using a specific case study of a 43-inch LED TV, which is a common home appliance in Korea. For this purpose, a CV survey of 1000 Korean consumers was conducted in 2016. Moreover, we used a one-and-one-half-bounded (OOHB) dichotomous choice (DC) question to derive the additional WTP responses and a spike model to analyze zero additional WTP responses. The remainder of the paper is made up of four sections: the methodology adopted in this study is explained in Section 2; the WTP model used here is described in Section 3; the results are presented and discussed in Section 4; and the paper is concluded in the final section.

2. Methodology

2.1. Goods to Be Valued

The object to be valued in this study is an eco-labeled 43-inch LED TV over a conventional 43-inch LED TV. More specifically, we assess the consumers' WTP a premium for an eco-labeled 43-inch LED TV over a conventional 43-inch LED TV. If the following three conditions are satisfied, a certified eco-label can be given to the producers of 43-inch LED TVs. First, an eco-labeled LED TV should be produced through a process emitting less waste water and waste. Second, during the course of its production, fewer pollutants, such as Pb, Cd, Hg, and Cr6+, which negatively affect the land, atmosphere, and human health, should be emitted. Third, the packaging material should be made of recyclable resources. The quality of an eco-labeled LED TV is the same as that of a conventional one. The only difference between the two is the PPM of the products. These points were explicitly conveyed to the respondents during the CV survey.

2.2. Method for Measuring a Premium of an Eco-Labeled 43-Inch LED TV: The CV Approach

A premium for an eco-labeled 43-inch LED TV should be understood as a case of a non-market good including environmental goods. The people's WTP for a non-market good constitutes the underpinning rule for the benefits of the associated policy [22], and can be gauged using certain preference techniques, a representative one of which is the CV technique. Arrow et al. [10] concluded that the CV method is able to generate credible information that can be applied in relation to decisions regarding administration and jurisdiction. The CV approach is likely to be in accordance with the general notion of microeconomics.

2.3. CV Survey Instrument and Sampling

We conducted a pre-test on the survey questionnaire with a focus group (30 people) to examine whether the questionnaire could be properly understood and to obtain the distribution of the WTP values. The pre-test results helped us to rectify the errors in the questionnaire and to refine the bids to be presented to the respondents. The final questionnaire consisted of (a) explanations of the general background and purpose of the survey; (b) a question on the issue of the additional WTP for an eco-labeled 43-inch LED TV; and (c) questions regarding household characteristics.

A professional survey company implemented a random sampling and field CV survey. In the CV survey, the respondents were asked to make a responsible decision about payment. To satisfy this condition, the survey firm selected and interviewed heads of households or home-keepers; the respondents' ages ranged from 20 to 65. We chose to use face-to-face interviews so that the respondents were provided with sufficient information on the objects to be valued. Based on the interviewers' comments, the interviewees gave their WTP responses without any particular difficulty. The trained interviewers carried out 1000 personal interviews at the interviewees' homes during June 2016.

2.4. Method of WTP Elicitation and Bid Amounts

In accordance with Arrow et al.'s [10] guidance on the CV approach, we adopted a DC question format. Open-ended questions are not encouraged, as they will generate an overestimated WTP [11]. Generally, interviewees are asked questions that have 'yes' or 'no' answers that indicate the interviewees' WTP a concrete amount for a non-market good; in this study, the questions specifically addressed an eco-labeled 43-inch LED TV.

The number of questions identifies the DC question form—a single-bounded (SB) or a double-bounded (DB) DC format. A SB DC question asks the respondent one question, but a DB DC question offers him or her two bids. As the additional question obviously gives a greater range for the WTP, DB questions are likely to be more efficient than SB ones [23]. However, many studies in the literature claim that some bias is captured when moving from an SB to a DB question [24–26]. In summary, the SB and DB formats may, respectively, suffer from statistical inefficiency and response bias. To overcome these complications, a OOHB DC question method is suggested by Cooper et al. [27]. The merits of using of an OOHB DC question, as employed in our study, are presented in Cooper et al. [27].

2.5. Payment Vehicle

The interviewees could easily reveal their true WTP the medium through which the amount would be paid. The medium is called the payment vehicle, and may be a tax, a fund, a donation, or an expenditure. The respondents should feel at home with the payment vehicle, and the goods to be valued should have a clear connection with it. For this reason, the payment vehicle used for this study was a 43-inch LED TV price surcharge. This is appropriate for our analysis and is also familiar to the respondent. Furthermore, some previous studies use price-added to goods [28–30]. Other former studies [3,12] also used a premium on the product price as a payment vehicle. Therefore, the premium is employed in this study as the payment vehicle. The WTP question was posed in the following manner: "Is your household willing to pay an additional given amount for an eco-labeled 43-inch LED TV over a conventional one?"

3. Modeling of WTP: OOHB DC Spike Model

The basic modeling of WTP using DC CV data is usually based on the work of Hanemann et al. [23], Cameron and James [31], and Cameron [32]. In particular, OOHB DC CV data can be analyzed following Cooper et al. [27]. There are N respondents. Several sets of two bids are determined before the CV survey is carried out and a set is randomly presented to the respondent. Any set offered to respondent i is made up of two bids, a lower bid (B_i^L) and an upper bid (B_i^U). About half of the interviewees are offered B_i^L as the first bid. If the answer is "yes", a follow-up question is asked concerning B_i^U. If the answer to this is "no", no further question is needed. B_i^U is presented to the other half of the respondents as the first bid. If the response is "yes", no further question is required. If the response is "no", a subsequent question regarding B_i^L is asked.

There are six possible outcomes to this process: "yes–yes" ($WTP > B_i^U$), "yes–no" ($B_i^L < WTP < B_i^U$), and "no" ($WTP < B_i^L$), from the first case, and "no–yes" ($B_i^L < WTP < B_i^U$), "no–no" ($WTP < B_i^L$), and "yes" ($WTP > B_i^U$) from the second case. Therefore, we can set up six binary-valued indicator variables, I_i^{YY}, I_i^{YN}, I_i^{N}, I_i^{Y}, I_i^{NY}, and I_i^{NN}, such that:

$$
\begin{aligned}
I_i^{YY} &= \mathbf{1}(i\text{th interviewee's answer is "yes-yes")} \\
I_i^{YN} &= \mathbf{1}(i\text{th interviewee's answer is "yes-no")} \\
I_i^{N} &= \mathbf{1}(i\text{th interviewee's answer is "no")} \\
I_i^{Y} &= \mathbf{1}(i\text{th interviewee's answer is "yes")} \\
I_i^{NY} &= \mathbf{1}(i\text{th interviewee's answer is "no-yes")} \\
I_i^{NN} &= \mathbf{1}(i\text{th interviewee's answer is "no-no")}
\end{aligned}
\tag{1}
$$

where $\mathbf{1}(\cdot)$ is an indicator function that is one if the interviewee's answer is consistent with its superscript, and zero otherwise.

When a considerable proportion of interviewees give zero WTP answers, because of their indifference towards the object to be valued, researchers need to pay particular attention to these zero WTP observations. We utilized a spike model to analyze our OOHB DC CV data with a number of zero observations. The spike model was originally proposed for SB DC CV data by Kriström [33], was adjusted for DB DC CV data by Yoo and Kwak [34], and is sometimes applied to OOHB DC CV data (e.g., [21,35]). Let the random variable for the WTP be W and the cumulative distribution function of the WTP be $H_W(\cdot)$. In our OOHB DC spike model, $H_W(\cdot)$ has the functional form:

$$
H_W(B;\alpha,\beta) = \begin{cases} [1+\exp(\alpha-\beta B)]^{-1} & \text{if } B > 0 \\ [1+\exp(\alpha)]^{-1} & \text{if } B = 0 \\ 0 & \text{if } B < 0 \end{cases}
\tag{2}
$$

where α and β are the parameters to be estimated. The spike, defined as the probability of the respondent's having zero WTP, is computed as $[1+\exp(\alpha)]^{-1}$.

Those interviewees who answered "no" when presented with $B_i{}^L$ as the first bid, or "no–no" when presented with $B_i{}^U$ as the first bid, were asked an extra question, "Do you have zero willingness to pay?". This is because they were separated into two groups: those who have a true zero WTP, and those who have a positive WTP that is less than $B_i{}^L$.

Consequently, we can define two more binary-valued indicator variables:

$$
\begin{aligned}
I_i^{TY} &= \mathbf{1}(i\text{th interviewee's additional answer is "yes")} \\
I_i^{TN} &= \mathbf{1}(i\text{th interviewee's additional answer is "no")}
\end{aligned}
\tag{3}
$$

Using Equations (1)–(3), we can derive the log-likelihood function of the OOHB DC spike model as:

$$
\begin{aligned}
\ln L = \sum_{i=1}^{N} \Big\{ & (I_i^{YY} + I_i^{Y}) \ln[1 - H_W(B_i^{U}; \alpha, \beta)] \\
& + (I_i^{YN} + I_i^{NY}) \ln[H_W(B_i^{U}; \alpha, \beta) - H_W(B_i^{L}; \alpha, \beta)] \\
& + I_i^{TY}(I_i^{N} + I_i^{NN}) \ln[H_W(B_i^{L}; \alpha, \beta) - H_W(0; \alpha, \beta)] \\
& + I_i^{TN}(I_i^{N} + I_i^{NN}) \ln H_W(0; \alpha, \beta) \Big\}
\end{aligned}
\tag{4}
$$

Moreover, we can obtain the estimates for α and β by applying the maximum likelihood estimation method to Equation (4). Using these, and the well-known mean formula, the mean WTP can be calculated as:

$$
E(W) = \int_{0}^{\infty} [1 - H_W(B; \alpha, \beta)]dB - \int_{-\infty}^{0} H_W(B; \alpha, \beta)dB = (1/\beta) \ln[1 + \exp(\alpha)]
\tag{5}
$$

4. Estimation Results

4.1. Data

We collected 1000 observations from the CV survey of randomly-chosen households over the entire nation. We used seven sets of additional WTP values, detected through a pre-test, as mentioned before: (4000, 12,000); (8000, 16,000); (12,000, 24,000); (16,000, 32,000); (24,000, 40,000); (32,000, 48,000); and (40,000, 60,000). The figures given are in Korean won, and the first and the second elements of each set are, respectively, the lower and the higher bids. At the time of the questionnaire, the exchange rate was USD 1.0 to approximately KRW 1171.

Table 1 shows the distribution of responses by each bid level. As expected, the proportion of those stating "yes" to an offered bid decreases as the bid amount increases. Zero additional WTP results in a "no–no" response or a "no–no–no" response, and Table 1 indicates that 480 households (48.0%) revealed zero additional WTP for an eco-labeled LED TV. This means that our strategy of adopting a spike model in the analysis of the OOHB DC CV data is appropriate.

Table 1. Distribution of the responses by the bid amount.

Bid Amount [a]		Lower Bid Is Presented as a First Bid [b] (%)				Upper Bid Is Presented as a First Bid [b] (%)				Sample Size [b]
Lower Bid	Upper Bid	yes–yes	yes–no	no–yes	no–no	yes	no–yes	no–no–yes	no–no–no	
4000	12,000	24 (16.8)	10 (7.0)	5 (3.5)	33 (23.1)	30 (21.0)	8 (5.6)	4 (2.8)	29 (20.3)	143 (100.0)
8000	16,000	25 (17.6)	10 (7.0)	5 (3.5)	31 (21.8)	25 (17.6)	4 (2.8)	3 (2.1)	39 (27.5)	142 (100.0)
12,000	24,000	19 (13.3)	13 (9.1)	7 (4.9)	32 (22.4)	30 (21.0)	5 (3.5)	4 (2.8)	33 (23.1)	143 (100.0)
16,000	32,000	20 (13.9)	11 (7.6)	8 (5.6)	33 (22.9)	27 (18.8)	5 (3.5)	8 (5.6)	32 (22.2)	144 (100.0)
24,000	40,000	18 (12.7)	10 (7.0)	6 (4.2)	37 (26.1)	24 (16.9)	6 (4.2)	9 (6.3)	32 (22.5)	142 (100.0)
32,000	48,000	16 (11.2)	12 (8.4)	11 (7.7)	32 (22.4)	23 (16.1)	3 (2.1)	6 (4.2)	40 (28.0)	143 (100.0)
40,000	60,000	17 (11.9)	9 (6.3)	7 (4.9)	39 (27.3)	18 (12.6)	5 (3.5)	10 (7.0)	38 (26.6)	143 (100.0)
Totals		139 (13.9)	75 (7.5)	49 (4.9)	237 (23.7)	177 (17.7)	36 (3.6)	44 (4.4)	243 (24.3)	1000 (100.0)

Notes: [a] The unit is Korean won; [b] The numbers in parentheses below the number of responses are the percentage of the sample size; At the time of the survey, USD 1.0 was approximately equal to KRW 1171.

4.2. Estimation Results of the OOHB DC Spike Model

Table 2 reports the estimation results. Judging from the *t*-values and the Wald statistic, we can reject both the null hypothesis that each parameter estimate is zero and the null hypothesis that all of the parameter estimates are zero at the 1% level. The estimate for the bid level is negative, which implies that a higher bid amount makes a "yes" response less willing. The estimate for the spike is 0.4820, which is the same as the percentage of the sample having zero WTP responses, as shown in Table 1 (48.0%). This demonstrates that the spike model applied here depicts the sample well. We found that the mean additional WTP is KRW 29,007 (USD 24.8) per product, and that this is statistically significant at the 1% level. For the purpose of accounting for the uncertainties pertaining to the computation of the estimates, we also report a 95% and 99% confidence interval, calculated using the parametric bootstrapping method with 5000 replications [36].

Table 2. Estimation results of the spike model.

Variables	Coefficient Estimates [d]
Constant	0.0720 (1.14)
Bid [a]	−0.0251 (−15.93) *
Spike	0.4820 (30.51) *
Mean additional WTP per product	KRW 29,007 (USD 24.8)
t-value	15.72 *
95% confidence interval [b]	25,701 to 32,969 (USD 22.0 to 28.2)
99% confidence interval [b]	24,827 to 34,158 (USD 21.2 to 29.2)
Number of observations	1000
Log-likelihood	−1200.35
Wald statistic [c] (*p*-value)	247.09 (0.000)

Notes: [a] The unit is Korean won, and USD 1.0 was approximately equal to KRW 1171 at the time of the survey; [b] The confidence intervals are calculated by the use of the Monte Carlo simulation technique of Krinsky and Robb [36] with 5000 replications; [c] The null hypothesis is that all the parameters are jointly zero, and the corresponding *p*-value is reported in the parentheses beside the statistic; [d] The numbers in parentheses beside the coefficient estimates are *t*-values, computed from the analytic second derivatives of the log-likelihood; The symbol * indicates statistical significance at the 1% level.

4.3. Estimation Results of the Model with Covariates

To examine the impact of a respondent's socio-economic characteristics on the probability of him or her answering "yes" to a given bid, it is necessary to consider the model with covariates. At this point, α in Equation (4) is easily changed to $\alpha + x_i'\gamma$, where x_i and γ are the covariate vector and the parameter to be estimated, respectively. Some related previous studies (e.g., [13,16]) used socio-economic variables, such as gender, age, income, education level, and family size as key factors to determine people's WTP for green appliances. For this reason, we also employ gender, age, income, education level, and so on, as covariates. The socioeconomic variables and the sample statistics used for the covariates are described in Table 3. Almost seventy percent of the respondents did not know about eco-label before the survey, and the mean monthly household income was KRW 4.45 million (USD 3800). Furthermore, respondents spend, on average, 2.52 hours per day watching TV.

Of the eight variables employed in this study, the population values for gender, income, and time variables are available from Statistics Korea (www.kosis.kr). According to Statistics Korea, the ratio of males, the average of household income, and the average number of hours of watching TV in a day are 50.0%, KRW 4.31 million, and 2.77 hours in a day, respectively, at the time of the survey. These values are quite close to the sample means (50.0%, KRW 4.45 million, and 2.52 hours in a day). Our CV survey was implemented using in-person face-to-face interviewing; thus, the response rate was almost one hundred percent. Therefore, it seems that our sample is reasonably representative of the national population.

Table 3. Definitions and sample statistics of the variables.

Variables	Definitions	Mean	Standard Deviation
Income	Monthly household's income before taxes (unit: 1 million Korean won = USD 854)	4.45	2.75
Knowledge	Dummy for prior recognition of information about eco-label before the survey (0 = do not know; 1 = know well)	0.69	0.46
Age	The respondent's age (unit: years)	46.50	9.50
Earner	Dummy for whether the number of person who earn a living in family of the respondent is multiple or not (0 = no; 1 = yes)	0.49	0.50
Child	The number of children in the respondent's family	0.82	0.95
Education	Dummy for educational level of the respondent in years being larger than twelve (0 = no; 1 = yes)	0.62	0.49
Time	The time the respondent spends on watching TV during the day (unit: hours)	2.52	1.37
Gender	The respondent's gender (0 = female; 1 = male)	0.50	0.50

Table 4 presents the estimation results of the model with covariates. A total of ten variables, including constant and bid amount terms, are used. All of the coefficient estimates in the model are statistically significant at the 5% level. The positive sign of the coefficient implies that the higher the value of the variable, the higher the likelihood of stating "yes" to a given bid. Since the LED TV is a normal good, the respondents with higher incomes have a higher tendency to report a "yes" response to a provided bid than others. One who already knows the existence of eco-label before the survey is more likely to say "yes" to a presented bid than others. We found that in order to increase sales of the eco-labeled LED TV, communication with the media that can provide consumers with accurate and objective information about eco-label is needed. The respondent's age has a positive correlation with the likelihood of answering "yes" to an offered bid. That is, older respondents tend to accept additional payment for the eco-friendly LED TV than others. The number of children in the respondent's family has a positive relationship with the possibility of responding "yes" to a suggested bid. For the purpose of environmental education, the parents with children are likely to prefer eco-friendly LED TVs to non-eco-friendly LED TVs. The respondents with higher education levels have a positive relationship with the likelihood of saying "yes" to a presented bid.

Table 4. Estimation results of the spike model with covariates.

Variables [a]	Coefficient Estimates	*t*-Values
Constant	−2.0772	−4.30 *
Bid amount [b]	−0.0275	−15.99 *
Income	0.0834	4.00 *
Knowledge	1.0000	7.22 *
Age	0.0325	3.76 *
Earner	−0.2980	−2.23 [#]
Child	0.1447	1.96 [#]
Education	0.4636	3.08 *
Time	−0.1852	−4.16 *
Gender	−0.4116	−3.09 *
Number of observations	1000	
Log-likelihood	−1140.41	
Wald statistic [c] (*p*-value)	357.57 (0.000)	

Notes: [a] The variables are defined in Table 3; [b] The unit is Korean won, and USD 1.0 was approximately equal to KRW 1171 at the time of the survey; [c] The null hypothesis is that all the parameters are jointly zero and the corresponding *p*-value is reported in the parentheses beside the statistic; The symbols [#] and * indicate statistical significance at the 5% and 1% levels, respectively.

On the other hand, the negative sign of the coefficient indicates that the higher the value of the variable, the lower the likelihood of stating "yes" to a given bid. The bid amount is negatively correlated with the possibility of a respondent's giving a "yes" response. Multiple-earner families are less likely to state "yes" to a given bid than a single-earner family. This is because multiple-earner families mean that the multiple earners' per capita income is less than the single earner's personal income when other conditions are all equal. Earner's lower per capita income seems to negatively contribute to the likelihood of saying "yes" to a bid. The time the respondent spends on watching TV during the day has a negative relation to the possibility of reporting a "yes" response to a presented bid. Korea is quite well equipped with mobile networks and, thus, Koreans are accustomed to watching TV programs such as drama, entertainment, and movies on their mobile devices while working, walking, moving, and taking a rest, even at home. Usually, the respondent who spends much time on watching TV usually spends more time on watching mobile TV and less time on watching an LED TV at home than others. The probability of a male respondent saying "yes" to a provided bid is less than that of a female respondent saying "yes" to a provided bid.

Based on these quantitative and qualitative results, the LED TV producers in Korea could obtain a number of useful implications for manufacturing LED TVs and developing concise, targeted product innovations and marketing strategies. For example, it would be effective to set high-income, older, highly-educated, and female consumers with children as marketing targets. In addition, market planners can easily know the incremental contribution of each variable to accepting a premium for eco-labeled LED TV and define an appropriate marketing policy.

4.4. Discussion of the Results

To examine the consumers' preference for an eco-labeled LED TV in monetary terms, we estimated the mean additional WTP for an eco-labeled 43-inch LED TV over a conventional one. In the course of the estimation, the most important issue was whether or not the sample was representative of the population. As addressed above, the sampling was conducted by a professional survey firm to ensure the randomness of the sampling and its consistency with the characteristics of the population. Another important issue is the response rate in the CV survey. Our CV survey was implemented using in-person face-to-face interviewing; thus, the response rate was almost 100%. Consequently, we cannot deny that our sample is representative of the population.

We use the mean additional WTP estimate from the model with no covariates, since the setting of the covariates may influence the mean additional WTP value if we use the mean additional WTP value from the model with covariates. The mean additional WTP a premium for an eco-labeled 43-inch LED TV over a conventional one is estimated to be KRW 29,007 (USD 24.8) per product, which is statistically meaningful at the 1% level. This value amounts to 3.9% of the price of a conventional 43-inch LED TV (KRW 750,000 or USD 640. 5) and can be interpreted as the external benefit of an eco-labeled LED TV over a conventional one. The corresponding 95% and 99% confidence intervals for the point estimate are KRW 25,701 to 32,969 (USD 22.0 to 28.2) and KRW 24,827 to 34,158 (USD 21.2 to 29.2), respectively. Overall, we can judge that LED TV consumers in Korea are ready to pay a significant premium for an eco-labeled 43-inch LED TV instead of a conventional one.

If the additional production costs of an eco-labeled 43-inch LED TV relative to the production costs of a conventional one are less than the premium, the scheme for eco-labels can be implemented successfully. However, if not, further action is needed to ensure success in implementing the eco-label application. For example, this might involve assigning a yield of a certain rate of the total output and offering a green fund to be operated from the eco-label premium. Moreover, various tax credits and other incentives can be made available by the government to enhance the eco-label. For instance, a sound incentive for manufacturers to develop more eco-friendly and efficient technologies for the production process and to use eco-friendly materials might be the provision of subsidies. Moreover, the information on the premium obtained from our study can be employed in determining the levels of tax reductions, tax credits, or subsidies necessary to foster eco-labeled products.

5. Conclusion and Policy Implications

Although the production costs and prices of eco-labeled products are higher than those of conventional ones, the use of greener products can lead to better environmental outcomes. Thus, the consumers' preferences for eco-labeled products should be investigated to understand the potential of markets with green products. In this study, we chose a 43-inch LED TV as the item to be valued, because it is a common home appliance in Korea. We attempted to assess the consumer's WTP a premium for an eco-labeled 43-inch LED TV using the CV approach. The survey was implemented using person-to-person interviewing by a professional polling firm. An OOHB DC question was used to reduce the response bias as well as to increase the statistical efficiency, and the spike model was applied to handle, explicitly, the zero additional WTP data.

The results provided us with various interesting insights in terms of both research and policy. First, the study gave us research insights concerning the application of the CV approach to measuring a premium for an eco-labeled home appliance. Extensive evaluation of CV methods in experimental settings suggests they are quite reliable. These survey instruments are becoming increasingly popular and show considerable promise for assessing the market potential of eco-labeled products. Overall, judging from the interviewers' comments, the CV survey was successful in eliciting the additional WTP values from the respondents. All the parameter estimates were statistically significant at the 1% level. The OOHB DC spike model fit our data well. Moreover, we found that the mean additional WTP for an eco-labeled 43-inch LED TV per product is KRW 29,007 (USD 24.8), and this value is significantly different from zero at the 1% level. Our results show that use of data from the OOHB DC CV survey is a reasonable way to provide information on a premium for eco-labeled LED TV over non-eco-labeled one. Thus, we can conclude that a combination of the CV method and the OOHB DC spike model is suitable for assessing a premium for an eco-labeled product.

Second, several policy implications emerge from the results. Our analysis provided a preliminary indication of the consumer's value of eco-labeled LED TV. The main finding is that consumers' concerns about eco-labeled LED TVs are on the rise, and that people are willing to shoulder some additional financial burden to purchase one. This finding is consistent with the findings of previous studies [3,12]. The OOHB DC CV techniques are based on the premise that the maximum amount of money an individual is willing to pay for a product is an indicator of the value to him/her of that product. Use of the OOHB DC CV technique would imply that the provision of eco-labeled LED TV should be encouraged when the total value of the product, defined as the sum of the price of non-eco-labeled LED TV and the premium for eco-labeled LED TV, outweighs the cost.

It is necessary to estimate the additional WTP for an eco-labeled LED TV in the early stages of development or the production of it. The premium amounted to 3.9% of the average price of a conventional 43-inch LED TV (KRW 750,000 or USD 640.5) at the time of the survey (June 2016). This value can be also interpreted as the external benefit of an eco-labeled 43-inch LED TV. It appears that LED TV consumers in Korea are ready to pay a significant premium for an eco-labeled 43-inch LED TV. Therefore, if the difference between the production costs of eco-labeled LED TV and those of non-eco-labeled one is less than 3.9% of the price of non-eco-labeled one, developing and selling eco-labeled LED TVs is profitable. If not, developing and selling eco-labeled LED TVs is not profitable and, thus, a government's subsidy or tax credit program for eco-labeled LED TVs can be introduced to promote the production and consumption of eco-labeled LED TVs.

Some more findings stem from our CV survey. First of all, a number of households were concerned about eco-labels and wanted a strong governmental introduction of eco-labeling for all home appliances. A next step is to clearly set the standard and range of eco-labeling. Therefore, it is necessary to find the optimal standard and range of eco-labeling after carefully examining the benefits and costs involved in the eco-labeling policy. Information on the public WTP for the eco-labeling policy is needed because it can be utilized for doing so. Evaluating the public WTP for expanding the range of eco-labeling to all home appliances is required as a second stage of this study. In the case that consumers were already familiar with the eco-label, they were more likely to state "yes" to a presented bid than other consumers. Eco-label promotion to the public can help consumers to think favorably. The logo is easy to recognize and can be found on the packaging of every product manufactured through an eco-friendly course of production. It is meaningful to place eco-labels on products because they give consumers useful information. We also found that in order to secure the success of the eco-labeling we need to communicate with the media that can provide consumers with accurate and objective information about eco-labeled products.

The results are a useful starting point in understanding the possible implications of eco-labeled LED TVs. It is desirable for the government and the industry to know how potential consumers of eco-labeled LED TVs perceive its premium. For example, the policy decision is to encourage more production of eco-labeled LED TVs, knowing the consumers place higher value on eco-labeled LED TVs than non-eco-labeled LED TVs. Moreover, the study contributes to the existing literature because the start of the labeling program supports to set the standard and range of new certification in a timely manner. If an eco-labeling policy is implemented, a consumer's additional WTP or premium for eco-labeled products will be conveyed through higher prices, thereby providing incentives for producers to produce more environmentally-friendly goods.

Acknowledgments: This work was supported by the Korea Institute of Energy Technology Evaluation and Planning (KETEP) and the Ministry of Trade, Industry, and Energy (MOTIE) of the Republic of Korea (no. 20164030201060).

Author Contributions: All of the authors contributed immensely. Seo-Hyeon Min designed the ideas and analyzed the data; Seul-Ye Lim wrote the majority of the manuscript; and Seung-Hoon Yoo contributed the main idea and various scientific insights and helped to edit the manuscript.

Conflicts of Interest: The authors declare no conflict of interest.

References

1. Kemme, M.R.; Lateulere, M. *Reducing Air Pollutant Emissions from Solvent Multi-base Propellant Production*; CERL Technical Report 99/71; US Army Corps of Engineers, Construction Engineering Research Laboratory: Champaign, IL, USA, 1999.
2. Hartikainen, H.; Roininen, T.; Katajajuuri, J.; Pulkkinen, H. Finnish consumer perceptions of carbon footprints and carbon labeling of food products. *J. Clean. Prod.* **2014**, *73*, 285–293. [CrossRef]
3. Milovantseva, N. Are American households willing to pay a premium for greening consumption of information and communication technologies? *J. Clean. Prod.* **2016**, *127*, 282–288. [CrossRef]
4. Ministry of Government Legislation. 2011. Available online: http://www.moleg.go.kr (accessed on 1 July 2016).
5. Korea Environmental Industry & Technology Institute. Eco-label certification in Korea. Available online: http://el.keiti.re.kr/service/index.do/ (accessed on 31 July 2016).
6. Kennedy, P.W.; Laplante, B.; Maxwell, J. Pollution Policy: The Role for Publicly Provided Information. *J. Environ. Econ. Manag.* **1994**, *26*, 31–43. [CrossRef]
7. EU. Directive 2002/95/EC of the European parliament and of the council of 27 January 2003 on the restriction of the use of certain hazardous substances in electrical and electronic equipment. *Official Journal of the European Union 13*, 19e22. Available online: http://www.niagara-video.com/images/rohs/suppliers-RoHS.pdf (accessed on 10 July 2016).
8. Sammer, K.; Wüstenhagen, R. The influence of eco-labelling on consumer behavior—Results of a discrete choice analysis for washing machines. *Bus. Strat. Environ.* **2006**, *15*, 185–199. [CrossRef]
9. Austgulen, M.H. Consumer Perspectives on Eco-labelling of Textiles: Results from five European Countries. Available online: http://www.hioa.no/eng/About-HiOA/Centre-for-Welfare-and-Labour-Research/SIFO/Publications-from-SIFO/Consumer-perspectives-on-eco-labelling-of-textiles (accessed on 26 April 2017).
10. Arrow, K.; Solow, R.; Portney, P.R.; Leamer, E.E.; Radner, R.; Schuman, H. Report of the NOAA panel on contingent valuation. *Fed. Regist.* **1993**, *58*, 4601–4614.
11. Mitchell, R.C.; Carson, R.T. *Using Surveys to Value Public Goods: The Contingent Valuation Method*; Resources for the Future: Washington, DC, USA, 1989.

12. Mostafa, M.M. Egyptian consumers' willingness to pay for carbon-labeled products: A contingent valuation analysis of socio-economic factors. *J. Clean. Prod.* **2016**, *135*, 821–828. [CrossRef]

13. Ward, D.O.; Clark, C.D.; Jensen, K.L.; Yen, S.Y.; Russell, C.S. Factors influencing willingness-to-pay for the ENERGY STAR label. *Energy Policy* **2011**, *39*, 1450–1458. [CrossRef]

14. Lanzini, P.; Testa, F.; Iraldo, F. Factors affecting drivers' willingness to pay for biofuels: The case of Italy. *J. Clean. Prod.* **2016**, *112*, 2684–2692. [CrossRef]

15. Gaspar, R.; Antunes, D. Energy efficiency and appliance purchases in Europe: Consumer profiles and choice determinants. *Energy Policy* **2011**, *39*, 7335–7346. [CrossRef]

16. Murray, A.G.; Mills, B.F. Read the label! Energy Star appliance label awareness and uptake among U.S. consumers. *Energy Econ.* **2011**, *33*, 1103–1110. [CrossRef]

17. Taufique, K.M.R.; Siwar, C.; Chamhuri, N.; Sarah, F.H. Integrating general environmental knowledge and eco-label knowledge in understanding ecologically conscious consumer behavior. *Procedia Econ. Financ.* **2016**, *37*, 39–45. [CrossRef]

18. Park, J.Y. Is there a price premium for energy efficiency labels? Evidence from the introduction of a label in Korea. *Energy Econ.* **2017**, *62*, 240–247. [CrossRef]

19. Park, S.-Y.; Lim, S.-Y.; Yoo, S.-H. The economic value of the national meteorological service in the Korean household sector: A contingent valuation study. *Sustainability* **2016**, *8*, 834. [CrossRef]

20. Lim, S.-Y.; Kim, H.-Y.; Yoo, S.-H. Public willingness to pay for transforming Jogyesa Buddhist temple in Seoul, Korea into a cultural tourism resource. *Sustainability* **2016**, *8*, 900. [CrossRef]

21. Kim, H.-Y.; Park, S.-Y.; Yoo, S.-H. Public acceptability of introducing a biogas mandate in Korea: A contingent valuation study. *Sustainability* **2016**, *8*, 1087. [CrossRef]

22. Brent, R.J. *Applied Cost-benefit Analysis*, 2nd ed.; Edward Elgar: Cheltenham, UK, 2006.

23. Hanemann, W.M.; Loomis, J.; Kanninen, B.J. Statistical efficiency of double-bounded dichotomous choice contingent valuation. *Am. J. Agric. Econ.* **1991**, *66*, 1255–1263. [CrossRef]

24. McFadden, D. Contingent valuation and social choice. *Am. J. Agric. Econ.* **1994**, *76*, 689–708. [CrossRef]

25. Bateman, I.J.; Langford, I.H.; Jones, A.P.; Kerr, G.N. Bound and path effects in double and triple bounded dichotomous choice contingent valuation. *Resour. Energy Econ.* **2001**, *23*, 191–213. [CrossRef]

26. Carson, R.T.; Groves, T.; Machina, M.J. Incentive and informational properties of preference questions. *Environ. Resour. Econ.* **2007**, *37*, 181–210. [CrossRef]

27. Cooper, J.C.; Hanemann, M.; Signorello, G. One-and-one-half-bound dichotomous choice contingent valuation. *Rev. Econ. Stat.* **2002**, *84*, 742–750. [CrossRef]

28. Kwak, S.-Y.; Yoo, S.-H.; Kim, C.-S. Measuring the willingness to pay for tap water quality improvement: Results of a contingent valuation survey in Pusan. *Water* **2013**, *5*, 1638–1652. [CrossRef]

29. Lim, K.-M.; Lim, S.-Y.; Yoo, S.-H. Estimating the economic value of residential electricity use in the Republic of Korea using contingent valuation. *Energy* **2014**, *64*, 601–606. [CrossRef]

30. Yoo, S.-H.; Kwak, S.-Y. Willingness to pay for green electricity in Korea: A contingent valuation study. *Energy Policy* **2009**, *37*, 5408–5416. [CrossRef]

31. Cameron, T.A.; James, M.D. Efficient estimation methods for 'closed-ended' contingent valuation surveys. *Rev. Econ. Stat.* **1987**, *69*, 269–276. [CrossRef]

32. Cameron, T.A. A new paradigm for valuing non-market goods using referendum data: Maximum likelihood estimation by censored logistic regression. *J. Environ. Econ. Manag.* **1988**, *15*, 355–379. [CrossRef]

33. Kriström, B. Spike models in contingent valuation. *Am. J. Agric. Econ.* **1997**, *79*, 1013–1023. [CrossRef]

34. Yoo, S.-H.; Kwak, S.-J. Using a spike model to deal with zero response data from double bounded dichotomous contingent valuation survey. *Appl. Econ. Lett.* **2002**, *9*, 929–932. [CrossRef]

35. Kwak, S.-Y.; Yoo, S.-H. The public's value for developing ocean energy technology in the Republic of Korea: A contingent valuation study. *Renew. Sustain. Energy Rev.* **2015**, *43*, 432–439. [CrossRef]

36. Krinsky, I.; Robb, A.L. On approximating the statistical properties of elasticities. *Rev. Econ. Stat.* **1986**, *68*, 715–719. [CrossRef]

MDPI AG

St. Alban-Anlage 66

4052 Basel, Switzerland

Tel. +41 61 683 77 34

Fax +41 61 302 89 18

http://www.mdpi.com

Sustainability Editorial Office

E-mail: sustainability@mdpi.com

http://www.mdpi.com/journal/sustainability

www.ingramcontent.com/pod-product-compliance
Lightning Source LLC
Chambersburg PA
CBHW051314020426
42333CB00028B/3331